EDWARD M. ALMOND AND THE US ARMY

American Warriors

Throughout the nation's history, numerous men and women of all ranks and branches of the US military have served their country with honor and distinction. During times of war and peace, there are individuals whose exemplary achievements embody the highest standards of the US armed forces. The aim of the American Warriors series is to examine the unique historical contributions of these individuals, whose legacies serve as enduring examples for soldiers and citizens alike. The series will promote a deeper and more comprehensive understanding of the US armed forces.

Series editor: Joseph Craig

An AUSA Book

EDWARD M. ALMOND AND THE US ARMY

From the 92nd Infantry Division to the X Corps

Michael E. Lynch

UNIVERSITY PRESS OF KENTUCKY

Scholarly publisher for the Commonwealth,
serving Bellarmine University, Berea College, Centre
College of Kentucky, Eastern Kentucky University,
The Filson Historical Society, Georgetown College,
Kentucky Historical Society, Kentucky State University,
Morehead State University, Murray State University,
Northern Kentucky University, Transylvania University,
University of Kentucky, University of Louisville,
and Western Kentucky University.

Editorial and Sales Offices: The University Press of Kentucky
663 South Limestone Street, Lexington, Kentucky 40508-4008
www.kentuckypress.com

Cataloging-in-Publication data is available from the Library of Congress.

ISBN 978-0-8131-7798-4 (hardcover : alk. paper)
ISBN 978-0-8131-7800-4 (pdf)
ISBN 978-0-8131-7801-1 (epub)

This book is printed on acid-free paper meeting
the requirements of the American National Standard
for Permanence in Paper for Printed Library Materials.

Manufactured in the United States of America

Member of the Association
of University Presses

For all the many other soldiers whose stories are yet to be told

Contents

List of Tables

List of Maps

List of Abbreviations

ACTS	Air Corps Tactical School
ADCOM	GHQ Advance Command and Liaison Group
AEF	American Expeditionary Forces
AFPAC	Army Forces, Pacific
AGCT	Army General Classification Test
AGF	Army Ground Forces
Amtrack	Amphibious Tractor
ASTP	Army Specialized Training Program
AWC	Army War College
BOV	Board of Visitors
CAG	Civilian Advisory Group
CASW	Civilian Aide to the Secretary of War
CCA	Combat Command A
CCB	Combat Command B
CCF	Chinese Communist Forces
CGSS	Command and General Staff School (later College)
CP	Command Post
CPVA	Chinese People's Volunteer Army
DMGO	Division Machine Gun Officer
DoD	Department of Defense
DSC	Distinguished Service Cross
EUSA	Eighth US Army (in Japan, prewar)
EUSAK	Eighth US Army in Korea
FEAF	Far East Air Forces
FEC	Far East Command (Pentagon usage)
FECOM	Far East Command (Far East usage)
G1	Personnel Office(r)
G2	Intelligence Office(r)
G3	Operations Office(r)
G4	Logistics Office(r)

GCMRL	George C. Marshall Research Library, Lexington, VA
GHQ	General Headquarters
GO	General Orders
IG	Inspector General
JCS	Joint Chiefs of Staff
KATUSA	Korean Augmentee to US Army
KMAG	Korean Military Advisory Group
MHI	Military History Institute, USAHEC
MMA	MacArthur Memorial Library and Archives, Norfolk, VA
MMI	Marion Military Institute, Marion, AL
NARA	National Archives and Records Administration, College Park, MD
NK	North Korea
NKPA	North Korean People's Army
NSA	National Security Act
NWC	Naval War College
OCMH	Office of the Chief of Military History
OCS	Officer Candidate School
PI	Philippine Islands
PLA	People's Liberation Army (China)
PMAG	Provisional Military Advisory Group (later KMAG)
PS	Philippine Scouts
RCT	Regimental Combat Team
RG	Record Group
ROK	Republic of Korea (South Korea)
ROTC	Reserve Officers Training Corps
SCAP	Supreme Commander, Allied Powers
SOOHP	Senior Officer Oral History Program, MHI
TACP	Tactical Air Control Party
UMT	Universal Military Training
USAFIK	US Army Forces in Korea
USAHEC	US Army Heritage and Education Center, Carlisle, PA
USO	United Servicemen's Organization
VMI	Virginia Military Institute, Lexington, VA
WDGS	War Department General Staff
WPD	War Plans Division (later Operations Planning Division)

Preface

Edward Mallory "Ned" Almond belonged to that generation of US Army officers who came of age during World War I and then ascended to senior command positions in World War II and the Korean War. Almond's early military life differed little from that of his contemporaries, who included such luminaries as General Omar N. Bradley. Ambition and the drive to excel made Almond and his peers stand out as young officers and destined them for future prominence.

While Almond's is hardly a household name today, he has a poor reputation among military historians. Almond exhibited many commendable traits throughout his thirty-six years in the Army. He displayed personal courage in combat, exercised strong leadership as a battalion and later a corps commander, demonstrated dedication and efficiency as a staff officer, and showed some capacity as an author and military innovator. He also left a reputation for aggressiveness, ambition, impatience, racial prejudice, and insecurity. In every position Almond held, he earned the respect of his superiors, including Generals George C. Marshall, Douglas MacArthur, and Matthew B. Ridgway. Almond's performance in an early assignment with then–Lt. Col. George C. Marshall marked him as a "Marshall man" and destined him for future success. Almond received his greatest accolades commanding the American troops who landed at Inchon, South Korea, on September 15, 1950. This amphibious flanking movement temporarily shifted the momentum to the United Nations forces during the Korean War. A dedicated, loyal officer and hard-driving commander, Almond enjoyed many professional successes. Nevertheless, he remains a controversial historical figure.

Alongside his positive traits and considerable achievements lurked the distasteful beliefs of a fervent racist and right-wing political zealot. Almond's vehement attitudes regarding African American soldiers serving in combat units overshadow his accomplishments. His tenure as commander of the all-black 92nd Infantry Division in World War II and his resistance to racial integration after 1948 provide case studies of his racism in practice.

Yet Almond was hardly alone in the US military or civilian society in harboring bigoted attitudes against African Americans. The possible causes for Almond's faults must be traced from his childhood through his long career. The intertwined contexts of America's military and civilian society need to be assessed as influences on Almond's beliefs. Such contemporary senior leaders as Gen. George C. Marshall, Lt. Gen. Mark Clark, and Lt. Gen. Lucian K. Truscott shared similarly low opinions of black men's ability to fight effectively. In addition, discriminatory policies in the form of segregation and Jim Crow laws pervaded the Virginia society of Almond's youth, as well as the civilian society of his adult life.[1]

Such an accomplished yet contradictory soldier has gone too long without a scholarly biography. While acknowledging Almond's faults, this book balances the historical ledger by arguing that he played significant roles in the Army's history that are worthy of careful consideration. This critical examination of Almond's life and career treats both the good and the bad, taking stock of this complex man who was so deeply flawed in some areas, yet supremely strong in many others.

Almond initially made his mark on history as the commander of the 92nd Infantry Division, one of only two African American divisions to see combat during World War II. The Army recognized Almond's skills as a trainer when selecting him for this billet, and that too is part of his story. The division's failure to perform well under fire embittered Almond, and he became an implacable opponent of the subsequent integration of the armed forces. The nation's civilian leadership pressed the issue in the post–World War II years, and the US Army eventually changed its segregationist policies. Almond's contemptuous opinion of black soldiers never wavered, however, and the racist positions he espoused in his later life tarnished his reputation.

Because Almond's attitudes made him a hard man to like, his historical reputation is tarnished by many inaccurate stories inspired by baseless rumors or exaggerations. One oft-repeated tale asserts that Almond achieved success and high rank only because he was the brother-in-law of George C. Marshall. In reality, Mrs. Margaret Crook Almond of Alabama bore no relation to the Marshall family of Pennsylvania, yet the story appears repeatedly in the historiography. This book dispels these and other myths about Almond but examines his shortcomings fairly.

The Korean War provided another opportunity for Almond to

excel on the battlefield, but it also mired him still further in controversy. Almond's abrasive personality and close relationship with Douglas MacArthur turned him into an unpopular figure. In addition to the racial controversies for which Almond is best known, he developed a reputation for personal animosity and interservice rivalry with Air Force and Marine officers. Almond held strong but informed views on each service's mission, and these opinions brought him into conflict with the Air Force chief of staff, Gen. Hoyt S. Vandenberg, and his own service chief, Gen. J. Lawton Collins.

Most historians of the period have focused on Almond's racist statements and find much to dislike about him. This spotlight on Almond's racism disregards his other qualities and skews the study of his performance. Many historians also attack Almond's relationship with MacArthur. Few, however, address the challenges Almond faced in Korea, such as the sheer scope of the mission, the inhospitable terrain, and the inadequate forces available.[2]

The existing historiography also overlooks Almond's personal side. The hard-bitten general had a family to which he was devoted. He was not immune to personal tragedy and lost both his son and his son-in-law in combat. Almond also possessed a deep sense of honor that he cherished throughout his life. When threatened, this concern about honor would lead to many of his later difficulties. These contradictions with the rest of his personality make Almond a complex man, and indicate the need for a much more nuanced perspective than the current historiography allows.

1

Coming of Age

1892–1916

On a warm September day in 1912, Edward M. Almond hopped off the train at Lexington station after the short train ride from his home in Culpeper, Virginia. Carrying the few personal possessions approved for new cadets, the young man walked across the campus of Washington and Lee University and onto the adjoining grounds of the Virginia Military Institute (VMI). After a long and tiring day of uniform and equipment issue, drills and barrages of verbal abuse from upper class cadets, Almond and the other new "rats" finally moved into their barracks. The first of many orientation lectures took place in Jackson Memorial Hall with Thomas J. "Stonewall" Jackson's immortal words emblazoned on one wall: "You may be whatever you resolve to be." Almond entered VMI resolved to become a soldier.

Almond's school years revealed his most notable qualities: commitment to a mission or task, an aggressive nature, a driving ambition, and intense loyalty. Jackson's injunction also instilled in him a deep sense of honor that he cherished throughout his life. He could not fail to appreciate a campus so immersed in history, and he drank it in. Jackson's admonition to maximize one's potential would greet Almond every day for the next three years, and those words formed the core of his personal philosophy. He quoted them countless times over the next six decades, always believing they played a central role in his life. Almond's can-do attitude and a natural inclination to work hard, earned him the sobriquet "Sic 'em Ned," which epitomized his approach to life and his profession.[1]

Edward Mallory Almond, nicknamed Ned by his family at an early age, began his march toward his destiny on December 12, 1892, in Luray, Virginia, as the first son born to Walter and Grace Popham Almond. A second boy, Malcolm, joined the family in 1895 and a sister, Judy, came along two years later. The Almond family had resided in the Shenandoah Valley since the early eighteenth century, generally around Orange and Page Counties but with relatives scattered throughout Virginia. Walter traveled the Shenandoah Valley and northern Virginia on horseback and by buggy, selling International Harvester farm equipment. The family lived comfortably but without wealth.[2]

Almond's family took little interest in its own history, though Ned tried to research the genealogy in his later years. He idolized his grandfather, David Edward Almond, and spent a good deal of time with the old man at his home in the nearby community of Slate Mills on Hawks Bill Creek. Almond particularly relished riding his grandfather's horse on the "race track" he imagined in a leafy glade at the farm. Almond's paternal grandmother doted on him, and he remembered her telling stories about her teenage years in the hotly contested Shenandoah Valley during the Civil War. His maternal grandfather, Thomas Popham, and a great-uncle, William Barton Mallory, had served in the Confederate Army. Many aged veterans of that conflict still made their homes there during Almond's youth. Almond reported that his grandparents and older people in the area spoke little of the war, but there was an undertone of bitterness because of all they had lost. He remembered, however, that the Spanish-American War "solidified the attitude of the average citizen toward national welfare rather than bitterness of the past war." Despite that feeling of national unity, Almond surely could not escape the influence of southern traditions and Confederate heritage.[3]

Almond grew up in the "Jim Crow" South and did not question the status quo, which derived from the landmark Supreme Court decision *Plessy v. Ferguson,* handed down four years after Almond's birth, which allowed segregation throughout American society following the doctrine of "separate but equal." He demonstrated no particularly racist tendencies beyond the societal norms of the day, but those norms were inherently racist. His racism found expression in the genteel paternalism exhibited by middle-class and upper-class whites of the region. Black people lived in "certain sections" of the towns of his youth, and he generally saw them only in subservient roles working on his grandfather's farm. Despite the prevailing Jim Crow environment, this limited contact with African Americans engendered a moderate outlook, shaping Almond's early years and carrying over into his military career.

This moderate attitude came from the prevailing views among southern whites, who considered themselves morally superior to blacks, whether or not their families had owned slaves. George T. Winston, president of the North Carolina College of Agricultural and Mechanical Arts, characterized paternalism this way:

> The Negro race is a child race and must remain in tutelage for years to come; in tutelage not of colleges and universities, but of industrial schools. . . . If he do not, he will remain for a while among the races of the earth a dull and stupid draught animal; and finally will pass away, incompetent. But, with the help of the white race he may obtain opportunity to develop his powers . . . and cultivate his gentler emotions, may train his physical strength into skill and power, may grow from childhood into mature manhood.[4]

The Virginia of Almond's youth did not experience racial violence to the degree that Georgia and other Deep South states did. For instance, there were more lynchings in Georgia in 1919 alone than in Virginia throughout the entire twentieth century, and in fact such violence had grown rare in Virginia by 1910. Moreover, the incidence of racial violence in the areas where Almond lived, the Shenandoah Valley and western Virginia, proved to be the lowest in the state. During the period of Almond's youth, eight lynchings occurred either in the Piedmont or the Shenandoah Valley region, but five occurred before Almond reached the age of ten (see table 1.1). Only one was in Page County, and well after his family had moved to Culpeper County. The last event recorded in the region occurred in Culpeper in 1918, but Almond was in France with the Army at the time. He would still have been aware of the violence undergirding the Jim Crow system, but there is no evidence that he or his family supported it.[5]

Table 1.1. Racial Violence in Western Virginia

Year	1893	1897	1898	1899	1900	1902	1904	1905
No. Racial Incidents	1	1	1	1	1	1	1	1
Almond Age	1	5	6	7	8	10	12	13

Source: Adapted from Brundage, *Lynching in the New South: Georgia and Virginia, 1880–1930*, 281, appendix A.

Almond grew up in an environment in which, though racial violence existed, its occurrence was contained by local white society's moderate views. Virginia differed from Georgia and other southern states in racial violence because of the post–Civil War change in the rural economy, which has been termed "patronage capitalism." In Virginia, this meant greater land ownership opportunities for blacks, and the shift from single-crop to multi-crop and livestock farming made for a more symbiotic relationship between black and white societies. Since Almond's father sold farm equipment rather than farming himself, his family was even further removed from the traditional farming gentry. The improving economy also led to a greater toleration of blacks in the region, and therefore whites were more tolerant of blacks' behavior. Further, the Virginia elite believed that social unrest and racial violence inhibited economic progress. The Virginia society of Almond's youth believed in the inferiority of blacks and kept them "in their place" through racial and class boundaries, but also believed blacks were naturally subordinate and those boundaries were necessary for social harmony.[6]

Almond's interest in the military began at an early age. Dr. Fred Amos, a neighbor in Luray and a VMI graduate, used to talk to young Ned about VMI and the military profession. Amos gave Almond four brass buttons from his old VMI "coatee," and Almond's mother sewed them onto a coat of similar design. The future general then formed a "military unit" of like-minded boys in the area, to "play soldier." When Almond was ten, his family moved to the somewhat larger town of Culpeper, hometown of the famed Confederate general A. P. Hill, and Hill's family still lived there. Professor T. W. Hendricks, a Culpeper High School history teacher, nurtured what would become Almond's lifelong passion for history.

When Almond grew older, his friend Walter Hitt encouraged him to join the Culpeper Minutemen, a local militia outfit that traced its lineage to the Revolutionary War–era unit of the same name. A similar organization had formed during the Civil War and served in the Confederate Army. Almond recalled that William Nalle, a former adjutant general of Virginia, visited the outfit often during its training assemblies. He advised the young soldiers on getting their company ready to go to camp, and encouraged all the young men in the area who had an interest in the military to join. Nalle had been a cadet at VMI when Robert E. Lee died and had been part of the five-man honor guard on the day of the Confederate hero's death and again at his funeral. Nalle doubtless regaled the young men with tales of that important assignment. As Almond's interest in history increased, he could not fail to appreciate these tangible connections to the Confederate past. The influence of such men, the comradeship of friends, and his feeling of connection to a military past nurtured his vocation.[7]

Through another family contact, Almond secured a state "cadetship," or scholarship, that paid for his tuition and books. These scholarships required cadets to perform some kind of state duty after graduation, such as teaching school. Almond received his appointment to VMI in the summer of 1912 and entered that fall. Before any of this, however, he faced a life-threatening illness. In the spring of his senior year of high school, he suddenly contracted appendicitis, which worsened into peritonitis. Almond's parents took him to the hospital in Charlottesville, where he endured four operations in ten days. His lengthy recovery complicated his first year at VMI.[8] As he later recalled: "I was also confronted with the fact that I had only been out of the hospital three months with a very serious operation. This would make it difficult for me to undergo the hardships of being a 'rat' and I made this known to the doctor on my appearance [at school]. The doctor saw the severity of my predicament and had me excused by the Commandant from strenuous training, not from drill, but for football, baseball, or from hazing that the "rats" were usually subjected to."[9] This experience may have evoked in him a feeling of insecurity. In the male-dominated society of a military school, he may have seen himself as a weakling. Being excused from normal cadet activities doubtless sped his healing, but it also affected his self-esteem.

Each new cadet entering VMI received the derogatory title "rat" for the first year, and joined the "ratline." Some of those rituals included "finning out," which required rats to throw back their shoulders while keeping forearms in a horizontal position to build endurance and discipline. Each new cadet also underwent "uncle rat" sessions on Saturday afternoons that subjected the rats to other humiliations, such as sitting naked in a bowl of ink while older cadets spun them around, with punishment for those who fell out. The upperclassmen also forced the rats to memorize poems or speeches for recitation on demand. These seemingly pointless customs promoted class unity through shared pain and eliminated those lacking the dedication and toughness to continue. Completing these rites of passage facilitated gradual acceptance into the cadet brotherhood. First-year cadets, or plebes, at West Point suffered a similarly harsh rite of passage.

During Almond's cadet years, VMI operated as an all-white, all-male bastion of southern masculinity. The Institute perpetuated many traditions in place since its founding in 1839, most notably a strict honor code imported from West Point, the service academy on which VMI's founders modeled their school. Though the honor code of the US Army officer corps never found explicit expression, every officer of Almond's time knew and understood it: an intangible sense of responsibility, belonging, and loyalty to one's peers. Most professional officers of the period came from West Point, and that institution's ethos and its honor code carried over into the officer's professional life after graduation. That code enjoined a cadet to not lie, cheat, steal, or tolerate those who do; expulsion awaited violators of these precepts. One of the VMI official histories described the code as follows: "The Honor Code is the daily application of the principles of ethics, honesty, and personal integrity by each cadet to the problems with which he is confronted. . . . It is, therefore, far more than just a set of principles for four years in the life of a cadet. It is a Code that must be strictly followed by a cadet, no matter where he may be, if he wishes to preserve the most priceless thing he has in his life—HIS HONOR."[10]

This immutable code and the brotherhood engendered by the school's military system remained powerful forces throughout Almond's life. That acceptance also underscored the sense of honor so central to military *esprit de corps*. The Institute expected cadets to abide by its honor code throughout their lives, and such expectations helped bond the cadets as students. For the many who ended up entering the Army, it linked them to brother officers reared with a similar ethic.[11]

Despite VMI's military school environment, few active-duty officers served as faculty members. Nevertheless, the state incorporated the Institute into its unorganized militia, and the faculty held rank and wore uniforms. VMI's superintendent, traditionally a retired or former military officer, wore the stars of a brigadier or major general, a distinction often based on his retired military rank. The Commandant of Cadets, however, was a serving Regular Army officer. As for the faculty, professors became colonels in the Virginia militia; associate professors, lieutenant colonels; assistant professors, majors; and instructors, captains and lieutenants. Conversely, West Point had a mostly military faculty with a few civilian exceptions. West Point's officer-instructors boasted little education beyond their West Point training. They had spent at least three years on active duty and would teach at the academy for two to four years. At both institutions, the older, tenured professors tended to stay in place for many years.[12]

VMI faculty evaluated each prospective cadet before admittance and assigned him to a class. Almond's high school record and exam results placed him in the third (sophomore) class in 1912. When Almond entered VMI, he found a rigid academic and military environment with classes conducted six days a week. Unlike civilian universities, VMI prescribed a strict schedule of classes for the entire Corps of Cadets, divided by class and then by section. The commandant transmitted all instructions to the Corps of Cadets through general orders. These orders covered everything from the course schedule to personal hygiene. Faculty divided each class into six sections for course scheduling (see table 1.2). The remainder of the schedule consisted of fieldwork and labs in such topics as drawing, military drill, and physical training.[13]

Table 1.2. Almond's Schedule of Classes for Fall 1912

Time	Days of the Week	Subject
8:00–9:00	Monday–Saturday	Trigonometry
9:00–10:00	Monday, Wednesday, Friday	German
9:00–10:00	Tuesday, Thursday, Saturday	Open
10:00–11:00	Monday, Wednesday, Friday	Descriptive Geometry
10:00–11:00	Tuesday, Thursday, Saturday	Physics
11:00–12:00	Monday, Wednesday, Friday	English
11:00–12:00	Tuesday, Thursday, Saturday	Latin
12:00–1:00	Monday–Saturday	Open
1:00–2:00	Monday–Saturday	Lunch

Source: General Order No. 6, Schedule of Classes, September 6, 1912, Order Books, 1912–1913, Virginia Military Institute Archives.

The school also maintained a rigorous exam schedule, even ignoring certain holidays. For instance, midterm exams for the first term (fall 1912) began on January 1, 1913. The cadets had one two-hour exam each day for three weeks, and anyone who failed an exam automatically repeated it. Any cadet found deficient after a review exam then took an oral exam.[14]

Almond excelled academically from the start of his education at VMI, earning top marks in Latin, physics, French, inorganic chemistry, surveying, dynamos and motors, electric lighting, boilers, electrical engineering, electrical power transmission, and general merit. He played no sports, saying, "I had no special class distinction as an athlete," but he managed the track team and served on the health committee. Team managers did more than take care of the equipment. They were responsible for planning meets, coordinating schedules, arranging transportation, and running the meets. Almond also served as associate editor of the student newspaper, the *Cadet*, during his senior year.[15]

Confederate Civil War influences permeated VMI during Almond's time there, and he witnessed many memorable events that underscored these ties. The Confederate "Lost Cause" mythology strengthened military traditions at southern military schools such as VMI. VMI revered no Confederate hero more highly than Thomas J. "Stonewall" Jackson, and Almond succumbed to that cult. Jackson had taught courses on natural and experimental philosophy (science) and artillery at the Institute from 1851 to 1861, and his spirit seemed to linger there. Professor Jackson had used six cannons, called the Cadet Battery, to teach artillery tactics. At the beginning of the Civil War, the Confederate Army pressed VMI's two 12-pounders and four 6-pounders into service. The 6-pounders, now nicknamed Matthew, Mark, Luke, and John, formed Poague's Battery of the Rockbridge Artillery and fired from the ridge on which Jackson made his famous stand at the First Battle of Bull Run, where he gained his immortal nickname "Stonewall." Federal forces destroyed one VMI gun during the Confederate retreat from Antietam in September 1862 and captured the other five in June 1864. Secretary of War Edwin M. Stanton returned the battery to VMI in 1866.[16]

When Almond arrived at VMI, four of these famous guns remained in training service, while a fifth fired the Institute's salutes. VMI retired the guns in a solemn ceremony on May 10, 1913, the fiftieth anniversary of Jackson's death. Almond participated in that ceremonial parade, led by the wartime commander, William T. Poague. A larger-than-life Jackson statue, dedicated one week before Almond's VMI appointment, overlooked the parade ground and signified Jackson's omnipresence.[17]

The Lost Cause also linked military virtues to religious ones, with the "Christian knight" Robert E. Lee and "Old Testament prophet-warrior" Stonewall Jackson as the prime exemplars of a noble army of martyrs. With the passage of a half century, time was claiming the last of that "noble Army." Almond could not fail to feel the impact of VMI's rich traditions, or the passing of iconic Confederates and their relations. The VMI Cadet Corps provided numerous escorts or parades marking key events, and Almond participated in several of them. General Lee lay buried at nearby Washington and Lee University, and the Lee family reinterred Lee's father, Richard Henry "Lighthorse Harry" Lee, in the family crypt in 1913 with a VMI cadet escort. The following year, Robert E. Lee Jr. passed away and joined the remainder of the family in Lee Chapel. A year after retiring Poague's battery, the Corps of Cadets also mourned the death of its namesake, William T. Poague, the VMI treasurer and former Confederate artillery colonel. Having commanded the famous battery early in the Civil War, Poague later exhibited heroic leadership while leading an artillery battalion in the Battle of the Wilderness. The Corps of Cadets escorted Poague to his final resting place near his old chief, Jackson, in Lexington.[18]

Almond later said that he learned about VMI traditions from other cadets and from some legendary instructors, but "the most prominent one I recall is Stonewall Jackson, of Civil War fame." Almond remembered, "Stonewall Jackson's statue on the edge of the parade ground was an inspiration as our company marched past it to parade or drill." Each cadet felt a special connection to Jackson. When the general's revered widow passed away during Almond's senior year, it must have been especially moving. The VMI faculty and graduating class honored the family by serving as escorts for the funeral in Lexington.[19]

As an all-male institution, VMI allowed female guests on post only for special events, such as "hops," as the cadets called dances. These included the Opening Hop, Thanksgiving Hop, pre-Christmas Hop, February Hop, Spring Dance, Easter Hop, the Ring Figure, and the Final German. Cadets treated their guests to lunch and dinner on the days they came to VMI, but Almond later lamented that he had little money and therefore did not date very much.

A man's friends often remember him differently than he sees himself, however, and this appeared to be true of Almond. His classmates remembered him as socially active. Almond carried on his flirtations both on the dance floor and in writing, as attested by classmates quoted in his class yearbook: "Say, girls, can't he dance?" one entry read. "They can't forget him and we can all see why." The dance cards he saved and preserved in a scrapbook reveal a healthy interest in the opposite sex and an active social life. His classmates joked that his future lay in becoming a dashing and romantically driven Marine officer, "having sweethearts in every port, and staying there just long enough to keep several of them jealous." They encouraged him to "Go to it, 'Ned,' old boy. 'Sic 'em.'" Whether this appellation first described his forceful nature or his pursuit of the ladies is unknown, but it stuck to him.[20]

World War I began in Europe during Almond's last year at VMI, but it had surprisingly little effect on cadet life. Almond recalled that the class did not discuss anything about such emerging technology as the machine gun and the airplane, nor did the faculty attempt to add anything to the curriculum based on current events. He reported that Col. Jennings C.

Wise, professor of law and economics, began swaying the cadets toward the British side early in the conflict. Almond did not remember any cadets of German extraction, or any who favored that side in the war.[21]

Under Almond's editorship, the weekly VMI newspaper, the *Cadet*, featured Institute news but also summarized the past seven days' important developments from other newspapers. The *Cadet* served as an official publication of the general athletic association, so the bulk of its news concerned VMI sporting activities. The September 16, 1914, issue, for instance, might well have carried news of the First Battle of the Marne that had just ended, or at least the beginning of the war. Neither appeared, however, in favor of articles on the football team and the recent death of Colonel Poague. The editions for the remainder of the year devoted scant attention to the war, never featuring more than one article related to the conflict. In the May 15, 1915, issue of the *Cadet*, the final edition of the academic year, Colonel Wise wrote a column titled "Submarine, Blockade, and Neutral Rights" that explained the laws of war and American neutrality rights in the wake of the recent sinking of the RMS *Lusitania*. For Almond's class, this appeared too late. The Class of 1915 graduated largely ignorant of military affairs in Europe and around the world.[22]

Despite VMI's reputation as a military school, its graduates did not automatically receive commissions, as West Pointers did. The small US Army required relatively few officers. Almond later remembered that "while in the days of my cadetship nobody [could] go into the Army unless there happened to be a vacancy [and] that was supposed to be given only to the top graduates of our school." Almond had excelled academically at VMI and graduated third in his class of sixty-five cadets in June 1915. Elated over surviving a demanding academic program but with no immediate military options, Almond sought civilian employment. He and his classmates joined a small minority of Americans with college educations, just a little over 3 percent of the population. Since Almond had majored in electrical engineering, he hoped to secure a job with Westinghouse or another big manufacturing firm. He also considered becoming a chemical engineer or a physics teacher. A man with Almond's drive surely felt the need to prove himself.[23]

Almond's friend Rutherford H. Spessard had finished first in their class and landed a teaching job at Marion Military Institute (MMI) in Marion, Alabama. He helped Almond obtain an interview with the school's president, Col. Hopson O. Murfee, who hired Almond to teach French, physics, and mathematics. MMI, a two-year college located about seventy-five miles southwest of Birmingham in the bucolic Alabama countryside, provided a military environment similar to VMI. Though founded in 1842, the school had shed much of its military image in the early twentieth century and had modeled itself after an English public school. When Almond arrived, however, the outbreak of World War I had pushed the school back toward a military stance. Almond knew that America's entry into the war loomed on the horizon, and he began angling for a commission shortly after he arrived in Marion.[24]

Almond's path to a military career would not be easy. With the Great War under way in Europe, the question of America's preparedness consumed the War Department and the US government. The War Department tried to proceed with military expansion, but public opinion remained divided. Many Americans considered military readiness unimportant, and even dangerously provocative. President Woodrow Wilson and the Democrats were initially opposed. The Republicans, encouraged by former president Theodore Roosevelt, had been agitating to increase the size of the armed forces since the outbreak of war in 1914, and by the next year, major newspapers and the more educated public had become convinced the nation was not prepared to defend itself. Most voters, however, perceived that the country faced little peril, as did their representatives in Congress When the German navy sank the British liner RMS *Lusitania* on May 6, 1915, with the loss of 123 American lives, however, the country's mood quickly changed. By the fall of that year, public support for preparedness had grown so much that Wilson could no longer ignore it. Though he remained opposed to any large military measures, he also faced an election in 1916 with widening fractures in his own party.[25]

In the spring of 1916, Almond enlisted a local attorney, J. G. Hiden, to aid his bid for an Army commission. Hiden had heard that a pending "Army Bill," might provide Almond with the opportunity he sought and recommended that Almond contact his congressman. "My understanding of the matter is that no designations will be made until after the bill passes," Hiden wrote. "I think it would be well for you to get what influence you can command and try to get your name designated to take the examinations."[26]

Ironically, Hiden recommended approaching Representative James Hay for assistance, evidently hoping that the congressman would be pleased to provide a little patronage. The Democratic representative since 1897 of Virginia's 7th District, which included Almond's home, Hay chaired the powerful House Committee on Military Affairs from 1911 to 1916. Unfortunately for Almond, Hay was a rabid opponent of preparedness and counted few friends in the War Department. From the beginning of the Wilson administration, Hay had battled Lindley M. Garrison, the secretary of war. Garrison was an able and vigorous administrator, determined to strengthen the Army and keep it free from political interference. He protested what he saw as congressional attempts to usurp the duties and powers of the War Department. As the country's mood changed, the *New York Times* and other major newspapers attacked Hay for his lack of support for the military. Feeling the pressure, Hay finally decided, despite his personal opposition, to endorse the administration's evolving policies.[27]

This contradiction reveals the serious difficulties President Wilson's party faced as he approached the election of 1916. Secretary of War Garrison proposed a moderate defense program designed to both appease the preparedness supporters and not anger the administration's friends in the Democrat-controlled Congress. That program, which went to Congress as the Army Bill, included a small increase for the Regular Army but also called for the creation of a new, federally controlled National Army to be kept on a reserve status.[28]

Garrison's National Army would consist of some 400,000 volunteers recruited over a period of three years, with the Regular Army providing the troops with training for short periods every year. Attacked from both ends of the political spectrum, the first version of this bill ultimately failed. Some congressmen feared that voluntary recruitment would fall short and be replaced by conscription. As a canny politician, however, Hay saw an opportunity to both reduce Garrison's influence and strengthen his party's support. He proposed an alternative Army Bill that focused on strengthening the National Guard through federal funding. The reworked Army Bill reached a final vote on March 6, 1916. Hay, having been adamantly opposed to preparedness, thus became its champion, albeit on his terms.[29]

The preparedness movement got a boost from other developments. Three days after the House passed the Army Bill, Mexican revolutionaries led by Francisco "Pancho" Villa raided Columbus, New Mexico, and triggered a punitive response by the US government. Tensions with Mexico and the growing war in Europe began changing the mood in the United States, and the preparedness movement gained traction. Hay's Army Bill reached the Senate, which made modifications and passed it. President Wilson signed the Army Bill as the National Defense Act of 1916 on June 3. The act provided for the federalization of the National Guard and increased its size. It also created the Organized Reserve Corps and the Reserve Officers Training Corps (ROTC), but most important for Almond's purposes, it authorized the recruitment of sixteen hundred more officers.[30]

Though the act authorized Army expansion, that growth moved slowly for the next ten months. On the eve of the US declaration of war with Germany in April 1917, the regular US Army contained only 133,111 soldiers, with another 76,713 National Guardsmen in federal service (see table 1.3). Over the next year and a half, the Army expanded to an unprecedented size. By the end of the war in November 1918, US Army strength stood at 4,176,297, which included 203,876 officers. This officer corps expansion gave Almond the opportunity he needed for a commission. He took a test-preparation course offered in August 1916 for potential Army officers and then passed the examination itself. Almond received a commission as a "provisional" second lieutenant of infantry in the riding hall at Fort Myer, Virginia, on November 30, 1916. After the ceremony, he returned to Marion Military Institute to resign his instructorship.[31]

Marion forever held a special place in Almond's heart, for there he

Table 1.3. Strength of the US Army as of April 1, 1917

Component	Officers	Enlisted	Total
Regular Army	5,791	121,797	127,588
Philippine Scouts	169	5,354	5,523
National Guard (Federal Service)	3,733	76,713	80,446
TOTAL	**9,693**	**203, 864**	**213557**

Source: Kreidberg and Henry, *History of Mobilization in the United States Army,* 221-22.

met the love of his life, Margaret Crook of Anniston, Alabama. Margaret attended Judson College, a women's school in town. Judson women often attended MMI football games and other cadet functions, and Almond fell for Margaret almost immediately. He had dated many women during his VMI years, but at Marion he only had eyes for Margaret. They spent their Sunday afternoons together, and those days acquired a special meaning for both of them.[32]

Almond's entry into military service made courtship and marriage difficult, but neither Ned nor Margaret allowed these problems to stop them. Almond's subsequent correspondence with Margaret reveals his love for her, his loneliness, and a fear that their separation might cause her to find another suitor. His letters indicate his devotion to Margaret, but they also reveal a bit of the insecurity that would color the rest of his life: "Well, dear, sometimes on Sunday afternoons, remember, where you are out there on the lawn with someone else, that away down on the border, in a tent all covered with dust and flapping in one continuous wind, there is someone always dreaming of "you and the future" and thinking how wonderful you are and who still offers up his little prayer every night "that she may not forget!"[33]

Almond proposed to Margaret in the spring of 1916 and met her parents, Samuel Leander and Ione Crook, at Christmas of that year. Margaret agreed to be married, but the couple made no definite plans until Almond received his commission in the Army. Almond sought Samuel Crook's approval, stressing his love for Margaret but striking a pragmatic tone calculated to impress his future father-in-law with his maturity. He promised to care for her and make plans for her support if he should be killed in action. Samuel Crook answered a short time later and gave his blessing.[34]

Almond's development from boyhood through college, his marriage, and entry into the Army set the pattern for his life and military career. Life in the postbellum South, with its strong Confederate and military influences, shaped his outlook. Almond no doubt developed attitudes toward black people early on that would become apparent only decades later. Neither he nor his contemporaries would have considered their views racist. The nation's social and legal framework guaranteed a separation of the races, and Almond accepted this as reality.

2

Introduction to Combat

1916–1919

Just after Christmas 1916, Almond reported to Fort Leavenworth, Kansas, for three months of Officer Candidate School (OCS). Almond joined the first provisional class, composed of some three hundred officers (including future general officers Thomas T. Handy, Lee Gerow, Leonard R. Boyd, and Withers "Pinky" Burress) who had recently taken the commissioning exam. This class included officers from the infantry, artillery, coast artillery, and cavalry. They all attended class together to receive basic military instruction before reporting to their respective units. All officers trained on basic military subjects, physical fitness, and equitation. They also received some basic infantry instruction, such as exercising and giving commands, with some field exercises.[1]

Upon graduating from OCS, Almond joined the 4th Infantry Regiment at Fort Brown, Texas, on March 22, 1917. Fort Brown was an old nineteenth-century post located at the southernmost point of Texas near the present-day town of Brownsville, just across the Rio Grande River from Matamoros, Mexico. Originally named Fort Texas, Fort Brown was founded in 1846 at the beginning of the war with Mexico to establish the southern boundary of the United States on the Rio Grande. When Almond arrived, the regiment was on border guard duty following General John J. Pershing's Punitive Expedition the previous year. Almond joined Company F, and soon assumed command while his company commander completed a special assignment.

Almond's letters to Margaret in Alabama reveal the love and devotion of a young man clearly smitten with his girl. In a relationship committed yet still new, he was trying out "Little Girl" as a pet name for her while addressing his letters "Dear Crook."[2] The letters proclaimed his longing for her, with a dash of bravado mixed in. One letter in mid-May 1917 mentioned that the regiment was moving to Gettysburg for training, then assured her that the Army would not deploy to France until it was trained, and when the Americans did go, "they'll be heard from, whoever they are," a reference to the VMI motto "The Institute will be heard from today." Almond also related the humorous aspects of military life, such as a recent ceremony in which he had commanded the company for the parade. As Almond marched around the last turn before passing in review of the commanding officer, two goats joined the formation and one marched beside him until the end. The reviewing officer and the audience found the incident hilarious, and Almond barely maintained his composure until he completed the parade.[2]

The regiment left Fort Brown on May 28 for Gettysburg, Pennsylvania. The War Department had assumed possession of the famous battlefield from the Gettysburg Battlefield Memorial Association by act of Congress in 1895 and would retain ownership until 1933. The declaration of war highlighted the need for large training areas, so the department set aside some sixty-two acres in the Gettysburg National Military Park for infantry regiments then forming at other locations around the country.[3]

The US Army's rapid mobilization and expansion caused several structural changes. Starting with a constabulary force of little more than 125,000 active duty soldiers employed in "penny packets" from the United States to the Philippines, the War Department sought to increase the size and strength of the Army to enable it to fight much larger and more capable European armies. When the war began, the regiment constituted the largest single unit in the US Army. In order to create the military force required to wage war on a European scale, the Army needed to expand along unprecedented lines. The commander of the American Expeditionary Forces (AEF), General John J. Pershing, anticipated the need for one million troops and an expanded organizational framework to project American power to Europe.[4]

The initial War Department mobilization plan envisioned a three-brigade division totaling some 25,000 troops. An Army War College force structure study based on initial AEF staff reports had determined that three brigades would allow divisions the flexibility required to rotate in and out of the line. Because of the need to get troops overseas quickly, however, the War Department modified the plan and activated only two brigades per division, with two regiments per brigade. Regiments consisted of three battalions of one thousand soldiers each, with each battalion divided into three companies. Each regiment also included a headquarters company, a supply company, and ordnance and medical detachments. With an attached machine gun company, the regiment totaled 3,832 men. Army leaders split and expanded the existing formations to form "cadres," or core elements for new larger units. Platoons grew into companies, companies became battalions, battalions became regiments, and regiments paired to form brigades. Brigades in turn also paired to form the so-called "square" division. In this way, the US Army quickly increased its size, though not necessarily its effectiveness.[5]

The 4th Infantry Regiment began reorganizing shortly after it arrived at Gettysburg in June 1917, becoming the cadre for the newer units then being activated. The regiment split into three parts, one of which retained the 4th Infantry Regiment colors and moved to the 3rd Division. The other two became the 58th and 59th Infantry Regiments. After this reorganization, Almond joined Company M, the machine gun company, in the 58th Infantry Regiment. The 58th Infantry occupied the famous Codori Farm, a thirty-three-acre tract on the southeast side of the Emmitsburg Road in Gettysburg.[6]

When Almond arrived, the company had only its soldiers, uniforms, and sixteen mules lacking saddles or harnesses. It lacked weapons of any kind, but did possess manuals and wooden guns for drilling purposes. Incredibly, the unit received only a few light machine guns and personal sidearms with which to train while at Gettysburg. Almond enjoyed seeing the places he had read about in high school and at VMI, and he later recalled: "The real first month's training at Gettysburg comprised mostly training of the animals and getting the men used to the mules. We would take the mules out for exercise along the battlefield roads that were famous in history for the battle of Gettysburg. . . . This was of interest to the soldiers as well as to the officers of the company."[7]

Almond and Margaret had nurtured their relationship despite his moving around, and his imminent deployment to war doubtless increased their urgency to marry. They set the date for August 4, 1917, Margaret's twentieth birthday, and she began planning the ceremony. The military's mission took precedence over an individual officer's personal plans, however, as Almond quickly discovered. One week before the wedding date, Almond received orders to go to New York to muster in National Guard outfits. This called for some fast work, precise timing, and a little luck. He completed his tasks at midnight on August 2–3, and then took the next train to Anniston. He arrived the following day, just in time for the wedding. After spending their wedding night in the Winecoff Hotel in Atlanta, the Almonds took a short honeymoon trip to New York City before returning to Gettysburg as husband and wife. Almond had found rooms with Mrs. W. C. Sheeley at 143 Springs Avenue in which they could live comfortably while Ned's unit prepared to sail for France. The early days of the Almond marriage were doubtless filled with dreams of the future, tainted by fear of the unknown. Margaret wrote to her parents after she had been in Gettysburg a month or so, telling them of her fears and joys, in a letter she titled "What Ned Means to Me." [8]

The War Department activated the 4th Infantry Division on December 3, 1917, and directed it to assemble at Camp Greene, North Carolina, under the command of Maj. Gen. George H. Cameron. The 58th Infantry departed from Gettysburg in November 1917 en route to Camp Greene, where it joined the 59th Infantry to form the 8th Brigade. That brigade joined the 7th Brigade (39th and 47th Infantry) and associated support units to form the 4th Division. The Army Act of May 18, 1917, authorized filling all units to maximum strength, federalized the National Guard, and authorized drafting up to one million men. The War Department also ordered all enlistees in the country to be sent to the 4th Division.

The soldiers moved south to a supposedly warmer climate but found instead a cold, deep, snowy winter. With few paved roads, the raw weather turned the camp and surrounding area into impassable muck. Conditions deteriorated to the point that supply trucks could not get into camp from nearby Charlotte, so food and other supplies came in by mule train. The soldiers lived in overcrowded tents throughout the winter months, each with a small stove providing the only source of heat. Soldiers cut their own firewood from the green timber surrounding the camp. The division chief of staff later credited the harsh conditions at Camp Greene with toughening the soldiers for what lay ahead of them in France, but the weather also seriously impeded military training. Between December 10, 1917, and March 4, 1918, the weather allowed only sixteen days of useful training. During one period in February, the regiment suspended training for more than a week so that soldiers could go out and clear roads around the camp.[9]

Camp Greene, one of the sixteen training posts developed quickly to support the rapidly expanding Army, experienced terrible overcrowding. Construction had begun on a 2,150-acre lot just west of Charlotte on July 23, 1917. Over the next two years, the US Army erected more than 6,000 tents, 326 mess halls, 377 showers, 4,212 latrines, 320 stables, and 275 other buildings, as well as twenty-two miles of roads and four and a half miles of railroad siding. The 3rd Division had been activated at Camp Greene on November 23, and it shared space with the 4th Division. New men came in every day, and these new men required mental and physical evaluations for fitness before they could move on to training. This constant influx of new men and removal of old or unfit ones made cohesive training difficult. The spring of 1918 brought some relief as the 3rd Division completed its stateside training and left Camp Greene for France, and the weather began to improve. Better conditions allowed the artillery brigade finally to shoot live ammunition in the woods near Gastonia, North Carolina, and the infantry began to exercise the skills learned in the classroom over the winter.[10]

After the division was activated, it compelled each regiment to transfer a small number of soldiers from each company to fill out three machine gun battalions, one to each brigade and one in general support of the division. The 10th Machine Gun Battalion would provide that general support, while the 11th and 12th Battalions supported the 7th and 8th Brigades respectively. With few senior officers yet assigned, the 8th Brigade commander directed Almond, now a temporary captain, to form the 12th Machine Gun Battalion. Almond activated the unit on December 1, 1917. At the beginning, Almond had eight officers, 150 soldiers, sixteen mules, and four wagons. All officers attended a two-week machine gun training course while the unit formed.[11]

After about three weeks, the battalion's permanent commander, Major H. J. M. Smith, arrived and assumed command as the unit grew to its authorized strength of 730 officers and men. Almond then took over Company A. Each machine gun company contained three platoons with four guns each, and each platoon typically supported a battalion of infantry. Commanders normally employed the platoons by themselves, but they could also mass their guns for additional firepower. The machine guns laid down covering fire at likely enemy positions out to about 1,000 yards, with some guns aimed at the expected front lines and others at potential observation points. Almond's unit would then advance with the infantry, synchronizing its movements to provide support whenever the troops moved.[12]

Almond entered the infantry, and specifically the developing environment of the machine gun unit, at an auspicious time. Before the First World War, the US Army had begun a modernization program that extended from the War Department down to individual units. Planners struggled with the numbers of officers, men, and guns for each machine-gun unit, a conflict reflected all the way up the chain of command as the War Department worked to refine responsibilities and create appropriate structures. Specifically, the department's inability to collect and interpret intelligence coming out of the war on new techniques and procedures stymied its development of machine gun units. The Army failed to appreciate this new weapon or to develop proper plans for it, and generally geared tactics toward the capabilities of a specific gun rather than automatic weapons in general.[13]

On April 23, 1918, the 58th Infantry Regiment began boarding trains for Camp Mills, New York, one of several embarkation stations established for soldiers en route to Europe. All the regiment's personnel received a twenty-four-hour pass to visit New York City as the unit conducted last-minute preparations for sailing, and Margaret rushed from Charlotte to New York by train to see Almond off as his unit departed. As she later wrote her parents, "I had no idea that Ned would get here till [this morning], when the phone call came for me, and I heard his voice once more. . . . goodness! how I wish for the old days back in Gettysburg! But I can't tell you how happy I am that I can see him now."[14]

Margaret stayed in the Garden City Hotel on Long Island and Ned visited her from Camp Mills as often as he could. Her letters reflect the pride she felt in her husband, and the fear of an Army wife watching her husband leaving for perhaps the last time: "Ned and I are being very happy and gay these last days. I blind myself to the fact that I must give him up. And I will try *very very* hard to be smiling when he goes. But one never knows how it will be in the end. When I get back to you I promise to make the best of it."[15]

The 58th Infantry sailed in stages from May 7 to 10, 1918, aboard five different ships sailing from different East Coast ports. Almond's 12th Machine Gun Battalion, plus an infantry regiment and Signal Corps and Air Squadron units, boarded a large British ocean liner, HMS *Aquitania,* at Hoboken. All the regiment's transports steamed to Halifax, Nova Scotia, where they met a convoy escort for the ocean crossing. The convoy carrying Almond's 8th Brigade sailed from Halifax on May 11, 1918. This convoy, one of the largest sent to France during the war, totaled some fifteen ships carrying 45,000 men.[16]

Misfortune struck the convoy early: HMS *Themistocles*, carrying the regimental headquarters and three rifle companies, developed engine trouble and returned to Halifax. After repairs, it sailed with a later convoy, but the soldiers aboard would not rejoin the rest of the regiment until mid-June. True calamity struck Almond's regiment almost within sight of their destination. Just after 2:30 a.m. on the cloudy morning of May 23, a German submarine evaded the convoy's five-destroyer screen in the English Channel and torpedoed HMS *Moldavia,* carrying Companies A and B. The daily lifeboat drills during the crossing paid off, and no one on the *Moldavia* panicked. Destroyers circled the stricken ship and picked up survivors in boats while the remainder of the convoy fled under escort for the Thames River and London. The 58th Infantry lost fifty-five men from Company B and one from Company A, but things could have been much worse. The survivors landed later that day in Dover and began receiving spare clothing from local citizens. The remainder of the regiment, having arrived safely at London, disembarked and boarded trains for Dover.[17]

After the 4th Division arrived in France on May 26, it traveled by rail to the village of Samer. This short movement exposed the green American soldiers to the horrors of war. Wounded soldiers, destroyed buildings, antiaircraft guns, and contingents of downtrodden German prisoners of war all bore witness to what awaited the 4th Division at the front. The US II Corps assumed control of the division and further assigned the newly arrived Yanks to the British 16th Infantry Division for training and supply. The British provided their American guests with British equipment and schooled them in their methods.

Almond's brigade settled in at LaTurne, France, with the 51st (Highland) Division for training on the Vickers machine guns and other weapons. The Americans lamented losing their Springfield rifles in favor of British Enfields for training. The men also disliked British rations, which were less filling and did not include coffee or sugar. After a couple of weeks of training, the 58th Infantry turned in the British gear and reclaimed its American equipment. On June 9, 1918, the regiment began a three-day move by both train and foot to Lizy-sur-Ourcq, where it would join the rest of the division. The ad hoc nature of World War I unit deployments has been forgotten over the years, but certain aspects of it provide a cautionary tale. The harsh winter at Camp Greene and the urgency to move overseas had prevented the 39th Regiment of the 7th Brigade from conducting any marksmanship training. On June 13, the men of the 39th Infantry Regiment finally completed their long-delayed first target practice.[18]

As the Americans moved closer to the front, they began assisting in trench construction, and also suffered some of their first casualties. The French 164th Division began training Almond's soldiers at Lizy-sur-Ourcq on the Hotchkiss machine gun. The Americans trained until the middle of July, but did little live-fire training and no combined arms training with artillery. They had lectures on collaboration with these units, but no practical exercise. The French instructors proved tough taskmasters, and they prepared the Americans well. Speaking through interpreters, the Frenchmen focused on the proper function and employment of the machine gun, and Almond considered this highly useful. Almond found the French-issued Hotchkiss machine guns heavy and unwieldy, but reliable and stable. Almond thought the French officers alert and educated, but sometimes emotional. He judged French units flexible and loyal to the cause, but undependable unless favorable conditions existed.[19]

The US Army's rapid expansion exacerbated the problem of finding enough experienced personnel to fill key positions. NCOs could be either draftees or career soldiers who came with a unit's original cadre. Among draftees, the Army tried to mold older, more seasoned men into NCOs. Almond's first sergeant, a career soldier, had a drinking problem, which made him unreliable. Almond's outfit contained a mixture of soldiers from different backgrounds and regions. Years later Almond remembered: "That was one of our problems. The educational advantage of most of our men was mid-high school or better, but there were some men who were illiterate and that had to be taken into consideration in their assignment to duty, especially a weapon like the machine gun which involved clinometers, compasses, and clearances in feet and yards."[20] The need for more officers drove enlisted men with good educations to Officer Training Camps (OTCs), but by the summer of 1918 the caliber of enlisted soldiers going to the OTCs had dropped. Those remaining in the ranks varied in education, experience, and aptitude.[21]

Unknown to Almond, tensions among the Allies ran high at the time the 4th Division reached France. General Pershing sought to accumulate enough American units in France to build an American-led army, but he faced significant pressure from Britain and France to amalgamate his force with the existing Allied armies. A German offensive in March 1918 had bled the Allies white and driven two large salients, or bulges, into the Allied line. The French, drained of manpower by three years of war in their own country, anxiously sought reinforcements. Pershing remained adamant that his American Army must ultimately operate as an independent partner of the Allied forces, but agreed to allow temporary "amalgamation" to stabilize the front.[22]

The Aisne-Marne Offensive, or the Second Battle of the Marne, gave Almond his first taste of combat. The Germans had launched an offensive on March 21, 1918, aimed at a weak British sector in hopes of splitting the Anglo-French alliance. The assault continued deep into the Allied lines in a series of offensives lasting into June. The resulting bulge formed a giant U shape roughly thirty-seven miles wide and twenty-eight miles deep, bounded on the south by the Marne River, with the Aisne and Vesle Rivers forming the open end. The Germans had anchored their defense near the town of Soissons on the northwest shoulder of the bulge while

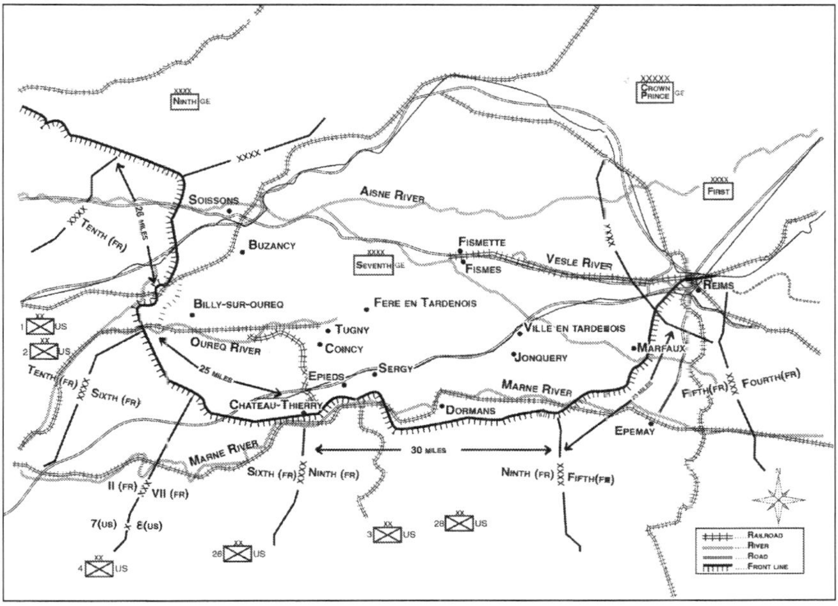

2.1. Second Battle of the Marne, July 15–August 6, 1918

fixing the southeastern corner on the town of Reims (see map 2.1). The Germans had planned another great offensive to begin on July 15, 1918. The French learned of this intention, however, and quickly organized a massive counterattack. With the 4th Division now consolidated near the Marne, the 58th Infantry began its final training before going into combat. The 4th Division conducted its last maneuver exercises on the brigade and division level, and sent liaison teams to observe British and French units in the trenches.[23]

Proximity to the front lines imbued this training with an urgency and realism impossible to attain in the States. Almond rated the 4th Division adequate in close-order drill and small-unit training, but it had not conducted any large-scale maneuvers, and he doubted its dependability in combat. His machine gun company had trained with its weapons but still lacked adequate experience. The artillery trained independently, and the division had no cavalry. The 4th Division would enter battle unprepared for combined arms operations—the sine qua non of modern warfare.[24]

Marshal Ferdinand Foch, Supreme Allied Commander, conceived a massive counterattack to begin on July 18 to reduce the salient. Foch planned to crush the bulge using five French armies, which included the newly arrived American divisions as well as French, French colonial, and British troops. The French Tenth Army, which included the US 1st and 2nd Divisions, would launch the main attack with five corps along a twenty-six-mile front (see map 2.1). The French Sixth Army, which included the American 4th and 26th Divisions, joined the Tenth Army at the Ourcq River and would assault a twenty-five-mile front in support of the main attack. The French Ninth Army, which included the US 3rd and 28th Divisions, was assigned to the longest stretch of the front along the Marne River, some thirty miles. This army would hold the front of the bulge and slow the retreating German armies. The French Fifth Army, which contained no American units, held a twenty-eight-mile front stretching northward toward Reims and would also slow the escaping Germans.[25]

Some of the American divisions went into the line intact, but the green 4th Division's brigades entered the French Sixth Army's sector on July 17 individually. The 7th Brigade was assigned to the French II Corps, while the 8th Brigade went to the French VII Corps. The 58th Infantry joined the French 164th Division, which formed three *groupements* or task forces, each consisting of three French battalions and one American battalion with its supporting machine gun company. The 3rd Battalion, 58th Infantry, and Almond's Company A, 12th Machine Gun Battalion, went to the reserve group mustered at Château de Brumetz, and reported no enemy contact between July 18 and 22.[26]

Although Almond was going into battle for the first time, he had much more to worry about than combat. Anxiety and insecurity would be expected on the eve of battle, but he did not dwell too much on the horrors of trench warfare. He calmed himself by focusing on his leadership tasks: "I was so concerned with the local problems of billeting the men for the night wherever we were, of getting them properly fed, from the field kitchens with a hot meal, and the animals fed, and the company to move out from wherever we were by daylight sometime the next morning, but I had little else to think about or to concern me, except in immediate requirements of the command of a machine gun company, trying to get into the battle area."[27] This penchant for checking the troops and eyeing every detail never left him.

After four days of combat, the Germans retreated and the French halted to regroup. The American regiments returned to 4th Division control and prepared for their next mission. The US I Corps assumed control of the 4th Division and committed it to battle as a unit on August 1, 1918. The 4th Division relieved the US 42nd Division in line and contin-

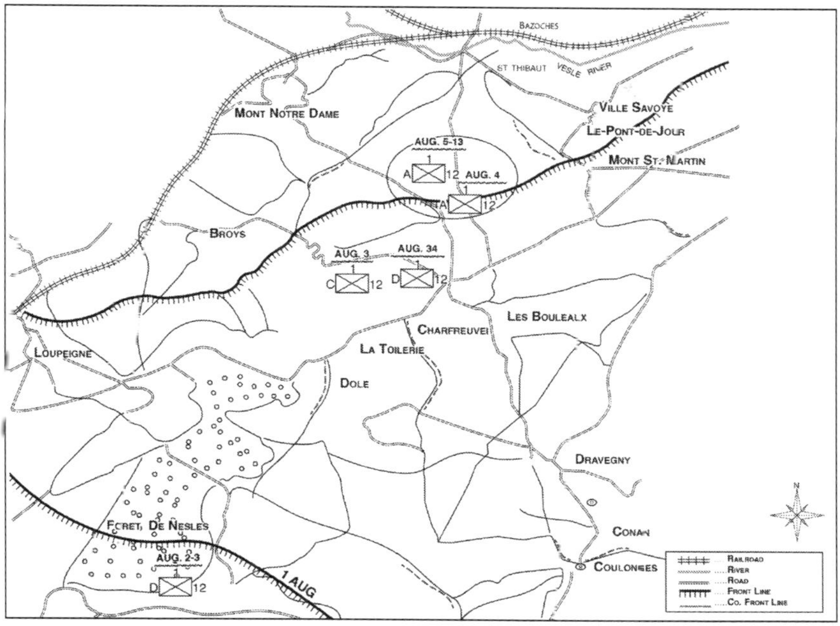

2.2. Attack on the Vesle, August 4–8, 1918

ued pursuing the Germans toward the Vesle River. After a daylong march through rain and mud, with several detours caused by enemy shelling and difficult terrain, the division's exhausted units halted for rest, having advanced only fifteen kilometers. The division attacked in the Forêt de Nesles on the night of August 2 and reached the south bank of the Vesle two days later (see map 2.2). Here Almond's battalion experienced its first real sustained contact with the enemy. The next day, the 8th Brigade renewed its advance to keep pressure on the retreating Germans, this time with the 3rd Battalion, 58th Infantry, and Almond's Company A, in the lead. Almond later recalled: "Our Battalion was used as one of the two assault battalions of the 58th Infantry of the 8th Brigade. My Company A, 12th Machine Gun Battalion, was attached to this battalion. We attacked at dawn from the area of Mont St. Martin and proceeded across the hilltops toward the Vesle on opposite banks—on the eastern bank as a matter of fact, and much of August 3 was occupied with our getting to where the enemy was entrenched in opposition and in strong numbers."[28]

The two battalions encountered withering small-arms fire from the

Germans across the river. Almond's friend and VMI classmate Rutherford H. Spessard took command of the 3rd Battalion, 58th Infantry, when that unit's commander was killed.[29]

From this first combat action, Almond placed himself at the front with his troops. On the evening of August 4, Almond seated himself in an observation post on the front slope of a hill overlooking the Vesle River. From there he could direct supporting fire for an American attack. The 3rd Battalion, 58th Infantry, advanced in a dispersed formation because of the Germans firing from the other side of the river. Almond sent his draft animals and carts to the rear and positioned his machine guns so that they could provide overhead fire across the stream. Just as Almond took a moment to eat, a shell exploded nearby and a fragment struck him in the head. He later remembered: "I had just opened a can of corn willy [corned beef] when a shell broke into our midst from across the stream, and although I had my helmet on it penetrated my helmet and the top of my head. My orderly who had brought me my supper was killed by another fragment, and a number of men in my vicinity were wounded also, and a couple killed."[30]

Medics evacuated Almond to an aid station and later to a field hospital where he recuperated. Almond's small but potentially deadly wound and his performance under fire earned him respect and a commendation. The 4th Division commander, Maj. Gen. George Cameron, later cited Almond's valor:[31] "Staggering to his feet[,] he issued the necessary orders for the welfare of his men, directing that they report to the next senior officer and after making an inspection to see that all were as well protected as possible from shell fire, he consented to be evacuated. His coolness, courage[,] and utter disregard of personal welfare were a great inspiration to his men."[32]

Lt. C. A. Burnett assumed command of the company but was wounded in a gas attack the next day, and Lt. Paul T. Baker replaced him. Almond did not suffer in vain, because his regiment successfully crossed the Vesle River and consolidated a position a few days after his wounding. His battalion's casualties in this action included four officers and eighty-eight enlisted men. His battalion and the rest of the 4th Division spent the remainder of August resting, refitting, and assimilating the lessons learned during the first month of combat.[33]

General Pershing had activated the US First Army on August 10, 1918, in preparation for the AEF's first offensive as a separate field army. Pershing sought to demonstrate the strength of the US Army, and its usefulness as an independent force, by crushing another salient in the Ger-

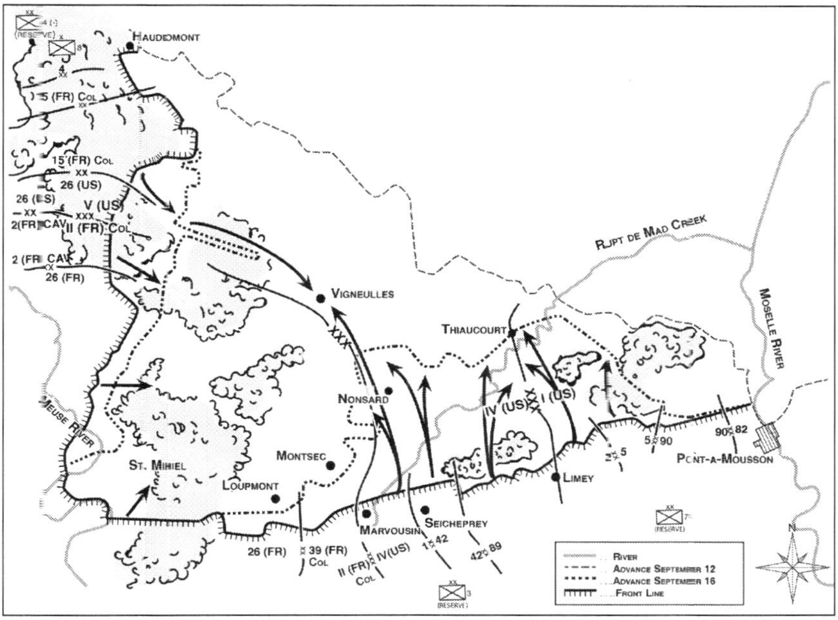

2.3. St. Mihiel Offensive, September 15–18, 1918

man line. For four years, the Germans had occupied a V-shaped bulge roughly thirty miles wide and twenty miles deep, with the point of the V anchored on the town of St. Mihiel (see map 2.3). Pershing had an audacious plan. He would commit an untried First Army with an inexperienced staff to attack both sides of the bulge simultaneously and crush it. Maj. Gen. John L. Hines would lead the 4th Division in this offensive after Maj. Gen. George Cameron took over US V Corps.[34]

Marshal Foch did not support Pershing's plan for the St. Mihiel offensive, because he intended to use the new US First Army in a much larger attack some sixty miles north in the Meuse-Argonne region. Foch acquiesced in the plan with the understanding that Pershing would throw the weight of the US First Army into the Meuse-Argonne region at the conclusion of the St. Mihiel operation. Fortunately, the unknowing Germans cooperated and began pulling out of the St. Mihiel salient shortly before the attack began. Pershing's First Army thus conducted its first combat action against a retiring enemy, which guaranteed an American success. Pershing launched his offensive on September 11, and the First Army achieved all of its objectives in two days. Pershing then began prep-

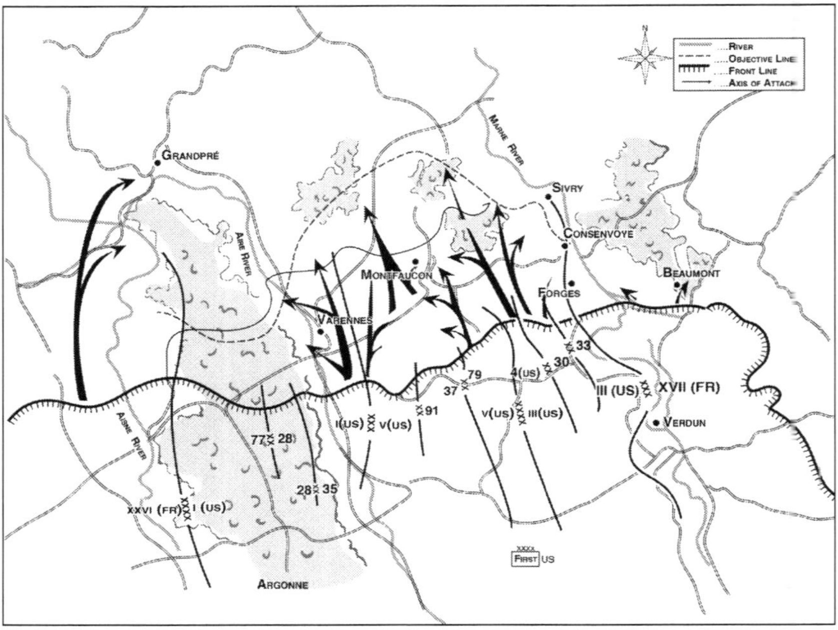

2.4. Meuse-Argonne Offensive, September 26, 1918

arations to join a larger combined Allied assault in the Argonne Forest, scheduled to begin on September 26.[35]

Foch's bold plan dwarfed all other previous Allied attacks, as it envisioned a simultaneous attack by American, French, British, and Belgian armies along a two-hundred-mile-wide front. Pershing planned to support the Meuse-Argonne assault with three corps attacking northwest between the Aisne and Meuse Rivers (see map 2.4). US I Corps (77th, 28th, and 35th Divisions) used the western zone of attack and shared a border with the French Fourteenth Army. US V Corps (91st, 37th, and 79th Divisions) occupied the center zone, while US III Corps (4th, 80th, and 33rd Divisions) attacked in the east and maintained an initial boundary with French XVII Corps at the Meuse River.[36]

Pershing kept one French and six American divisions in reserve. The three-phased plan aimed the weight of the attack at the Kriemhilde Stellung, the key German defense system in the area. The Germans had anchored the defense on the high ground in the center of the sector, with its flanks protected by the Argonne Forest on the west and the Meuse River on the east. Pershing planned the first phase, a seven-to ten-mile advance to capture the heights at Montfaucon and then Romagne and Cunel. Phase II would clear the Argonne Forest to the west while pushing the advance in the center another ten miles. His final phase envisioned an assault across the Meuse River, clearing the heights on the east bank and capturing Mézières. Pershing imagined this enormous undertaking would require no more than a few days.[37]

Almond had tried to rejoin his brigade before it entered the St. Mihiel offensive, but a three-week stay in the hospital and a short convalescent leave to Biarritz prevented that. Fortunately, Almond had caught the eye of the division's machine gun officer (DMGO), who convinced the new 8th Brigade commander, Brig. Gen. Ewing E. Booth, of the young captain's skills. The DMGO urged that they try to expedite Almond's return so he could take command of the 12th Machine Gun Battalion. Booth did so, and recommended Almond's promotion to temporary major.[38]

General Booth enjoyed a reputation for loyalty to his subordinates, and Almond earned that fidelity. Almond performed well and impressed Booth, who respected Almond's work, and the two remained professionally close after the war. Almond nurtured that relationship by sending a congratulatory note when Booth received the French Croix de Guerre, which elicited a warm, self-deprecating response. The US Army officer corps remained a closed society, bound by honor and personal connections, and officers commonly remained in touch. This correspondence initiated by the subordinate to the superior officer also hints at Almond's insecurity as well as his knack for making the right connections. The correspondence continued for many years after the war, and Booth became one of Almond's mentors.[39]

Almond rejoined his regiment on September 26, 1918, just as the 4th Division kicked off its assault in the Meuse-Argonne. In this last large-scale American attack of the war, Maj. Gen. Robert L. Bullard, US III Corps commander, ordered the 4th Division to attack north along the west bank of the Meuse to seize the town of Cuisy and support the attack on the main corps objective of Montfaucon. The 4th Division, with 7th Brigade in the lead and 8th Brigade following, encountered tough resistance in difficult, marshy terrain, but it captured Cuisy and Septsarges early on September 26. The 8th Brigade moved into the division lead on September 29 and continued to advance toward the forest at Bois des Ogons and the heights of Cunel. Almond took command of the 12th Machine Gun Battalion on October 1 and ensured his troops did not sit idle. He instituted a series of weapon shoots intended to demoralize the enemy and cause as much damage as possible. Almond ordered every machine gun in the battalion to fire simultaneously for five minutes at known German positions several times throughout the day. The battalion fired more than 400,000 rounds of ammunition in this manner, and the effect was devastating. When the infantry renewed the assault on October 4, they found large numbers of dead Germans killed by machine-gun fire. Intelligence reports later revealed that the firing had also broken up a counterattack in the area. It was a lesson Almond would not forget, and a technique he was to use throughout his combat career. The 4th Division advanced into the Bois du Fays but ground to a halt in the face of withering machine gun and artillery fire. Unable to proceed further because the AEF divisions also bogged down, the 4th Division established a defensive perimeter.[40]

General Pershing activated the US Second Army on October 12 and named General Bullard to command it. Pershing assigned Almond's 4th Division along with the 7th, 28th, 3rd, 35th, and 92nd Divisions to the new army. The 4th Division remained in place for two more weeks, until General Bullard pulled it out of the line for rest on October 19. After leaving the front, the division marched for seven days to a rest area where it stayed for four days, then moved again to another camp to receive new equipment and replacements. Almond and his battalion joined other Second Army units in a new sector on November 6, in preparation for a new large assault planned for November 12. The campaign had been expensive for the 4th Division, which lost 45 officers killed and 199 wounded, with 1,120 soldiers killed and 6,048 wounded in twenty-four days, the longest consecutive period of any division. Almond's 12th Machine Gun Battalion lost 4 officers and 186 men.[41]

On the morning of November 11, 1918, as Almond moved his battalion from the Second Army assembly area in preparation for the next planned offensive, he and his men began hearing rumors about an imminent armistice. Almond later recalled, "We therefore were in a state of fluidity when a motorcycle rider came down the road yelling, 'The war is over, the war is over!' Nobody in the battalion believed it and they all yelled back, 'Oh! Yes, Oh! Yes, we know but you are a liar.'[42] Almond quickly discovered the rumor's truth, as hostilities ceased.

General Pershing created the US Third Army for the occupation of Germany and assigned to it III Corps with 1st, 2nd, and 32nd Divisions; IV Corps with 3rd, 4th, and 42nd Divisions; and VII Corps with 5th, 89th, and 90th Divisions. The 4th Division began marching to Germany on November 20, arriving in its new occupation zone on December 17. Almond billeted his battalion two days later in the town of Sehl on the west bank of the Moselle River, where it remained until the spring of 1919. In April of that year, the battalion displaced from Sehl to the town of Kripp on the Rhine River, and shortly thereafter to Remagen, where it awaited final orders to return to the United States.[43]

Almond began collecting information for a unit history while commanding the 12th Machine Gun Battalion during the last days of the occupation. He had the history printed and sent copies to many friends and influential acquaintances. He sent a copy of the book to Maj. Gen. Mark L. Hersey, who had taken over the 4th Division in October. Almond continued this practice for the remainder of his career. In addition to providing some of the first, and at times only, histories of the units concerned, the practice cemented relationships with peers and superiors. These histories also served as a canny bit of self-promotion for Almond and shored up his sometimes shaky self-esteem.[44]

Almond's experiences in the First World War taught him some enduring lessons about the value of training. War in Europe had changed the US Army a great deal, and Almond experienced much of that change. Almond also began to exhibit some of the professional traits that became the hallmarks of his career: aggressiveness, personal courage, loyalty, commitment to his mission, a knack for training, and tireless attention to detail. Almond finished the war as a temporary major, having been awarded a citation and a wound badge. When the War Department revised the awards system in the 1930s, the Silver Star replaced the citation and the Purple Heart replaced the wound badge. He had shown personal courage and aggressiveness and demonstrated tactical initiative that marked him as a bright and capable officer. The coming years saw him develop and mature professionally, and his experience and training helped prepare him for continued service. He stayed in the Army as it demobilized, and in the coming years he met and adapted to other challenges.

3

Soldier as Teacher

1919–1933

After nearly a year of occupation duty in Germany, Almond's 12th Machine Gun Battalion sailed back home aboard the USS *Von Steuben*. On what must have been a bittersweet occasion, Almond discharged the remaining soldiers and deactivated the battalion at Des Moines, Iowa, as the Army shrank back to peacetime size. The new National Defense Act of 1920 limited the peacetime Regular Army to 280,000 enlisted soldiers, a restriction that would remain in place until 1941.[1]

The Army also drastically reduced the number of commissioned billets, forcing Almond to compete with his brother officers for retention on active duty. A board of officers evaluated all those competing for the positions to determine their fitness for future service. The board considered the officers' performance records and their commanders' recommendations. Almond's commander, Brig. Gen. E. E. Booth, praised him effusively and highlighted his strong traits:

> He commanded the Battalion in a highly satisfactory manner, in battle, on the march into Germany, and in the training area after arrival in Germany. He had one of the best disciplined and smoothest running organizations I have ever seen. He has excellent tactical judgment, is aggressive and courageous, and possesses most of the qualities so desirable in a commanding office[r] on the field of battle. In the training area he is equally capable, enthusiastic, and energetic and above all is able to gain and keep the loyalty and enthusiastic support of the officers and men of his organization.[2]

Almond's performance in combat, and recommendations such as Booth's, earned him a Regular Army appointment. Having recently commanded first a company and then a battalion in combat, Almond longed to return to an assignment with soldiers. The US Army's drastic postwar reduction, however, made that highly unlikely. Like many of his contemporaries, he would wait more than ten years for another command opportunity. General Booth told Almond that he might as well accept that staff postings would become the norm for a few years anyway. Moreover, in keeping with the ongoing demobilization, Almond lost his temporary major's rank and reverted to captain in January 1920.[3]

Almond's next assignment surprised and pleased him. The War Department ordered him back to Marion Military Institute as the professor of Military Science and Tactics. He did not seek to return to his wife's home, but he certainly welcomed it. Almond assumed responsibility for conducting student military training prior to commissioning. He later professed not to enjoy teaching, but this is the disingenuous claim of the man who wished to be remembered only as a soldier. In fact, Almond was born to teach, and those who are so gifted teach regardless of whether or not they are formally "teaching." Almond taught and mentored in every staff and command assignment in his career. A good teacher is also a good student, and Almond's talent did not end with graduation. A voracious reader with an inquisitive mind, Almond was a lifelong student of his craft. He held four teaching assignments during his career and performed well in them.

Almond's VMI experience helped him land the Marion job, because his classmate Rutherford H. Spessard had returned to Marion as commandant of cadets and had requested him by name. Marion Military Institute was a junior college, and it prepared cadets to take entrance exams for the US Military Academy and the US Naval Academy. After the Reserve Officer Training Corps (ROTC) program began in other civilian colleges nationwide in 1920, Almond converted the military science program at Marion to an ROTC unit. Starting a new ROTC unit and ensuring the cadets met US Army standards required a lot of hard work, and Almond's forceful nature suited his new mission. His cadets performed well during his first year at Marion, gaining "honor school" designation at the first annual inspection. The keen competition among schools pitted ROTC instructors against each other, and Almond enjoyed besting friends and colleagues such as Capt. Alexander "Sandy" Patch at Staunton (Virginia) Military Academy. The time at Marion also saw the growth of Almond's family. The Almonds welcomed daughter Margaret in September 1920 and son Edward Jr. in December 1921.[4]

After four years at Marion, Almond received orders to attend the Company Officers Course at Fort Benning, Georgia. Almond found the school curriculum a stimulating mixture of tactics, logistics, history, map reading, and various other military disciplines. The largely combat-experienced instructor group expected the students to draw on their experiences as well. Almond excelled in the course and remained at Fort Benning after graduation, joining the Infantry School Tactics Department. Almond's experience commanding an AEF machine gun battalion, and the time he devoted to additional study, made him a natural choice to teach machine guns and supporting weapons.

He also made an important connection: Lt. Col. George C. Marshall served as the assistant commandant of the Infantry School during Almond's years at Fort Benning, and Almond caught his eye. During this period, Marshall noted the officers who demonstrated special skills and abilities. Though they did not know it at the time, those officers became "Marshall men," destined for high rank and position. Almond served with several future general officers at Fort Benning, including his fellow tactics instructors, Majors Clarence R. "Ralph" Huebner and Omar N. Bradley. Working with these men gave Almond exposure to their skills, and they surely learned things from him.[5]

Marshall marked Almond's abilities as an instructor, and Almond owed some of his later success to the impression he made on the future US Army chief of staff. Marshall and Almond had never met before, but Marshall had many occasions to observe the younger officer both in the classroom and in the field. Marshall, a 1901 VMI graduate, knew that Almond also hailed from the Institute, but that carried no weight. As Almond later recalled, "General Marshall never let such associations, especially of people he hadn't seen for years, interfere with his actions toward an officer, especially a junior officer."[6]

Fort Benning proved the perfect assignment to develop infantry tactics. Though characterized by lean budgets and public neglect, the postwar years benefited the Army intellectually, as many of its officers used the time for study and self-improvement. Lack of command opportunity meant Almond spent fourteen of the twenty-three interwar years as either a student or a teacher. Almond devoted much of his time as an instructor to overhauling classes and refining theory, and many hours on horseback reconnoitering the routes and positions for each practical exercise. Class development involved evaluating US Army doctrine, and changing it where necessary. Almond taught in the offense section of the tactics department, and naturally focused on the use of machine guns. He wrote an article for the influential *Infantry Journal* that crystallized his thoughts based on his wartime experiences. Titled "Let Machine Guns Support the Attack," it argued that the Army possessed adequate machine gun doctrine but many commanders had failed to use it properly in combat and therefore did not achieve the desired results. Almond's teaching responsibilities included other supporting weapons, such as mortars, in addition to machine guns. He also penned an article defining emerging tactics for mortars, titled "Smoke: The Infantryman's Third Estate." These articles indicated Almond's dedication to his craft as he worked to refine the tactics and procedures he had learned during the war.[7]

Almond joined many of his peers in scholarly explorations of assorted technical issues facing the Army after World War I. Junior officers of the period combined their combat experience with additional thought and training to propose new solutions to problems or to suggest different tactical techniques. Future World War II general officers such as Marshall, Dwight D. Eisenhower, and George S. Patton Jr. contributed articles on a variety of topics to professional journals such as *Infantry Journal.*

Marshall set the tone in 1921 with "Profiting by War Experience," a holistic look at learning the lessons of the Great War. Eisenhower and Patton both examined the future of tanks in the Army, and Patton explored cavalry operations as well. Other officers destined for high command also participated in the Army's intellectual foment. An article on some aspect of machine gunnery appeared at least annually in *Infantry Journal* between the wars, beginning in 1920. Of the twelve monthly issues of *Infantry Journal* that year, seven featured articles related to machine guns. This reflected the service's fascination with a relatively new but important weapon, and it demonstrated that Almond was not alone in his desire to be at the cutting edge of new military technology. These young officers sought to distill the tactics, techniques, procedures, and lessons learned from the Great War into new doctrine for a modern American army.[8]

The military's role in projecting the nation's power also provided grist for the Army officer corps's intellectual mill. The War Department addressed the citizen's role in society, and considered citizenship training important. Officers taught classes to soldiers on the US Constitution, Communism, Bolshevism, pacifism, the National Defense Act of 1920, voting responsibilities, venereal diseases, and sanitation for civil life, in addition to normal military training such as military courtesy and chemical warfare. The War Department believed this training would make the soldiers both better citizens and better soldiers by inculcating appropriate skills and values. The civics lessons helped enlisted men understand the military's place in the nation, while the training in hygiene and sanitation made them healthier soldiers.

Demonstrating this ethos, Almond offered an idealistic picture of citizenship in his first article in *Infantry Journal*, "Training for Citizenship." This article revealed much about Almond's personal attitudes. He identified four characteristics: the Christian religion, a clear and concise understanding of the republican form of government, love of country in peace and in war, and the principles of health and hygiene. Referring to spiritual grounding, Almond wrote that "the first essential, a Christian religion, needs no discussion: it is a mental state without which any individual attempting to qualify in true citizenship would prove a failure; it is axiomatic."[9] The remainder of Almond's article stressed patriotic duty. He argued that basic civics lessons would make for better-informed citizens and soldiers, and that they must understand the Constitution, the three branches of government, and the rule of law. Love of country meant supporting it in peace and in war, preparing to defend the nation, and rejecting pacifism. Almond also raised the controversial notion of Universal Military Training:

> Each prospective citizen should prepare himself for his vocation in life, understanding that the best citizen is the sturdy, home-loving, property-owning individual who has a definite aim always before him, but in addition to this vocation should be that of bettering himself to serve (whether man or woman—there is a place for all) his country in time of emergency; his country from the standpoint of armed defense, needs him only in time of war, but when war comes the nation does not want encumbrances, it wants men and women trained in the elements and essentials of the service for which they are needed.[10]

Finally, Almond identified health and hygiene as the last crucial elements for citizenship, arguing that the nation required healthy citizens. "What does an ignorant and illiterate individual know of the essentials of a healthful community?" Almond asked. "Who but the good citizen is going to correct the illiterate?" Almond had also experienced trouble with illiterate and uneducated soldiers during the Great War, and he cited statistics in which the US Army found 30 percent of the draftees to be unfit for service. Educated men made better soldiers.

Almond intended his article as a call for education and preparedness. As he did countless times throughout his life, Almond echoed his boyhood hero's cardinal maxim to close his argument: "Stonewall Jackson once said 'you may be whatever you are resolved to be,' certainly any man or woman of ordinary intelligence may be a good and true citizen; certainly it should be a fundamental of every education to teach citizenship of the right type, impressing upon the student his obligation to[,] as well as the benefits of[,] a republican form of government."[11]

Almond envisioned this article as a guide for brother officers assigned to command American and native units in the Philippines. The United States had seized the Philippine Islands as a colony after the Spanish-American War, which exposed the US Army to sustained contact with its inhabitants. Since nearly every officer could expect to spend at least one tour in the Philippines during the 1920s and 1930s, the article reflected the Army's paternalistic attitude toward the Philippine Scouts and other non-Caucasian soldiers. Army officers would not merely exemplify the traits in the article but must also inculcate them in the native population. This attitude of protective racism typified the US Army officer's worldview during Almond's formative years. Almond had not yet been to the Philippines at this stage of his career, but he had begun to reflect prejudices he absorbed from his fellow officers.[12]

The officer corps of the early twentieth century, whose paternalism stemmed from accepted norms in a white, mostly Protestant, genteel society, accepted discrimination as a fact of life. The racism and anti-Semitism prevalent in the officer corps surely influenced Almond during his career, probably more than his southern upbringing. Army officers of this period subscribed to, and were in fact taught, the theory of "scientific racism," a spin-off from Social Darwinism that used biological evolution to explain why the races differed. Unlike biological evolution, which makes each generation stronger, Social Darwinism holds that "inferior" races, defined as blacks, Jews, and other nonwhites, cannot be changed and that their inherited racial traits have been passed genetically from generation to generation. This deterministic theory grouped physical, cultural, and intellectual attributes of these races, and held that neither improved social circumstances nor education did anything to change them. The eugenics movement popular during the 1920s and 1930s promulgated these theories, supposedly supported by science that proved that the black person's potential for unrestrained violence was inbred and natural.[13]

On the other hand, the movement believed the integrity of the "superior" white race had triumphed many times over the nonwhite races, with natural selection leaving only the strongest whites to survive. Adherents to this philosophy believed that white men possessed "inherent racial aptitudes" for thinking and fighting and should therefore rule the world. They also believed the United States should end immigration of these "lower" races, and they abhorred miscegenation.[14]

The officer corps embraced these attitudes, and Army schools reinforced them. West Point cadets read Darwinian racial theory before World War I, and Army War College students read such works as Lothrop Stoddard's *Racial Realities in Europe*. Junior officers of the early 1900s could not fail to be influenced by the US Army chief of staff, General Leonard Wood, who wrote to his good friend Theodore Roosevelt, "We have enough national weaknesses and humiliation from the Negro to avoid further trouble by the introduction of races [i.e., Asians] with which we can never mingle." As these junior officers rose through the ranks, they passed on such views, which they had absorbed as impressionable "shavetails."[15]

After Almond departed the Infantry School, he maintained contact with the staff and faculty there and provided critiques of the program. He wrote a detailed letter to Colonel Marshall outlining the two most important deficiencies remaining in infantry training. Almond first asserted that practical instruction in night operations required considerable improvement, pointing specifically to two exercises conducted essentially as demonstrations. Almond argued that these exercises "were of no value because, in [their] execution, [they] were allowed to become a joke among students, who were given nothing of especial importance to do." A third exercise, created only the year before, seemed no better. Almond contended that the Infantry School's night instruction, "when considered in connection with the importance to be attached to the movement of troops, against an enemy, under the protection of night seems rather a pitiful attempt to give officers a working knowledge of one way [of operations]." Almond felt even more strongly about training for long-distance maneuver. Reflecting on his five years at Fort Benning, Almond said he had never seen troops or officers experience the real problems they would face in the field. Students, he wrote, needed to experience the "difficulties of maintaining contact, maintaining organization of combat groups, conforming to prescribed directions of attack, and the cooperation necessary for effective sustained action in an advance over a considerable distance—for example, 2000 or 3000 yards in varied terrain."[16]

Officers required this training, he submitted, in order to arrive at the distant objective with their units intact and ready for action without delay. He then gave a short example from his own experience during the Great War, in which one of the companies in his battalion made a long advance and experienced great difficulties due to the officers' inexperience in making these types of attacks. Almond wrote warmly and politely, but gently lectured the assistant commandant on the failings of the Infantry School. Though Marshall's answer does not survive, Almond heard that the Infantry School changed the course the following year. Marshall appreciated such candor from his officers and encouraged them to challenge the status quo. This sort of professional engagement, and Almond's performance as an instructor, helped make him a "Marshall man," which would profoundly affect his future.[17]

Almond applied for the Command and General Staff School (CGSS) at Fort Leavenworth, Kansas, near the end of his Fort Benning tour. Theoretically, the Army's intellectual milieu provided the opportunity for the brightest officers to get ahead. The selection process at that time was not centralized, and therefore uneven, sometimes favoring officers with senior-level connections. Whatever the reason, Almond received orders to CGSS in 1928. He arrived at Fort Leavenworth in August of that year and received promotion to permanent major at the same time.[18]

The CGSS curriculum changed in 1928 to a two-year program. The course covered tactical use of troops, staff duties, military law, field operations, general application of artillery and logistics, and equitation. The cavalry, of course, steadfastly maintained that horses still had an important operational role since automobile usage in the military remained limited. Almond himself believed that cavalry might still have a role on the battlefield either in rough terrain or in use as mobile forces between larger troop formations. The Army still regarded horsemanship as an important skill for commanders and staff officers, and it remained an important source of exercise. While the CGSS course included discussions of tactics, grand tactics, and strategy, it focused on the principal staff functions of personnel, intelligence, operations, and logistics. As the course grew more complex, students learned to maneuver multiple arms such as infantry, cavalry, and artillery in combined arms operations, which Almond remembered had been so necessary during the last war. He also found logistics, which included hospitalization and medical evacuation, one of the most important parts of the course, because he had little training in it before.[19]

Almond received orders to the Philippines after he completed his studies at CGSS in 1930, and he began preparing the family for the move. The children, Margaret (Peggy), soon to be ten, and Ned Jr., nearing nine, would attend an American elementary school established for the military and diplomatic families assigned to the Philippine Islands. As they would be away from family for the duration of the stay in the Philippines, Almond spent several weeks in Anniston to allow the children time with their grandparents, who doted on them. In August he and his family boarded the US Army Transport *US Grant* in Hoboken, New Jersey, and sailed via the Panama Canal to Manila.[20]

After settling the family in quarters at Fort McKinley in Manila, Almond took command of the 3rd Battalion, 45th Infantry Regiment, Philippine Scouts, in October 1930. Under the US Army rank authorizations of the time, majors commanded battalions, so Almond received no promotion. A colonel commanded the regiment, with a lieutenant colonel as executive officer. The remaining officer leadership contained an even mix of Americans and Filipinos who had attended American military schools. Filipinos filled all the NCO positions and made up the lower ranks. The officers got along well together, but some Filipinos reported that they had received better treatment in the United States as students than they did in their own country from their American counterparts. The battalion's organization, weapons, equipment, and personnel mirrored an American infantry battalion.[21]

The US Army had created the Philippine Scouts in 1901 as a native soldier force with American officers. American troops had occupied the Philippines and fought the insurgents loyal to rebel leader Emilio Aguinaldo in the wake of the Spanish-American War. As the first Americans chosen to officer the Philippine Scouts returned to the States at the end of their tours, enlisted men recruited from American units in the archipelago replaced them. As the Scout establishment grew and matured, Filipinos took some of the lower-ranking officer positions. The Philippine Scouts recruited each of the one-hundred-man companies from a specific area to give it cultural and linguistic homogeneity.

The War Department reorganized the Philippine Scouts as part of the Regular Army beginning in June 1921, assigning them unit designations with the suffix (PS). The scouts formed one "square" infantry division with mixed active and inactive units, designated the Philippine Carabao (often Anglicized as Caribou) Division (PS), after the water buffalo native to the islands. This division contained the 23rd Infantry Brigade (PS), consisting of the 45th and 57th Infantry Regiments (PS) (both active); the 24th Infantry Brigade (PS) (inactive) with the 43rd Infantry (PS) (active) and the 44th Infantry (PS) (inactive); and the 12th Field Artillery Brigade (PS) (active). The Philippine Department, the division's higher headquarters, contained other units not assigned to the division. These included the 91st Coast Artillery Regiment (PS) (active) and the 26th Cavalry Regiment (PS) (active). While other cavalry outfits stateside began losing personnel because of declining budgets and the retiring of horses due to the new technologies offered by automobiles and other vehicles, the 26th maintained its strength until World War II.[22]

Almond's experience reflects the US Army's position in the Philippines during the 1920s and 1930s. The War Department saw Japan as the greatest threat to US possessions in the Pacific, and it developed War Plan Orange to prepare for a possible Japanese attack, but its commitment to the Philippines as part of War Plan Orange waxed and waned over the decade. The Philippine Division's mission changed as the War Department shifted defensive forces in the Pacific from the Philippines to Hawaii and back again. This yielded a combined force too small to protect all of the island of Luzon, and too big to fit in the fortress of Corregidor.[23]

The Army dispersed the Philippine Division throughout the islands to fulfill its defense mission under that plan. The division had established headquarters at Fort McKinley in Manila with the 45th Infantry Regiment headquarters and 2nd and 3rd Battalions there as well. The 1st Battalion split its time between Manila and the Baguio Recreation Area, in the mountains some 150 miles north of Manila. The 57th Infantry Regiment had its headquarters and all infantry battalions stationed at Fort McKinley, while cavalry and artillery staged at Fort Stotsenburg, thirty miles northwest of Manila.

Almond enjoyed his time in command, but the heavy administrative burden endemic to service in the Philippines irritated him. In a peacetime Army, the non-tactical details of supporting an installation had grown to consume the battalion. As Almond discovered, the Philippine Division devoted much of its limited training time to parades and ceremonies. The long monsoon season limited training time in the jungle, allowing Almond only one month a year to maneuver his battalion. The situation frustrated Almond, but all the commanders found themselves in the same predicament. Almond made the best of his reduced training time by concentrating on one or two specific missions. In 1932 he conceived a plan to cross a river using only the battalion's organic equipment. Army doctrine, and Almond's wartime training with the British Army, taught him that most commanders used specialized units or engineer equipment to assist in a river crossing. He collected several articles on past river crossings in preparation for his own mission. He reasoned that an infantry outfit might not have specialized assistance available and should therefore be prepared to make a crossing without it.[24]

Almond assigned his 3rd Battalion a challenging task: cross a 400-

foot, unfordable watercourse (eighteen feet deep, current five feet per second), with all its weapons and transport, using only its organic equipment. Almond's battalion consisted of three rifle companies and one machine-gun company, along with their pack animals and wagons for transporting heavy equipment. For three months the 3rd Battalion trained to execute the mission. This was Almond at his best as a trainer. Officers and men attended instruction sessions, trial and error experimentation, swimming lessons, and rehearsals. The training culminated on December 13, 1932, with a grand demonstration of the techniques the battalion had mastered. Senior commanders from both the 23rd Infantry Brigade and the Philippine Division turned out to watch the show. The brigade commander hosted the demonstration and invited Mrs. Theodore Roosevelt Jr., wife of the governor general, as a special guest. The Malayan Motion Picture Company filmed the entire event. Almond shrewdly planned spectator seating, had a program printed, and arranged for photographers to record the event. To make sure his guests came away with the correct impression, he assigned himself the role of narrator. This gave Almond a lot of positive attention, and no doubt boosted his ego.[25]

Having staged a successful demonstration of military ingenuity, Almond next set out to evaluate it. He provided a detailed report of his men's training and performance, offering his own critiques and suggestions as to how units should prepare to perform this task. Almond then prepared an article, "Methods of Stream Crossing by Combat Units," that appeared in *Infantry Journal* in April 1933. This work received an enthusiastic response and was reprinted in the *Cavalry Journal* of August 1933. In February 1934, Almond recommended that the information in the article be used in a new or revised field manual on stream crossing. He also submitted the film that the Malayan Motion Picture Company had created to the War Department for use as a training film. The War Department lost little time in adopting the production, and it became Signal Corps Training Film 20, *River Crossing*. Almond's attention to detail and relentless advertising of the exercise marked him both as a dedicated trainer and a canny self-promoter.[26]

Almond received congratulatory notes and requests for information on the article over the next several years. Maj. Gen. Paul B. Malone, III Corps Area commander, wrote to commend him on his work and mentioned that he had entertained similar thoughts, but most of his soldiers had recently assumed control of the Civilian Conservation Corps (CCC) camps in his area, which left him too shorthanded for such training. The 4th Infantry Regiment training officer asked Almond for guidance, as that unit was planning identical training. The chief of engineers published a short extract of the article in the periodic "Information Bulletin" he sent to all engineer officers and noted the similarities between Almond's methods and training planned by his branch. As long as seven years after the article first appeared, Almond continued to receive requests for more information. The chief of infantry contacted Almond in 1940 and requested more photographs and his updated thoughts, suggesting these should go in a field manual. In a small professional Army, Almond was gaining renown as a trainer.[27]

While Almond distinguished himself professionally in the Philippines, he left few documents to reveal his feelings about the archipelago's people. It seems likely that he was influenced by the attitudes of previous generations of US Army officers who served there. Most judged the Filipinos on a racial basis, and therefore considered them of a lower grade or quality than white men. These white officers believed that the Filipino mind works differently than the American mind, and every US Army field manual of the time argued that Filipino officers could not be expected to be as good as American officers.[28]

When asked later about the quality of Filipino officers, Almond responded, "They were good officers within their capabilities." This condescending assessment reflected white officers' basic attitude toward native troops. In the Philippines they expressed the same paternalist attitude toward native soldiers that Almond had experienced with respect to African Americans. Indeed, the US Army even imported the segregation policies it found comfortable, ensuring that the American officers did not have to mix socially with the dark-skinned Filipinos.[29]

Almond noted that Filipino NCOs and enlisted men were good and obedient but did not adapt well to unexpected conditions. He cited an example in which troops would deploy "by the book" regardless of whether or not this was tactically sound, such as when the ground made textbook moves difficult. For instance, the textbook method might require the unit to deploy from a line formation to a combat formation 500 yards from the enemy. Almond recalled, "If the ground between 500 yards [from the enemy] and the enemy position was swampy and difficult to negotiate in, they [Filipinos] would deploy [to a combat formation] anyhow, which is not using your judgment but following the book." Despite these reservations, Almond generally thought well of his subordinate officers, including the Filipinos. He wrote warm personal letters to each of his company commanders when he left the Philippines, praising their performance and thanking them for their service.[30]

Tragedy also marked Almond's tour in the Philippines. On July 29, 1931, Almond struck and killed a Philippine pedestrian while driving outside Manila. A report on the accident, termed unavoidable, appeared the next day in the *Manila Daily Bulletin*. The victim had apparently stepped from behind a bus and directly into Almond's path. Almond picked up the stricken man and rushed him to the Philippine General Hospital, where he later died. Local police briefly took Almond into custody but later released him to US Army officials.[31]

Almond concluded his tour of duty in the Philippines in June 1933, and returned to the States to attend the US Army War College at Washington Barracks in Washington, DC. With the world in the depths of the Great Depression, President Herbert Hoover had ordered the War Department to require its officers to take one month of leave without pay, and to do so away from their duty stations. Almond chose to take his month at the end of his tour, and with Army War College classes starting in September, he had a full three months to travel. Almond and his family had enjoyed the time they spent in the Philippines. Margaret (Peggy), now age thirteen, and Ned Jr., eleven, had the adventure of a lifetime as the Almond family made a leisurely trip home, spending a week in Hong Kong, with side trips to Macao and Canton, and three weeks in Shanghai. They then proceeded to Tokyo for another three-week stay, and on to Peking for yet another three weeks, followed by a week in Tientsin. The trip to Tientsin included a side trip to Korea, over much the same ground Almond would cover with X Corps nearly two decades later. The family also spent time with Almond's friend Maj. Charles L. Bolté, then posted to Korea, who would shortly join Almond at the War College and later also command a division in World War II. They then returned to Peking for another three weeks. The family experienced near tragedy when Almond's daughter Peggy contracted dysentery and almost died on the return voyage.[32]

Living overseas at government expense had protected Almond's wife and children from the worst financial difficulties of the Great Depression, but the rest of his extended family was not so fortunate. Margaret's father lost his entire savings to an unscrupulous business partner, and he was forced to seek support from Almond and other family members. Almond pledged to help within his limited capabilities; the episode doubtless reminded him of the pragmatic promises he made when asking permission to marry Margaret.[33]

Almond had spent most of the years since the end of the war in a teaching capacity, either as a trainer or as a commander. Senior officers had recognized his skills, and his reputation was growing. He had also entered the intellectual milieu of the professional journal, penning several articles and adding to the growing doctrinal discourse. Almond combined his knack for training and attention to detail with a flair for public relations and created a well-respected training event that garnered him respect years afterward. He had also commanded nonwhite soldiers in a segregated Army, a preparation for the challenge he would face later.

4

Education of a Senior Officer

1933–1941

Officers found entrance to the Army War College competitive, and Almond's selection surely gratified him. This course differed completely from the CGSS, which focused on operations at the tactical level of corps and below. The Army War College curriculum examined the political, economic, and social matters that influenced the conduct of war. One study of the school pointed out that the War College also taught officers the "duties of the War Department General Staff . . . the joint operations of the Army and Navy . . . [and] the strategy, tactics, and logistics of large operations." From a higher-level planning perspective, the officers attending the War College during this time received excellent preparation for the global conflict in which they would shortly find themselves. Almond recalled that "the War College course was a great advance in intellectual pursuit of national events, whereas the staff course dealt more with the operation of troops."[1]

Almond joined a class destined for high command, including his friend Maj. Omar N. Bradley and forty-five other future general officers. The class consisted mostly of US Army officers, though each of the other services sent officers; Capt. William F. Halsey was in the naval contingent. In addition to the stimulation provided by US Navy and Marine Corps officers, the State Department sent some of its senior staff. The class also attended talks delivered by government officials, right up to cabinet secretaries, and the US Army chief of staff. The visitors presenting special lectures during Almond's year constituted a governmental "who's who." Maxwell H. Hamilton, assistant chief of the Division of Far Eastern Affairs, War Department General Staff, presented "The Situation in the Far East." For financier Bernard Baruch, who had chaired the War Industries Board during the Great War, the topic was "Industry in War"; for Maj. Gen. Fox Conner, former chief of operations (G3) of the American Expeditionary Force, it was "The Allied High Command and Allied Unity of Direction," and for Maj. Gen. Hugh A. Drum, the US

Army's deputy chief of staff, "The War Department General Staff and the General Council." These presentations and many others gave Almond and his classmates insights into important aspects of senior leadership and the preparation for war.[2]

Seven periods of intensive study constituted the Army War College curriculum: the G1 (Personnel) Course, G2 (Intelligence) Course, G3 (Operations) Course, G4 (Logistics) Course, War Plans Course, Conduct of War Course, and Individual Studies Period. Each course focused on field army or higher-level planning, and used a combination of lectures and group projects. At the outset of each course, the class received committee and sub-committee assignments, with a question or problem that each committee would tackle. Each student chaired at least one committee or subcommittee during the year. Course length varied according to the subject matter, but each committee received a schedule and timeline for rehearsals and briefing. The committee then met and developed a plan to address the question.

The War College functioned as the "thinking" branch of the War Department General Staff (WDGS) and routinely addressed questions posed by that agency. The War College commandant solicited input from both the general staff and the chief of infantry for research topics to support ongoing requirements. The record does not indicate whether students' preferences played any role in these committee assignments. Each committee shared its plan with the class and faculty and led a general discussion, then received a critique. The faculty sent some committee plans to the WDGS for further discussion.

The War College courses, starting with the class of 1933–1934 and continuing for the next several years, displayed remarkable prescience. Many of the students' plans, in Almond's class and the years following, focused on coalition war planning. This built on the experience of the last war and anticipated the nature of the next. While the students worked on the plans, they filled the roles of all the senior staff sections and conducted themselves accordingly. Almond's class of 1934 planned for a war in which the United States fought in a coalition against Japan, while the class of 1935 examined the United States in a war with Nazi Germany. The class of 1936 planned for a war against the Central Coalition (Germany, Italy, Austria, Hungary), and the following year's class studied the possibility of war against both Japan and Germany.[3]

Each course presented the officers with opportunities to study new aspects of military operations. During the G1 (Personnel) course, Almond's morale committee worked to "study and report on the measures taken to raise and maintain the morale" of both the Allies and the Germans during the Great War. The committee also analyzed current War Department plans for maintaining American soldiers' wartime morale and plans for lowering the enemy's morale. Almond's committee defined morale as a state of mind, synonymous with the individual's spirit, and determined that early battle success, good leadership, rewards and decorations, and recreation and welfare maintain morale. After studying how other countries addressed the issue, the committee then recommended that the military assume active leadership in the moral and patriotic education of the nation, with the states providing obligatory patriotic education courses in colleges and schools. Other recommendations included better officer training on the human elements of command, and that the military assume control of welfare work in wartime through a civilian agency.[4]

One of the other committee reports that came out of Almond's class addressed "Negro Manpower in the Military Service." Almond did not serve on this committee, but all committees briefed the full class on their findings. The study began by analyzing African, French, and British blacks to set up a comparison with African Americans. It included a demographic study of American blacks throughout the nineteenth and twentieth centuries. The study outlined black military service beginning in ancient times and describing its use during America's wars. The committee devoted its most detailed treatment to the Great War, finding that it offered the best opportunity for analysis due to its scope, duration, and cultural relevance, since all of the students had served during that war. The study found that more than 2.5 million blacks had registered for the draft, representing 9.63 percent of the total registrants. Of the more than 2.8 million American men inducted, 369,710 were black; approximately 344,000 of those entered before September 1918, or 12 percent of the total number of men inducted. Some 180,000 served in France, and 40,000 of those saw combat. Induction medical evaluations found 70 percent of whites and 75 percent of blacks fit for service. Yet draft boards tended to induct more blacks in order to reach the numbers required, because of their higher rates of hospitalization and the perception that black soldiers lacked the stamina of white soldiers.[5]

Blacks had a much higher admission rate to hospitals in 1918, at 200.4 per thousand as opposed to only 121.6 per thousand for whites. Similarly, deaths from disease totaled 20 per thousand among whites, 39 per thousand among blacks. The Army discharged whites for disability at the rate of 62 per thousand, blacks at 175 per thousand. This led the committee to determine that "the great difference between the superior stamina of whites over negroes is due to a large extent to the susceptibility of the negro to infections and contagious diseases." Those beliefs dated to the Civil War, and most post–Civil War studies indicated that black soldiers by nature lacked the stamina of white soldiers. Most of the data from the period points to the supposedly "innate" physical weaknesses of the black soldier, and the War College committee echoed this belief. More recent studies have shown, however, that socioeconomic status played a larger role in mortality rates than did race, with poor white soldiers suffering at the same rate as black soldiers.[6]

The War Department mobilization plans envisioned inducting soldiers by geographic area. This study analyzed existing black manpower in each area and estimated intelligence levels based on figures from the last war. Intelligence testing revealed that 25 percent of whites attained an intelligence rating in the middle, or C group, while only 5 percent of blacks did so. Median mental ages of the two groups were 13.1 for whites, 10.1 for blacks. Using a 1920 survey of officers who had commanded black troops in the World War, the committee further determined that "the negro is unfit for command in combat and the negro unit is inferior in combat to a corresponding white unit." Since the US Army attached great importance to precedent, this statement confirmed for Almond and his classmates the correctness of a racist worldview.[7]

With this information as background, the committee set out to examine how best to utilize black soldiers in the future, based on several assumptions. First, the committee assumed black males would furnish a share of combat troops proportionate to their population, within the limits of their qualifications. The committee reasoned that exempting blacks from such service would "result in a dangerous and unwarranted disturbance of the normal economic and social relationship existing between whites and Negroes in certain sections of the United States," and that political pressure from the "negro intelligentsia" and southern governors could force the administration to act. Second, white and black officer candidates must meet the same physical and mental requirements. Third, training a black unit would take twice as much time as training a similar white unit. Fourth, using African American troops only in noncombat units would reduce difficulties. The fifth and final assumption was that mixing whites and blacks in the same unit, except for officers and some specialists, would be undesirable. The committee essentially repeated the findings of previous studies.[8]

The committee's assumptions reflect the typical white officer's view, and in fact the War Department's official view. Three basic beliefs underpinned US Army policies toward the utilization of black troops as late as 1940. First, blacks should be segregated into separate units because the system had proved satisfactory, because the issue involved social questions that the Army could not address alone, and because severe social disruption would result from integration. Society remained segregated, and the majority of whites supported that segregation. Second, racial characteristics, primarily inferior intelligence, made black soldiers unsuitable for modern warfare. Third, black officers should not be utilized, because experience had revealed a lack of leadership character and because of the inherent distrust of blacks for black direction.[9]

The committee used these studies and the foregoing information to reach an unsurprising conclusion: if required for war, two black divisions should be mobilized using the existing black Regular Army regiments as the nuclei. This recommendation offered the comfort of precedent, since the US Army had formed two black divisions in the last war, and the assurance of political acceptability, since the move would appease the black community. The committee believed that keeping divisions segregated would increase the morale of both black and white troops while preserving the combat efficiency of the white units. The committee rationalized that these divisions could be used in the least important theaters of operation and in noncritical areas. If black divisions entered combat, the committee believed, attack and defense frontages must be reduced to increase their staying power. The committee recommended assigning white divisions to supporting roles to guard against breakthroughs in the black divisions. This report probably confirmed Almond's paternalist expectations concerning how the Army should deal with black soldiers. Its utilization of black soldiers in World War II would closely parallel the committee's recommendations, but this indicates the War Department tendency to follow precedent, rather than the prescience of Almond's class.[10]

The G2 (Intelligence) course prepared Almond for the job he would fill after graduation: drawing up intelligence estimates. Each committee developed intelligence estimates on its assigned area of the world, which supported a specific "color" plan from the War Department. The WDGS had developed color-coded war plans during the 1930s to address specific countries or regions and the particular threats in each. Almond's committee completed an estimate for use in preparing for war with the British Commonwealth of Nations (Red). Despite the fact that scenarios such as war with Great Britain became increasingly unlikely with the rise of Germany, Italy, and Japan as potential foes, the curriculum included these options to give the students an opportunity to plan for many possible contingencies, including multi-theater war. These assignments also required the officers to plan for joint and coalition operations. Their analysis had to consider the potential enemy's geographical, political, economic, psychological, and military situation, evaluate all reasonable lines of action open to that enemy, and propose the course the enemy would pursue in a war with the United States. Almond would use the same criteria in preparing his own estimates some six months later but with different foreign powers in mind.[11]

The G3 (Operations) course laid the foundation for both the Preparation for War and Conduct of War courses that followed. Again using student committees, the class studied six major themes: joint, strategic, and mobilization planning; training, organization, and equipment; defense against specialized threats; coastal defense; military aviation; and structure of the Regular Army. Many students served on more than one committee. The course directive required students to look critically at current plans and operations to assemble and interpret facts, reach conclusions, and make recommendations to any part of the national defense.[12]

Almond's subcommittee number 6 studied the adequacy of the existing Regular Army structure. The National Defense Act of 1920 had authorized a peacetime establishment of 280,000 men, but Congress had failed to appropriate sufficient funding to support such a force. That caused personnel levels to dip to 50 percent of authorized strength, preventing units from being able to perform their assigned missions. The most crucial of these included overseas stationing, coastal defense, and providing a "striking force" prepared to go immediately into combat. At the local level, manpower shortages prevented efficient unit small-arms training, the soldier's basic skill.[13]

The War College's Conduct of War course combined an appreciation for military history with practice in war planning. Each committee analyzed several battles, grouped in categories. Almond and his committee analyzed retreat and pursuit aspects of the Battle of Gettysburg, the German Somme Offensive, and the Vittorio Veneto Campaign from World War I. The committee reported its findings to the rest of the class. To prepare for the next critical phase of war planning, the committee then conducted a reconnaissance of the northern United States in reference to either the Red (Great Britain) or the Crimson (Canada) war plan, after which Almond's staff group used the historical analysis and reconnaissance to work on actual war plans. Almond and his friends assumed the role of III Corps Area (consisting of Pennsylvania, Maryland, and Virginia) staff and examined the corps's mobilization plan in light of War Department guidelines. These strictures specifically applied to each current commander for him to use in planning relevant color-plan support. The purpose of this course was to acquaint the officers with the complexity of a large-scale mobilization, which would be necessary sooner than any of them realized.[14]

The G4 (Logistics) course allowed the student to study all of the economic and industrial requirements for waging modern war. Almond served on a committee that examined how the War Department procured supplies and determined the national industrial base's adequacy in the event of a large-scale war. Almond and his classmates considered two questions during the G4 course. First, the committee analyzed the current Industrial Mobilization Plan to determine whether it adequately controlled economic and industrial efforts to support a war, and if not, to recommend modifications. The committee would also recommend legislative changes to support the plan. The committee then examined War Department supply procurement plans to determine whether they were flexible enough and whether the industrial load was appropriately distributed.[15]

The final period of the War College year, Individual Studies, assigned the students specific questions to examine under the supervision of a senior officer or faculty member. As the culmination of the AWC courses, this study period allowed students to apply all of the knowledge they gained throughout the year to study some of the Army's critical problems. The Army War College commandant queried both the War Plans Division (WPD) of the War Department General Staff and the chief of infantry to determine their research requirements, and each provided a list of the most important topics. Unlike the random committee selection throughout the year, some officers received specific assignments based on their experience. Many of these officers completed assignments that seemed prescient, given their later positions. For instance, the US Navy's Capt. William F. Halsey, future Third Fleet commander during World War II, tackled "Japan's Attitude at the Forthcoming Naval Conference," while Lt. Col. James A. Ulio, the future adjutant general of the US Army, studied laws and policies for appointing general officers.[16]

Despite the emphasis on individual study, many officers paired for their projects. Almond worked with Maj. Dale D. Hinman under the guidance of Col. Robert M. Beck Jr., the director of the War Plans Division. Having the WPD director supervising certain studies indicated the War Department's interest in these questions and their potential answers.

The question assigned to Almond and Hinman involved a realistic contingency: "Would the inclusion of an expeditionary or strike force as an addition to the Four Army Plan be suitable to the defense of our nation and simplify our procedure in War Planning? If so, a) What changes in war planning procedures would be necessary? b) What would be the effect on our war reserve policy?"[17]

Chief of Staff General Douglas MacArthur had reorganized the US Army in 1932 with a general headquarters and four field armies oriented geographically to cover both coasts and the Canadian and Mexican borders. This so-called Four Army Plan allocated a total of eighteen corps headquarters and fifty-four divisions to the four armies, despite the lack of sufficient troops to support it. The US Army could not fill four divisions quickly, to say nothing of four field armies. Nevertheless, the War Department had recently published the Mobilization Plan of 1933 based on the Four Army Plan, and Almond's class worked to develop details for the plan.[18]

Almond and Hinman produced a report titled "The Provision of an Expeditionary or Striking Force as an Integral Part of the Four Army Plan," which built on the work Almond had already done as committee chair during a previous course. Almond recommended reorganizing the standing Regular Army and National Guard to provide a strike force. The study produced a detailed report, including cost figures, proposed stationing locations, and projected ports of embarkation under various color-plan scenarios. There is no surviving WPD critique of the document, but the War Department never adopted such a plan, in view of the many other mobilization difficulties caused by personnel and budget shortages. This project and the year's course of study gave Almond a thorough understanding of operational and strategic planning.[19]

After graduation from the Army War College in 1934, Almond's next assignment sent him to the Intelligence (G2) section of the War Department General Staff, despite his having neither an intelligence background nor language skills. Taking a snapshot of the WDGS in November 1941, 33 percent of the 645 graduates in Army War College classes from 1934 through 1940 went on to serve in the War Department. From Almond's class, 20 of the 84 members, or 23 percent, went to the WDGS.[20]

Branch chief Col. William R. McCabe assigned Almond to the Latin American section under Col. Fay Brabson on the basis of his service record and demonstrated capabilities. The assignment disappointed Almond a little, because he considered G2 slightly less prestigious than either G3 (Operations) or G4 (Logistics), but he made the most of it.

Almond had once again made his mark in a school environment and caught the eye of a senior officer. His hard work and intellect, rather than language skills or intelligence training, had landed him the job.[21]

American authorities believed political instability in Latin America during the 1930s made the region all the more susceptible to the Nazi influence then spreading across Europe. The Latin American section gleaned information from the military attachés assigned to each of the twenty countries in South America with which the United States had relations. Almond's assignment was to "observe" the nineteen nations of South America while his colleague Lt. Col. John Breitling Coulter watched Mexico. The Latin American Section's mission reflected the War Department's growing concern about America's neighbors in the Western Hemisphere. American leaders believed a Nazi incursion into Brazil posed the greatest potential threat in South America, and they developed War Plan Purple (later renamed Violet) to prepare a US response. Almond and Coulter classified the envoys' reports under five general headings: geographic, political, economic, military, and social. The section also received, classified, and analyzed information from sources other than the attachés. Almond respected the attachés and found them highly capable. He posed specific intelligence questions to the attachés and assisted in debriefing those officers when they returned from their assignments. The chief of intelligence made nominations for the attaché assignments based on the person's interests and language ability, but the State Department held final approval.[22]

The so-called Chaco Wars from 1932 to 1935 between Bolivia and Paraguay threatened to deprive the United States of certain natural resources such as tin and precious metals. The area occupied much of Almond's time while he was in G2. Almond analyzed the size, equipment, and personnel of Bolivia's army, which was much larger than Paraguay's. American authorities took an interest in the fact that the Bolivian army benefited from German training and leadership. Almond determined that Bolivia could not win the war, primarily because it had disregarded the logistical difficulties in operating more than a thousand miles from its bases. The Bolivians, a heterogeneous army primarily from the uplands and deserts, had trouble fighting an ethnically homogeneous army in the forests of its home.[23]

Almond enjoyed G2, but he hoped to get out and do something that would better prepare him to return to the field. He lobbied hard for a seat in the next Air Corps Tactical School (ACTS) class when his G2 assignment concluded in 1938. Almond hoped that ACTS would "improve [his] professional knowledge of the powers and limitations of Military Aviation."[24] He cited considerable flying experience while on field maneuvers in the United States and in the Philippines, and he "felt that there was a great need for ground officers understanding the capabilities and possibilities of the Air Force in support of ground operations." Significantly, Almond did not wish to become a pilot; he sought this posting to make him a better and more well-rounded infantry officer.[25]

Almond reported to ACTS at Maxwell Field, just outside Montgomery, Alabama, in June 1938. This assignment surely pleased his wife, Margaret, as she would once again be living close to her family. The yearlong course of study at ACTS, a predecessor of the Air War College, focused on three areas: observation, attack, and bombardment. The class consisted primarily of pilots, and Almond and the few ground officers in the class would receive "observer" certification. Almond thought that the Air Corps focused too much on bombing and fighter operations. Later he recalled asking in class about support to ground forces. The instructor's response that "no one had ever asked for it" outraged Almond. He thought that Air Corps officers concerned themselves too much with strictly air operations rather than close or tactical air support for ground troops. This observation, made almost forty years after the fact, surely reflects Almond's bitter hindsight based on his Korean experience. Almond maintained his observer certification throughout his career and used observation airplanes extensively in both World War II and Korea to assist him in controlling his units on the ground. Study at the Air Corps school also doubtless enhanced his understanding of air operations, contributed to his self-assurance, and colored his relations with future US Air Force senior officers such as his ACTS instructor Capt. Earle E. Partridge.[26]

Despite Almond's desire for a field assignment, there were still few available after he completed the ACTS course in 1939. He had received a promotion to lieutenant colonel while stationed at Maxwell, which further limited his assignment opportunities with troops. Ever thirsty for professional knowledge, Almond lobbied to attend the Naval War College (NWC) at Newport, Rhode Island, for academic year 1939–1940 and received one of the two seats given to Army officers. Almond believed in learning the capabilities of the other services: "I thought the Army, Navy, and Air Force required understanding of each other, and I wanted to be sure that I understood the method of operation and the capabilities of the Navy just as I had desired to do likewise with the Air Force."[27] He believed these two schools, combined with his combat experience, would serve him well if he ever attained high command. Almond recalled that the NWC course focused primarily on naval engagements but included a section on amphibious operations. He found the curriculum at the Naval War College more strategically oriented than at the Army War College.[28]

With the outbreak of war in Europe in September 1939, new US Army Chief of Staff Gen. George C. Marshall had recommended to President Franklin D. Roosevelt that the Regular Army and National Guard be increased in size. The five Regular Army divisions were all understrength, lacking even enough soldiers to bring them to the authorized peacetime strength of 280,000. Congress had failed to appropriate funds for more than 165,000. Roosevelt declared a national emergency on September 8 and authorized small increases: 17,000 additional troops for the Regular Army and 43,000 for the National Guard by executive order. He also directed Marshall to begin bringing the active and National Guard divisions up to full peace strength. The WDGS commenced planning for larger future increases that would require congressional action as the country drew closer to war.[29]

The fall of France in June 1940 accelerated wartime mobilization planning for the United States. The mobilization plans developed during the late 1930s had focused on defense of the Western Hemisphere, but US involvement in the European war seemed increasingly likely. Congress authorized the president to federalize the entire National Guard for one year beginning in September 1940, and simultaneously passed the Selective Service Act that began the first peacetime draft in the nation's history.[30]

Almond found himself caught in a frustrating predicament upon graduating from the Naval War College in 1940. The War Department had promised to assign an Army officer for the NWC faculty, and after his graduation the Navy, impressed by his performance in the course, selected Almond. Almond had not seen troop duty since 1933, and he doubtless saw the mobilization and subsequent expansion of the Army as an opportunity not to be missed. Desperate to command troops once more, Almond sought to escape yet another teaching assignment, despite the clear accolade he had earned. Almond's superiors acquiesced, but only partially. He was released from the Newport assignment but quickly learned that the Army meant to return him to the War Department G2, which he had left only two years earlier. Almond implored Maj. Gen. George V. Strong, the WDGS deputy chief of staff, G2, to release him from this assignment as well. He wanted to return to line service to put to practical use what he had learned since 1933.

The particular problem facing the War Department at the time concerned Mexico. With a possible revolution brewing south of the border, Maj. Gen. Sherman Miles, assistant chief of staff, Military Intelligence Division, WDGS, regarded Almond as an experienced Latin American affairs hand. War Plan Green had posited just such a situation, and the General Staff prepared to execute it. Almond argued strongly that his friend Lt. Col. John B. Coulter, who had the Mexico desk during Almond's previous tour in G2, would be a better choice. Coulter hailed from Texas and spoke Spanish, had served recently with troops, and had logged two border tours, credentials Almond lacked. Coulter, however, had recently assumed command of the 4th Cavalry Regiment in South Dakota and was unavailable. General Strong insisted that Almond was the man for the job they had in mind, and the orders would stand. Col. John Magruder of G2 told Almond, perhaps to soften the blow, that his reputation had gotten him the job. General Miles promised to consider Almond's request to return to troop duty after the Mexican emergency ended. The decision disappointed Almond, but the ego stroke must have pleased him.[31]

War Plan Green planned for American intervention in Mexico to stabilize the government and prevent further incursions by Nazis or Communists known to be operating in Latin America. Mexico's government had been unstable for many years and by 1938 had developed close ties to Francisco Franco's fascist regime in Spain. Franco's relationship with Nazi Germany at this time increased American fears about Nazi intervention in Mexico, and War Plan Green remained an annual War College exercise. When no revolution came, Miles honored his pledge to Almond and released him in late 1940.[32]

In January 1941, Almond moved to Providence, Rhode Island, as the G3 (Operations) officer of the newly organized VI Corps under Maj. Gen. Karl Truesdell, with Almond's friend Col. Charles Ryder as chief of staff. As the War Department reorganized to meet the demands of an expanding Army, it began to activate new corps headquarters to train and supervise the activating and mobilizing divisions. The VI Corps, one of the first corps headquarters activated, consisted of the Regular Army 1st Infantry Division at Fort Devens, Massachusetts, and the 26th Infantry Division, a National Guard unit in the Boston area. Both divisions had significant personnel shortages, each being more than 5,000 soldiers short of its their authorized peacetime strength. Moreover, each had begun conversion to a new "triangular" configuration, based on three infantry regiments rather than the four regiments in two brigades that had been the case during World War I. The 1st Infantry Division had started the conversion process in January 1940 and was nearly finished. The 26th Infantry Division, the first of the National Guard divisions mobilized in September 1940, had only just begun its conversion. These units received priority for draftees entering the Army.[33]

With all units at varying stages of readiness, VI Corps needed to inspect them and develop training plans to bring them up to standard. Almond designed maneuvers to test their capabilities. He found many units "woefully weak in basic training and small field operations." The VI Corps conducted a field maneuver in August 1941 that employed the 26th Infantry Division, 1st Infantry Division, and 101st Cavalry Regiment (an African-American unit) together with several artillery units in a field force that Almond called "very effective." The same units later went to the Carolina Maneuvers, held on a vast tract of land covering sixteen counties in North and South Carolina from September through November 1941. The attack on Pearl Harbor occurred as units returned to the Northeast after completing these maneuvers, and Almond suddenly found himself catapulted into the position of VI Corps chief of staff.[34]

The years following World War I had proved fruitful for Almond. He performed well in a variety of assignments and attracted the attention of officers destined for high command who would remember his achievements. Almond received comprehensive education, training, and experience; few other future general officers attended two senior service colleges, and none attended all three. Almond committed himself fully to any task, and consistently excelled. Such dedication would guide him through his next challenge: training and commanding black troops. No white officer sought this task, but having received the mission, Almond threw himself into it. It would prove to be the most difficult assignment of his career.

5

Almond Takes Command

1941–1943

On a crisp December Sunday afternoon in 1941, Col. Ned Almond, VI Corps assistant chief of staff, G3 (Operations), sat in Griffith Stadium in Washington, DC, watching the National Football League's Washington Redskins play the Philadelphia Eagles. His VI Corps had finished the General Headquarters (GHQ) Carolina maneuvers, a two-phased exercise on the border of North and South Carolina pitting large units against one another in what proved to be the last peacetime exercise of its kind. Operating as part of the First Army (Blue Force), VI Corps had performed well, and its units had begun to move back to their home stations in New England. Almond had stopped off to see the game and later recalled hearing an announcement over the loudspeaker for all officers to return immediately to their units. Almond quickly learned of the attack on Pearl Harbor, which galvanized the American military as the Army once again expanded to fight a world war.[1]

While the prewar Regular Army consisted of five divisions on active duty, and two more were activated in 1939, the fall of France in June 1940 had made Americans feel more vulnerable to German aggression, and the War Department began activating additional divisions as the Army expanded. When President Roosevelt federalized the National Guard in September 1940, those eighteen divisions began mobilizing as well. One week later, Congress had authorized the nation's first peacetime draft. By December 1941, the US Army had mobilized or activated thirty-six divisions.[2]

Following America's declaration of war, VI Corps Chief of Staff Brig. Gen. Charles W. Ryder moved to the 90th Division and corps commander Maj. Gen. Karl Truesdell selected Almond to replace him. With the first wave of wartime promotions, Almond advanced to brigadier general in January 1942. His first general officer assignment quickly followed: he would report to Fort Huachuca, Arizona, as assistant division commander of the black 93rd Infantry Division. En route to Fort Huachuca, Almond attended a short course for general officers at Fort Leavenworth, Kansas, to prepare them for their new duties. Upon completion of the course, he arrived with his family at Fort Huachuca in April 1942.[3]

The War Department addressed wartime mobilization as an engineering problem, not a social one. The Army needed to field more divisions and other units than ever before and obtain millions of men to fill them. Feeding, clothing, housing, equipping, and training a mass army, while simultaneously establishing the infrastructure to support it, strained the War Department's capabilities. After Pearl Harbor, the WDGS approached this seemingly insurmountable task in a logical and orderly fashion. The staff developed a schedule that activated divisions at the rate of more than two per month from February 1942 to September 1943, along with hundreds of support units.[4]

Civilian industry needed to convert to wartime production to make all of the tools and weapons the Army would require. Some of this conversion meant increased production of known war materials, but it also included the development of different products. Supply and equipment production required a precise sequence so that supplies would arrive at the training bases when soldiers did. The technical specialists in the War Department developed not only new equipment and weapons but also the manuals to go with them. The massive, complicated planning effort demanded by this mobilization reinforced the idea that winning the war was largely an engineering problem to be mastered.

Solving the puzzle in such a way made sense to the War Department staff, but this approach ignored the difficult social and human issues of the day, such as segregation. The War Department believed such issues fell outside its basic responsibilities, and neither America's civilian nor its military leadership felt the need to address them. Almond and the War Department found themselves at the confluence of several powerful forces. The War Department saw the need to build the Army and win the war as paramount, outweighing all other considerations. African American leaders, on the other hand, seized on the war to advance the fight for racial justice. They argued for a greater combat role for black servicemen, and some pushed for an end to segregation in the service, but the US Army's leadership and much of white America proved unreceptive to radical racial change. When the United States entered World War II, segregated facilities were the norm across the country. The 1896 US Supreme Court decision *Plessy v. Ferguson*, 163 US 537 (1896) had established the nation's "separate but equal" doctrine and fostered the poisoned racial environment that would affect the US Army's use of black troops during World War I and World War II.[5]

War Department officials struggled to find places to train black soldiers, because white communities objected to having thousands of black soldiers in their proximity. The Army chose Fort Huachuca, a remote desert post located some seventy miles south of Tucson in the southeast corner of Arizona, to train the 93rd Infantry Division. Historically associated with black units, Fort Huachuca featured plenty of wide maneuver space, varied terrain, and room to build ample housing for the 20,000 troops who would inhabit the post. The base also had the advantage, as the War Department saw it, of being situated far from large white communities.

Maj. Gen. Charles P. Hall, a Mississippi native, activated the 93rd Division in May 1942, shortly after Almond reached Fort Huachuca. All new infantry divisions used the "triangular" formation, with three infantry regiments, one artillery regiment, one engineer regiment, and various supporting arms. Upon activation, the 93rd Infantry Division assumed control of three black regiments. The 25th Infantry, one of the two black Regular Army infantry regiments authorized by statute, had called Fort Huachuca home for decades. Its personnel had served for many years in a unit with a high percentage of reenlistments. The 368th Infantry had activated in January 1941 as a separate regiment of draftees, also at Fort Huachuca. The 369th Infantry Regiment, originally a National Guard unit from New York, activated in May 1942 to round out the division. Known as the Harlem Hellfighters, the 369th had been part of the 93rd Division during World War I and had acquired a proud record in combat.[6]

To facilitate rapid expansion, the War Department designated each division as "parent" for one activating later. As new divisions mobilized, each parent division provided a "cadre" of 172 officers and 1,190 enlisted men for its "child," no later than thirty days before activation. The department also began expanding old bases and building new ones to meet the increased demand for troop housing and training. Under the Troop Basis of 1942, the War Department planned to activate four black divisions, two in 1942 and two in 1943. The 93rd Infantry Division would activate first, and would then provide cadre to the 92nd Division, activating later in the year. The 92nd Infantry Division would be composed entirely of draftees, and would provide cadre to the 105th Division, scheduled for activation in 1943, which in turn would parent the 107th Division. The subsequent War Department decision in 1943 to create only ninety divisions prevented the last two divisions from being activated. The War Department customarily assigned new brigadier generals slated for division command first as assistant commanders in other divisions for a short training period before sending them to their own commands. For instance, Almond's friend Ryder spent a few months with the 90th Infantry Division in training and then led the 34th Infantry Division throughout the war. When Almond received his assignment to the 93rd, he must have suspected that he might later command the black division scheduled to activate later in 1942, though years later he claimed surprise at his selection for such an assignment. Three months after Almond arrived at Fort Huachuca, he received a telegram directing him to Fort McClellan, Alabama, to form the 92nd Infantry Division. The record does not indicate that he asked for the 92nd specifically, but he had pushed for a troop assignment.[7]

The War Department carefully selected its senior officers. Army Ground Forces (AGF) Commander Lt. Gen. Lesley J. McNair personally recommended prospective division commanders to Army Chief of Staff Gen. George C. Marshall, who trusted McNair's judgment. Despite the short time Almond had spent in VI Corps, he had performed well and impressed General Truesdell. He had also attracted positive outside attention. Almond believed he owed some of his early success to the fact that certain people, such as Brig. Gen. Mark Clark, AGF chief of staff, observed his performance and reported on his fitness.[8]

Because the Jim Crow–era military placed little confidence in the ability of African Americans to become steady soldiers, the Army especially needed to find the right officers to lead black divisions. A special investigation in mid-1942 informed Marshall that the War Department had assigned mediocre men to command black troops in units then being activated, which had caused problems. This prompted Marshall to recommend: "Difficulty in handling colored troops almost without exception can be attributed to a lack of knack on the part of officers assigned to this duty. Officers must be carefully selected, with the primary requirement the ability to handle negroes. Such officers can accomplish much, whereas officers who may be better trained in a military way, but without the knack, not only fail in accomplishing the task but create the conditions which breed trouble."[9]

Marshall knew that troops were quick to notice when their leaders were not capable, and that inevitably led to discipline problems. With this in mind, he declared: "The Secretary of War directs that the current practice in this regard be examined critically in all commands . . . and that such corrective measures be taken as will insure the assignment to negro units of officers of especially high professional qualities, particularly judgment and common sense, tact, initiative and leadership."[10]

This letter, distributed one month after Marshall named Almond to command the 92nd Infantry Division, indicated the Army leadership's attention to the issue of placing good commanders over black troops. Marshall clearly saw Almond as the right man for such an assignment, and his opinion would not vary throughout the war.[11]

There was, however, a more sinister connotation. Almond felt Marshall gave him the 92nd Infantry Division to help black troops succeed, and that Marshall had special reasons for believing him qualified to command black soldiers: "I think that General Marshall felt that General Hall, who was in command of the Ninety-third Division when I was Assistant Division Commander and [who] was from Mississippi, understood the character of the Negro and his habits and inclinations. The artilleryman at that time was General William Spence from North Carolina as I recall, who also had that understanding of Southern customs and Negro capabilities; the attitudes of Negroes in relationships thereto. I think that my selection for the Ninety-third and Ninety-second Divisions was of the same character."[12]

Almond's assumption reflects the War Department's paternalist outlook toward black soldiers. Marshall and the Army's senior leaders looked for the best leaders possible for black troops, but they believed those leaders came from the descendants of an oppressive culture; only the oppressors could understand the oppressed. Marshall clearly saw "the ability to handle Negroes" as a leadership skill distinct from those necessary for leading white soldiers. Many of the officers selected for general officer positions in the 92nd, 93rd, and 2nd Cavalry Divisions had served with Marshall either as instructors or as students. Marshall believed these officers had the aptitude required to help train the black soldiers and get their divisions into fighting shape. As for those officers whom Marshall did not know, he told McNair, "If [the officer] was highly successful with colored troops I think he should be considered for advancement." Marshall's statement captures the War Department's outlook: if the officer could command black troops, he could do anything. The paternalist leadership would never see the black soldier as equal to the white soldier.[13]

Marshall's habit of identifying solid performers early and then promoting them is well known. These officers' association with Marshall undoubtedly influenced their wartime assignments, but first General

McNair needed to recommend them. He based those recommendations on the officers' efficiency ratings, experience, succession of assignments, and finally seniority. A relationship with Marshall, though useful, did not guarantee preferment. Southern heritage aside, Almond got the 92nd Division because McNair and Marshall believed he was capable. McNair continuously monitored senior officers to ensure they sustained high standards; the War Department relieved many division commanders before their units reached combat. Almond succeeded, not because of a relationship with Marshall, but because he met the War Department's criteria for success at the time. He was not an anomaly, he was part of the system.[14]

Almond's prewar experience and career path had been typical of that of his contemporaries, and he and other officers tapped for division command entered the war with approximately the same degree of experience. Almond had also made a name for himself before the war as a trainer, a desirable skill in a fast-expanding Army. His brother officers regarded him as hardworking and successful. This reputation gave him the opportunity to rise professionally.

In the course of the war, 197 men commanded the eighty-nine divisions that served in combat. On average, the typical division commander was forty-seven years old in 1940 with 25.3 years of service; Almond was forty-eight, with 26 years. Marshall considered age an important factor in command selection. As soon as the mobilization began, Marshall started pushing out older officers and promoting younger ones. He reasoned that younger officers possessed the stamina and vigor necessary for combat, and he therefore set upper age limits at each grade. Almond fell well within the War Department limits for a major general, which extended to age sixty-two.[15]

The officers' assignment patterns varied, and thus Almond's experiences matched those of his brother officers in some areas but differed in others (see table 5.1). The smaller size of the US Army during the interwar years limited opportunities. Many officers secured long command tours, which benefited the officers who held them but meant fewer opportunities for others. Most future division commanders averaged 98 months in command from platoon through regimental level. In this area Almond fell well below the average, with only 65 months of command, including his World War I service and his battalion command in the Philippines.[16]

Serving on the staff of a corps headquarters or below provided an officer with useful experience in how to train, support, and control tactical units. Almond spent a mere eighteen months on a corps staff, nearly two years less than his peers, but most of this time came during the mobi-

Table 5.1. Assignment Time Comparison

Function	Average (Months)	Almond
Command	98	65
Corps Staff	41	18
Major Command	42	45
Instructor	66	98
Student	42	74

Source: Adapted from Wade, *World War II Division Commanders,* graphs 11–16.

lization period from 1940 to 1942 and thus provided excellent preparation for his division command. Higher-level staffs, such as those assigned to numbered armies and the War Department, provided an entirely different level of experience that enabled the officer to understand much larger and more complex operations at national level. In this, Almond's experience in high-level staff assignments at the War Department mirrored that of his peers.[17]

Most officers spent a significant amount of time as instructors. This gave them a deep understanding of various specialties and, combined with education and experience, made them particularly qualified officers. Almond's ninety-eight months of teaching at various levels, the bulk of his assignments during his pre–World War II career, were well above the average and afforded him the opportunity for thorough understanding of training principles. Finally, the US Army provided many educational opportunities for officers. During the interwar years when promotions stagnated and other opportunities dried up, rising officers had plenty of time for schooling. Almond spent nearly three more years in school than did his peers, which reduced his command time but endowed him with other valuable skills.[18]

Promotion analysis of this officer cohort reveals wide disparity in company-grade ranks, lieutenant to captain, but great similarity at the field-grade level, major to colonel (see table 5.2). Most of these officers had joined the Army between 1915 and 1917, but some entered earlier. Those who entered before Almond spent more time in the lower grades. Though Almond graduated from VMI in 1915, this placement did not make him a professional contemporary of the 1915 West Point class that produced so many generals. Since Almond received his commission in late 1916, his contemporaries are more properly those officers commissioned with the VMI and West Point classes of 1917. VMI produced only one other future division commander that year, Maj. Gen. Lemuel C. Shepherd, who went on to command the 6th Marine Division. The West Point class of April 1917 produced many general officers, but only eleven of these commanded divisions in World War II. When the United States entered the Great War, promotions had accelerated for everyone. Almond therefore spent comparatively little time as a lieutenant and captain, reaching temporary major by 1918. After the war, however, Almond and his peers reverted to permanent lower ranks. Almond spent a total of nine and one-half years as a captain, and a similar length of time as a major. His time as a major and as a lieutenant colonel matched that of his peers.[19]

Table 5.2. Time in Grade Comparison

Rank	Average (Years)	Almond
2nd Lieutenant	2.3	0.6
1st Lieutenant	2.2	1.0
Captain	5.6	9.5
Major	9.6	9.3
Lieutenant Colonel	3.2	3.1
Colonel	1.0	0.5
Brigadier General	1.0	0.5

Source: Adapted from Wade, *World War II Division Commanders,* graphs 3–10.

Almond and the other division commanders were selected in a specific order based on the division activation schedule, and placing Almond in that order helps rank him among them. War Department practice identified division commanders, assistant division commanders, and division artillery commanders no later than seventy-eight days before the division activation date. Almond received orders on July 3, 1942, assigning him to command the 92nd Infantry Division, scheduled to activate in October. The War Department activated twenty-five new infantry divisions between March and September 1942; all but two of the commanders selected were senior to Almond in time of service. This date provides an approximate "order of merit" for those selected to command. These data indicate that Almond's qualifications for command equaled those of his contemporaries.[20]

Almond knew that the 92nd Division had emerged from World War I with a poor reputation, and he later claimed to have found little specific information on how and why the division failed. There was no official history of the 92nd Division's World War I experience published until 1944. The Army War College Historical Section, however, had produced a short study in 1923 with which Almond must have been familiar from his time as a student. The study analyzed Inspector General (IG) reports from the 92nd Division's World War I mobilization experience to evaluate the division's training and performance. One of the few consistent findings from the scanty information available concerned the basing of the division. The 92nd had been scattered among seven bases, and all inspectors recommended consolidation. The Army had activated the 92nd Division on October 17, 1917 at seven widely separate bases: Camp Funston, Kansas; Camp Grant, Illinois; Camp Dodge, Iowa; Camp Sherman, Ohio; Camp Dix, New Jersey; Camp Meade, Maryland; and Camp Upton, New York. Several of the IGs reached the same conclusion: "The brigades should be consolidated so the brigade commander can supervise the training." One report concluded: "It is likewise doubtful whether the colored officer can be trained to properly perform their duties—it is certain that they are not up to the standards of the white officers." The War Department's failure to heed its own study about stationing of units indicates its failure to understand the racial problem, because it did not accept that black officers could be trained.[21]

Because the division was so fragmented, there was no overall division-level evaluation. The reports indicated that some posts experienced shortages of clothing, or clothing of proper sizes, and nearly all reported shortages of weapons. The study found many of the same problems Almond would find in World War II: poorly educated draftees with low intelligence made for poor soldiers and gave little "bench" for NCOs. As would be the case during World War II, all of the field-grade officers and some captains were white, with African Americans constituting a small percentage of the officer complement.

Capt. William J. McCaffrey, the division headquarters commandant, reported to Fort McClellan in the summer of 1942 as the first officer assigned to the 92nd Infantry Division. McCaffrey had grown up in Boston, graduated from high school in 1932, and spent three years working in the fur business. Receiving an appointment to West Point in 1935, he graduated with the class of 1939. McCaffrey was commanding a rifle company in Panama when the United States entered World War II, and he feared he would miss the action. When McCaffrey had completed enough time in the assignment to receive a furlough, he went home to the United States, ostensibly to see his family. While there, he reported to the Officer Replacement Pool at Little Rock, Arkansas. Seeking an assignment to a combat unit, McCaffrey accepted the headquarters commandant position open in the 92nd Division. McCaffrey did not know the 92nd was a black division until after he took the job, but that did not matter to him. He had no idea at the time how much the assignment would affect his career. Despite the rank and the twenty-two-year difference in their ages, McCaffrey would become Almond's confidant and closest friend for the remainder of Almond's life.[22]

The War Department selected general officers with input from Army Ground Forces. To assist Almond in his mission of forming the 92nd, the War Department gave him one officer who had already served successfully with black troops. The department recalled Col. John E. "Joe" Wood from Liberia, where his 41st Engineer Regiment (Colored) was deployed building a runway and guarding the strategically important Firestone rubber plantation. A lifelong bachelor and a contemporary of Almond's, Wood had received a commission in the Corps of Engineers in 1916 after graduating from both the University of North Carolina and MIT. He commanded an engineer unit in France during the First World War and later served in the Philippines and in Washington. The War Department formed Wood's regiment in August 1940 using volunteers from the 9th and 10th Cavalry Regiments. The 41st gained a reputation as the "Singing Engineers" because its members sang spirituals while marching. They earned respect for their parades, which they executed with great ceremony and precision.[23]

Wood believed he possessed the ability to get black troops to perform well. Promoted to brigadier general, he reported to the 92nd Infantry Division in August 1942 as assistant division commander. Wood considered himself the best trainer in the Army, and he had great confidence in his soldiers. He believed his skills had won him command of the 41st Engineers, and that Marshall had noted his knack for training black soldiers. This was probably true, but Wood lacked tact. Almond and Wood had similarly forceful personalities, and each considered himself an outstanding trainer. They each felt the pressure and pride of being "Marshall men." They initially clashed, and Almond assigned Wood to supervise administrative tasks, reserving training for himself. Although Almond and Wood shared many traits, it is clear that they were incompatible.[24]

McCaffrey later claimed Wood "was an old redneck boy, who had no sensitivity towards the enlisted men whatsoever and his attitude was that 'they're all thieves, rapists, and murderers and we got to run them that way.'" As for Almond, McCaffrey thought him an excellent trainer who knew exactly what a division was supposed to do: "He'd been chosen by General Marshall personally. I think General Marshall considered him probably the best potential division commander the Army had to offer and gave him the hardest division to train and a division that had a lot of political impetus behind it but was an unknown quantity. I firmly believe from listening to General Marshall when he came to visit us that he figured if Ned couldn't do it, nobody could do it, and he was giving the black troops the best possible leadership they could have." McCaffrey's observation confirms Marshall's paternalist attitude toward black soldiers, and also indicates that Marshall gave Almond a lot of latitude. Such an observation from an unknown junior officer reveals much about Marshall's beliefs.[25]

Wood believed that West Point produced the best officers, and he routinely requested specific graduates by name for his unit based on their records. He brought one such officer with him from Liberia, Capt. Edward L. Rowny, a Baltimore native who graduated from West Point in 1941. Rowny's first assignment as a newly commissioned second lieutenant had been Wood's 41st Engineer Regiment. Despite Rowny's obvious affection for a man he considered a mentor, he later admitted that Wood had a paternalistic, though benevolent, attitude toward black soldiers, and supported the "separate but equal" concept, believing that blacks and whites would be happier living and working separately. A bright officer, Rowny thrived after his transfer to the 92nd Division. McCaffrey later called Rowny "the smartest guy I've ever run into—absolutely brilliant." Like McCaffrey, Rowny would develop a lifelong friendship with Almond.[26]

Col. (later Brig. Gen.) William H. Colbern joined the 92nd Infantry Division as its artillery commander following a stint with the 1st Infantry Division at Fort Indiantown Gap, Pennsylvania. Colbern, a 1916 VMI graduate from Lee's Summit, Missouri, held a variety of positions in a career pattern that differed markedly from Almond's. Originally commissioned in the infantry, Colbern also served in two other combat branches. He began his career with the 37th Infantry Regiment during World War

I. After the war he went to the Philippines, then shortly afterward joined the 15th Infantry in Tientsin, China. Colbern transferred to the artillery in 1923, but later attended both basic and advanced cavalry schools and the Polish cavalry school at Gruziadz, Poland. After teaching stints in both the cavalry and field artillery schools, Colbern commanded in the 14th Field Artillery Regiment and then attended the Command and General Staff School. In 1938 and 1939, Colbern served as the American defense attaché in Warsaw until Poland fell to the Nazis. He next held a variety of short assignments, culminating as executive officer of the 1st Infantry Division Artillery at Fort Indiantown Gap, Pennsylvania. He received orders to the 92nd Infantry Division in February 1942.[27]

The War Department prescribed a set of training courses for the division's officers, which varied according to their prospective positions. The courses began on July 22, 1942, with a three-day orientation at Army Ground Forces (AGF) in Washington, DC, followed by five days of maintenance instruction at Holabird Quartermaster Base in Baltimore. The officers then split up for training at different locations: Almond and future division commanders went to the CGSS at Fort Leavenworth for a month of instruction, while Wood and Colbern went to the Infantry and Artillery Schools, respectively. Each division commander and his principal staff arrived at their division's training camp no later than thirty-seven days before activation, with the cadre and the remaining officers arriving a week later. Almond and his division staff met at Fort McClellan, Alabama, on September 2, 1942, to begin preparations for activating the 92nd Infantry Division on October 15. The division's remaining 13,000 recruits would arrive for training in the two weeks after activation. The division would be assigned to the Second Army and ultimately III Corps for training.[28]

Basing a black division in the heart of the Deep South posed some serious problems. The War Department directed camp commanders to respect local customs whenever necessary. Brig. Gen. H. T. Mayberry, for instance, commanded the Tank Destroyer School at Camp Hood, Texas, from 1942 to 1944. He reported after the war that he maintained separate messes and barracks for whites and blacks, both officers and enlisted. Though some people protested this policy, Mayberry reasoned that orders bound him to conform to the established social customs in that part of the country.[29]

Drawing on the practice used during World War I, the War Department opted to split the division among several different bases in order to reduce the potential for racial problems with local communities. Whereas

Almond's World War I counterpart, Maj. Gen. Charles Ballou, had seen his division scattered widely with no real thought to cohesion, Almond at least had the relative advantage of having each of his Regimental Combat Teams (RCTs) based together. The RCTs, which consisted of an infantry regiment of three battalions plus a field artillery battalion of three batteries, would train together, affording some degree of unit cohesion. The division headquarters and special troops activated at Fort McClellan, Alabama, with combat teams split among three other bases: Camp Atterbury, Indiana; Camp Breckinridge, Kentucky; and Camp Robinson, Arkansas. Support units trained at Fort McClellan, as did the 600th Field Artillery Battalion, the divisional artillery unit. No other division in the US Army trained in such a decentralized fashion for such an extended period. Aside from the logistical disadvantages inherent in such a setup, this arrangement inhibited proper training and retarded cohesion. The 92nd would remain separated for six months.[30]

With Almond's division split among four different posts, he needed to keep constantly on the move to supervise his operations. He conducted a commander's reconnaissance at each of the installations his soldiers would occupy when the unit activated, and he made detailed notes, which he then passed to the division staff. He inspected each of the key training areas and noted deficiencies. The initial visits reflected all of the problems expected in activating a new unit at a new post: equipment and housing shortages, uniform infractions, and construction delays for both buildings and training facilities. He also noted the attitude and helpfulness of each post commander.

Almond and his staff remained in constant motion, visiting each of the RCTs every few days. Almond encountered immediate troop support difficulties. He and his subordinate leaders commanded their respective units but not the bases at which they trained, and they had to rely on post commanders to provide supplies for their troops. Much as his predecessor General Ballou had, some twenty-five years earlier, Almond experienced problems in securing the necessary housing, training areas, equipment, and recreation facilities for his troops. These difficulties stemmed from three roots. First, the War Department activated large numbers of troops and built infrastructure simultaneously. The WDGS attempted to synchronize the activation and construction schedules, but inevitable building delays left many posts with housing shortages. Second, the attitude of the local populace and the post commanders also affected the type of support the black soldiers received. Almond wanted a hospitable civilian community nearby that could provide entertainment for the soldiers in their off-duty hours to buoy morale. He assessed this local support on each of his visits to his respective units. Third, the necessity for separate facilities for black soldiers also affected housing availability. Almond did not challenge the status quo, but he worked hard to ensure that his soldiers received adequate recreational facilities, and he directed his staff to take appropriate action immediately to secure them. As a division commander, Almond could not decide US Army policy, but he did build soldiers' morale by ensuring they had the proper support. Posts that trained black soldiers routinely segregated enlisted mess halls and barracks, but Almond strove to provide his soldiers with adequate facilities. Almond quickly learned that providing "equal" facilities was even more difficult than providing separate ones. He also ordered officer messes to be integrated, as a way of helping bring in the new black officers.[31]

Almond began inspecting his four bases in August 1942, and his reports back to his staff reflect his earnest desire to support his soldiers. He began at Fort McClellan, a large installation with some 29,000 acres in the barracks area and 25,000 additional acres of maneuver area. This post would house his division headquarters, divisional artillery, and all the division support elements such as the quartermaster, ordnance, medical, military police (MP), engineer, and signal units. When all Almond's units arrived, he expected to have 3,000 men and 160 officers at the base. With more than 26,000 white soldiers and their 1,200 officers already at Fort McClellan, obtaining space for housing and training required some coordination. The post commander proposed a scheduling plan for training areas, but he still lacked enough separate mess halls and barracks to support the black soldiers, with no off-post quarters available. Almond also deemed the post hospital and laundry sorely deficient. He believed the training areas were generally adequate, but his staff made several requests to modify the overall training schedules to allow the 92nd Division access to ranges and training areas. The post commander had already taken steps to expand and improve these facilities. Most important for Almond, he pronounced the post commander a frank man willing to assist the 92nd in getting settled.[32]

Col. Sterling A. Wood commanded the 371st Regimental Combat Team, consisting of the 371st Infantry Regiment and the 599th Field Artillery Battalion, would train at Camp Robinson, Arkansas, a former Civilian Conservation Corps camp and World War I training base. The War Department began converting the 45,000-acre installation just outside Little Rock in September 1940 to accommodate 42,000 troops in two regimental training camps: a Branch Immaterial Replacement Training Center and a Medical Replacement Training Center. Almond found Camp Robinson tackling the same problems he had encountered at Fort McClellan but less prepared for large numbers of troops, with the billeting area wholly inadequate. Persistent construction delays frustrated Almond. He learned during his visit to Camp Robinson in August 1942 that barracks construction had been delayed for five weeks. Furthermore, the post quartermaster and ordnance officers had received no instructions to issue equipment to the 92nd Division personnel. Almond worked with the post commander to get things corrected, but such problems continued to slow mobilization.[33]

The situation at Camp Robinson demonstrated the US Army's attitude toward black soldiers. All soldiers received a handbook describing camp life including administration, training policies, support facilities, and military courtesy. The booklet highlighted the missions of the two training centers and the Eighth Service Command that operated the post. The pamphlet underscored the troop segregation by identifying the four theaters on post with their names, locations, and opening times and then adding, "There is also a theater for colored troops," indicating that black troops were merely an afterthought.[34]

Since the bases offered few recreational opportunities for black soldiers initially, Almond looked for activities off-post to help entertain his men. The theater at Camp Robinson offered some diversion, but it could not serve the entire 371st Combat Team. Almond worked to locate a building to house a black United Servicemen's Organization (USO) for his troops, since segregation did not allow 371st personnel to use the white soldiers' USO. He also worked with the post commander and city officials in nearby Little Rock to provide buses from the post to town. City officials seemed agreeable to accommodating the soldiers. Almond noted the local civilians' attitude as he visited each base: "Improving among those who count. City authorities are considering means of handling colored activities. Colored MPs and policemen appear probable." He also made notes on logistical arrangements: "A division of available busses will be arranged. A building for a large USO club is being arranged for by 1 September."[35]

Camp Atterbury, Indiana, home to the 365th RCT, consisting of the 365th Infantry Regiment and the 597th Field Artillery Battalion, differed somewhat from the two southern posts. Located thirty miles south of Indianapolis, this 40,000-acre base already hosted the newly activated 83rd Infantry Division and had enough housing for all the soldiers assigned there. The barracks were originally designed for medical units rather than infantry, and Almond requested some modifications, but he largely accepted the quarters available to his soldiers. Post supply had almost all the individual equipment the troops required on hand and ready for issue. The local civilians' attitude toward black soldiers "was improving in nearby towns of EDINBURG [*sic*] and FRANKLIN," Almond noted, but "COLUMBUS has no Negro population and it is difficult to interest people in taking a helpful attitude." He reported that both Indianapolis and Franklin had USO clubs and Columbus would soon have one. He also observed that the post had an ample number of both black and white Military Police units.[36]

Of the four installations Almond visited, he discovered the worst conditions at Camp Breckinridge, Kentucky, home of the 370th RCT, consisting of the 370th Infantry Regiment and the 598th Field Artillery Battalion. The 33,000-acre base, located about thirty-three miles south of Evansville, Indiana, also housed the 98th Infantry Division. He found few facilities ready for his troops and seemed doubtful that any would be ready when the cadre arrived in September, nor when the rest of 370th Infantry arrived in October. He considered the post commander "cooperative," a somewhat weaker description than he had given the others. The surrounding communities' attitude toward the arrival of black soldiers also differed notably from that in other areas. "Much improvement is to be desired," Almond wrote. "Post C.O. has made request for cooperation of all Kiwanis, Rotary, and other Clubs; many promises are received, but little action; his special services officer is not useful and he is being replaced." Almond observed that nearby cities were only slightly more helpful: "EVANSVILLE and HENDERSON have rented USO (Colored) Clubs; MORGANFIELD promises, but nothing results." Many division commanders dealt with shortages in housing, equipment, and training facilities as they built up their commands, but Almond experienced much greater difficulties than his peers because of the nation's social climate.[37]

While the black press clamored for an end to "separate but equal," most whites, and the War Department leadership, resisted such a move. With *Plessy v. Ferguson* as a guiding principle, the War Department regulations required units to conform to state and local laws in civil matters. Almond ordered his staff judge advocate (legal officer) to examine the racial laws of each of the four states in which his unit trained. Maj. Harrison W. Gebhardt summarized the Alabama, Kentucky, Arkansas, and Indiana state constitutions and their associated codes for Almond and his key staff. Alabama had the most restrictive laws, while Indiana had the least, but the concept of "separate but equal" had been the law of the land for nearly fifty years and affected all four states to a certain extent. Each one prohibited marriage, cohabitation, adultery, and fornication between whites and persons of color, and declared such marriages null and void. These were not merely local customs but state laws.[38]

Almond provided guidance to each of his regimental commanders, explaining the local laws. He concluded each memo with this pragmatic paragraph:

> The existence of these laws and customs is a fact. The personnel of this division must avoid any activity or conduct that will interfere with military training or with the discipline of the command. It is not our function to attempt to alter the existing order. The problem is social, not military. When we remember that numbers of persons have devoted their entire lifetimes unsuccessfully trying to change these ways of living, we are forced to realize that any effort by this division to that end would be an improper diversion of its time and energy, and contrary to the interests of National Defense. The men of this division will receive fair and just treatment, and they will obey the laws of the state and its communities.[39]

By disposing of the race question early on, Almond hoped to keep focus on his main mission: preparing his division to go to war. With unit cadres in place and inductees beginning to arrive, the 92nd Infantry Division officially uncased its colors in a formal activation ceremony at Fort McClellan on October 15, 1942. Each of the regiments sent representative cadres to Alabama for the ceremony and conducted concurrent activation ceremonies at their bases. During the observances at Fort McClellan, Almond enjoined the soldiers to work hard, while building esprit de corps:

> The 92nd Division is primarily a combat division. In many ways the division is like a great giant; a defect in the structure of any part reflects on the whole. . . . All parts must work together in order to perfect the division. One of my principal aims is to produce a first class battlefield unit. I promise fairness to every officer and man; the best leadership of which your officers and noncommissioned officers are capable; and adequate, modern equipment with which to train. High battlefield morale involves the ability to endure hardship with a smile; success on the battle-

> field hinges on spirit, courage, and cooperation. Stonewall Jackson said, "You may be whatever you resolve to be." You are the 92nd Division. What you become depends on your resolution.[40]

Almond's attitude was clear: training the division and getting it ready for combat were his priorities. Repeating the Stonewall Jackson quote that had sustained him since VMI days, he challenged his black soldiers to strive for excellence. He assumed that line would motivate them as it had him, and his use of it demonstrates his faith in their individual abilities. He failed to grasp, however, the racial overtones he projected by recalling such a prominent Confederate's words. Almond later said that he decided not to make his mind up on any black soldiers' capabilities until he saw the 92nd Infantry Division for himself, and he ordered his officers to do the same. He believed that if they worked hard enough, they could accomplish anything, and he refused to admit failure before he tried. He seemed to relish the challenge.[41]

When the division activated, most of the officers were junior for the positions they filled. All battalions were commanded by white majors (still following prewar custom), and most of the companies were commanded by white lieutenants. War Department policy called for black combat units to receive African American officers as they became available. The Army initially had difficulty providing enough black officers. Regulations required a minimum Army General Classification Test (AGCT) score of 110 for Officer Candidate School (OCS), which eliminated most black soldiers from consideration. The 1942 "Negro Officer Troop Basis" set the 92nd Infantry Division as the Army's second priority for allocation of black officers. In August of that year, blacks comprised only 817 of the 244,000 officers in the US Army, or 0.33 percent. The number of officer slots for African Americans steadily increased throughout the war as more black units activated, but assigning the officers became more difficult. Some black officers failed in their assignments, which then condemned the lot in the minds of many white officers, who were predisposed to believe they would all fail anyway.[42]

The method of assigning black officers also caused problems, both for the officers themselves and for the units they joined. Replacement and School Command notified Almond that the officers would arrive in groups or "blocks" after each OCS graduation. The first group of black infantry lieutenants was scheduled to arrive in October and would be assigned to the 370th RCT. As each block of officers integrated into the command, a corresponding number of white officers would be released for reassignment. This process would continue until all the lieutenant positions were filled by black officers. The division had activated with 550 white officers and only one black officer, the division chaplain. Eventually, all lieutenants in infantry companies and artillery batteries would be African American. At twenty-five black lieutenants per infantry battalion and eleven per artillery battery, this amounted to 25 percent overstrength.[43]

The practice, however, had flaws. The Army sometimes delayed assigning blocks of officers to units, breeding frustration and boredom. When the block arrived and displaced an equivalent number of white officers, the abrupt shift destroyed whatever esprit de corps the unit had. Many of the black officers had no leadership experience, but white superiors generally attributed their mistakes to their race rather than their inexperience. This exacerbated the problems between black officers and enlisted men, who often thought of these officers as second best. The disruption then set back training several weeks. Almond did not record his feelings about receiving the black officers, merely accepting it as part of the mission. Moreover, he made it clear to disgruntled white officers who wanted to transfer out of the division that they must serve wherever the Army assigned them. He granted few releases to white officers before their black replacements had arrived and received sufficient training. While Almond was willing to readily accept black lieutenants and captains, he evinced less enthusiasm for the few black field-grade officers sent to the 92nd.[44]

As the 92nd began its training, Almond knew the War Department would keep a close eye on him and his division. He intended to assess both the officers and the training system in order to provide feedback to the War Department on how his division, with its distinctive racial composition, was shaping up. After the first group of black officers had been with their units for about a month, Almond asked regimental commanders to provide general remarks on their efficiency, ability, and leadership compared to white officers of similar rank and experience. He also asked them to note the officers' military attitude and interest, discipline, aggressiveness, physical endurance, command ability, and training deficiencies and to recommend changes to the Officer Candidate School course to address them. Finally, Almond asked the commanders to list any duties the black officers were assigned requiring perseverance, diligence, decision, concentration, and to assess the proficiency they attained in these duties.[45]

The response Almond received in those reports sounded positive and helpful notes. All commented that it was much too early to render any solid analysis, but they seemed equally encouraged by what they had observed to that point. The three infantry regimental commanders noted some deficiencies, but all three balanced these findings with positive comments. They also noted that black officers exhibiting deficiencies would probably do better with more training and experience.

For instance, Col. Walter A. Elliott of the 365th Infantry noted that his officers' physical endurance was excellent, but he rated their discipline, attitude, and interest as only satisfactory. Elliott's black officers lagged behind their white peers in leadership, command ability, and aggressiveness. He ended his evaluation on a hopeful note: "Colored officers have been given an assigned duty which requires perseverance, diligence and concentration. Degree of proficiency attained—satisfactory." Elliott made no recommendations for changing OCS to better prepare the officers.[46]

Col. A. R. Walk, commanding the 370th Regimental Combat Team, commented, "Relative efficiency and leadership of colored officers as compared with white officers, seems to be slightly lower as a whole." He rated them deficient primarily in discipline, and recommended the officer candidate course put more stress on that aspect of training. Walk saw no difference between white and black officers in their military attitude and interest. But he noted, "Their commands do not bring as cheerful and willing response [from the soldiers] as the white officers'." This subjective appraisal may in fact reflect Walk's personal bias. Lt. Col. Robert G. Ross of the supporting 598th Field Artillery Battalion noted that while black officers displayed good technique, "the response from colored troops is generally passive." He recommended more OCS instruction on the administrative duties of the artillery lieutenant to better prepare him to be productive in his job.[47]

The last regimental commander, Col. Sterling A. Wood of the 371st Regimental Combat Team, rated his black lieutenants as "sorely deficient" in leadership, but he appreciated that they had never been given the opportunity to lead before. Wood recommended that the officer candidate course give them additional practical experience. Overall, however, this first report was simply too early. Lt. Col. Otto Ellis of the 599th Field Artillery, which supported the 371st RCT, reported that none of the battalion's eight black lieutenants had been in place long enough to evaluate and that three had arrived the day he tendered his report.[48]

Training soon became the greatest of all the Army's "engineering problems." The troops' aptitude and their inability to train bedeviled

Almond and the 92nd Infantry Division leadership from the outset as it had their Great War predecessors. The War Department developed detailed plans for assessing, classifying, and training tens of thousands of soldiers who had varying levels of education and no military experience. The standard US Army–wide method of assessing suitability for service, the Army General Classification Test, measured the soldier's capacity for learning and grouped the men into five categories, with the fastest learners going into Category I, down to the slowest in Category V. The Army expected that the smallest numbers (fewer than 10 percent) would be in Categories I and V, with 24 percent in each of Categories II and IV and nearly 38 percent of the population in Category III.[49]

The soldiers in the 92nd scored significantly lower than white soldiers. The War Department had designed the AGCT to yield a median score of 100, with the scores grouped into five categories in the form of a bell curve. Most officers came from Category I, while Category II provided additional officers and the bulk of the NCOs, and Categories III, IV, and V supplied private soldiers (see table 5.3). The actual test scores came close to the expected numbers for white soldiers across the Army. Black soldiers did not fare as well, with nearly half of them in Category V, one-third in Category IV, about one-eighth in Category III, and the remaining small fraction in Categories I and II. The scores for 92nd Infantry Division soldiers fell below the expected Army average in all categories and even below averages for other black soldiers in Categories I, IV, and V. The 92nd averages were slightly better than black soldiers Army-wide in Categories II and III, but 13 percent of the soldiers were illiterate and could not be tested.[50]

Table 5.3. AGCT Scores Comparison

Category	Expected Army Average	White Soldiers Armywide	Black Soldiers Armywide	92nd
I	7%	6.6%	0.4%	0%
II	24%	28.0%	3.4%	10%
III	38%	32.1%	12.3%	15%
IV	24%	24.8%	34.7%	41%
V	7%	8.5%	49.2%	21%
Illiterate				13%

Source: Adapted from U. Lee, *Employment of Negro Troops*, 244, table 5; Goodman *A Fragment of Victory in Italy: The 92nd Infantry Division in World War II*, 4, 52.

The situation improved a little as some black soldiers washed out and others replaced them. The educational levels meant that the 92nd Division soldier lagged well behind his white counterparts in other divisions. Only some 20 percent of black soldiers had a high school diploma, while 38 percent had less than an eighth-grade education. Black soldiers encountered difficulty with training because of educational defects caused by decades of "separate but equal" schooling that was anything but equal. Despite this evidence, some officers did not believe that these early educational inequalities explained the instabilities the unit later experienced in combat.[51]

The AGCT seemed to favor white soldiers because the wording of the questions often did not permit the black soldiers to understand the problem. They encountered questions couched in a social construct familiar to most whites but alien to most undereducated African Americans. While those socioeconomic differences might have been real, the Army had few options for personnel assessment. The notion of providing separate tests for black soldiers did not occur to Army leaders. Experience in combat later revealed a correlation between battlefield performance and AGCT scores. African Americans in the South had consistently fewer opportunities for education than did those from other parts of the country, and they earned proportionately lower AGCT scores as well. The higher-scoring men from the North went to the division headquarters and special troops, while the majority of the infantry came from the low-scoring South. Almond would later report that his division's more technical arms, such as artillery and engineers, did well, while the infantry consistently failed in combat.[52]

These educational difficulties prevented the 92nd Infantry Division from holding to the same training schedule as other divisions. The War Department prescribed a training period of 42 weeks, or a scant 10 months, for an infantry division; the 92nd trained for 22 months. The training program consisted of three phases. Individual training would take 13 weeks, with up to four weeks of flextime to allow for receiving men and matériel. Unit training required 13 weeks, and combined arms training 14 weeks. The divisions would then complete large-scale maneuvers and final pre-deployment training to maintain a sharp edge while awaiting overseas movement.[53]

Despite the October activation ceremony, recruits continued to join the 92nd Division's scattered elements until December. The individual basic training period began on December 14. As Almond's soldiers began to fail in training, they went to remedial training classes. All training centers had a "casual camp" to provide additional training for soldiers unable to keep pace with their comrades. When the soldiers attained proficiency, they returned to their units, but some never reached the appropriate level and required replacement. This constant cycling of soldiers into and out of the casual camps, along with newly arriving replacements, contributed to the division's difficulties in reaching the required training levels.[54]

The training schedule for infantry units assumed that the soldier had no previous training of any kind, and therefore all started at the most basic level. The thirteen-week cycle opened with preliminary individual tasks such as military customs and courtesy, field sanitation, drill and ceremony, physical training, and rifle marksmanship. Men assigned to the weapons platoons received additional instruction on mortars and machine guns. The training grew progressively harder, adding weekly road marches, tactical training at the squad and platoon level, and night operations. The twelfth and thirteenth weeks brought together company and battalion training. The training schedule consumed forty-four hours per week. With the addition of fatigue details, drills, ceremonies, and other events, the soldiers had little time to relax. For the 92nd Division, this period was scheduled from December 14, 1942, to March 13, 1943. When all soldiers had successfully completed the course, the unit would begin training at regimental level.[55]

Almond and his officers encountered difficulty completing the unit's training at every stage. "Rifle marksmanship, for example, required three to four times as much ammunition," Almond later recalled, "before we went to record . . . [firing] and consequently more time in combat firing." The men required much more training and more effort from the instructors because of their educational deficiencies. The division established special night schools to teach soldiers to read. At one point the division had more than two thousand men in these literacy schools, taught by officers and NCOs assigned to the division. Despite this, testing and inspection revealed many training failures that required instruction. At the end of the individual training period, III Corps headquarters inspected the division and found it deficient. The 92nd received a four-week extension, through April 9, in order to retrain on individual skills.[56]

The first couple of years of the war had been tumultuous for the Almond family too, with moves from the US Naval War College at Newport, Rhode Island to Washington to VI Corps headquarters at Providence, Rhode Island, to Fort Huachuca, and finally to Fort McClellan, all in less than two years. The children had grown and left the home, and their experiences somewhat mirrored Almond's own experience during World War I. His daughter Peggy had married Lt. Thomas T. Galloway on his graduation day from West Point, May 29, 1942, and he departed immediately for flight school. Peggy would remain with the Almonds while her husband was away in training, and also after he deployed to Europe with his outfit. Their son, Tommy Jr., was born on August 28, 1943. Ned Jr. graduated from West Point in June 1943 and received a commission in the infantry. He reported for infantry training immediately.[57]

Some historians have judged Almond harshly for his attitudes toward black soldiers, but his approach mirrored that of the War Department and much of white society. Others deplore his apparent lack of prewar command experience, but available evidence indicates that Almond matched his peers in every respect. Almond's previous performance marked him as a successful officer and gave him the opportunity to command at division level. General Marshall had recognized that commanders of black troops must be selected with even greater care than others, and Almond believed he possessed the "knack" that Marshall required for such duty. But while Almond had achieved success in the system as it existed, the system itself failed black units. The problems caused by using racially segregated divisions had started to become apparent to the white Army leadership, and they would become more so as the units progressed through training. The War Department's acceptance of local racial policies made Almond's job all the more difficult for both logistics and unit cohesion. He would soon see exactly how many problems the unit separation had caused.

6

Trouble at Fort Huachuca

1943–1944

Having operated at four widely separated bases for more than six months, Almond received orders in April 1943 to move the 92nd Infantry Division to Fort Huachuca, Arizona. The 93rd Infantry Division had completed its training and moved to the Louisiana Maneuver Training Area. After a month and a half of training and exercises opposing the 85th Infantry Division, the 93rd would move to the California-Arizona Maneuver Area at Camp Clipper, California, for additional training until December. The division would then embark for the Southwest Pacific Theater of Operations in January 1944. Almond could expect a similar training pattern for his division, although his ultimate combat destination was unknown.[1]

For the first time since the 92nd Infantry Division's activation, Almond could finally train his entire division in one place. He found Fort Huachuca better equipped to handle his troops than their previous bases, since all necessary facilities had been in place to support the 93rd Infantry Division. The 92nd enjoyed the use of good training facilities and few equipment shortages of any consequence. Despite the disadvantages associated with a remote post, the Arizona desert at Fort Huachuca proved to be an excellent training site. The weather, though hot, remained dry so that training could continue unhampered throughout the year. The post also offered varied terrain, and wide-open spaces that provided plenty of room for units to maneuver.[2]

The move to Arizona from the four widely separated bases consumed a month of Almond's training time. With all basic and individual training now complete, the division would use Fort Huachuca for battalion- and regimental-level instruction. The RCTs had completed individual and company-level training before arriving at Fort Huachuca, but they had yet to function as cohesive units. Combined arms training began on May 10, 1943, and constituted the final fourteen-week period before the division-level "D" exercises, which were scheduled to begin on

August 16. The division had numerous training failures, however. Nine of the division's eighteen infantry battalions needed to repeat their combat firing tests, as did two of the artillery battalions. Almond requested extensions through January 1944. Upon completion of the "D" exercises, the 92nd would deploy to Louisiana for large-scale maneuvers with other divisions. Shortly after these tests began, Almond convened the "92nd Infantry Division Tactical School," designed to prepare all officers for combined arms training. He published a directive describing the makeup of the regimental combat team, and included a description of RCT operations.[3]

Though Almond had gained a reputation as a trainer, his first experiences maneuvering large formations led to difficulties. During one of the tests, Almond abruptly changed the order of march of some of the units. With little time to disseminate the new instructions, the convoys became confused and ended up scattered throughout the training area. Almond blamed the division's operations (G3) officer for the mistake and relieved him, replacing him with Maj. William J. McCaffrey. This move reflects a bit of Almond's basic insecurity, because he blamed a subordinate for his own mistake. McCaffrey later reported the man to have been a competent officer who served well in other units during the war.[4]

This was not the only time Almond's zeal for training and his tendency to micromanage led him to subvert his own system. McCaffrey later recalled an incident in which the 370th and 371st Infantry Regiments encountered coordination problems. The two regiments found themselves at odds over a firing range, each believing it had rights to use it. The regimental commanders approached Almond, and the general queried McCaffrey. McCaffrey had assigned the range to the 370th, but Almond had allowed the 371st to use it. As McCaffrey later recalled, he told Almond: "Well, if you're going to be the G3 you don't need me. I'd like to go to one of the regiments." Almond dismissed the two colonels. He said, "You shouldn't talk to me that way. I'm the division commander." McCaffrey said, "You can't be the division commander and G3, it won't work. If you're going to be G3, you don't need me." Almond started to laugh and said, "Okay, you're G3." After that, said McCaffrey, "I told him exactly what I thought."[5]

This was not the last time that McCaffrey would directly challenge Almond, and so began the close, trusting relationship between the two men that lasted until Almond's death. The situation illustrates Almond's tendency to micromanage and to skip his own chain of command, a trait he retained throughout his career. Almond needed a strong subordinate such as McCaffrey to keep him in line, and in return the man earned Almond's undying respect. This relationship, the most important of his professional life, allowed Almond to mask his insecurity somewhat, as he now had a "sounding board" to help him.

Almond began leading black troops at a pivotal time. The Army had raised two black divisions during World War I, but those soldiers' wartime and postwar experiences had hardened their resolve and that of the African American community. The Army needed to do more than simply appease a society that was no longer willing to accept whatever the white leadership would allow. Black soldiers returning after World War I used their veteran status to fight for civil rights and the dignity of African American people.[6]

As the nation moved toward a war footing in 1940, African Americans were no longer content to accept the small accommodations the military made merely to placate agitating black leaders. Many of them were bitter, believing that their service and sacrifice had not been rewarded with the full benefits of citizenship. Several of these veterans pushed the Roosevelt administration for greater racial equality in the armed forces. Moreover, as the sons of these veterans prepared to fight another war, they refused to accept the status quo and demanded an end to discriminatory practices.[7]

The black press had begun pressuring President Franklin D. Roosevelt to broaden opportunities for African Americans as early as his first term. African American educator William Pickens penned an article criticizing Roosevelt's appointment of white men as ambassadors to Haiti and Liberia, and chiding him for employing blacks only in menial labor positions around the White House. By the election of 1936, however, Roosevelt had appointed several prominent African Americans to what became known as the "black cabinet," which he used to include community leaders and thus gain support among northern black voters. These government appointments won over the black press, which then swung its support behind the president. One African American activist likened the black cabinet to the rim of a wheel, connected to the center by the "spokes" of the government agencies. "Roosevelt is our hub of progress, inspired by faith in God and the people of a great nation he is the center around which everything governmental revolves." The *Kansas American* also called for the black community to support Roosevelt just before the election, and enumerated the large number of government jobs held by African Americans.[8]

By 1940, however, much of the African American community vocally opposed government segregation policies, and black newspapers continued to apply pressure. African Americans urged Roosevelt to consider appointing even more blacks to high positions. FDR's Republican opponents fanned the flames, and his unprecedented third term seemed in doubt. The African American community's cries reached a crescendo when, some two weeks before the election, the Army promoted eighty-four white officers to brigadier general while passing over Col. Benjamin O. Davis, the Army's senior black officer. The black community recalled the War Department having also ignored Lt. Col. Charles Young, then the nation's highest-ranking black officer, in 1917. Ignoring Davis proved to be too much for many black newspapers, such as the *Pittsburgh Courier*, the *Baltimore Afro-American,* and the *Kansas City Plaindealer,* which then urged their readers to vote for Republican Wendell Willkie instead of Roosevelt. Other notables such as African American boxer Joe Louis and white labor leader John L. Lewis did the same.[9]

Roosevelt had gained most of the black vote in 1936, and the potential loss of significant numbers of black voters alarmed him. He worked through Gen. George C. Marshall, US Army chief of staff, to appoint Davis as a brigadier general, over the opposition of Secretary of War Henry L. Stimson, and Secretary of the Navy Frank Knox. Roosevelt also appointed William H. Hastie, then dean of the Howard University Law School, to a top-level post with the title Civilian Aide to the Secretary of War (CASW). These moves, coming only days before the election, drew support from some, but cynicism from others. The African American newspaper *Cleveland Gazette* argued that Roosevelt had acquiesced "in the face of the vigorous and united race press."[10]

Recognizing that FDR had appointed Hastie and Davis merely to pacify the black community and win back the vote, the newspaper continued to support Willkie. Roosevelt was reelected, but part of his traditional support base, the African American community, had eroded. William H. Hastie, a longtime favorite of Roosevelt, had been an easy choice as CASW. He had served in several positions in the black cabinet, and the president had appointed him as the first African American federal judge in 1937. He had resigned in 1939 to take the position at Howard, and he accepted Roosevelt's offer of the CASW position in 1940.[11]

From the outset, Hastie had a different view of his position than did Secretary of War Stimson. Stimson saw Hastie's position merely as a "clearinghouse" for African American complaints. Emmett Scott had held a similar position in the Great War, but the post was largely symbolic and used primarily to inspire patriotism in the black community.

Hastie had no intention of taking a passive role, and he chose to attack the biggest racial problem: segregation. He hoped to work from inside the administration, influencing policy and developing strategies to end racial discrimination. Hastie represented the new generation of African-American intellectuals who were determined to change the discriminatory practices of the last war, even as the nation prepared for the next.[12]

Army leaders also assumed that General Davis would not challenge the Army's segregation policy and that his appointment would placate the black community, but it too was problematic. Davis was approaching mandatory retirement on his sixty-fourth birthday. After briefly commanding the 4th Cavalry Brigade, a reserve formation being raised to wartime strength, he retired and was immediately recalled to active duty as the War Department special inspector general (IG) for matters pertaining to black soldiers.[13]

Despite Davis's qualifications, he owed his star to politics and therefore needed to tread a careful path. He also self-identified with the "old Army," seeing himself as a professional officer first, a black man second. Davis dealt skillfully with both the black press and the white War Department hierarchy, each of which trusted him to advance their agenda. He did not ignore race problems, but he presented a more pragmatic view than Hastie and tended to deal with racial incidents as they came. He toured military bases and investigated complaints from black soldiers, determining whether the reported "injustices" stemmed from mere soldier dissatisfaction with military life or from true racial discrimination.[14]

Davis sometimes irritated the black community when he seemingly supported discriminatory War Department policies, but he saw himself as part of the Army's senior leadership. In some cases Davis spoke plainly in his reports, but his boss, US Army Inspector General Maj. Gen. Virgil I. Peterson, toned them down. In one report, for instance, Davis stated that segregation remained the main cause of strained race relations in the Army. He suggested the government use the Army to bring about changes, such as instituting better race training for white officers. He also recommended against sending large numbers of black soldiers from the North to train in the South. Peterson omitted some things from Davis's final report to the War Department, but he retained these two suggestions.[15]

The 92nd Infantry Division experienced some of the same kinds of turbulence other divisions did. Almond had received orders in February 1943 just before the move to provide three hundred men as cadre to the 364th Infantry Regiment at Camp Van Dorn, Mississippi.[16] Ironically, the division's consolidation at Fort Huachuca caused morale problems. The War Department accepted that dispersing the division to four different posts would affect training, as it had during World War I, but it did so to preserve social order. Consolidating the regiments, however, brought new problems, because antipathies that had been dormant while the regiments were separated became more obvious when they came together at Fort Huachuca. The three RCTs had developed independent attitudes and unit esprit de corps while training separately, and uniting them destroyed some of that spirit without building any loyalty to the division. The 93rd Infantry Division, formed from two regular regiments and a draftee regiment, faced a similar problem, but not to the degree that the 92nd would. The individual regiments had built some degree of unit identity, but Almond found building division-level unity difficult.[17]

The division had adopted the nickname Buffalo Division during World War I, as a nod to the heritage of the 367th Infantry Regiment, then assigned to the division. The 367th had previously borrowed the moniker from the original Buffalo Soldiers, the 9th and 10th Cavalry Regiments. Those cavalry troopers had earned the sobriquet in the late nineteenth century from their Indian foes, who both saluted their fighting spirit and poked fun at their tight, curly hair. The unit patch also featured a buffalo. Almond made several bold attempts to build division-wide morale. For instance, he imported a live buffalo as a division mascot, and named it Buffalo Bill. The animal attended all division ceremonies, and sometimes proved to be a source of entertainment as well as pride. It once broke loose on the parade field during a ceremony, to the amusement of all present. Drawing on the buffalo symbol, Almond ordered a buffalo to be painted on every division vehicle bumper, both to identify his vehicles and to stimulate unit pride.[18]

He also started a division newspaper, the *Buffalo*, that operated throughout the war. He directed each regimental commander to provide news and photos to the editor on a weekly basis. Each issue also carried the news of the famous African American celebrities who visited the troops, including boxer Joe Louis, entertainers Eddie Anderson and Hattie McDaniel, and singer Lena Horne, whose nephew served with the 92nd. While these morale-building measures seemed logical, and in fact similar to those adopted in many other divisions, not all of Almond's soldiers embraced them. PFC Troy Johnson of the 365th Infantry later recalled that the US Army's *Stars & Stripes* was "a good paper but the unit paper was trash."[19]

Many soldiers found the harsh desert conditions at Fort Huachuca much harder to tolerate than those they had experienced at their eastern camps, and it had a deleterious effect on their training. The problem surfaced when large numbers of soldiers claimed medical disabilities during a twenty-five-mile road march. Most of these ailments turned out to be feigned, and the "straggling" troops returned to duty, but some two thousand continued to seek medical excuses to avoid further training. Almond later noted, "It is doubtful if any such mass movement occurred in the training of any white divisions. This probably was the first indication of racial instability and for disinclination to enter combat."[20]

The medical problems black soldiers experienced were not new; they dated at least to the Civil War. During that earlier conflict, white soldiers were found to be generally healthier than black ones. Many blacks suffered a lifetime of malnutrition, a condition they shared with white soldiers from urban slums. The black soldiers, moreover, having come from largely rural environments, lacked the immunity to disease that many white soldiers had developed. Inadequate health care for black soldiers when they did get sick reduced their vigor. This inadequacy included ignorance, such as the supposition of black soldiers' resistance to malaria, insufficient numbers of doctors for black regiments, inferior training for those available, and simple racist attitudes that valued black soldiers less than white ones. Combined with the typically primitive medical care of the era, and exacerbated by combat conditions, these factors ensured that black Civil War soldiers suffered a much higher death rate from disease that did their white counterparts.[21]

Black soldiers entering the Army in the 1940s still suffered from inadequate civilian health care, inadequate or nutritionally deficient diet, and differing cultural standards that produced a higher rate of social diseases, much as their forebears in the 1860s had. This resulted in higher rejection rates for military service for black soldiers. Doctors found that 60 percent of African Americans and 50 percent of whites accepted for general service between November 1940 and December 1943 were completely healthy, with those remaining having only minor problems. The soldiers accepted only for limited service, however, had more significant problems: white soldiers predominantly had trouble with teeth and eyes, while black soldiers had venereal diseases. When excluding VD, rates of other serious medical problems were roughly equal in the black and white populations for these limited service personnel. Black soldiers, however, tended to suffer from inadequate reporting. The examining station often noted only the most serious defects for black soldiers, so other conditions went unrecorded. Venereal disease became the primary limiting factor for black soldiers and, combined with educational deficiencies, seriously reduced the number of African Americans available for induction. These two defects eliminated more than 50 percent of the black registrants on their first examinations, compared to less than 40 percent of the whites.[22]

There were, then, some legitimate medical issues. But the straggling hinted at larger morale problems in the division. Brig. Gen. Davis inspected the 92nd Infantry Division twice in 1943, and his findings illuminated a racial basis for many of the division's woes. Davis conducted his first inspections of the 92nd in February and March of 1943, just before the move to Arizona. He rated morale superior at three of the four posts, with no "complications" between the white and black officers. Davis also gave Almond high marks in his report: "The Division is commanded by Major General E. M. Almond, U. S. Army, who appears to be most active and efficient, as do the members of his staff. General Almond has shown special aptitude for a command composed of colored and white officers and a colored enlisted personnel. He has secured and maintained the greatest respect and admiration of the colored officers and enlisted personnel by his fairness and sympathy with their problems."[23]

Five months later, Davis arrived at Fort Huachuca with Truman K. Gibson, acting CASW. Gibson had replaced William Hastie, who had resigned the post in January to protest the War Department's segregation policies. General Marshall directed Davis to investigate conditions at Fort Huachuca after receiving reports of racial problems in the 92nd Division. Some of the problems included lack of promotions for black officers, bad food, segregated officer mess halls, several assaults on soldiers, and General Almond's alleged use of racially offensive language in a public forum while talking to soldiers. This followed a visit in June by Lt. Gen. Courtney Hodges, commander of the Third Army, who had also reported on conditions.[24]

Davis remained at Fort Huachuca for five days, interviewing soldiers and observing training and other activities. Davis needed to use all his skills during the investigation. He was able to develop a rapport with the African American soldiers that would have been impossible for a white officer, and thus uncover some of the underlying causes for unrest in the division. At the same time, he was a Regular Army general officer, and able to distinguish between legitimate racial incidents and simple soldier complaints about military life.

Many of the black officers had become convinced that the 92nd's white officers were prejudiced—and with good reason, as some clearly were. Some attributed this attitude to General Almond, claiming they overheard him use the word "nigger" while speaking at a barbecue. After investigating this incident, Davis decided that Almond was the victim of a misunderstanding. Though an acceptable word at the time, Almond often pronounced the word "Negro" as if it were spelled "N-I-G-R-A, later viewed as mere code for the epithet." Davis had suggested at one of the first meetings of the Advisory Committee on Negro Policies that the committee direct commanders to use the term "colored" instead of "Negro," for exactly this reason.[25]

Almond's officer promotion policy became one of the black officers' main grievances, and Davis found the policy discriminatory and unjust. Black officers contended that the promotion and assignment policy should be the same for all officers, since they all had to make the same sacrifices. Almond analyzed officer promotions within the 92nd Infantry Division and gave Davis the results. Division policy mirrored the War Department's guidelines, which based promotion on merit and demonstrated efficiency, with seniority and experience being basic factors. Almond noted that the division had activated with 550 white officers and one black officer. Some of the white officers had been in the Army longer and therefore had seniority and experience. As new black officers joined the division, white officers left in accordance with Army policy to allow the black officers to command black troops. By the time of Davis's inspection, nearly half of the lieutenants in the division were black. Almond reported that his commanders had evaluated all of the lieutenants for potential promotion, and the first black officer in the division advanced on January 1, 1943, two and one-half months after the unit activated. Since then, 9 percent (34 of 386 assigned) of all black lieutenants who had joined since activation had either received or been recommended for promotion. The division's white lieutenants advanced in rank at a higher rate, 38.7 percent (173 of 447 assigned), but most of these officers had more experience than the black lieutenants (see table 6.1).[26]

Table 6.1. Comparison of White and Black Lieutenant Promotions

	Assigned July 1, 1943	Commissioned Before September 15, 1942	Promoted Since Arrival	Percent
White	447	447	173	38.7
Black	396	27	34	8.1

Source: Adapted from memorandum, Headquarters, 92nd Infantry Division, "Subject: Study of Promotion of Colored Officers of 92nd Infantry Division," July 8, 1943, Box 18, Davis Papers.

The confusion and anger over promotions among the black officers likely stemmed from two factors. First, the original War Department policy limited black officers to company-level assignments. This prevented them from moving to staff positions and potentially reaching higher ranks. Second, many saw promotions as awards, rather than recognition of the capability for an increased level of responsibility. Black officers believed white officers received promotions for being "good ol' boys" or favorites of various commanders.[27]

Quick promotions for black officers presented problems. While second lieutenants could expect to advance quickly to first lieutenant as they learned their jobs, training to operate effectively as captains, majors, and lieutenant colonels required time and experience. Newly inducted officers, most of them recent OCS graduates, could not quickly grasp the necessary skills for higher-level leadership. Fast promotions had become the norm during the First World War, and the pattern held true during the Second. White officers generally had more military experience than their black counterparts, and therefore received promotions at a faster rate. Gen. Courtney Hodges, commander of US Third Army, had found the division's white officers to be above the average of those in other divisions.[28]

Progressing to the field-grade ranks and the correspondingly more complex responsibilities was even more difficult. This explanation seemed logical, but many black officers did not understand it. Two of the division's black officers, Capt. Jehu C. Hunter and Capt. Major Clark, wrote after the war that seeing so few black senior officers reduced confidence in the rest. They argued it "confirmed in the minds of many enlisted soldiers of the division that their black commissioned leaders were not full-fledged officers, confounding leadership problems at the platoon level where the need for trust in commissioned officers is critical."[29]

A segregated officers' mess was another sore spot. Col. Sterling A. Wood had segregated the 371st Infantry Regiment officers' mess upon arrival at Fort Huachuca in defiance of the division standard. The African American officers left the mess in protest, and Almond relieved Colonel Wood. His replacement integrated the mess and invited the black officers back, and the issue died away. This was not the first difficulty with Wood; Davis had given his regiment the lowest marks in the division on his previous inspection. Wood was an avowed racist who made no pretense of his feelings, and he shocked even other white officers with some of his comments. Eugene Johnston, a white officer and recent OCS graduate who would remain in the division throughout the war, served initially in the 371st and saw Wood firsthand. Wood made sure that all the black officers knew where he stood, saying, "I understand colored people. I had a plantation in Alabama." It was Wood who told his black officers, in a phrase often attributed to Almond: "You people constitute ten percent of the population of this country, and I'm going to see to it you suffer ten percent of the casualties." Among the RCT commanders, only Wood had requested 25 percent "overstrength" of white officers, in addition to the black officers. Despite Almond's quick action to get rid of Wood, his attitude had spread throughout the 371st and the rest of the division.[30]

Almond established a School of Application and Proficiency to educate officers who failed to meet training standards. The school was intended for any officer who required remedial training, but no white officers attended it. This angered the black officers, who assumed that Almond found only blacks deficient. The instructors' attitudes reinforced that point. The African American officers therefore considered such a school a punishment. General Hodges had inspected the school and ordered Almond to close it, but only because it interfered with training time. Almond later reported that some officers had done well enough in the school that he had cancelled their reclassification. The black officers interpreted this closure as confirmation of their position.[31]

Davis's investigation revealed that the soldiers' perceptions of Almond's policies inhibited the results Almond hoped to achieve. For instance, one of the issues that prompted Davis's inspection concerned black officers confined in the stockade. Two of them had complained to a congressman, who referred the matter to the US Army IG. Davis investigated these cases and determined their offenses to be worthy of court-martial. He later explained that it appeared to the troops that Almond had resorted to the remedial school and court-martial procedures to get rid of unfit officers, rather than using the reclassification system. Davis noted that division leaders should have recognized these officers as unfit and sent them for reclassification, the process for demoting and removing unfit officers, before they committed their crimes.[32]

Appearances to the contrary, Almond was ruthless about removing bad officers regardless of rank, position, or race. For instance, by the time Davis visited, Almond had replaced the commanders of two of the three infantry regiments, and he would replace the third before deploying the following year. At the time of Davis's visit, Almond had twenty black officers being reclassified, and another thirty-three black officers and two white field-grade officers were being prepared for reclassification. The commander and the inspector general had similar motivations: Almond to make the best of what he had, and Davis to make sure only the best remained.[33]

During Davis's inspection tour, he was shocked to observe firsthand an incident that demonstrated the tensions at work in the division. General Almond invited Davis to attend the dedication ceremony of a new athletic field, and when Almond rose to speak, the troops booed him. This display of disrespect surprised and disappointed Davis and humiliated Almond. Davis believed the incident showed Almond the degree to which morale had suffered since the division's arrival at Fort Huachuca.[34]

After final discussions with the division's officers and selected enlisted men, Davis departed to complete his report. As he worked through several drafts, the report became shorter and more terse, but the draft versions combined with the final version provide a complete picture of his findings. Davis determined that widespread disaffection in the 92nd stemmed from distrust between the white and black officers, both of whom deserved a measure of blame for the situation. Davis found that "white officers of the Division in admitting the dangerous state of affairs blamed [outside influences] for the inefficiency and poor performance of the Negro officers," while the "Negro officers on their part blamed (a) bad racial attitudes of the white officers of the Division (b) their inability to obtain promotions."[35]

In assessing the racial climate in the division, Davis pointed out that white officers had grounds to resent their black counterparts:

> There can be no question that some of the Negro officers are seriously lacking in character. It is likewise a fact established by personal observation that many of the officers do not comprehend the full meaning of discipline. There is no question, particularly in view of the extremely limited number of complaints from enlisted men, that the Negro officers furnish nearly all of the difficulty now being experienced in the Division and contribute materially by their own action and deficiencies to the difficulty. . . . There is no question but that many of the Negro officers have miserably and utterly failed to conduct themselves as officers and that many more have lacked in certain basic requirements. Whether these failures are due to the attitudes that have developed or have produced them is moot and useless discussion. The existence of the deficient officers is a fact.[36]

Davis made no personal comments on these thoughts, but the actions of these few officers no doubt angered him. As an African American officer of long Regular Army service, Davis saw what damage these few individuals could do to the advancement of other black officers, and he had little patience for soldiers who did not follow regulations. Those officers mistrusted their white peers and superiors, however, because of the demonstrated racist attitudes of some of the whites. Davis concluded that the promotion system, the remedial school, the court-martials, the segregated mess hall, and the undisguised attitudes of some of the officers, all made the black officers feel that "they were not officers in the Army of the United States, but colored officers in some special sub-section of a colored Army." Davis determined that "the record shows that in all cases where white officers deviated from [Almond's] policy of fairness, action has been taken. Such officers were transferred, court-martialed, or disciplined under [Article of War] 104." He conceded that the time required for investigations sometimes delayed the disciplinary action, so it was not always clear to the soldiers that the offender had been punished.[37]

Davis believed that Almond was earnest in his efforts. "General Almond himself has been diligent and conscientious in applying himself to the training of his division," Davis found, "He has not however received the necessary cooperation from his junior officers." Davis believed that both the white and black officers had failed in this regard.[38] In the final report, however, Davis identified Almond's one important failing:

> General Almond has, in the opinion of the inspector general, overlooked the human element in the training of this Division. Great stress has been placed upon the mechanical perfection in the execution of training missions. Apparently not enough consideration has been given to the maintenance of a racial understanding between white and colored officers and men. The execution of ceremonies with smartness and precision, and the perfunctory performance of military duties is taken as an indication of high morale. This is not true with the colored soldier. He can be driven to perform without necessarily having a high morale. . . . However, General Almond appears to be an able officer, and it is believed that now—since he is well aware of the situation and because of the fact that in all cases of unfairness or misconduct involving racial issues he has taken remedial action—action will be taken to remove the causes of unrest.[39]

Almond had been slow to realize that he had significant racial problems in the division. He focused on building and training his division, and that included strict adherence to regulations, directives, and customs of the service. Almond felt the scrutiny of the War Department, with high-level visitors coming nearly every month to check on the outfit's progress under wartime pressure. In the prevailing Jim Crow environment, Almond believed that his job was creating a fighting force, not finding racial harmony. Davis believed the incident at the baseball field had removed the scales from Almond's eyes, and he began to realize the degree of the racial problems plaguing the division.[40] Davis concluded his report with an endorsement of Almond, but also a prod to the War Department to investigate the current promotion policy:

> That Major General Edwin [*sic*] M. Almond, the commanding general, is honest, sincere, and is now aware of the causes of this unrest; and if the special War Department policy as to the promotion of Negro officers is rescinded, and colored officers are promoted and treated the same as white officers, he will be able to overcome the present conditions. There is no question as to General Almond's professional fitness, and it is believed that he is thoroughly imbued with the idea of fairness and justice. . . . The only criticism that might be levelled against General Almond is the failure on his part to realize the extent of the problem confronting any commander of Negro troops. He must appreciate for example that fact that discriminations and inequalities exist towards the Negro soldier. He must further appreciate the fact that the Negro soldier knows this and this knowledge is increased by the columns in the Negro press. . . . In short, the lower echelons of command have not put across in the 92nd Division, General Almond's ideas.

The remainder of Davis's report took aim at the paternalist attitude that held that southerners had a special "knack" for dealing with black soldiers: "Further, he must realize the junior officers from the south do not know the Negro merely by reason of accident of birth. Many of them are sincere, earnest and well-intentioned but do untold harm."[41]

Davis's observation confirms the prevailing view in the War Department that those officers who had grown up in a culture as oppressors must somehow better understand those they oppressed.

After Davis's report reached the Inspector General, the War Department studied the request and took action. The War Department staff analyzed the officer promotion rates for the major commands, Army Ground Forces (AGF), Army Service Forces (ASF), and the Army Air Forces (AAF), and determined that an average of 25 percent of the black officers in each command were qualified for promotion. Insufficient data existed from the three commands to enable a comparison to white promotion rates, but there appeared to be no significant variation in the application of War Department policies.[42]

Based on this review, the War Department issued a revised policy for assigning black officers. Previously, black officers had been limited to service with certain types of units, but the revision allowed reassignment to any unit composed of black enlisted personnel. It also clarified that black officers would receive promotion in accordance with current regulations, and that white officers would transfer to other assignments to make room for black officers as they became capable of the required duties. These promotions would include staff positions as well, and officers promoted within a division would normally remain assigned to it.[43]

The change in assignment regulations gained the division six field-grade officers. With their arrival, the 597th Field Artillery Battalion, commanded by Lt. Col. Wendell T. Derrick, and 600th Field Artillery Battalion, commanded by Lt. Col. Marcus H. Ray, contained only black officers. These officers had come from black National Guard outfits. The division's artillery commander, Brig. Gen. William H. "Red" Colbern, rated Derrick and Ray highly, and though they had very different command styles, their battalions performed well. Colbern had not previously commanded black troops, but he had a positive opinion of them. Colbern believed the soldiers regarded their officers on the basis of performance. As he later related: "To be perfectly frank, I was very highly pleased with the performance of the battalions having all Negro officers. They did much better than I expected them to do. . . . It doesn't make a nickel's worth of difference to the general run of Negro enlisted men whether his officer is white or black, just so long as the officer knows his job, is a good disciplinarian, and has the welfare of the men at heart."[44] Colbern intended to sound a positive note about soldiers, but a white general could not know exactly how black privates felt about their officers, white or black. He did not consider black officers equal to white ones, but he acknowledged good performance regardless of race.

After finally completing all individual, unit, and combined arms training, the 92nd Infantry Division conducted its division-level, or "D," exercise in December 1943. The division then departed in January 1944 for the Louisiana Maneuvers, but not before suffering a critical loss of personnel. Almond was ordered to release another three hundred men as cadre for the 2nd Cavalry Division at Fort Clark, Texas. He lost seventeen more men, most of them noncommissioned officers, who volunteered for a new all-black airborne unit, the 555th Parachute Infantry Battalion, then being formed at Fort Benning, Georgia.[45]

The Louisiana Maneuvers were the final exercise in the division's pre-deployment training, conducted in a 2,400-square-mile area in central Louisiana. The exercise was intended to give soldiers and their outfits the opportunity to operate as closely as possible to the way they would in combat. The Fourth Army ran the maneuvers, which began February 7 and included XVIII Corps headquarters, the 44th Infantry Division, the 75th Infantry Division, the 8th Armored Division, II Tactical Air Division (Army Air Forces), and corps support troops, in addition to Almond's 92nd Division. These large-scale training operations had changed little in overall concept since Almond's days as VI Corps G3 (Operations) officer in 1941, but in practice each cycle of training brought new challenges. AGF headquarters adapted each new "maneuver period" to emphasize the areas identified as lacking in the previous period.[46]

The exercise consisted of five phases: division maneuvers, river crossings, advance to contact, defense, and meeting engagements. The maneuvers began with "flag exercises," designed to allow troops and their commanders to practice some tactical movements before beginning the more complex exercises. After the flag exercises, the maneuver director designated one of the divisions as the defense while XVIII Corps practiced tactical operations with the remaining three divisions. The units rotated the defense mission, so that all got the maximum opportunity to work on a variety of combat tasks.[47]

Despite Almond's tone-deaf approach to soldiers' racial complaints, they remained "his" soldiers, and he protected them fiercely. One incident during the Louisiana Maneuvers stands out as an example of Almond's attitude toward civilian harassment. Sergeant Elvyn V. Davidson, a noncommissioned officer with prewar cavalry experience and some college education, led 1st Platoon, Company F, 370th Infantry. His unit encountered trouble as it moved through a small town in Louisiana. The local sheriff and his posse, facing down tanks and half-tracks with shotguns, stopped the convoy and refused to allow it to move through the town. Almond arrived shortly thereafter, and the sheriff told him, "Well you can't bring them damn black troops through here." Almond exploded. "[Don't] tell me what I can't do! If you don't get the hell outta the way, we'll tear this damn town down!" The sheriff offered Almond a compromise, saying the black soldiers could travel through as long as they stayed on just one street. Almond brusquely told his soldiers, "Just run that damn tank through that building over there." Davidson recalled the impact that this incident had on Almond's troops: "From that day on the guys really began to like him, because he was not going to, that's his troops and you didn't tell him what he could do with his troops. We walked through Main Street, and half the buildings got knocked down by tanks, guys swinging the guns around on the half-tracks, you know. They'd knocked down a couple of buildings; the sheriff didn't bother us anymore. You know the government had to pay for it, but that's all right. They remembered us forever!"[48]

Major McCaffrey, the division G3 (Operations) officer, found the Louisiana Maneuvers very effective and believed they saved lives once the division deployed. Almond also had good reason to be pleased. Lt. Gen. William H. Simpson, Fourth Army commander, rated the 92nd Division "very satisfactory" after the completion of the training, while the white 75th Division was only "satisfactory." This indicated that Almond had built an effective fighting unit, despite the earlier troubles. McCaffrey said Almond handled the division flawlessly, but one of the "umpires," a colonel, faulted him for using improper radio security. This humiliated Almond and added to the feelings of stained honor. A man with his fragile self-esteem could not have appreciated the chiding, especially from a junior officer. After completing the maneuvers on April 3, Almond returned his unit to Fort Huachuca to conduct additional training.[49]

Throughout the division's training, Almond had been at odds with the War Department over his planned employment. As early as July 1943, Almond had heard rumors that the War Department had activated the division merely as a "sop" to the black community, and it would not actually go to combat. The black press jumped on this because of its innate suspicion of the Army's white leadership, but the rumor had some basis in fact. Only one of the 93rd Infantry Division's regiments, the 25th, had actually seen combat after deployment. The other two had been broken up and used for other duties.

Intensifying the rumors, the other two black divisions planned for activation in 1943 and 1944, the 105th Infantry Division and the 107th Infantry Division, had been cancelled, and the future of the mixed-race, horse-mounted 2nd Cavalry Division remained uncertain as late as 1942. Activated in 1941 with a unique organization combining white and black troops, the 2nd Cavalry Division consisted of the existing Regular Army

4th Cavalry Brigade and its African American 9th and 10th Cavalry Regiments, plus the white 3rd Cavalry Brigade, made up of the 2nd and 14th Cavalry Regiments, to be raised through conscription. Mixing white and black troops in the same division was never a popular decision, and in the spring of 1942 the War Department removed the 3rd Brigade from the 2nd Cavalry Division to form the nucleus of a new armored division. The 2nd Cavalry Division remained only partially filled until 1944, when it added another African American cavalry brigade. The War Department deployed the division to North Africa in 1944, but then deactivated it and sent the troops to service units. The 2nd Cavalry Division was thus never used in a combat role.[50]

The War Department Advisory Committee on Negro Troop Policies counseled Army Chief of Staff Gen. George C. Marshall in 1943 that he should send more black combat units overseas, but Marshall declined. This became the preeminent racial issue in the Army for the next while. The committee argued that training the black troops without deploying them would be a waste of time and resources, but convincing the War Department took nearly a year. Marshall remained doubtful that black soldiers could be used in combat, and he sought other ways to employ them. In October 1943, Marshall had become concerned about the number of troops assigned to Washington's antiaircraft units who were not rotating overseas, and he directed Maj. Gen. John T. Lewis, commander of the Military District of Washington, to investigate the situation. Marshall then suggested that black soldiers replace those white soldiers in Washington. Marshall mentioned that it might "be a good thing to bring in here a much larger proportion of negro troops, chauffeurs, depot men, etc." Citing the issue of local support, Marshall noted that "Washington can absorb the negro soldier population much better than most any other city except possibly Chicago or New York, and with their presence here we would not feel that we were holding back personnel that we would wish to get overseas as quickly as possible." Marshall clearly saw the stationing of black troops in Washington as a way to avoid sending black troops overseas while still giving the appearance of using them in an important role. Almond would have to overcome this reluctance in order to get his division into combat.[51]

Racial violence in Harlem, Detroit, and Los Angeles in 1943 prompted the War Department to send African American units overseas to reduce the trouble at home. While these overseas deployments may very well have had that effect, there was a war in progress, and the soldiers were being trained to go into combat.[52] Assistant Secretary of War

John J. McCloy made getting the 92nd Infantry Division into combat a priority, reasoning that deploying black divisions overseas would help reduce racial tension and achieve a national objective. McCloy argued, “Ten percent of our people are colored and we have to use [them]. We make a clerk out of a farmer. It is a vital National Policy to make a military asset out of that part of the population.” General Davis’s influence on the committee and his assessment based on his Fort Huachuca inspection also swayed the decision to deploy the 92nd Infantry Division.[53]

Despite the War Department’s confidence in Almond, it lacked conviction about black troops, and the division’s poor training performance at Fort Huachuca amplified those fears. Almond assured his troops that the 92nd would see action as an intact division, but the rumors took their toll on morale and compounded training problems. Almond later remembered protesting to Lt. Gen. Lesley J. McNair, the commanding general of Army Ground Forces, “General, you can’t let me down on this purpose. I promised these officers and I tried hard to do a good job and so have they and I promised them if they stood behind me, I would stand behind them.” Almond sought to validate all the training the division had completed. McNair told Almond he would see what he could do. Almond’s plea worked, and the War Department scheduled the full division to deploy. General Marshall made one last quick inspection of the 370th Regimental Combat Team as it paraded before deployment. Evidently impressed, Marshall commented to Almond as he departed, “I think they are all right. Go ahead.” Almond took this as a final affirmation that he and his troops were ready. On April 4, 1944, Almond triumphantly told his troops that their training had paid off.[54]

Almond’s words, indicating his pride in the unit and his pleasure at seeing it accepted for deployment, came as welcome news to the division’s officers and men, jaded from months of speculation as to whether or not they would ever go to combat:

> Four days ago, I was visited by three Officers from Washington, with instructions that this Division is slated for combat duty in an active theater in the near future; that the first element to leave is a combat team, and that combat team is the 3-7-0! . . . Now what does that mean? There is not a man here who does not realize the importance of it. This is *a* Colored Division, with both white and Colored Officers. This is a cohesive military unit. You have just shown it. This is a unit that the Colored race should be proud of, and they will be before we are through; and not

> only the Colored race, but every American who knows enough to read about his war. . . . you must take great satisfaction in the fact that you are now about to actually prove your worth.[55]

The 370th Regimental Combat Team would deploy first, followed by the remainder of the division. Almond hoped to ensure the combat teams' success by removing soldiers who had failed training repeatedly. He replaced these officers and men with transfers from other divisional units. Some new replacements came from the recently cancelled Army Specialized Training Program (ASTP), which gave the division a much-needed leavening of college-educated men. The Army diluted that infusion of superior troops by sending unfit black soldiers from other units all over the United States to Fort Huachuca to join the 92nd Infantry Division. Hondon B. Hargrove, a black captain in the 597th Field Artillery, said that these foul-ups posed a serious problem for the division in its preparation to go overseas. Almond left behind some three hundred men in casual camps classified as unfit for overseas service; that number grew to more than a thousand as other black units dropped soldiers as well.[56]

Almond had taken on one of the most difficult jobs in the US Army. He dealt with all the normal challenges a division commander faced, such as housing, feeding, training, and equipping his unit, while scrambling for the same scarce resources coveted by his colleagues. But Almond's task was made all the more difficult by the educational limitations of his troops, the prevailing social environment, and growing pressure from the black community and his officers. He chose to ignore the social difficulties in order to focus on the military ones and get his unit ready for combat. He would shortly find out whether or not he was successful.

7

Initial Success in Italy

1944–1945

Early on the morning of July 15, 1944, Col. Raymond G. Sherman led the 370th Regimental Combat Team, "Sherman's Raiders," up the gangway and onto the deck of the SS *Mariposa* in Newport News, Virginia. A light rain peppered the soldiers as they settled aboard their seagoing home. The *Mariposa,* a converted cruise ship, left the dock at 12:15 p.m. headed for an undisclosed destination. Many of the soldiers had never been on a ship before and began to get seasick. The *Mariposa* made a fast solo crossing to Gibraltar, then joined a convoy as it approached Africa. Nine days after leaving Hampton Roads, the ship docked in Oran, Algeria. As the soldiers debarked and boarded the US Navy transport USS *George C. Squier*, they experienced a new kind of segregation: the ship's store offered ice cream "For Navy Personnel Only." Not until the ship left Oran did the Buffalo Soldiers of the 370th learn their destination: Italy.[1]

Almond had selected Sherman's Raiders to lead the way because he believed it was the best of his three infantry regiments, and he consistently rated Colonel Sherman highest among his infantry commanders. Sherman became another of Almond's most trusted subordinates, and Almond maintained a first-name relationship with Sherman after the war. Brig. Gen. Joe Wood led Task Force 92, consisting of the 370th Regimental Combat Team and the 92nd Division's headquarters advance element, off the ship and into Naples on the evening of July 30, 1944. Recently promoted Lt. Col. William McCaffrey, division G3, served as the task force executive officer. After a long trek north to join US Fifth Army forces at Viareggio, Wood reported to Maj. Gen. Willis D. Crittenberger, commander of the US IV Corps, who assigned the 370th RCT to the 1st Armored Division on August 17. This effectively integrated the 1st Armored Division to regimental level for a brief period of time.

One of Sherman's soldiers, Cpl. Ivan J. Houston, joined the 370th RCT during the Louisiana Maneuvers after the War Department cancelled the Army Specialized Training Program (ASTP) in March 1944. Houston had grown up in Los Angeles and attended the University of California at Berkeley, his father's alma mater. He enlisted in the Army Reserve in July 1943 after two semesters and received orders to active duty after completing a third semester at Berkeley. His excellent Army General Classification Test (AGCT) score won him a place in the ASTP, and he reported for basic training on January 23, 1944. Assigned to the 3rd Battalion's headquarters, Houston respected both the battalion's white and black officers. Black lieutenants commanded the Headquarters and I, L, and M Companies, while a white captain led K Company. The battalion commander, Lt. Col. Clarence W. Daugette, a white former National Guardsman from Alabama, recommended all black lieutenants for promotion shortly after the battalion moved to Italy.[2]

After an unopposed landing at Reggio di Calabria on the tip of the Italian boot, the Allied conquest of southern Europe had begun in earnest on September 9, 1943, with the invasion of Salerno. The Allied Armies in Italy, commanded by British general Sir Harold Alexander, consisted of two formidable armies. Lt. Gen. Mark Clark's US Fifth Army comprised four corps headquarters controlling thirteen divisions and three separate brigades. The British Eighth Army, under Lt. Gen. Sir Oliver Leese, also contained four corps with eleven divisions and seven separate brigades. The two armies had attacked relentlessly northward, finally capturing Rome on June 4, 1944. The world's attention was diverted at the time, however, to the invasion of northwest Europe at the Normandy beaches in France. Gen. Dwight D. Eisenhower's European strategy required additional units for a second landing in southern France, intended to coincide with the Normandy landings, but shifted to August when the capture of Rome took longer than expected. Operation Dragoon, the second invasion, launched on August 15 with an assault on Marseille on France's Mediterranean coast.[3]

The combat units needed for Operation Dragoon had come from Italy, stripping more than half of the Fifth Army's combat strength. Rome's capture had changed the Italian campaign, and with it unit requirements. By August, the Allies had paused at a line along the Arno River, with a 180-mile front. The Germans held a series of defensive lines north of Rome while the Allies continued attacking. The Mediterranean Theater commander in chief, British general Maitlin Wilson, needed to keep the German armies in Italy tied down so they could not reinforce German armies in France.[4]

The German army had anchored its defense in mountainous northern Italy in the Gottesstellung, or "Gothic Line." Clark faced Lt. Gen. Joachim Lemelson's Fourteenth Army, which included the 16th SS Panzer Grenadier Division (Reichsführer SS); the 65th, 362nd, 334th, 350th, and 715th Grenadier Divisions; the 26th Panzer Division; the 3rd and 29th Panzer Grenadier Divisions; and the Luftwaffe's 20th Field Division and 4th Parachute Division. None of these units was at full strength, but the Allies would still find it difficult to dislodge them.[5]

Wood and the 370th RCT arrived in Italy at a transitional time. When the Fifth Army halted at the Arno River, the units needed rest and refitting. One of the US Army's most battle-hardened divisions, the 1st Armored had just begun a long-overdue reorganization. The War Department had redesigned the armored division structure, making it lighter and more agile, while also changing to newer tanks to make it more lethal. The 370th joined the 1st Armored during this refitting process to give the Buffalo Soldiers time to acclimate to a combat environment, the customary introduction method for new units. While Maj. Gen. Vernon E. Prichard, commander of the 1st Armored Division, conducted organizational and equipment changes, he assigned small portions of the division's zone to the 370th. He gradually increased that sector's size until the RCT became accustomed to its mission.[6]

Unlike the infantry divisions, armored divisions used a flexible "task force" organization, with its subordinate organizations consisting of three "combat commands" composed of both infantry and tank battalions. The reorganization removed the last vestige of the old organization, the infantry regimental headquarters, replaced by combat commands carrying the designations A, B, and R (Rear). Besides this change, several antiaircraft units had reorganized into infantry units and been christened Task Force 45. The German Air Force could no longer challenge the Allies in the air, making redundant the large numbers of antiaircraft artillery units originally planned and fielded in Italy.[7]

With the pending arrival of the 92nd and the Brazilian Expeditionary Force (BEF), a division-sized unit, General Clark realigned the corps and divisions. Clark assigned US IV Corps the western part of the sector, with the units arranged as follows, west to east (see map 7.1): Task Force 45; the 1st Armored Division including the 370th RCT; the BEF; and the South African 6th Armored Division. Maj. Gen. Geoffrey Keyes's US II Corps in the eastern portion controlled the US 34th, 85th, 88th, and 91st Infantry Divisions. Clark also temporarily supervised the British 13th Corps under Lt. Gen. Sir Richard McCreery, consisting of the New Zealand 2nd Infantry Division, British 1st Infantry Division, British 6th

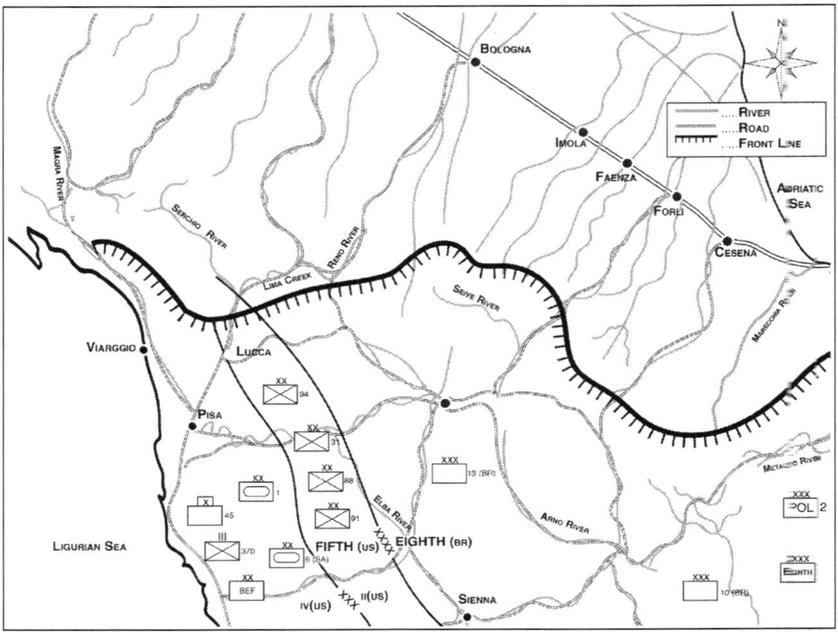

7.1. Gothic Line, September 1944

Armored Division, and Indian 8th Division. After completing this shift, the Fifth Army occupied a thirty-five-mile front anchored on the Mediterranean coast from the mouth of the Arno River, west of Pisa, to the Elba River, twenty miles west of Florence (see map 7.1). The British Eighth Army, after several organizational changes, now consisted of the British 5 and 10 Corps, Canadian 1 Corps, and Polish 2 Corps.[8]

The Fifth Army began its Gothic Line assault on August 31. A mere week after its arrival, the 370th RCT received its first major mission, an assault on Monte Pisano, a hill roughly ten miles long by seven miles wide. The IV Corps would cross the Arno River and protect the Fifth Army's left flank while supporting II Corps in the main effort, attacking on Monte Pisano and Monte Albano. Joining Col. Hamilton Howze's Combat Command A (CCA) near Pisa, the 370th RCT quickly saw action. Its introduction to combat began with patrolling, the basic small-unit activity. Its early experiences included company-sized attacks, limited artillery firing, and reconnaissance missions across the Arno River. To take Monte Pisano, Colonel Howze gave Sherman the 1st Tank Battalion, and Sherman detached one rifle company to Combat Command

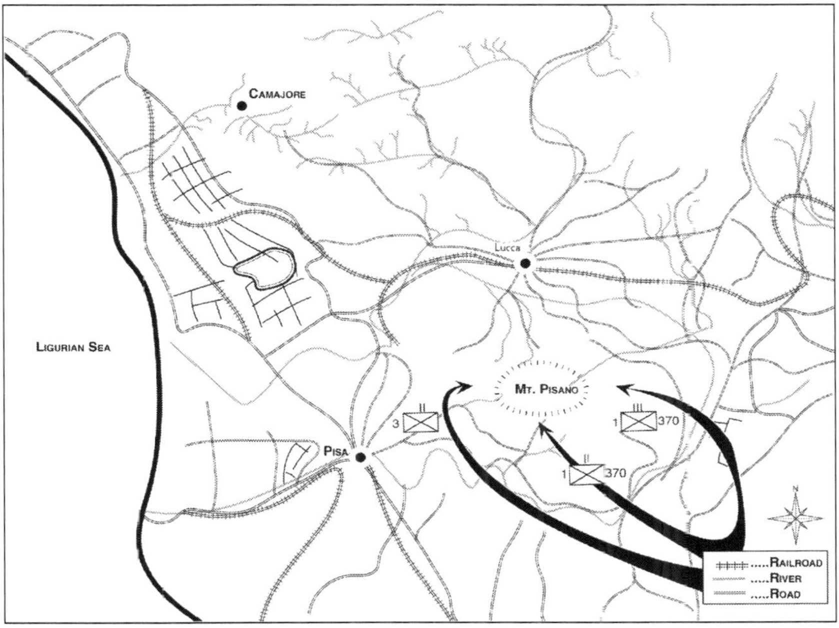

7.2. Attack on Monte Pisano, September 2–5, 1944

B (CCB). The 370th RCT attacked Monte Pisano from three directions: 3rd Battalion from the west, 2nd Battalion from the south or center, and 1st Battalion from the east (see map 7.2). CCB struck northeast toward Altopascio. Success in this operation, with few casualties, gave the soldiers confidence and helped the unit build cohesion. The 370th RCT enjoyed excellent artillery support from both its own 598th Field Artillery Battalion and the 1st Armored Division's 91st Field Artillery Battalion, and quickly took the objective. The 370th then consolidated and moved toward a new objective, Bagni di Lucca. By September 4, CCA had arrived outside the city of Lucca, and German resistance stiffened.[9]

The 3rd Battalion, 370th RCT, relieved the 14th Armored Infantry Battalion and assumed a three-mile sector. Corporal Houston recalled that the "courteous, efficient, battle-wise veterans of the all-white 1st Armored Division soon put us at ease and began teaching us the rudiments of war." Houston worked in the battalion intelligence (S-2) section and appreciated the maps and overlays he received. The 370th garnered attention at the highest levels, as Crittenberger sent a couple of officers to observe 3rd Battalion's arrival, to see how it functioned as a unit. General Clark also visited them soon after they arrived. "I tried in particular to welcome the 92nd Division," Clark recalled. "General Marshall was eager to give an opportunity to prove the ability of Negro troops in battle." Clark's recollection some six years after the event gives Marshall more credit than is due, given the latter's reluctance to send black soldiers to combat. Clark questioned a colonel about any major problem he might have, and the officer (unnamed, but probably 2nd Battalion commander Lt. Col. George O. Weber) replied that one of his lieutenants was overdue for promotion. Clark borrowed his aide's captain's bars and promoted Lt. Charles F. Gandy on the spot, giving Gandy the distinction of being the first 92nd officer to be promoted in combat. The incident garnered favorable comment in the black press and Gandy became a celebrity at home. That same press sorrowfully reported him as a casualty just a few weeks later.[10]

The attack of IV Corps had succeeded better than anticipated, and on September 4 Clark slowed its advance to prevent it from exceeding the II Corps's attack pace. He ordered aggressive patrols to ensure the enemy did not move east to oppose II Corps. The 370th crossed the Serchio River on September 10 and commenced a series of missions with the 1st Armored Division operating in flexible task forces. These small operations with rapidly changing task forces prepared the 370th RCT well for its combat role in the fluid atmosphere of Fifth Army. Many alterations reflected shifting mission requirements, but some may have reflected the US Army's institutional reluctance to entrust black troops with important operations alone.

The Fifth Army intended to keep the 1st Armored Division available as a mobile task force for the Po Valley and began consolidating its units. CCA pulled off the line to move in support of the US II Corps assault on September 18, and the 370th RCT took over that portion of the line. The rest of the 1st Armored Division gradually turned over its entire sector to the 370th by September 25. For the first time, 370th RCT units would operate independently under Task Force 92 control. General Wood took charge of the 1st Armored Division's CCB and of Troop D, 81st Cavalry Reconnaissance Squadron, in addition to the 370th RCT. After a few days of joint patrolling, CCB rejoined the 1st Armored Division in II Corps, and the 370th RCT remained to hold a sixteen-mile sector.[11]

The 370th had earned respect during its first exposure to combat, having advanced nearly twenty-one miles. While it had not yet met strong resistance, the RCT had nonetheless worked well with its white counterparts. The officers and men had become somewhat accustomed to combat conditions. The unit made mistakes and discipline lapsed, but this was typical for most green units. Both Colonel Sherman and General Wood saw promise and a developing esprit de corps. Wood sounded one cautionary note, however. "They are not aggressive," he wrote, "but will go willingly anywhere their officers take them, they will stay where they are led." Later events would prove Wood wrong.[12]

The 92nd Infantry Division staff and remaining elements began arriving in early October in the port of Livorno. Almost immediately the division suffered the loss of one of its senior officers as Col. Frank E. Barber, the division chief of staff, died in a German artillery attack on October 3, his third day in Italy. Almond arrived at Task Force 92's headquarters in the town of Viareggio on October 5 and assumed command. He immediately called for McCaffrey and installed him as chief of staff. Almond then pulled Maj. Thomas St. John Arnold, executive officer of the 598th Field Artillery Battalion, up to division headquarters as the G3.[13]

While awaiting the arrival of the 365th and 371st RCTs, the task force began acquiring nondivisional units that would support the division during combat. These included the inaccurately named 2nd Armored Group, consisting of the 434th and 435th Anti-Aircraft Artillery Battalions, now dismounted and fighting as infantry; the 751st Tank Battalion; the 894th Tank Battalion; a chemical company; two antiaircraft artillery batteries; and an Italian engineer company. With the 370th and these new outfits, Almond assumed control of the coastal sector, stretching from the Ligurian coast inland for twelve miles. Crittenberger ordered Task Force 92 to assault the German 42nd Jaeger Division on Mt. Caula, a 1,200-foot massif. This was the first objective leading toward the eventual capture of the city of Massa, about fourteen miles north of Viareggio. Task Force 92 held IV Corps's left flank while maintaining contact with the BEF on its right. The 371st RCT arrived at Viareggio on October 31, with the 365th RCT arriving on November 8, and by November 13 all of the division's elements were in place.[14]

On November 28, General Clark attached the 366th Infantry Regiment, another African American unit, to the division. The 366th had served in the 92nd Division during World War I, but it began World War II as a separate infantry regiment activated on February 10, 1941, at Fort Devens, Massachusetts. Unlike the division's other infantry regiments, the 366th boasted all-African-American leadership. The 366th had arrived in Italy in May 1944, where it initially guarded air bases for the Fifteenth Air Force. As Clark's infantry requirements became more urgent, however, Brig. Gen. Don Brann, Fifth Army G3, requested the regiment from the Fifteenth Air Force. The regiment relinquished its air-base guard mission on October 28 and arrived in Livorno on November 26 for attachment to the 92nd Division. Brann inspected the unit and found it fit, but determined it required more training and equipment. Placing it with Almond seemed to make sense.[15]

Almond's relationship with the 366th Infantry Regiment differed from that with the other regiments from the beginning; he surely saw these new troops as "outsiders." Whatever antipathies he may have had toward the soldiers of the 92nd, they remained "his" soldiers: he had spent more than two years forming and training the unit, and he had affection for them. The 366th soldiers were strangers. Hondon Hargrove had joined the 366th before the war and later moved to the 597th Field Artillery. Hargrove recalled Almond's welcoming speech to the regiment upon its joining his division: "Your Negro newspapers have seen fit to cause you to be brought over here, [and] now I'm going to see that you suffer your share of the casualties."[16] First Lt. Edward W. Brooke of the 366th, later a US senator from Massachusetts, also heard Almond's remarks and remembered his "angry and condescending tone" as he shouted through a bullhorn. Almond's gruff and tactless words, echoing those of Col. Sterling Wood to the 371st, doomed his relationship with all of his soldiers. Corporal Houston of the 370th RCT testified that his comrades also grasped Almond's ambivalent attitude toward the 366th. Hargrove reported that other soldiers told him that Almond said he had not asked for the regiment and did not need them, but he would make them fight since they were there. There is no way to verify this last statement as any more than hearsay, but that is somewhat beside the point: the perception among the soldiers of Almond's attitude is clear.[17]

As a separate infantry regiment rather than a full combat team, the 366th had only three infantry battalions and a cannon company, with no artillery battalion or engineer company. Almond introduced the 366th to the combat area in the same way the Fifth Army had introduced the 92nd, by dividing it up among his RCTs for training purposes. He retained the 1st Battalion under division control, sent the 2nd Battalion to the 370th RCT, and sent the 3rd to the division training area. He distributed the remaining units by individual companies throughout the division. While this had been sound practice for divisions entering the line, it proved disastrous for the 366th. The regiment had lost cohesion during months of guarding dispersed air bases and lacked the necessary unit training to bring it back up to readiness. Splitting the units also undercut the regimental commander and staff.[18]

Almond did not trust Col. Howard D. Queen, the 366th Infantry Regiment's commander, as much as he did his white regimental commanders, and their relationship was rocky from the start. Almond later revealed that he found the 366th "less capable of carrying out instructions which involved the movement of troops in a defensive line, and especially offensive operations." Queen requested that his men receive three months of refresher training before returning to an infantry role. The officers received three weeks of additional leadership instruction, and the regiment conducted marksmanship training, but the tactical situation did not allow Queen to receive the additional training time he requested.[19]

Two weeks after the 366th joined the 92nd, Queen requested relief from command due to the mental and physical strain associated with the treatment he and his unit had received since joining the division. Queen's departure deeply disturbed the regiment. The men felt great loyalty to him, since he had led them nearly from the outfit's activation, and they never forgave the perceived mistreatment that drove him away. Many of the 366th's officers privately felt that Queen's medical complaints were legitimate and that he was not ready for combat duty. They also believed his successor, Lt. Col. Alonzo Ferguson, the former regimental executive officer, was a much better commander. Those facts, however, did not erase the pain of Queen's departure and the implementation of new command arrangements.[20]

Almond should have welcomed the 366th, a unit encumbered by none of the supposed disadvantages of his own infantry regiments. As one of the Army's four separate black infantry regiments, the 366th had the advantage of containing volunteer soldiers from northern states rather than the draftees from the South who filled the 92nd. In addition to long-serving NCOs, the regiment also boasted many soldiers with a high school education, contrasting with the majority of the 92nd's soldiers, who had not even passed fourth grade. The regiment had originally formed with white senior officers, but black officers shortly replaced them.[21]

Almond overlooked an important characteristic of the 366th Infantry's officers. They formed a very tight team. Since educational opportunities for African Americans were limited, many of these men had attended the same colleges. Howard University functioned essentially as the 366th Infantry's "West Point," producing 77 of its 125 officers. Wilberforce University produced 26 more officers for the 366th, with another 9 coming from other universities. Regardless of these officers' origins, they had formed personal bonds long before they entered active duty. Of the Howard graduates, for instance, the captains and first lieutenants came largely from the classes of 1930–1932 and 1934–1935, while the majority of the second lieutenants came from the classes of 1939–1941. The classes of 1932, 1934, and 1940 each produced seven classmates who served together in the 366th. These personal relationships no doubt strengthened the professional relationships in the regiment.[22]

The officers of the 366th had, on average, more education and experience than their counterparts in the other regiments. All but twenty or so of its officers had received their commissions before 1940, and some junior officers as early as 1930. With few active duty opportunities available to blacks, these officers received reserve commissions and began civilian careers. Some even went to graduate school; seven officers had master's degrees, two had law degrees (not including the division's lawyers), and one had a PhD. This made for a very mature junior officer corps, much more advanced than that of other regiments, which should have proved to be an advantage in combat.

Lt. Gen. Lucian K. Truscott replaced General Clark as commander of the Fifth Army on December 16, 1944, and Clark moved up to command the 15th Army Group (formerly Allied Armies in Italy), which supervised the US Fifth Army and British Eighth Army. Clark had moved combat teams around the Fifth Army sector frequently, and Truscott continued the practice. This allowed the veteran divisions in the line to rotate regiments out to rest, and it provided additional training for the 92nd Infantry Division's green units. As with the 370th Infantry Regiment's initial experience, these movements integrated the 92nd and other divisions for brief periods of time. For instance, the 365th RCT spent more than a month in the 88th Infantry Division line, while the 370th sent battalions to the 6th South African Division and the BEF. While this provided valuable combat experience for these units, it also undermined regimental and division cohesion in the 92nd Infantry Division.[23]

Almond planned an attack for Christmas Day as part of the Fifth Army's general offensive toward Bologna. He intended to launch the 370th RCT, with the 2nd Battalion, 366th Infantry, attached, to capture the town of Lama di Sotto on the east side of the Serchio River. Almond moved the 2nd Battalion, 370th RCT, into Sommocolonia and other units into adjacent towns to prepare for the attack. The 92nd Division's initial probing action before the attack had yielded much stronger reactions than anyone expected, perhaps warning Almond that he faced a greater threat than he initially realized.

By mid-December, intelligence revealed German divisions massing opposite the 92nd's line west of the Serchio and at La Spezia, intending to strike toward Livorno, possibly as a complement to the large attack then under way in the Ardennes, based largely on the Fifth Army G2 assessment. Truscott immediately countered the expected thrust, moving two 85th Infantry Division RCTs into the IV Corps sector. Almond received the 337th RCT from the 85th Infantry Division, as well as the 19th (Gurkha) and 20th (Sikh) Brigades from the British Army's 8th Indian Division.[24]

General Crittenberger visited Sherman's 370th Infantry command post at Fornaci on December 23 and assured him that the 8th Indian Division would reinforce him. Sherman impressed Crittenberger with his determination to fight on and hold his position. "Colonel Sherman's stand there at his Regimental Command Post was as good a piece of business as I saw during the entire fight," Crittenberger remembered. A few minutes after Crittenberger left, the Germans overran Fornaci, but Sherman and his staff managed to escape.[25]

Almond cancelled his planned attack on Christmas Eve in view of the changes in the German strength and began preparing to withdraw. Before he could move his forces, the Germans attacked the lead element of the 2nd Battalion, 366th Infantry, in Sommocolonia and nearly surrounded it. The battalion initiated a fighting retreat, leaving two platoons to cover the town. Failing to reinforce Sommocolonia after several attempts, Almond ordered the remaining seventy soldiers there to abandon their posts. Of these, one officer and seventeen men escaped back to American lines. Lt. John Fox, a forward observer from Cannon Company, 366th Infantry Regiment, calmly continued to call artillery fire on the advancing Germans until he was himself surrounded. He then directed fire on his own position, acknowledging the danger to himself and his team. Fox and his radio operator died in the resulting barrage, but it also stopped the attack and killed approximately one hundred Germans.[26]

This event and its aftermath illustrated Almond's poisoned relationship with the 366th and confirmed his racist predilections. Division artillery commander Brig. Gen. William H. Colbern recommended Lieutenant Fox for the Distinguished Service Cross (DSC), the nation's second highest award. That award recommendation, however, disappeared. The unintended loss of such a significant award in bureaucratic channels, especially one initiated by a general officer, is unlikely. This probably means that Almond stopped the award at division level; in any case, it never reached IV Corps. Almond did not believe in awarding decorations for failed missions, however valorous his men's conduct may have been. Almond may also have opposed such a high decoration for black soldiers, failed or not; his own writings and oral history omit any mention of the Sommocolonia action.[27]

Ironically, this award led to some of the first postwar research on the 92nd Infantry Division in Italy. Hondon Hargrove did not witness the event but knew many soldiers who did. He campaigned for years after the war to force the Army to award Fox the DSC, which his widow finally received in April 1982. It was an honor richly deserved and long overdue. The story might have ended there, but some fourteen years later President Bill Clinton ordered a review of high decorations in World War II to determine if senior commanders had overlooked African Americans. The Fox case proved this to be true and illustrated an Army leadership unable or unwilling to recognize African American heroes. Almond's failure to honor Fox's heroism and sacrifice underscores his grudge against the "outsiders" of the 366th and indicates his growing antipathy toward black soldiers in general. The review commission recommended that President Clinton upgrade Fox's DSC, and the president presented the Medal of Honor to Fox's widow on January 17, 1997.[28]

The failure of the Serchio Valley attack left Almond bitterly disappointed. Even though the Fifth Army faced a threat along its whole front, Almond must have felt that the entire Allied force in Italy believed he needed to be rescued. One of his units, albeit a new and unfamiliar one, allowed its personnel to flee the battlefield, and he had required the assistance of another unit to get the soldiers back. The 8th Indian Division remained in control of the Serchio Valley, inside his sector, until January 10, 1945. General Truscott transferred the 135th RCT from the 34th Infantry Division, as well as a couple of tank battalions, to strengthen the 92nd. Almond no doubt welcomed the reinforcements, since the 365th RCT remained with the 88th Division in the II Corps sector and the German attack seemed to be weighted in the Serchio Valley. A man of his pride, forceful nature, and basic insecurity, however, could not help but see this as a stain on his honor. His division had failed in a conspicuous way, and he must have felt great shame and pressure to improve. Failure haunted him, and what he experienced in December 1944 affected his outlook for the remainder of the war.[29]

The enemy operation was merely a reconnaissance in force, though Almond did not know that at the time. German general Hans Roettinger, who had been the German Army Group C chief of staff, reported after the war that he intended mainly to get German units back to their origi-

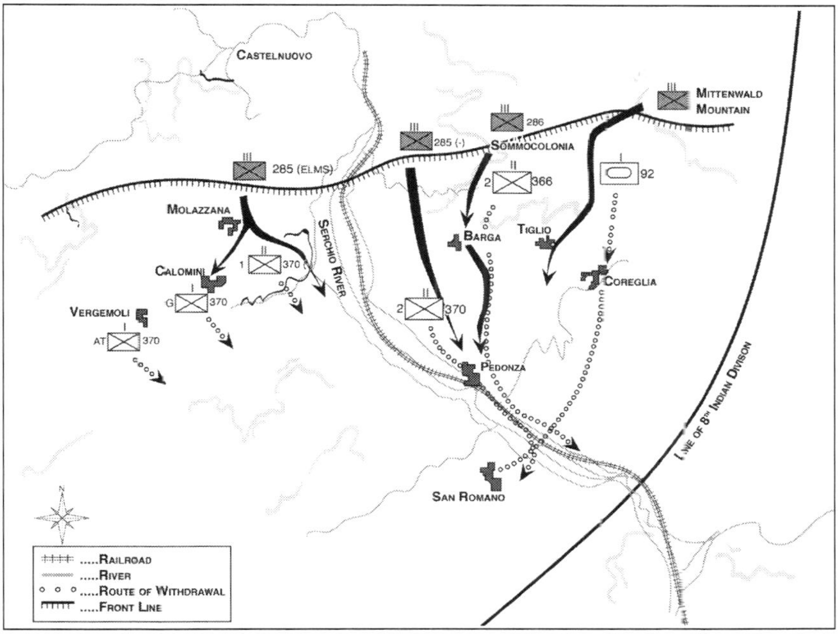

7.3. Serchio Valley Christmas Attack, December 25–26, 1944

nal lines to prepare for a larger offensive. He perceived the 92nd Infantry Division sector as the weakest part of the American line. Any larger push would have required more forces than Army Group C had available. In a postwar interview Generalleutnant Otto Fretter-Pico, commander of the 148th Grenadier Division, said that he stopped his attack near Fornaci due to lack of forces, but his objective was to stop the Allied movement toward Bologna by diverting resources, and he felt he had accomplished that objective. Regardless, the Germans massed at a point they deemed weakest: the 92nd Infantry Division sector (see map 7.3). According to Fretter-Pico, "The weaknesses of your [American] deployment in the Serchio Valley in December 1944 were that your troops were deployed on a front which was too long for the troops available, and your reserves were too far in the rear area which prevented their being deployed immediately."[30]

Truscott ordered the Fifth Army to postpone further actions and prepare for another large-scale offensive to begin about April 1, essentially ceasing combat operations for the winter. In the meantime, he directed Crittenberger to plan a limited objective attack in IV Corps's area for position improvement, particularly in the 92nd Infantry Division area. Fifth Army restricted artillery ammunition use to accumulate stockpiles for the spring offensive, but small-arms ammunition remained unlimited. As both sides settled in for a bitterly cold and snowy January, Almond instituted "weapons shoots," repeating his old machine gun battalion's practice during the First World War. He directed the 92nd Division's infantry components to fire every small caliber weapon for five minutes at varying intervals throughout the day. As in 1918, he intended to keep the Germans off guard, never allowing them to rest. Almond's battalion commanders believed that the shoots gave their soldiers confidence by seeing and hearing a full battalion's firepower, while ensuring that all weapons functioned properly in a cold and wet environment. German commanders interviewed after the war confirmed the shoots' effectiveness, reporting that the intermittent fire inflicted casualties, lowered morale, and restricted movements.[31]

The winter brought tragic personal news for Almond as well. His son-in-law, Capt. Thomas Galloway, US Army Air Forces, was confirmed killed in action, after having been listed as missing in action since the previous August. Captain Galloway flew a P-38 Lightning, a fighter designed as a bomber escort. While on a fighter "sweep" in northwest France on July 24, 1944, Galloway collided with another P-38. The other pilot, 2nd Lt. Neil W. Kemper, successfully bailed out, but reported that he did not see any other parachute. Kemper landed in a field, and local French resistance members took him to safety in a nearby house. He spoke no French and his rescuers spoke no English, so they communicated using a French-English dictionary. He asked several times about Galloway. Later another local man came in with Galloway's name and service number. He confirmed that Galloway was dead and had been buried in a French cemetery with flowers on his grave. Galloway's family did not receive notification of the captain's death until Kemper could make his way back to American forces. The news reached Peggy Galloway at the Crook home in Alabama, where she had taken little Tommy to live with Margaret Almond. Galloway had completed more than thirty missions before his death and had been awarded three Air Medals and the Purple Heart. The War Department promoted Galloway posthumously to major in August 1944.[32]

Almond also learned that his son had been wounded in action. Capt. Ned Almond Jr. commanded a rifle company in the 157th Infantry Regiment, 45th Infantry Division, in France. As his regiment approached the German border, the younger Almond received a minor shrapnel wound and required brief hospitalization. His letters to his father, mother, and sister downplayed his wound: "I wasn't hit bad—just a little piece in my back just underneath the right shoulder blade. The medics have already cut it out. . . . I wrote mother and told her so a WIA [Wounded in Action] telegram would not worry her." After Thomas Galloway's death, the family's fears for Ned Jr. intensified. Displaying an irrationality bred of anxiety, the Almond family hoped that the younger Almond's relatively minor wound would "insulate" him against something worse. General Almond could not escape worrying about his son as he planned a new operation in his coastal sector.[33]

8

Winter of Discontent

1945

Intelligence reports in early 1945 revealed that some German units were withdrawing north. Moreover, reliable sources had reported that German troops had withdrawn from the 92nd Division's front, and Truscott requested a plan for an early attack to determine the enemy situation in this sector. To facilitate a IV Corps advance toward Massa, Almond conceived a bold plan in January 1945 to open the coastal route. Operation Fourth Term, no doubt named to commemorate President Roosevelt's 1944 election, would test German coastal defenses and capture Monte Strettoia, which overlooked Highway 1. This key road paralleled the coastline, and capturing it would open that route to the American advance on Massa. The attack would also maintain pressure on the Germans and threaten their supply lines. Almond envisioned a three-pronged, two-phased assault, with the main effort on a narrow coastal front and a diversionary thrust in the Serchio Valley to the east (see map 8.1).

Almond aimed to secure the high ground at Montignoso that dominated Highway 1. With this hill in friendly hands, IV Corps units could safely advance to Massa. Almond directed the 370th and 371st RCTs to make the main attack to seize German-occupied Monte Folgorito, which dominated the Ligurian coastal area. The Allies would need to clear that area in order to get to Massa and then Genoa. The 371st faced a series of seven steep hills leading to Monte Folgorito. These hills, coded with American names from south to north, would serve as intermediate objectives for the 1st and 2nd battalions of the 371st to "leapfrog" toward the final objective, the summit of Monte Folgorito itself. The 2nd Battalion would take the first objective, Monte Caula, or Rockyridge, and the 1st Battalion would capture Maine. The battalions would bound alternately, taking Florida, Georgia, and finally Ohio 1, 2, and 3 before the final assault on Monte Folgorito.[1]

The 370th faced three hills blocking its path to assault Monte Fol-

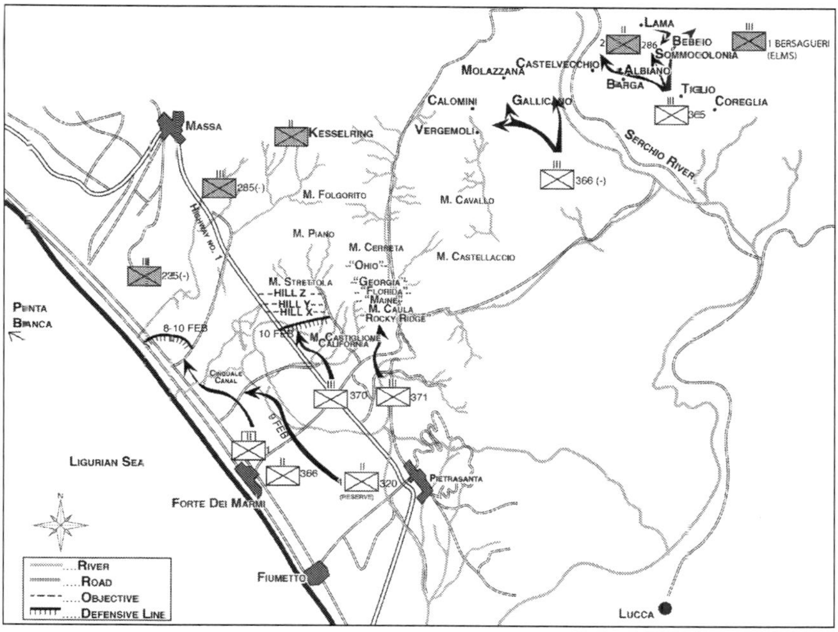

8.1. Operation Fourth Term, February 8–11, 1945

gorito. As with the hills in the 371st sector, each hill provided an intermediate objective. The division staff code-named the Strettoia hills X, Y, and Z. The 3rd Battalion would lead the assault, taking Hill X, a 450-foot terraced hill situated in front of the others. The 2nd Battalion would then capture Hill Y, a 600-foot peak just to the northwest of Hill X. This would then allow 1st Battalion to capture Hill Z, another 600-foot prominence to the east of Hill Y.

The division would also force a crossing of the La Foce (Cinquale) Canal. Almond created a special task force built around 3rd Battalion, 366th Infantry, crossing the canal at the beach, but he no longer trusted the all-black leadership of that unit to conduct the important coastal assault. He ordered Ed Rowny, now a lieutenant colonel commanding the 317th Engineer Battalion, to relinquish that command and form a composite task force and prepare it for this mission. Rowny selected an infantry officer, Capt. William H. Holbrook, as his executive officer. Rowny's Task Force 1 contained the 3rd Battalion, 366th Infantry, and several units attached from the 1st Armored Division: one medium tank company, one tank destroyer platoon, one chemical mortar platoon, one engineer platoon, and the 27th Field Artillery Battalion. These additions gave the task force the power to punch through German defenses.

Another diversionary effort pushed into the Serchio Valley (see map 8.1). The 365th RCT, with two battalions of the 366th Infantry, would attack toward the town of Castelnuovo on the Lama di Sotto ridge. Almond held one battalion of the 370th RCT in division reserve. Phase II of the operation would end on the line of the Frigido River if the enemy withdrew that far.[2]

Almond saw advantages in this plan. The coastal attack would divert forces from the main attack. By seizing the line of the Frigido River into Massa, the coastal drive would also put the southern edge of La Spezia Harbor within artillery range, thus facilitating its capture. Almond also hoped that a successful attack would improve morale in his division, helping him and his soldiers in getting over the Serchio Valley debacle in December. On the other hand, the plan carried some risks. Almond feared that if the attack failed, it would lower the division's morale even further. The enemy held the heavily fortified high ground protected by extensive minefields. "Offensive actions in the directions indicated might not be decisive," Almond warned, "and would cause only small immediate difficulties to the enemy." He must have proposed the attack under these circumstances out of desperation to restore the 92nd's confidence and blot out the shame of the previous December.[3]

General Truscott approved Operation Fourth Term on February 3, 1945, but restricted Almond to Phase I objectives, holding open the possibility of continuation to Phase II if the situation permitted. Truscott warned that there were "increasing indication[s] additional enemy forces may be in process of withdrawal from Italy. Our enemy order of battle may no longer be accurate."[4]

Almond's Operation Fourth Term seemed perfectly to fit Truscott's requirements.[5] Every plan for combat operations involves assumptions that, if proven unfounded, could derail the mission. Almond made four conjectures, three of which were actually unsubtle requests to IV Corps and Fifth Army to stop meddling with the 92nd Division's units. First, Almond requested that the 6th South African Division return the 3rd Battalion, 370th RCT, to his control. He also requested that Fifth Army place two brigades from the 8th Indian Division at his disposal. Almond further asked that all troops in the Serchio Valley sector remain under General Wood's operational control during the mission, requesting higher headquarters to leave his division alone. That final appeal probably reflected Almond's frustration with the many changes that Crittenberger, Clark, and now Truscott had imposed on his division. The fluctuations in the 92nd's order of battle due to detachment and attachment had degraded his ability to control it adequately. Finally, Almond believed that the enemy forces in his sector would not be strengthened before he completed the operation. Intelligence available at the time supported this assumption.[6]

Almond received abundant external support from IV Corps and higher command levels. The 370th RCT received three tank companies, one tank destroyer platoon, one engineer company, forty assault boats for the planned crossing of the Frigido River in Phase II, and three chemical mortar companies. The 371st RCT also received three tank companies, two tank destroyer platoons, one engineer company, and one chemical mortar company. General Colbern received one heavy (8-inch howitzer) and two medium (155 mm howitzer) artillery battalions from IV Corps for general support, and two light (105 mm howitzer) artillery battalions to reinforce the combat teams' own artillery battalions. Fifth Army also coordinated heavy aerial bombardment and naval gunfire support.[7]

As soon as Almond received his superior's approval, he and his staff began detailed planning and training in earnest. Rowny began preparing for the assault with training and rehearsals, moving the task force to a quiet area south of Viareggio to practice tank-infantry operations on a beach area similar to what it would encounter during its mission. The task force continued these rehearsals for two days, while other division units moved to their positions for the attack. As these preparations continued, the division staff planned the mission's support requirements. The Fifth Army G3 staff arrived on February 5, 1945, to coordinate air support and promised maximum effort. After the staff had completed all coordination, Almond designated H-Hour, D-Day as 6:00 a.m., February 8, 1945.[8]

Units in the Mediterranean Theater of Operations had developed a specific method of integrating air support with ground fire based on British practices. Pilots typically had difficulty hitting targets on the ground, and they had no habitual relationship with the infantry forces. The infantry could see the targets but had no reliable means of communicating with the airplanes. "Rover Joe" and "Horsefly" became the means of effectively integrating ground and air operations. Rover Joe placed a US Army Air Corps observer with the ground forces, enabling these units to quickly identify targets and have them attacked by air. Horsefly put an observer in a spotter plane above the battle, allowing even greater flexibility and responsiveness. By February 1945, Fifth Army had thoroughly integrated the two proven concepts in all operations.[9]

Shortly before H-Hour, Generals Truscott and Crittenberger arrived at Almond's headquarters to observe. The 27th Field Artillery Battalion began firing at 5:45 a.m. to cover the sound of the tanks warming up, and the chemical mortar platoon laid down a smoke screen to obscure the canal crossing. The units moved forward at 6:00 a.m. and most initially reported progress, but they quickly ran into trouble. The first two tanks hit mines, blocking the approach routes. The engineers discovered that the Germans had laid these antitank mines two levels deep, with one layer just below the soft sand surface and another three feet down. The Germans had also scattered antipersonnel mines among the other mines, making the beach a formidable obstacle. As the engineers struggled to clear safe lanes, German artillery began raining down from the large coastal guns at Punta Bianca, further slowing progress.

By 10:00 a.m., all units had crossed the canal, and the Task Force 1 command post moved forward. As Rowny moved across the mouth of the canal, an artillery shell landed in the middle of his command group, sparing him but killing or injuring seven of his nine subordinates. Rowny later reported, "The entire mouth of the canal appeared to turn red with blood." The constant shelling also inhibited communications, as it kept cutting field phone wire to the rear. Rowny relied on couriers to stay in contact with division headquarters. Despite these problems, two of the rifle companies succeeded in their initial objectives quickly, and the entire force had gained 1,200 yards by 5:00 p.m.[10]

The task force had sustained heavy casualties, however, and badly needed rest. Rowny's language in his after-action report and his postwar writings indicate that he respected the 366th's black leadership more than Almond did. He later described Maj. Willis D. Polk, the 3rd Battalion's commander, as "gallant" and complimented his behavior under fire. Polk refused to let a wound take him out of the fight. As Rowny reported, "He told me that he wanted to reassure me that . . . he would have to be hit harder than he was to make him stop." Polk died shortly afterward in an artillery barrage, and received a posthumous Silver Star. Polk's death had left Capt. Raymond Diggs in command of the 3rd Battalion. An experienced officer who had received his commission through ROTC in 1933, Diggs immediately ordered all units to advance and clear the beach. Having achieved Task Force 1's initial objectives, Rowny established a defensive perimeter and reoriented the task force for the attack the next day inland toward Highway 1. He also received Company B, 370th RCT, to help stabilize and reinforce the line.[11]

The day had been expensive: Task Force 1 lost three officers and ninety enlisted casualties, with another ten non-battle injuries. Captain Holbrook received four wounds while directing the attack. Intelligence reports later revealed that the attack along the beach and across the canal had surprised the Germans, but they recovered quickly. Rowny repelled five counterattacks during the night, the last of which completely broke through the left flank and exposed the battalion command post.[12]

The 92nd Division's attack in the hills began well. While the 365th RCT and 366th Infantry (minus 3rd Battalion) maintained the right flank of the division sector, the 371st RCT attacked with two battalions abreast and one in reserve against initially light opposition. The advance grew more difficult as it proceeded, however, and stalled about 10:30 a.m. after going some 800 yards. The difficult terrain and well-placed German defenses stymied the 371st RCT's efforts to push forward. After reorganizing, the regiment moved forward again at 2:00 p.m. against much heavier German artillery and small-arms fire. The 2nd Battalion, on the east flank, also encountered a minefield that stopped its progress.[13]

The 370th RCT attack also began well but quickly encountered heavy opposition. Attacking on a narrower front than the 371st, the 370th attacked in a column of battalions with its 3rd Battalion in the lead. This advance also stalled around 10:30, but individual American companies began maneuvering to outflank well-placed automatic weapons. The 3rd Battalion had achieved its first day's objectives by 2:00 p.m., and the other battalions began to consolidate and reorganize. The 3rd Battalion repelled a counterattack at 4:00 p.m., but then disaster struck. A German mortar barrage that began around 5:00 p.m. killed some key leaders and disorganized the leading elements of both the 2nd and 3rd Battalions. Many soldiers fled back down the hill, erasing any gains made during the day. Casualties were light, but there were a few stragglers. The 370th began reorganizing and consolidating during the night.[14]

Almond evaluated the air support his division received that day as effective, with 226 sorties flown in support of the 92nd's operations. He also said that artillery support had worked well, with close coordination between assaulting and supporting units. Almond rated his armor support highly but faulted the engineers for failing to clear tank routes adequately. The soldiers on the ground did not share Almond's enthusiasm for the 92nd's air support. Cpl. Ivan J. Houston reported that during one of the attacks on Monte Caula, an American P-47 strafed his battalion's positions for over an hour. Houston contends that different colored flares on the ground may have confused the pilot, even though the plane was low enough that the soldiers could see the pilot's face. Some of the soldiers took their shirts off to show that they were African Americans, but the plane flew too fast to distinguish people on the ground.[15]

Almond's impetuous nature often got the best of him, especially when he felt pressure to perform. As these attacks ground slowly forward, the 92nd artillery used ammunition at a terrific rate. General Crittenberger saw the attacks bogging down and called Almond to tell him to call them off to keep from wasting ammunition. As the argument became heated and Almond grew insubordinate, Colonel McCaffrey unplugged the telephone line, cutting off the conversation. Almond, already furious, exploded at McCaffrey, "You're through, pack your bags." Five minutes later, a cooled and chastened Almond recalled McCaffrey, who admonished his boss, "As a division commander, you can't tell corps commanders to shove it." The incident illustrated Almond's impatience with restrictions from higher headquarters, and his continuing reliance on McCaffrey to be a moderating influence.[16]

The first day's results disappointed Almond, but the attack had not been entirely futile. The division had gained an average of 800 yards along the front, surprised the enemy with the initial flank attack, and begun developing intelligence on the enemy along the front. Given the scale of this operation, the 92nd Division had not suffered heavily. Its losses numbered 10 officers, 206 enlisted, and 42 non-battle injuries, with the heaviest casualties sustained by Task Force 1. Almond became concerned about straggling. The 3rd Battalion, 366th Infantry, also reported the highest number of stragglers: 110 out of the division's 121 came from this battalion. At 6:00 p.m. Almond ordered the attacks to continue again at 6:30 the following morning. All of the 92nd Division's elements spent the night consolidating their positions, reorganizing as required, and repelling counterattacks. The Germans fired heavy-caliber artillery all night long, and those shells fell with particular frequency in the Task Force 1 coastal sector.[17]

Dawn brought bad weather to the Ligurian coast, grounding aircraft and hampering artillery support. Rowny had attempted to bridge the canal and clear mines during the night, but heavy mortar and artillery fire interdicted those efforts. A IV Corps engineer unit also arrived to try to bridge the canal, but were prevented by enemy fire. Maintaining wire communications and receiving supplies from the rear had become nearly impossible. Task Force 1 resumed the attack at 6:40 a.m. under the cover of a smokescreen, but gained no ground. Twenty minutes later a German counterattack broke through the left side of the task force, causing the troops there to recoil toward the rear. So many troops fled their positions that some companies in the 3rd Battalion, 371st were reduced to as little as one quarter of their strength.[18]

Rowny and Captain Holbrook stopped the flight and put their troops back in position, but another counterattack in the same area again sent soldiers running to the rear. Rowny kept the remaining soldiers in line while the XO rallied the fleeing GIs, reorganized them into a unit, and returned them to their positions. By noon, Germans occupied many of the positions the troops had abandoned, and Rowny ordered a counterattack at 1:00 p.m., but he cancelled the assault when one company reported that their rifles would not function.[19]

Almond saw the difficulties along the coast. He ordered the commander of the 1st Battalion, 370th Infantry, Lt. Col. Harold R. Everman, to take the remainder of his outfit to reinforce the 3rd Battalion, 366th, and take over the sector from Task Force 1. Everman arrived and toured the position with Rowny shortly afterward. As Everman assumed command, the task force dissolved and the sector became an extension of the 370th RCT with the 3rd Battalion, 366th Infantry attached. Rowny moved to the rear and the following day assumed command of the troops south of the Cinquale Canal, both to catch and reorganize stragglers and to maintain communications.[20]

The remainder of the 370th RCT struggled as well. The Germans had moved tanks into the center of the 370th's sector on Highway 1 during the night, and the American attack at 6:30 a.m. met stiff resistance. Straggling continued and casualties mounted, with 8 officers, 98 enlisted men, and 17 non-battle injuries. Colonel Sherman spent the afternoon consolidating and reorganizing the line to fill holes left by stragglers and casualties, and stabilizing the former Task Force 1 sector. Corporal Houston recalled that the 3rd Battalion, 370th Infantry, lost many officers, both white and black. The fall of popular officers shook morale in many companies. Commanders who succumbed to shell shock had an even more debilitating effect on their men. Nothing unnerved troops more than seeing previously strong leaders break down. Corporal Houston reported that he and a captain found most of Company L hiding in a schoolhouse, shell-shocked, after their popular commander, Capt. Clarence Brown, suffered the same fate. On Sherman's right flank, the 371st continued its advance over steep terrain against a well-placed enemy, which had been reinforced with at least one more company during the night. The 2nd Battalion continued to try to clear the minefield while the 1st Battalion made limited gains in its sector, and regimental casualties remained light: 1 officer, 19 enlisted, and 26 non-battle injuries.[21]

The second day's assault had yielded no gains for the 92nd, while the division sustained 15 officer casualties, 183 enlisted casualties, and 58 non-battle losses. The official reports opted not to describe these non-battle casualties in detail, but other evidence indicates some involved self-inflicted wounds. Capt. Jack F. Runyon, commanding Company D, 371st Infantry Regiment, later reported that at least two of his soldiers had shot themselves in the foot to keep from going any further forward. Straggler totals also continued to mount, with another ninety-two soldiers having fled the battlefield. Almond increased the number of MPs on the division straggler line.[22]

Almond, Crittenberger, and Truscott took stock of the situation at 6:00 p.m. on February 9. With few gains to show for the first two days, Truscott urged Almond to call off the attack. Desperate to prove that the 92nd could succeed, Almond asked for one more opportunity. "I pleaded with [Truscott] to allow me to continue the attack to the extension of our ability to proceed," he later remembered. Truscott delayed a decision pending discussions with his staff, but asked Almond what he would need to continue the offensive. Almond required sustained air support, but said he could carry on with the forces and ammunition available. Truscott agreed to allow Almond to keep attacking. This would provide the final test of whether or not the 92nd Infantry Division could muster any offensive power. Almond ordered the next attack to go forward at 6:00 the next morning. During the night, Captain Holbrook was killed by a mine while trying to maintain communications with division headquarters. Rowny later reported that he had recommended Captain Holbrook for the Medal of Honor for his exploits, but that recommendation was stopped at division level. Sometime later, Colonel McCaffrey told Rowny that he too had been recommended for the nation's highest award. His nomination had also stopped at division headquarters. This underscores the notion that Almond did not want to reward "failing" efforts, even for his favorites.[23]

Colonel Sherman launched the attack at 6:00 a.m. on February 10. The 370th had experienced significant problems on the offense's first day, and Almond took steps to reinforce the unit. He attached the 3rd Battalion, 371st, to the 370th and released the 3rd Battalion, 370th, from division reserve. Sherman passed the 3rd Battalion, 371st, through the 2nd

Battalion, 370th, to reestablish the lines abandoned the previous day and then press on to Hill Y. The 3rd Battalion encountered little opposition and quickly secured its objective, but the Germans soon counterattacked. The enemy preceded its infantry assault with a mortar barrage, killing Lt. Col. Arthur H. Walker, the commander of 3rd Battalion, 371st Infantry. Maj. John B. Hazel took command and repelled the German attack, but the assault rattled the units, and men fled back down the hill. Companies became badly disorganized because of large numbers of stragglers, and the battalion spent the remainder of the day regrouping and consolidating positions.[24] The other two battalions of the 371st made slow progress on the steep hills. The 1st Battalion captured its initial objective, but German counterattacks later pushed the battalion back down the hill. The 2nd Battalion finally cleared the minefield in its zone and captured its objectives as well. The 371st lost 5 officers and 30 enlisted men, along with 49 non-battle injuries. The 1st Battalion, 370th Infantry, in the coastal sector with the 3rd Battalion, 366th Infantry attached, made no progress at all. The Germans attacked early in the morning and forced a temporary withdrawal before the 92nd's supporting artillery and tanks repulsed the assault, but succeeding German attacks finally forced the units to move back 500 yards.[25]

The third day of Almond's offensive had proved to be the most futile. With a total of 10 officers and 137 enlisted casualties, plus another 106 non-battle casualties, the 3rd Battalion, 366th Infantry, had lost its offensive capability. Straggling had begun to drain the division as much as German-inflicted deaths and wounds. The 3rd Battalion, 366th Infantry, had disintegrated on the third day. The battalion lost 260 stragglers on that day, more than its total number of casualties for the entire operation. Faced with mines and a well-placed enemy occupying steep terrain, the soldiers fled singly and in groups. Almond's subordinate commanders needed to reorganize their units several times a day to plug holes left by soldiers who abandoned their positions. Each company and battalion also used NCOs and officers to track down soldiers hiding in houses or caves in the area and bring them back to the line. Regimental straggler lines caught more, but some managed to get all the way back to the division straggler line, where Military Police apprehended them.[26]

After three days of limited gains and ineffective attacks, Almond reluctantly called off his offensive at 8:00 p.m. on February 10 and ordered the 370th and 371st to consolidate and withdraw to their original positions. Colonel Everman pulled back the 1st Battalion, 370th Infantry, across the Cinquale Canal, and sent the 3rd Battalion, 366th

Infantry, now deemed combat ineffective, to a rehabilitation area south of Viareggio to reorganize and refit. The withdrawal proved to be diffi-cult as well, with both regiments repelling counterattacks and suffering casualties.[27]

The straggling that had already been growing steadily during the limited operations over the winter reached dangerous proportions during the attack in February. The 366th Infantry's supposed cohesion based on its prewar service collapsed under the pressure of battle. The regiment sustained 347 casualties, more than any of the division's organic regiments. The number of stragglers exceeded the number of casualties in the division as a whole, but especially in the 366th Infantry. The death of one battalion commander had a traumatic effect, but that cannot explain how one regiment can suffer such a disproportionate number of casualties and stragglers. Military Police apprehended 630 soldiers from the 366th at the division straggler line, which accounted for 60 percent of the stragglers in the division. The 366th's casualties and stragglers amounted to 28 percent of the regiment's authorized strength of 3,472 (see table 8.1). Almond must have felt that his misgivings about these "outsiders" were justified.[28]

Table 8.1. Casualties and Stragglers for All Units, February 8–11, 1945

	Killed		Wounded		MIA		Total	Stragglers
	Off.	Enl.	Off.	Enl.	Off.	Enl.		
365th RCT	0	15	6	184	0	11	216	200
370th RCT	3	22	15	159	1	63	263	244
371st RCT	1	13	3	90	0	5	112	0
Rest of Division	3	6	7	42	0	0	58	0
366th Infantry	0	14	15	300	0	18	347	630
758th Tank Bn	0	0	0	2	0	0	2	0
760 Tank Bn	0	1	0	12	0	0	13	0
TOTAL	7	71	46	789	1	97	1,011	1,074

Source: Memorandum, Headquarters, Fifth Army (Assistant Chief of Staff, G1), to Chief of Staff, Subject: Casualties, 92nd Inf. Div., and Supporting Troops, February 11, 1945, Box 41, Almond Papers.

The 92nd Infantry Division captured ten prisoners during the three-day operation, yielding information on both the main enemy units and the commitment of some reserve units. Some of these were divisional reserves, but others had come from higher-level organizations, including the tank company that 370th Infantry encountered near Highway 1. The attack also exposed twenty-one previously unidentified German artillery positions. Unfortunately, these artillery units had devastated Task Force 1 in the coastal area. Prisoner reports indicated that American aerial bombardment and artillery had proved extremely effective, with total enemy losses estimated at 25 percent, and 36 percent in the coastal zone. The prisoners also indicated that the attack surprised the Germans. They made plans to withdraw if necessary, destroying bridges and mining secondary roads.

Later intelligence reports revealed the Germans did blow up some critical bridges. Despite this, the enemy did not intend to give up any key terrain without a fight. Almond also speculated that this attack forced the enemy to expend a lot of ammunition, and that it hurt their ability to run future operations—another attempt at finding a positive outcome. Almond summarized the results of the attack and declared that the intelligence gained outweighed any tactical failures. He no doubt intended both to bolster his men's morale and to protect his own standing among his superiors.[29]

Only the 371st had managed to retain any of the ground it gained, some 800 yards, but it still fell short of its objective. Bitterly disappointed, Almond launched an investigation into what caused his units to fall short. He appointed General Wood to head a board consisting of the division chief of staff and all the regimental commanders and the engineer battalion commander, each of whom investigated his own outfit's performance. All evidence pointed to the infantry as the weakness, with other arms having performed their missions well. Almond submitted a preliminary report to General Truscott on February 11, 1945, which made evident his frustration. Despite the positive tone of his report, the 92nd Division had failed badly, and Almond knew it. He described the preparation for the assault in language that was accurate in some places but not in others. He correctly presented the amount of reconnaissance his men had conducted, but he exaggerated the success of the fighter-bomber air support: "The attack was supported by heavy initial artillery concentrations on the enemy positions and by thorough and adequate artillery support throughout the operation. This was supplemented by excellent fighter-bomber support." Almond also downplayed the obstacles his men encountered on the ground: "The terrain was difficult and strongly organized but not heavily garrisoned."[30]

The remainder of the report focused on what went wrong. Almond credited his troops with a good initial attack, but said things fell apart when they had to either stay in place or continue beyond their initial objectives. When enemy opposition stiffened, Almond reported, "most of our front line elements not only failed to act aggressively to overcome local opposition by employing fire and maneuver, but these units repeatedly disintegrated, 'melting-away' to the rear at every opportunity." Numerous reports by both black and white officers at all echelons and in all units confirm this. There is little doubt that this "melting away" occurred on a wide scale. Almond blamed the lack of cohesion on poor junior officer leadership and lack of mutual trust and confidence, but failed to mention the heavy-caliber artillery at Punta Bianca that mauled the attack along the beach. Colonel McCaffrey later pointed out that the 92nd contained many good officers, both black and white, but the weak ones dragged down the entire division. He offered an interesting commentary on black soldiers' feelings about the war: "Even in combat we had wonderful engineers, first rate artillerymen, and mortar gunners who could put more rounds in the air than anybody. Where we were lacking was in the rifle companies and that was based, I think, essentially on lack of personal confidence in each other. There were many brave and effective officers, black and white, in the 92nd Division, but the chain is only as strong as its weakest links in the rifle companies."[31]

Almond's report documented his own lack of confidence in his soldiers for the first time and confirmed rumors about his feelings toward the 366th Infantry. There is no doubt that the infantry, and especially the 366th, "melted away" and failed to accomplish its objectives. Almond had planted the seeds for that failure: his "welcome" to the regiment upon its arrival, in which he promised to make them suffer their share of casualties, must have affected the soldiers' desire to perform. This created a "self-fulfilling prophecy," or more properly the Pygmalion Effect, which psychologists define as "acting in accordance with the expectations of another." The reverse of the Pygmalion, the Golem Effect, occurs "when subordinates realize leaders' low expectations" and therefore fail to perform adequately. These effects come from stereotypes or reputation, and then confirmatory evidence maintains them. One study determined that "in general, low performers were individuals who obtained low scores on mental ability tests or did not have the required experience and education to fulfill job requirements." When leaders expect different performance, the subordinates perform differently. Almond's low expectations of the 366th stemmed from the regiment having been "forced" on him, and on his suppositions of their potential. The higher straggling rates for the 366th would seem to confirm Almond's assumptions about that all-black unit. The overall dismal performance, however, affected how he thought about the rest of the division.[32]

The failed attack and the investigation that followed profoundly affected Almond, and no doubt fueled the insecurity that gnawed at him. He believed he had done his best to train these soldiers, yet they had not only failed to accomplish their mission, they had fled the battlefield. Almond concluded that black soldiers could therefore never succeed as infantry, and reported as much to General Clark: "In my opinion the failure of this operation is due almost entirely to the unreliability of the infantry units as shown by their repeated withdrawals in the face of enemy fire and small, though determined, hostile counterattacks; the withdrawals, by our infantry, take the form of panics, or disorderly retirements with little heed to command and leadership, particularly the weak leadership in the platoon echelons. Little if any determined offensive spirit to meet the enemy at close quarters existed in most of the infantry units."[33] This signaled a change in Almond. Having grown up in a racist era in a racist Army, he had so far absorbed the prevailing culture but not exhibited it any more than his peers. After these events of February 1945, though, Almond became more outspoken in his racist views.

General Wood's investigating board filed a report that condemned African American soldiers in nearly all respects. This report, which Almond approved and provided to his superiors, contended that black officers failed to meet minimum infantry standards, lacked "pride, aggressiveness, [and] a sense of responsibility," and had no capacity for command above the grade of captain. Almond argued that these officers did not understand the merit promotion system, an issue that clearly still rankled since his encounter with General Davis the year before. He further argued that the black NCO exhibited similar faults and "cannot be developed in self-confidence and consequent leadership within reasonable time for emergency infantry combat use. He lacks pride, is careless and undependable, and cannot induce enlisted men under his command to follow him in danger—principally because he himself is afraid of infantry combat."[34]

As far as the common black soldier was concerned, Almond contended:

> (1) The negro soldier, like the noncommissioned officer, lacks pride and trust in his fellow soldier. He distorts facts, is unreliable and fears the "unseen" such as the enemy at night and enemy artillery or mortar fire. Constant supervision fails to insure his care and maintenance of equipment. His regard for health, especially contraction of venereal disease and foot ailments, is very low.
>
> (2) The negro soldier can be trained in modern combat methods, but this requires a longer time than for white troops, even if both have the same AGCT scores. He is patient and willing but no amount of training of his infantry rifleman will insure his application of sound principles under fire or even in the forward combat area.[35]

Almond concluded with a paragraph that clearly outlined his feelings:

> Finally, I must express my high appreciation of the efforts of those white officers who have served for long periods with this division. In future employment of Negros, including white officers in the organization, a service time-limit policy must be decided upon and enforced. The theory of unstinting service wherever ordered in our Army is a noble one and has been my constant precept and my constant nature is a fact, not a theory, and a reasonable assurance to white officers, assigned to negro troops, that there is some limit to such assignment is essential to the high type of efficient service demanded of these officers.[36]

Almond concluded that three and a half years of experience in training and combat had convinced him that the black division concept was a failure. He argued that, in the future, the US Army should not create black units larger than regimental size, and they should be integrated at regimental level with white units.[37]

Almond needed a way to survive the disaster, and the investigation provided salve for his wounded spirit by absolving him of blame. He was fortunate that the prevailing US Army attitude saved him. General Marshall had given Almond the 92nd because he believed Almond could make black troops succeed if anyone could, but no one in the white leadership really believed black units capable of success. Had Almond commanded a white division, he surely would have been relieved of command. All of Almond's superiors, however, all the way up to Under Secretary of War Robert P. Patterson, sympathized with his plight and believed he had done as well as could be expected. Since none of them expected much from the 92nd, there was no question of relieving Almond. Truscott called Almond's attack "well planned, well organized, and well supported." Truscott's biographer, Wilson A. Heefner, believed that while Truscott himself harbored no personal racial bias, he accepted the "racial mindset" that also prejudiced Clark and Marshall. That worldview allowed Almond to remain in command.[38]

Almond had lived by the military dictum that "units don't fail, leaders do," but he seemed to forget this philosophy following his division's poor showing in February 1945. He insisted until his death that his black infantry had failed despite good leadership. Still, his role in the failure continued to trouble him. Lt. Col. Edward L. Rowny worked for Almond again in the future and remained close to him for the rest of his life. Rowny believed that Almond never fully came to terms with the contradiction. Almond's blame-fixing aside, he must have continued to feel his honor still carried a stain. He would nurse that wound for the rest of his life, and it made his declarations on race increasingly vehement.[39]

9

Tragedy and Redemption

1945

The winter of 1944–1945 had not gone well for Maj. Gen. Ned Almond. Brutal weather conditions, his son's wounding, his son-in-law's death, and his division's two conspicuous failures on the battlefield all must have affected his morale. For the most part, however, Almond kept his inner feelings well hidden. Both Col. William J. McCaffrey and Lt. Col. Edward L. Rowny later reported that Almond's indefatigable spirit and tremendous work ethic kept him moving.

Gen. George C. Marshall toured Italy in the spring of 1945 and visited Almond just after the disaster at the Cinquale Canal. Facing Marshall must have been hard for Almond. The renowned and powerful general could radiate a terrifying presence even under less stressful circumstances. McCaffrey later recalled a visit Marshall made during the division's training at Fort Huachuca. McCaffrey, then the G3, drove Marshall's aide in a jeep, while Almond followed with Marshall in a staff car. McCaffrey drove just past the officer in charge to allow Almond room to stop in front of the man. Rather than stopping in front of the officer, however, Almond pulled ahead as well. Marshall left the car and reprimanded McCaffrey for wasting his time, making him walk back to the officer. "I thought Major General Almond would speak up in my behalf," McCaffrey remembered, "but I immediately noticed that he had a brace on as rigid as mine."[1] The episode reflected poorly on Almond, who did not have the moral courage to defend his subordinate, and on Marshall, who chose to publicly dress down the junior officer in front of his superiors. It also demonstrated the aura of fear that Marshall generated with his mere presence. This must have weighed heavily on Almond's mind as he awaited Marshall's arrival. Marshall knew that the 92nd Infantry Division lacked offensive capability, and he seemed to recognize Almond's embarrassment over his failure. Almond later reported that General Marshall looked at him with an eagle eye and said, "You have had a heck of a time in the last two weeks, haven't you?" Almond replied that he had, and Marshall asked what it would take to make the division perform. Almond placed his hand on a map at his regiments' rear boundaries and said, "General, give me everything above that line," meaning replace all the 92nd's infantry. Almond further explained that "my infantry regiments won't close with the enemy and won't hold their ground if attacked. My artillery is first rate. My logistics work well, engineer and ordnance perform excellently. I have a competent, experienced division staff, but the infantry regiments aren't functioning well enough." Marshall ordered Almond to select the best soldiers from all three regiments and put them in one regiment, and then told him he would transfer the famed 442nd Infantry Regiment (Nisei) and the white 473rd Infantry Regiment to the 92nd Division.[2]

Truman K. Gibson, the civilian aide to the secretary of war, had been concerned about the 92nd Division since the debacle in December. When reports revealing the latest failure reached Washington, Gibson decided to fly to Italy to investigate. He landed on February 26, the same day the news of the battle hit major newspapers and magazines in the States. Going straight to Lt. Gen. Joseph T. McNarney, now the Mediterranean Theater commander, Gibson discovered the plan to pull the 92nd Infantry Division off the line, and he objected immediately. Almond's report, verified all the way up through the command chain, horrified him. Gibson persuaded McNarney to delay the 92nd's withdrawal from the line until he could personally investigate the situation.

Gibson reported that he spent one week with the 92nd Division moving from Livorno to Viareggio, interviewing more than eight hundred officers and several hundred enlisted men. His investigation uncovered some essential truths, such as the reports of panicked troops "melting away," but he also determined that Almond and his officers had failed to search for the underlying causes of such behavior. He also reported that the officers he interviewed blamed the retreats on replacement soldiers, some 2,600 of whom had transferred from service organizations into the 92nd before the assault, with no combat training. Gibson was told that many had never fired a rifle, and he declared, "No other single observation was repeated [by company officers] in more instances than this one."[3]

The exact numbers of replacements and their origins cannot be verified, but historical accounts agree with Gibson's assessment of the replacements. He determined that the replacement system for black soldiers differed from the system for white solders. He reported that the 92nd received some new men from the 372nd Infantry, a separate black regiment, and found them well trained. Most of the division's green soldiers, however, came from the Disciplinary Barracks in Africa or the East Coast Processing Center that received captured AWOL soldiers. The remainder of the replacements came from the division's overstrength, which had deployed with it and which included its "Q-minus" men, those deemed psychologically unfit for battle. Almond had argued against taking them, but in the end the War Department ordered him to do so.[4]

Gibson credited Almond with good intentions: "It would appear that . . . Negro officers and many of the enlisted men feel that the command is not interested in the success of division and that decisions have been made as to purposely reflect discredit on Negro officers and enlisted men. Nothing, of course, could be further the truth; General Almond and all of his officers were intensely interested in turning out an efficient division from the material that was given them to work with."[5]

Nevertheless, Gibson concluded that race relations within the 92nd differed little from what he and General Davis had seen at Fort Huachuca in 1943. Lagging promotions for the African American officers continued to affect their confidence, because by this time many black second lieutenants had more experience than their white peers. During that earlier inspection, Almond had claimed that officer promotions required merit, efficiency, seniority, and experience, and that black officers lacked these qualities in relation to their white peers. Almond had argued that time and experience would help them gain what they needed. By February 1945, those officers had completed another year of training and seen more than six months of combat. They possessed the requisite seniority and experience. Combat surely identified those who lacked merit, but this could not apply to all. Almond's earlier pledges of fairness to the officers did not ring true. Furthermore, Gibson found that black officers received promotions only when they fulfilled accepted, typically subservient, stereotypes. If true, this made the situation doubly difficult for black officers. Promoted officers would be Uncle Toms to their black soldiers or fawning yes-men to white commanders, or both. Gibson found that "white officers scapegoated black troops with all the prejudices of men who did not want to command African Americans."[6]

One of the command's attempts to provide experience or strengthen units backfired. Almond and his commanders often moved officers between platoons, companies, and battalions, either to bolster flagging units or to increase these officers' opportunities. The frequency of these moves, however, debilitated some outfits. Veterans Jehu Hunter and Major Clark reported that these frequent changes of leaders prevented the "development of trust between the leaders and the led that evolves into comradeship and combat effectiveness."[7]

Discovering that a large percentage of the 92nd's soldiers fell into the lowest Army General Classification Test categories evidently shocked Gibson, though this was not news to the War Department. Almond and others had identified this issue since the division's activation. Gibson suggested that appeals to racial pride, such as those contained in the newly published Army Service Forces Manual M5 (Training), *Leadership and the Negro Soldier*, would help improve the division's morale, and said that the 92nd Division's field-grade officers should be happy to cooperate in such a project. Gibson's conclusion precisely described the conditions that caused the division's failure: "It was difficult to inculcate pride in self, combat spirit, or love of country in soldiers trained in the hostile environment of the South." He warned that future use of black soldier employment should focus on "recognizing correctible deficiencies rather than in forming generalizations from the career of this particular unit."[8]

Gibson soon found himself thrust into the center of controversy. He conducted a press conference with war correspondents in Rome after concluding his investigation, a decision he later regretted. He told Assistant Secretary of War John J. McCloy that he gave the press conference because, though the reporters knew the 92nd Infantry Division had failed, they did not know why. He wanted to set the record straight and add context. The white press eagerly anticipated Gibson's comments because he was a black War Department representative and the first government official to offer the press a candid appraisal of the division. Gibson noted that the 92nd's experience did not prove that black men lacked combat ability. "There is no question in my mind about the courage of Negro officers or soldiers and any generalization on the basis of race is unfounded." In listing the division's faults, however, Gibson mentioned the "melting away" and the literacy issue. His comments elicited howls of protests from the black press in the United States. The *Pittsburgh Courier* called Gibson an "Uncle Tom," while the *Chicago Defender* called for Gibson's ouster under the screaming headline "Somebody's Gotta Go!" The National Association for the Advancement of Colored People (NAACP) later passed a resolution expressing a "lack of confidence" in Gibson and called for his ouster.[9]

American war correspondents in Italy, both black and white, disagreed with the stateside newspapers' characterization of Gibson. The *Afro-American*, based in Baltimore, defended Gibson, saying that his feelings were nothing new and that newspapers that had reported in Italy knew the facts before Gibson went overseas. The *Norfolk Journal and Guide* went even further in addressing the division's reported "melting away": "The term may prick us painfully, but Mr. Gibson might not have been as wrong as some would like to believe he was." Few grasped the irony of this outrage. Gibson noted in an interview with the Washington edition of the *Afro-American* that it was hard for him to "see how some people can on the one hand argue that segregation is wrong, and on the other hand blindly defend the product of that segregation." The April 1945 issue of the journal *A Monthly Summary of Trends in Race Relationships* supported Gibson, arguing that "Negro newspapers have been almost unanimous in holding [that] Jim Crow makes for less than maximum fighting efficiency, but many of them are embarrassed to find evidence of the correctness of their contention." The black community in the United States found itself trapped between the need to decry segregation and the desire to deny its most visible results.[10]

The US Army manual to which Gibson referred, *Leadership and the Negro Soldier*, had warned that the white press had very little to say to African Americans, so black newspapers filled the void. Black soldiers had to read these newspapers if they wanted to get news on black issues, and that may have exacerbated the situation. The black press kept soldiers informed of the various racial incidents that flared up during the war. The extant memoirs from black 92nd personnel fail to mention the Port Chicago ammunition ship explosion and subsequent mutiny of black sailors at another ammunition storage facility in 1943, but they were surely aware of it. The black press covered that story and its aftermath until after the war. Likewise, Almond's soldiers surely knew about the Philadelphia transit strike in 1944. Perhaps the Detroit race riots commanded more attention than the other events, however, because Nazi propagandists used the news of the riots to try to sow dissension between white and black soldiers and among the Allies. Each of these events drove home to black soldiers the ugly fact that African Americans inhabited a separate but unequal society.[11]

Despite the distractions caused by Gibson's inspection, press conference, and subsequent report, the overhaul of the 92nd Division went forward. Almond first removed the 366th Infantry Regiment from the line and returned it to Fifth Army control. He then accepted the 442nd and 473rd Infantry Regiments and placed them in line, while withdrawing the division's three organic infantry regiments. Once again selecting Col. Ray Sherman's 370th RCT as the lead element, Almond began to reorganize. Sherman identified his worst soldiers and sent them to the other two regiments, while the other regimental commanders selected their best soldiers and sent them to Sherman. Decorated soldiers, or those with the Combat Infantryman's Badge, transferred to the 370th. After the reorganization, the 365th and the 371st would go to the division training area and continue training, and perhaps be used in a limited role elsewhere. Almond assured Truscott that leaving the officer and NCO leadership in place in the 365th and 371st Infantry Regiments would ensure those units could retrain properly.[12]

The 92nd's reorganization moved approximately 70 officers and 1,400 enlisted men into the 370th RCT while removing 52 officers and 1,350 soldiers. Significantly, only white officers remained with the 370th RCT, though some black officers transferred in. While Almond's infantry components experienced a major shakeup, the organic artillery and service units remained unchanged. After the substandard infantry left the division, the 92nd's artillery and other support units formed new combat teams with the 442nd and 473rd Infantry Regiments.[13]

The 442nd Infantry Regiment arrived when the division's morale had reached its lowest ebb. Despite the Nisei soldiers' growing renown, they were outsiders themselves. The Japanese American soldiers comprising this outfit may have had some inkling of how it felt to be outsiders in a white man's Army. The 100th Infantry Battalion (Separate), core of the future 442nd RCT, had formed in 1942 with second-generation Japanese American, or Nisei, troops from the Hawaii National Guard. The Japanese termed first-generation immigrants Issei and called the third generation Sansei. The battalion had white senior officers, most with long service in Hawaii. The 100th Battalion trained and deployed to Italy as a separate unit. The War Department had authorized the 442nd RCT to form in January 1943 to expand opportunities for Nisei soldiers. The original 442nd RCT contained three infantry battalions, a field artillery battalion, and an engineer company. The combat team arrived in Italy in May 1944 minus one battalion that remained in the States to train replacements. The 100th Battalion then joined the 442nd to give the RCT the full complement of infantry.[14]

The Nisei troops had earned a reputation for toughness even during stateside training. In 1942, Second Army commander Lt. Gen. Ben Lear sent a letter to all his subordinate commanders to report on the 100th Battalion's training. During his inspection, he found the troops eager and moving at the double time to accomplish all missions. They maintained march discipline even during a heavy rain, operated radios correctly, used maps and aerial photographs accurately, and aggressively patrolled their flanks on any march. Lear emphasized that he observed no straggling at all; his only criticism was the unit's tendency to "bunch up" because rear elements tended to push ahead too fast. Junior officer control was "better than satisfactory" in all cases. Lear sent this report to alert commanders to these troops' quality.[15]

Many Nisei soldiers had endured forms of racial discrimination rivaling what their new black comrades had experienced. The US government had interned many thousands of Japanese American families in detention camps after Pearl Harbor, fearing that anyone of Japanese descent was a potential spy or saboteur. These families lost their homes and businesses and remained confined throughout the war. The War Department did not fully trust the Nisei troops to fight against the Japanese army, so the 442nd was earmarked for Europe. The US Army first consolidated Nisei draftees at Camp Robinson, Arkansas, and finally at Camp Shelby, Mississippi. Despite their experiences with detention centers, some segregationist practices in the South confused soldiers unused to "whites only" drinking fountains and segregated buses and restrooms.[16]

In August 1943 the 100th Infantry Battalion embarked for Italy, where it quickly proved its mettle. Lt. Gen. Mark Clark attached the 100th Battalion to the 133rd Infantry Regiment, 34th Infantry Division, on September 5, 1943. The battalion fought in the toughest battles of the Italian campaign: Salerno, Anzio, Cassino, and Rome, with nine of its soldiers receiving the Distinguished Service Cross (DSC) and the battalion earning a Presidential Unit Citation. After the 100th Battalion joined the 442nd, the newly reorganized RCT fought from Rome to the Arno, garnering another nine DSCs. After two months of brutal combat, the 442nd RCT went to southern France with invasion forces for Operation Dragoon. The 442nd matched its Italian performance in France, earning a Presidential Unit Citation and numerous individual decorations in its two months of combat there. After a brief rest, Gen. Dwight D. Eisenhower, Supreme Allied Commander in Europe, released the 442nd on March 20, 1944, to return to Italy to join the 92nd Infantry Division. The 442nd RCT left France minus its artillery battalion, which had been attached to the 69th Infantry Division. After drawing new personal equipment, the unit finally arrived in the 92nd Division area on April 3, 1945. Almond had gained a veteran unit renowned for its aggressiveness and success in combat. He issued the 442nd the unit equipment turned in from 366th RCT and assigned Col. Virgil R. Miller, the 442nd's commander, the Serchio Valley sector. He also detailed the 597th Field Artillery Battalion to support the regiment, completing the combat team.[17]

The 473rd Infantry Regiment's experience in Italy symbolized the changing nature of the Italian campaign. The recently organized command consisted of four battalions originally formed as the 434th, 435th, 532nd, and 900th Anti-Aircraft Artillery Battalions. With the Allies enjoying air superiority, Mediterranean Theater commander Lt. Gen. Joseph T. McNarney deactivated these superfluous units in January 1945 and reorganized their soldiers as infantry. The Fifth Army placed these battalions under the 2nd Armored Headquarters and sent them to train as infantry for sixty days. After only thirty days, however, the four battalions received orders to the 92nd Infantry Division. Almond attached an artillery battalion, and the newly rechristened 473rd RCT went into the line. Almond soon determined that the 473rd's commander, an armor officer, was not the right man for the job. He went to General Clark to request a replacement. Clark offered him Col. William P. Yarborough, an already well-known airborne commander. Yarborough had commanded one of the Army's first parachute infantry companies and had later commanded a battalion that led the airborne assault during the Allied invasion of Sicily in July 1943. Yarborough then led his battalion in the parachute assault that began Operation Dragoon. Almond welcomed the arrival of this proven leader, and Yarborough quickly welded the 473rd RCT's disparate elements into a fighting unit.[18]

Almond proposed replacing the 365th Infantry and 370th Infantry units in the coastal area immediately with the 473rd RCT, while using the 365th Infantry as a replacement training regiment. Almond believed this process would take two to three weeks and requested the press not be notified until the training had been completed. Truscott overruled Almond on replacing the units in the coastal sector with the 473rd RCT, believing it would attract too much attention. Truscott preferred to position the 473rd in the more vulnerable Serchio Valley, which he felt the "unreliable" African American troops there could not hold. Citing a crucial need for engineers that required converting some antiaircraft artillery units, Truscott recommended converting the 366th Infantry to a General Service Engineer (GSE) unit. GSE regiments were smaller than infantry regiments, so the number of soldiers in the 366th Infantry Regiment would equal two full GSE regiments, with enough white officers to lead both. Finally, Truscott ordered Almond to prepare another limited-objective attack in his sector using all three regiments, ensuring he used the 370th RCT. Leaving out the 370th, Truscott feared, would attract adverse comment from the black press.[19]

As the spring of 1945 brought warmer weather to Italy, General

Clark readied the 15th Army Group for what he believed would be its last major offensive. He envisioned a final push northward through the Apennine Mountains into the Po River Valley. That area featured a thirty-mile-wide plain running northwest to southeast between the Alps and the Apennines. The plan sent both the US Fifth and British Eighth Armies through the mountains into the valley, across the Po, and then north toward Verona. The Eighth Army, already located in the relatively flat region on the Adriatic coast, would attack northwest toward Ferrara and Verona along Highway 9 with a secondary effort along the coast toward Venice. The Fifth Army would deliver the more important thrust by pushing directly north through the mountain passes. Highway 64 divided II Corps in the east from IV Corps in the west. The Fifth Army would bypass Bologna to the west and the Eighth Army would bypass Bologna to the east, thus effectively encircling the city. The two armies would then proceed abreast to the Po River and force a crossing. Once past the Po, the Eighth Army's main effort would shift to the northeast toward Venice and Padua, while the Fifth Army attacked straight north toward Verona and west toward Milan.[20]

Truscott's Operation Craftsman for Fifth Army envisioned a main and a secondary effort (see map 9.1). The main effort had IV Corps advancing abreast from the mountains and into Milan while II Corps advanced north to capture Verona. The 365th and 371st Infantry Regiments detached from the 92nd Infantry Division and remained under IV Corps control covering the corps's left flank. The 92nd Infantry Division, operating under Fifth Army control, would attack along the coast toward Genoa.[21]

Almond launched his division's part of Operation Craftsman, which he dubbed Operation Second Wind, on April 5, 1945. The plan mirrored many elements of the ill-fated Operation Fourth Term, with Massa again as the main objective. This time, however, Almond abandoned the treacherous route along the beach and ordered the three regiments to advance in the same sectors the 370th and 371st RCTs had used in February. The terrain climbed steadily higher from west to east, from sea level at the coast to as high as 3,000 feet in the mountainous Apuan region. The IV Corps temporarily cut the Serchio Valley from the division's twenty-two-mile sector. Almond ordered the 442nd RCT to bypass Massa and seize Monte Brugiana. He designed the attack to go east of the Monte Caula–Monte Cerreta ridge, along a line from Monte Folgoriti to Monte Belvedere to Monte Brugiana (see map 9.2). In addition to the newly added and reorganized infantry regiments, Almond received heavy reinforce-

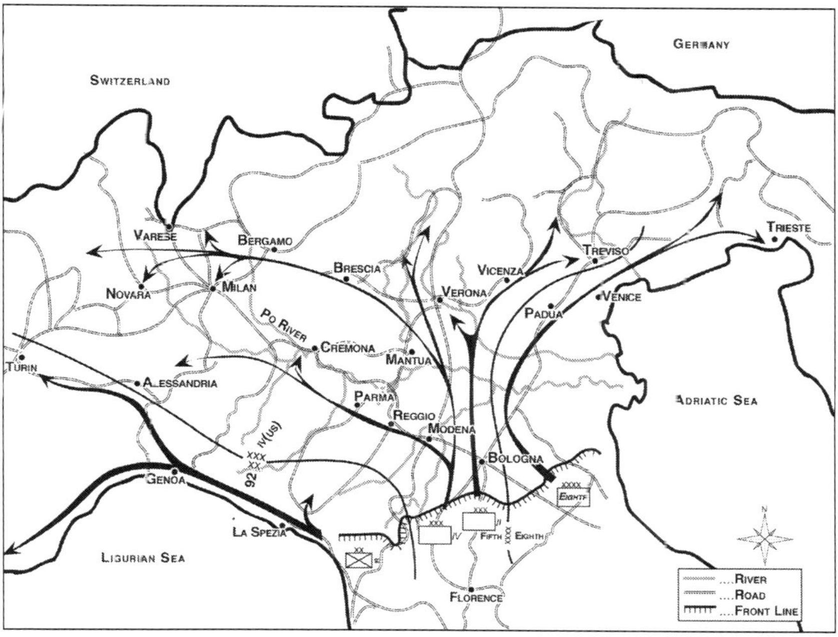

9.1. Operation Craftsman, April 14–May 2, 1945

ments. These units included the 760th Tank Battalion (minus two companies), 758th Light Tank Battalion (Colored), 679th Tank Destroyer Battalion (Colored), 894th Tank Destroyer Battalion (minus two companies), 329th Field Artillery Battalion, and 530th Field Artillery Battalion (155 mm) (minus one battery), plus a British antiaircraft artillery unit and several other support units. The operation's success hinged on silencing the guns at Punta Bianca, so Almond also received significant air support from medium and heavy bombers. The 442nd had already gained the 599th Field Artillery Battalion, and Almond attached the 329th Field Artillery Battalion (detached from the 85th Infantry Division), the 758th Tank Battalion, and one platoon from the 894th Tank Destroyer Battalion.[22]

The 442nd RCT possessed a brilliant record before joining the 92nd Infantry Division, and its men knew it. Moving back to Italy seemed strange at first, but then someone told them that they were going to "rescue" the 92nd Division. PFC Ben Doi of the 100th Infantry Battalion reasoned, "Why would they have to move us from Italy to France to Italy?

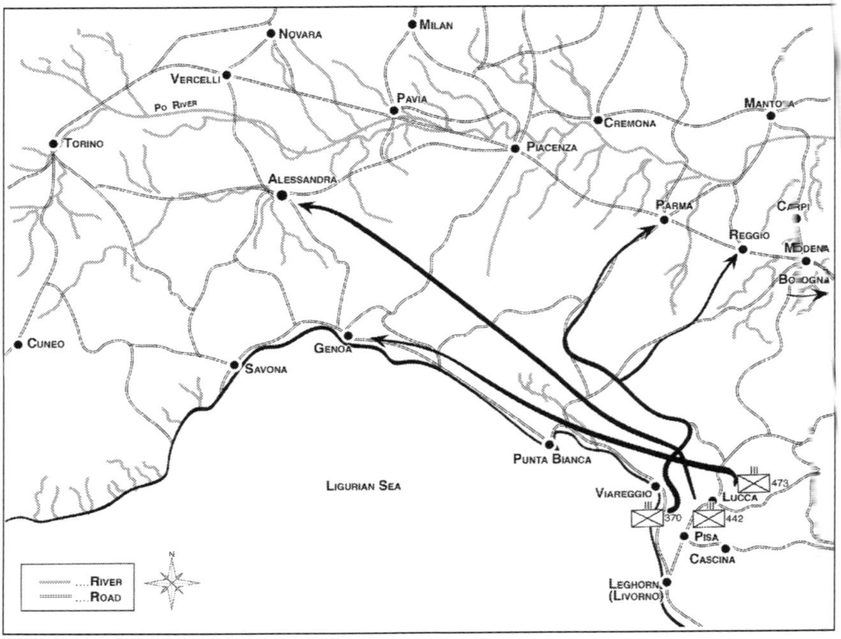

9.2. Operation Second Wind, April 5–12, 1945

Because those guys weren't doing anything at all for six months." This idea was common among the Nisei soldiers. "We were going to replace the 92nd Infantry Division on the line because they couldn't do the job," recalled PFC Masaru Ishida, also of the 100th Battalion. "They wanted us to break that line."[23]

Not all the Nisei thought the 92nd's personnel cowardly or lazy. PFC Robert Ichikawa, Company E, 442nd RCT, recalled meeting a wounded black soldier, an artillery forward observer, in an aid station. The soldier told Ichikawa that he knew the 92nd had a bad reputation, but he wanted to be up front "to prove that everybody ain't chicken in the 92nd." Tech Sgt. Al Takahashi of the 100th Infantry Battalion saw clearly the reason for the black troops' failure and sympathized, saying, "You can't blame them for not fighting, the way they treated them. God, they treated them terrible."[24]

As fellow victims of discrimination, some found common cause with their new black comrades. Perhaps none was more eloquent than 2nd Lt. Daniel K. Inouye, later a US senator from Hawaii. Inouye lost his arm in April 1945 in a vicious action that garnered him the DSC, later upgraded to the Medal of Honor. Inouye led an attack on a defended ridge guarding an important road junction. He led his platoon in a sweeping movement around one side to capture an artillery and mortar position, then assaulted the main enemy position on the ridge top. The enemy had emplaced three machine guns in bunkers and rock formations, set to deliver a crossfire down the slope. Inouye crawled up the hill toward the nearest machine gun and hurled two grenades, destroying the emplacement but receiving a wound in the process. Shortly thereafter, he received a second wound from a grenade that shattered his right arm. Despite these wounds, Inouye continued to lead his platoon until they overcame the enemy and captured the ridge. His platoon had killed twenty-five enemy soldiers and captured eight others. He refused evacuation until after he secured his platoon in a defensive position. Inouye recalled in an interview many years later that he had received seventeen blood transfusions from African American soldiers after losing his arm. "I was saved by Negroes. . . . The only way I could say 'thank you' was to join them in their battle on civil rights."[25]

Almond assigned Col. Sherman's reorganized 370th RCT the relatively flat coastal route along Highway 1 and gave the mountainous inland route to the 442nd RCT (see map 9.2). He kept 2nd Battalion, 473rd RCT, in division reserve while sending the remainder of the regiment to the Serchio Valley to block German reinforcements that might try to move toward the coast. The 370th RCT's mission included driving through the lower hills through Massa to the Frigido River. In addition to its own 598th Field Artillery Battalion, the 370th had the 597th Field Artillery Battalion, the 706th Tank Battalion, and that portion of the 894th Tank Destroyer Battalion not attached to the 442nd RCT. The 370th RCT moved up Highway 1 toward the Strettoia Hills, quickly covering more than two miles, and occupied a hill halfway to the objective. The Germans quickly counterattacked, though, and the soldiers began melting away under fire, erasing any gain the units made.[26]

When the 370th RCT reorganized, it had replaced all black company commanders with white ones but left some black lieutenants in place. One of them, 2nd Lt. Vernon J. Baker, remained in Company C. Capt. John F. Runyon commanded Company C in the 370th RCT assault on April 5. The company moved quickly against light opposition and reached its first objective, a hill overlooking Massa. Runyon had briefed Company C's 142 men, many of whom had just joined the organization, that the division had not yet performed well and that this was their opportunity to "bring credit to Negroes in combat." Runyon later reported that the men took his words to heart, and he had great confidence that they would accomplish their mission. The company quickly outpaced the battalion's other companies, and the regiment could not get reinforcements to it. Baker led the company's attack until machine-gun fire from several positions halted the advance. Baker crawled forward to one position and destroyed it, killing three Germans. He attacked an enemy observation post and killed two enemy soldiers, then called his men forward. Baker and one of his soldiers attacked two more machine gun nests, killing or wounding the four enemy soldiers occupying these positions.[27]

Baker later provided a disturbing account of the action, claiming that Captain Runyon had panicked and run off the hill, taking the only radio and leaving Baker and his men alone. Baker's charge is serious, though he failed to mention it to his battalion commander after returning to headquarters. Baker made clear his disdain for all white officers in a memoir he wrote more than sixty years after the war, a work heavily influenced by decades of discrimination. He clearly hated Runyon and believed he was a coward.

Runyon's report at the time, however, told a different story. After the attack's initial success, it began to slow down because of heavy enemy mortar and machine-gun fire. The heavy casualties the company suffered took a toll on the other men's morale, and they began to flee. Runyon called for reinforcements, but the battalion had none to send. He then ordered the company to withdraw in two groups. Runyon knew the some of the men were disappointed, and he said that Lieutenant Baker made a tearful plea to stand fast and fight it out, and Runyon knew that Baker "was willing to sacrifice his own life in an effort to win our battle." Baker and Runyon made one last effort to stabilize the men in a defensive position, but the loss of several noncommissioned officers made it impossible. At that, Runyon reported, "Lieutenant Baker, who had throughout the day displayed magnificent courage, volunteered to cover the withdrawal of the first group." Baker covered his wounded as they evacuated by drawing the enemy's fire. Unfazed by a grueling day in combat, Baker led a battalion advance through enemy minefields the following evening. Regardless of how Baker may have regarded white officers, Captain Runyon clearly respected Baker and recommended him for the DSC.[28]

Several weeks after the action, Baker received orders to report to Almond at division headquarters. Speaking in curt terms, Almond told him to write a report describing his action on the hill, and then abruptly dismissed him. Baker later recalled that Almond's attitude insulted and disappointed him, but he went back to his unit and prepared the report as ordered. The account became part of the record that justified his award of the DSC. The brusqueness and aloofness Almond displayed in Baker's presence were qualities that the manual *Leadership and the Negro Soldier* had warned white commanders to avoid. Almond tended toward abrasiveness with everyone, however, and division commanders did not have much time to lavish on second lieutenants. Baker believed that his entire chain of command hated him, except for his battalion commander, yet those same leaders approved the DSC recommendation.

Baker seethed with anger at Almond, who symbolized all the discrimination he and other black soldiers experienced, an attitude that has become embedded in the war's historiography. Baker felt a final indignity at the award ceremony in which he received the DSC. By tradition, those soldiers receiving the highest awards are decorated first, and Baker should have been first. When the soldiers lined up for their awards, however, Almond took the leading position. He received a Silver Star, a lower decoration than Baker. Baker then received the first DSC awarded in the 92nd Infantry Division. This small slight angered Baker for the rest of his life.[29]

Decades after war, Baker's record was reviewed along with many others in the investigation ordered by President Clinton. That review resulted in the upgrade of his DSC to the Medal of Honor. The president presented the Medal of Honor to Baker, the only living recipient among seven African American soldiers so honored, in the same ceremony in which Lt. John Fox's widow accepted his posthumous award.[30]

After some initial success, the 370th RCT attack began to bog down. Almond committed the division reserves on April 7 to try to invigorate the assault. Minefields stalled the tank attack, while the formidable battery of six 152 mm guns, four 128 mm guns, and numerous 90 mm guns at Punta Bianca pinned down the American infantry. The Army Air Forces had bombed the guns for four straight days and even destroyed one, but the threat remained. On April 8, Almond switched the 370th and 473rd RCTs, giving the 473rd the lead in the assault (see map 9.2). The 370th went to guard the division right flank in the Serchio Valley, which had been returned to the division sector. By April 9 the 473rd had pushed through the minefields and artillery fire to reach the outskirts of Massa. With the 442nd moving on the city from the north and the 473rd entering from the southwest, the Germans began withdrawing from the city during the night of April 9. The 473rd occupied the city on that day, but the Germans intended to stop the assault at the Frigido River. They mounted a fierce defense along that stream, and the Punta Bianca guns continued to pound the city. In one four-hour period, German artillery fired more than 11,000 rounds into the city.[31]

After the 370th and 473rd RCTs switched places, the 473rd continued toward Genoa while the 442nd pushed on toward Alessandria. The 442nd RCT attack in the mountains was going much better than the 370th's assault along the coast. The 442nd ran into several log bunkers and machine gun emplacements that slowed progress, but with the air support and naval gunfire they captured several positions the first day. On the second day, the 442nd captured Monte Cerretta and moved toward Monte Belvedere. Committing its reserve 2nd Battalion, the 442nd RCT seized Monte Belvedere, the 2,800-foot peak overlooking Massa, in a cold rain on April 7. The 442nd then crossed the Frigido River and took Monte Brugiana on April 10. This completed the division's encirclement and capture of Massa, and the 442nd RCT entered the recently abandoned city of Carrara on April 11, 1945.[32]

The 442nd had accomplished more in the first six days of its attack against a well-established enemy than the 92nd's organic regiments had done in five months. Platoon Sergeant Frank Kimura of the 442nd's Company M judged the black soldiers of the 92nd Infantry Division harshly. "They couldn't break the line in six months, and we did it in four to six hours." Kimura boasted. "They were more or less cowards as far as I was concerned." The regiment's attack had turned the 92nd's mission from a diversionary effort into a full-scale offensive.[33]

As Almond had done during training, he toured the division area, constantly assessing the tactical situation. He spent most of every day of the offensive moving from unit to unit, personally monitoring their progress and giving guidance to his commanders. He focused exclusively on visiting his forward elements and left the headquarters operations and planning to his chief of staff. He began each day with an operational briefing with the division's principal staff officers. He would issue or modify orders at the end of the half-hour meeting, and then leave immediately to visit units.

Some days he traveled by jeep, driving himself, and he often drove fast. He also flew in his L-19 spotter plane. He had never lost his love for flying and liked to refresh the skills he learned at the Air Corps Tactical School. His aides kept notes on where he went, whom he saw, and the orders he issued. The aides then passed this information back to headquarters to keep the staff in touch with Almond as he hopped from one battalion to another. Almond returned to headquarters late in the evening for a briefing on the day's activities, and then developed plans for the next day's operations.[34]

On April 12, Almond returned from a long day of checking out progress. President Franklin D. Roosevelt's death had been reported that day over the radio. Almond received his mail, but put it in his pocket and sat down to eat a late dinner in his trailer. After dinner he opened a letter from his wife and was stunned to read that his son, Ned Jr., had been killed in action. "I suppose you know that our precious Ned was killed in action in Germany on March 19th," Margaret began. "The telegram just arrived." Her letter was poignant and remarkably brave:

> These are the things I want you to know. That I love you deeply with all my heart. All through the years—as our young son was growing up. All through the agony of my soul—you have been a wonderful husband and father. Your letters to him were a source of great joy. He mentioned them always Thank God. . . . You are away from me now and I must walk alone for our loss is together, in our only son. . . . I want you to know I am going to carry on, as you would want me to do. So do not worry about me. You and Peg and I have Tommy—all that is left of our threesome. He is a perfect little boy and with us he is waiting for you after the war is won.[35]

Despite Almond's rank and position, he had received no notification from the War Department, and his first news came with this letter from his wife. When the news became known, he received numerous condolence notes from his fellow general officers, and General Marshall wrote notes to both Almond and Margaret.[36]

The death of Ned Jr., coming just four months after Almond lost his son-in-law, Thomas Galloway, crushed him. He called Col. William McCaffrey over to his trailer and told him the news. McCaffrey was concerned about Almond's mental state. "Do you want me to call the doc to give you a shot so you'll sleep?" McCaffrey asked his stricken chief.[37] Almond refused, and told McCaffrey not to inform the corps headquarters of his personal tragedy. Almond vowed he would not allow his bereavement to interfere with his duties. He then wrote a touching letter to his wife:

> Tonight your letter came to tell me that Ned had been killed.

> For some days now I've had a premonition that something had happened to him but last night your letter of 29 Mch said you had a note from him on 18 March and it reassured me. . . . He was a fine boy. I shall always mourn his loss but with unmeasured pride that he had a part in destroying as many cursed Germans as he could. . . . Your letter is a brave one and I am very proud of you that you can be as true a soldier in your way as he was in his.
>
> You, Peggy, Tommy and I have proud memories of Tommy and Ned and we have the courage not to whimper as so many do; they died noble deaths for many less noble. But they served their native land with the supreme honor and sacrifice. Nothing is higher. When I come home we must make a fine man of Tommy and we have no better models than Tommy and Ned were. . . . I won't urge you to be brave for you have already demonstrated that so I say, be proud of Ned and take much satisfaction in having raised a fine boy who has born[e] himself nobly. All my love and I wish I could be with you for a moment to say I love you and that we shall bear our grief in nobleness.[38]

Almond sought the full details concerning his son's death, writing Ned's regimental commander, Col. Walter P. O'Brien, to ask for more information. The unit adjutant later provided a report of the fatal action, and where Ned Jr. had been buried. The loss of Tommy and Ned Jr. deeply affected the family. From Almond's first letter home, the family began to rally around Tommy Galloway Jr. as a symbol of youth and continuity in the family. Almond always doted on his grandson, but after Ned's death, Tommy Jr. replaced him as his lost "son." They remained very close for the remainder of Almond's life.

By a tragic coincidence, General Crittenberger had received word of the death of his own son just days earlier. After Almond wrote to Margaret, he sent a letter to Crittenberger consoling him for his loss and notifying him of Ned Jr.'s death. "You and I appreciate, by these events and those surrounding us here, the full measure of the tragedy of war; and after this one is over, may God forbid another. I just wanted to take this means of sympathizing with an old friend."[39]

Almond's lifelong dedication to soldiering helped him cope with this heartbreaking situation. By concentrating on his duties, he kept from being consumed by grief. The division's chaplain, Lt. Col. Louis J. Beasley, wrote to Margaret Almond a few days afterward to express his condolences and to report on Almond's well-being. He said that the division's officers had heard about Ned Jr.'s death on Friday, April 13, at their daily regular meeting. Almond opened the proceedings by announcing President Roosevelt's death and then sat down. At that, the chief of staff announced that Ned Jr. had been killed. Awkward silence followed, and then McCaffrey dismissed the officers. Chaplain Beasley tried several times to see Almond after the conference, but the general remained too busy to talk. Finally Beasley was able to pull Almond away from work on Sunday morning, April 15. Afterward he wrote his letter of condolence to Margaret, and reassured her that the general was coping well:

> I had a very long talk with him. As with any other father the experience is a most painful one for him, and as is typical of him he gave expression to his emotions and inner pain as is so characteristic of him. However, in the midst of it all, he gathers himself together and prosecutes his task here, relentlessly. Such are the traits of the strong man. . . . He is still the indefatigable worker you have known through the years. He is well and looks none the worse after seven (7) months of combat. Where he gets the strength he exerts day and night is still a baffling problem to all of us.[40]

Beasley concluded by noting that, even with Almond's tremendous daily responsibilities, and now great personal sorrow, he still maintained his sense of humor and could "have a good hearty laugh at times." The letter comforted Margaret Almond, and it also underscored the chaplain's relationship with Almond himself. Beasley's tactful discussion of Almond's emotions belied the latter's tough reputation. Beasley had been the division's only black field-grade officer for most of its training period, until the arrival of the new artillery commanders.[41]

As a chaplain rather than a line officer, Beasley had a different relationship with the division commander. Almond surely appreciated his attempts to help, and this cemented their relationship. Almond trusted and accepted Beasley, and they would remain in communication for years after the war. Beasley evidently also enjoyed a good relationship with the senior staff, as Colonel McCaffrey also corresponded with Beasley until the end of the clergyman's life.[42]

Despite Almond's deep sense of loss, the ongoing attack remained his primary concern. The Fifth Army began its main attack toward the Po Valley on April 14, and enemy resistance stiffened all along the line. The 92nd Division's attack had gone well, forcing the Germans to commit their reserve, the 90th Panzer Grenadier Division, which weakened the enemy center just as the Fifth Army attack commenced. The guns at Punta Bianca, despite heavy bombardment, continued to direct devastating fire on the advancing American RCTs. Almond spent the next five days attempting to destroy these guns. He dedicated a tank destroyer battalion (36 guns) and one 8-inch howitzer to targeting the Punta Bianca position. Each time the big guns fired, the tank destroyer battalion fired 60, and sometimes as many as 180, 76 mm rounds at it. The guns on the Punta Bianca peninsula were grouped in three or four batteries, inside concrete casements, and protected by antiaircraft artillery tanks and self-propelled artillery. The larger German guns could hit effectively all the way to the southern end of the 92nd Division's sector, but Almond could not range them with his own artillery until he captured Massa.[43]

The 365th and 371st Infantry Regiments, now stripped of their organic artillery and detached from the 92nd, held the west, or left, side of the corps line under IV Corps control. For the first time since they entered combat, these units seemed to grasp their mission. The commanders now realized that units perform well when they understand the mission and their leaders believe in them, harking back to the Pygmalion Effect. The 371st Infantry Regiment commander, Col. James Notestein, was thrilled with his unit's performance and proudly wrote Almond on April 15: "For the first time our troops maneuvered on level ground in superior numbers, with superior supporting fires. While companies had stragglers after the Co's were hit by artillery and mortar concentrations, each outfit came back with the idea that they were good and that the Tedeschi [Germans] were not invincible. You have told them these same things for six months, but this is the first time they believed it. "[44]

This must have been bittersweet news for Almond. These regiments were performing well in combat, with "substandard" soldiers but by following his training ethic. He could only attribute the RCT's success to the change in environment after it left the division. While Notestein credits Almond, the "change in environment" was a negative reflection on Almond's leadership. Whether the decisive factor was leaving Almond's troubled division or Notestein's positive attitude is unknown, but the change was noticeable. After this performance, General Truscott gave Notestein a larger portion of the sector.[45]

The 473rd RCT had reached the Carrione Creek on April 11, yet another obstacle the Germans used to great defensive advantage. This stream marked the first of the German "Winter Line" defenses, and the enemy stopped the assault in both the 442nd and 473rd sectors. The uncharacteristically rapid advance of Almond's infantry had outpaced the division's support capabilities. The attack stalled under a furious enemy artillery barrage, and Almond's guns were too far back to deliver effective counterbattery fire. American infantry slowed considerably as the enemy committed reserve forces to strengthen the defense, and the 92nd's supply trains struggled to keep up with front-line units. For five days the infantry continued to push forward in small increments while the tank destroyers, artillery, naval gunfire, and aerial bombardment worked to reduce the guns at Punta Bianca. The American bombardment finally forced the German gunners to withdraw on April 20, allowing Almond's advance to move much faster.[46]

When Almond launched the 442nd and 473rd attacks in the coastal region on April 8, he had moved the 370th to the division's right flank. The change of mission seemed to invigorate the soldiers. While the 442nd and 473rd RCTs continued their attacks, the 370th RCT made steady progress in a patrolling role. The enemy elements in the region included remnants of nearly a dozen understrength German and Italian units, which were withdrawing under continued attacks. On April 15 the enemy artillery increased markedly in the Serchio Valley, and the 370th soon discovered that this covered a full-scale withdrawal from the area. Based on this intelligence, Almond ordered Sherman to push forward and capture Castelnuovo, which fell easily on April 20. Almond then ordered the 473rd to seize Genoa on April 24. The 442nd was to follow and protect the northeast flank, and the 370th to drive north on Highways 62 and 63 through the Cisa and Ceretta passes, the only routes available for the withdrawing enemy to escape to the Po Valley. The German 148th Panzer Grenadier Division and the Italian Bersagleiri Division would thus be pushed into the path of the Brazilian Expeditionary Force and US 34th Infantry Division, at that time moving up the Po Valley to the northwest. The 473rd liberated Genoa on April 27, a day after the remaining German garrison had surrendered its positions. By May 25 the 92nd Division had traveled so far beyond Fifth Army lines of communication that Truscott passed control of it to Gen. Mark Clark at 15th Army Group.[47]

Genoa's capture effectively ended combat operations in Italy. Several Axis remnants held out for a couple more days, but by April 30 all resistance in the area had ceased. The 370th RCT had forced the two divisions it was pursuing to surrender to the BEF, the first large-scale surrender in Italy. The remaining German commands established a ceasefire and surrendered on May 2, 1945. With the war in Italy over, Almond established his occupation headquarters in Genoa. The 92nd

Division reverted to IV Corps control and assumed occupation of the Ligurian region. The 442nd and 473rd RCTs established roadblocks at the Swiss and Italian borders to prevent small enemy units from escaping and to collect prisoners of war. Crittenberger returned the 365th and 371st Infantry Regiments to Almond's control on May 10 and withdrew the 442nd and the 473rd Infantry Regiments, minus the artillery battalions, the following week. Almond immediately launched a "rehabilitation" program, inspecting each battalion and decorating soldiers. He held nightly parades and memorial services for the fallen.[48]

On June 6, 1945, Almond and the 92nd Infantry Division received their greatest honor of the war. They returned the ashes of Genoa's greatest hero, Christopher Columbus, to his home city. Genovese officials had removed and hidden the ashes and accompanying papers early in the war to keep them safe. Almond formed the division in the Piazza della Vittoria in front the massive War Memorial Arch. Capt. Harold Montgomery led Company H, 370th RCT, which escorted the urn containing the remains on a horse-drawn caisson draped with the Italian flag. Almond laid a wreath at the ashes after depositing them in their place of honor in City Hall, and then gave a short victory speech to the assembled soldiers and citizens of Genoa.[49]

Almond invited his staff to his trailer to celebrate V-E Day. The cessation of hostilities in Europe brought new assignments for both units and men. Almond had received orders sending Lt. Col. Ed Rowny to the War Department's Operations Planning Division (formerly War Plans Division) three months previously, but Almond had refused to release him. When Almond found an officer such as Rowny that he trusted, he mentored him and guided his career. As with McCaffrey, Almond had come to depend on Rowny, and Rowny earned Almond's lifelong respect and trust. With the Germans finally beaten in Italy, Almond released Rowny, who departed one week after the German surrender.[50]

Shortly after the war ended, Almond took leave in June to find his son's grave and learn more about the action that killed him, and he granted Brigadier General Wood leave at the same time. Brigadier General Colbern had already left for a new assignment stateside, so McCaffrey ran the division for about a month. McCaffrey believed that Almond did not like Wood, so he preferred that McCaffrey be in charge. Almond found Ned Jr.'s grave in a temporary cemetery in the Rhone Valley, but he initially had difficulty locating Tommy Galloway's resting place.[51]

Colonel McCaffrey also left the division shortly after Almond returned to Italy from France. The German surrender did not end the war. The War Department then devoted its full attention to the invasion and conquest of Japan. McCaffrey and many other colonels received regimental commands in the invasion force. McCaffrey took leave and then reported to the War Department for briefings. He remained there after Japan's surrender eliminated the need for an invasion.

Immediately after the German surrender, the War Department ordered all general officers in the European and Mediterranean Theaters of Operations to evaluate their subordinate generals and colonels for promotion. Truscott and Crittenberger both rated Almond superior. Each general was required to rank his subordinate generals in order of promotion recommendation. Crittenberger rated Almond second among the five major generals he supervised. Truscott endorsed Crittenberger's rating, but said that he would rate Almond first instead of second among his major generals. When Truscott rated all fifteen of his general officers, he rated Almond fourth among them. He rated only corps commanders Crittenberger and II Corps commander Maj. Gen. Geoffrey Keyes and the 1st Armored Division commander, Maj. Gen. Vernon Prichard, ahead of Almond.[52]

Almond received transfer orders while Truscott was away on a special mission in China. A little while later Truscott sent Almond a farewell letter that read: "In your kindly understanding of the problems of your men you have contributed immeasurably to the cooperation between the races, which is such an integral part of the great American Idea, for which we have fought this war. . . . a grateful nation is indebted to you for the superior devotion to duty and outstanding performance which characterized all your efforts in the leadership of the 92nd Division during its training period in the states, and throughout its period of service in Italy."[53]

The last six months of the war had brought both professional triumph and personal tragedy for Almond. After the division's failures in December and February, he certainly felt pressure to perform. The division's reorganization brought the opportunity for redemption, and he wanted to justify General Marshall's faith in him. Almond had good reason to be proud, as the new organization performed very well in combat. He must have believed Marshall's trust in him was justified. Ironically, Almond had shifted from commanding one of the most segregated units in the US Army to commanding the most integrated division. The 92nd Infantry Division during those months reflected a unique structure in the Army, with integration down to regimental level. The division's success after the restructuring seemed to justify his previous findings about black soldiers.

Creating one regiment with all the best soldiers from the other regiments seemed to help that regiment succeed, while adding the two other regiments seemed to give the division the confidence it needed to regain the initiative. Almond did not know it at the time, but this integrated unit's success would become one of the arguments for the integration of the rest of the Army.

Ironically, America's black press seized upon Almond's own postwar decoration as evidence of the division's exemplary performance. The *Afro-American* quoted Almond's citation for the Distinguished Service Medal, highlighting the many problems the 92nd faced in its combat operations but crediting the division with tying down one Italian division and two German ones. The article also reported that the division "attacked vigorously, seized the dominating terrain . . . and, in ensuing operations, captured La Spezia and the vital port at Genoa." This opportunity for reflected glory aside, the black press did not harbor a high opinion of Almond.[54]

The elation Almond felt at finally seeing his unit succeed, however, could not assuage the crushing sadness he felt at his son's death. His letters home to Margaret reveal a father's anguish, his seething anger at the Germans, his love for and devotion to his only grandson, and his steadfast intent to carry on with the mission. Almond's tremendous work ethic and dynamic personality helped him push past his personal grief and focus on his mission. Nevertheless, the sense of failure, and therefore inadequacy, haunted him. His new assignment offered him the opportunity to start again, to put all the personal and professional problems of the previous three years behind him. It would also present great challenges. Almond believed that "units don't fail, leaders do" in his heart, and though he outwardly blamed soldiers, he could not help but feel the mortification of personal failure. Despite the accolades and awards, that feeling would push him to work even harder to be successful in his future assignments.

10

New Challenges in Japan

1946–1950

As America once again demobilized after a large war, Ned Almond remained in uniform, becoming part of the officer corps that would lead the Army through its next conflict. This represented an important juncture in Almond's career, as he moved quickly from combat to demobilization and then to occupation duty. Almond received orders in July 1945 to relinquish command of the 92nd Infantry Division to General Wood and report to Camp Swift, Texas, near Austin, to command the 2nd Infantry Division for the planned Japanese invasion. Almond admitted he was anxious to command a "white" division in another war zone, clearly an opportunity to redeem himself. After an appropriate farewell ceremony, Almond departed for home on August 12. He and Margaret vacationed in White Sulphur Springs, West Virginia, and in Miami before he reported to Camp Swift. He took command of the 2nd Infantry Division on September 14, 1945.[1]

The 2nd Infantry Division had recently returned from Europe to train for the planned invasion of Japan and possessed a similar structure to the 92nd Infantry Division, organized around three infantry regiments: the 9th, the 23rd, and the 38th. Each of these regiments formed the base of a regimental combat team with appropriate artillery and support units attached. The Pacific war had ended before Almond's arrival, so his mission had also changed. Almond soon found himself trying to establish discipline over a large number of soldiers who felt they had done their duty and just wanted quick discharges.[2]

Almond took command as the Army's demobilization process reached its most turbulent time. Instead of conducting invasion training, the War Department designated the 2nd Infantry Division as a "Discharged Area of Separation" for eight other divisions about to be demobilized. Those other divisions sent groups of soldiers to the 2nd Infantry Division's "casual camps" to await final demobilization and release from the Army. Most GIs simply did not understand the rules for demobilization, and many did not have enough combat points to qualify right away. These men quickly became disciplinary problems, as they saw no further need to continue adhering to military regulations.

The formula for discharging soldiers after V-E (Victory in Europe) Day was based on an Adjusted Service Rating (ASR) score. The ASR assigned points to each soldier based on length of service, length of time overseas, combat experience and decorations, number of minor children, and the needs of the Army. After V-J (Victory over Japan) Day, however, the War Department moved to a system based primarily on length of service. Beginning in January 1946, those with three and a half years of service were released, dropping to two and a half years by April, then two years in July. This contributed to the chaotic process. Almond answered hundreds of requests from congressmen, senators, families, and employers asking to know when certain soldiers would be released.[3]

Unlike his experience forming the 92nd Division, when Almond arrived at Camp Swift he found a cohesive cadre of combat-hardened officers, several of whom he would later recall for service in Korea. Col. Philip D. Ginder commanded the 9th Infantry Regiment, and Almond would shortly make him his chief of staff. Lt. Col. Frank T. Mildren served as the division G3. Mildren was commissioned into the infantry after graduation from West Point in 1939 and assigned to the 2nd Infantry Division, where he advanced rapidly and commanded battalions in the 23rd and 38th Infantry regiments. He remained with the 2nd Infantry Division when it returned to the States after the war, and was its G3 when Almond arrived to assume command. Col. John H. Chiles, commander of the 23rd Infantry Regiment, had spent the entire war in the 2nd Infantry Division. He had commanded a battalion in the 9th Infantry Regiment before taking command of the 23rd Infantry.[4]

After the initial rush of demobilization, Almond tried to settle his new division and its remaining troops into training. He tried implementing a normal training plan as he had in the 92nd, but the constant personnel turnover hindered his efforts. Despite the important changes under way in the Army at the time, such as moves toward Universal Military Training (UMT) and desegregation, Almond was more concerned with the specific challenges he faced. In this postwar environment, the troops and even some of their senior leadership had lackadaisical attitudes toward training that helped eat away at readiness. The 38th Infantry Regiment's commander, Col. Francis H. Boos, identified the problem in a note to Almond. Boos had talked to Lt. Gen. Clarence Huebner, V Corps commander, about the division's training difficulties, and Huebner's response shocked him. Huebner did not understand why Almond was so focused on training. Boos quoted Huebner: "You people are too worried about training, you have a mission and you have the men. So if you're ready, you're ready and there's no training problem; so just sit." Boos believed he had some convincing to do, showing that training and morale were important issues, to which Huebner finally agreed. "He finally allowed as how this matter of training, morale, and keeping men properly occupied was a real problem but nothing much to bother you after the problems you've had in the past," Boos reported. "He seemed of the impression that whatever problems we may have [in] the division is a shining light in handling them compared to conditions everywhere else. And I found the same impression among many others I talked to."[5]

Fortunately for Almond, not everyone shared Huebner's opinion. Almond's boss, Maj. Gen. John P. Lucas, Fourth Army commander, chided Almond in the fall of 1945 for letting discipline slip, noting, "The fact that the war is over is no excuse for slackening in the standards of military courtesy, appearance, or discipline." Such mixed messages from senior officers no doubt stung Almond as he worked to mold his new command. By September 1945, Almond forecasted that the demobilization of eligible soldiers would be complete by March 1946, and the division would stabilize at about 10,000 soldiers and be prepared to train.[6] By December, however, the division strength had dipped to 8,076.

With the war over, the issue of black soldiers in the Army came to the forefront, as the Truman administration explored the idea of desegregating the military. On October 1, 1945, Secretary of War Robert P. Patterson ordered Lt. Gen. Alvan C. Gillem to convene a board of officers to study the idea. From the beginning, the Army's wartime efforts had focused on personnel efficiency rather than fairness to black soldiers. Patterson directed the board to develop a policy for using black soldiers in both wartime and peacetime in order to achieve maximum use of available manpower. The War Department hoped to learn from its experiences in the two world wars, eliminate certain problems, and use its soldiers more efficiently.[7]

The move also helped relieve the growing political pressure from the black community. The black press immediately took up the cause of ending segregation, and used the combat experiences of the 92nd Infantry Division as evidence for doing so. *Pittsburgh Courier* columnist George Collins argued that the division's history proved: "No matter how many Negro units, in no matter how many branches of the service the Army may organize, the fact of segregation, the pandering to the racial ideas of a small segment of the Nation, serves only to vitiate the purpose for which those units are formed, to weaken the total defense power of the Nation."[8]

Collins placed Almond at the center of the division's problems. The debate still raged a year later, as *Pittsburgh Courier* special correspondent Roi Ottley argued that "the Negro troops lacked confidence in their white command, believing it to be incompetent, unsympathetic, prejudice[d], and often stupidly vicious." Ottley concluded that it was "a wonder that the division did as well as it did do."[9]

The board considered more than seventy studies on black soldier and unit performance during both world wars, including Almond's reports on the 92nd Division and Truman K. Gibson's report of his visit to Almond's command. The material also contained information on the black experience in the European Theater of Operations, training reports from Army Ground Forces (AGF), and information from the 93rd Infantry Division and other Pacific units.[10]

In addition to gathering documentary evidence, the board conducted fifty-two interviews with commanders from all over the US Army. The 92nd Infantry Division provided the most extensive combat experience for black soldiers during the war, so its record received the closest scrutiny. The board interviewed Almond, Colbern, McCaffrey, Rowny, and Lt. Col. George O. Weber, one of Almond's former battalion commanders. The board also called Generals Willis D. Crittenberger and Benjamin O. Davis Sr. and Col. Benjamin O. Davis Jr. Civilian board respondents included the two civilian aides to the secretary of war, William Hastie and Truman K. Gibson. Maj. Gen. Henry H. Johnson, the former commander of the 93rd Infantry Division, was the only member of that organization called to testify. The board did not shy away from senior leaders, and interviewed Gen. George C. Marshall and Gen. Jacob Devers, the AGF commanding general. Almond took little further interest in the issue of black troops after he testified before the Gillem Board, but the Army's slow reaction to that board's work illustrates the attitudes prevalent in the service at the time.[11]

The Army interpreted the Gillem Board results as justification for maintaining "separate but equal" facilities under the pretense of giving black officers equal rights. In a society still dominated by Jim Crow customs, the federal government failed to challenge local traditions. The Army's decision confirmed the notion commonly mouthed by whites that, while partial integration was possible and even necessary, full integration was not realistic. Army leadership acknowledged that units could be integrated down to the regimental level, but not below except in extraordinary circumstances. This reaction to the Gillem Board reflects the institutional prejudice that existed throughout the US Army, and that Almond and other leaders supported and encouraged. These leaders doubtless saw this as benevolent paternalism rather than racism. As these meetings and decisions occurred, however, Almond remained remote from them. After his brief testimony, Almond left his previous problems behind, ignoring the issue that would form such a large part of his legacy.[12]

In February 1946 the War Department ordered Almond to move the 2nd Infantry Division to Fort Lewis, Washington, a more permanent station with adequate housing and training facilities. Camp Swift had been a temporary wartime training base and would be closed as the defense establishment began to contract. In April the division headquarters and two of its RCTs moved to Fort Lewis via San Francisco, where they participated in a welcome parade for Gen. Joseph Stilwell as he arrived to take command of the Sixth Army at the Presidio of San Francisco. The 38th Infantry Regiment had received a large number of soldiers from the inactivating 10th Mountain Division. That regiment went to Fort Carson, Colorado, for summer mountain training, followed by winter training at Camp McCoy, Wisconsin, before rejoining the 2nd Division at Fort Lewis, where the remainder of the division would be conducting amphibious training.[13]

The postwar drawdown produced turbulence throughout the military establishment. While many units returned to the United States for demobilization, many remained overseas for occupation duty. While the soldiers and junior officers rotated home according to the points plan, new draftees and recruits took their places. By 1946 the War Department had begun rotating general officers based on their length of service overseas. Many American general officers in the Pacific had been deployed there for the entire war, and were anxious to come home. Almond had spent comparatively little time overseas, since his unit deployed in late 1944, so he was among those generals eligible for foreign duty. The Army Ground Forces G1, Maj. Gen. David G. Barr, offered Almond a choice of assignments: the attaché position in Moscow, or serving in General Headquarters, US Army Forces, Pacific (GHQ, AFPAC) in Japan under the legendary General of the Army Douglas MacArthur. Almond later said he had no use for Communists, and he refused the Moscow assignment. Another opportunity opened at about the same time. Lt. Gen. Charles E. Kilbourne, VMI's superintendent, was nearing retirement, and he approached General Marshall to see if Almond would be available to replace him. Almond appreciated the chance to return to his alma mater, but he declined. As much as he loved VMI, the job would have required him to retire. Having rejected those two options, Almond accepted the Tokyo assignment.[14]

There were other potential opportunities for Almond as well, though he did not know it at the time. His friend Maj. Gen. Al Gruenther mentioned to him in the fall of 1947 that the War Department had considered Almond to replace Gruenther as deputy commandant of the National War College, but nominated Maj. Gen. Lyman Lemnitzer instead because he was already in Washington and familiar with the NWC. The War Department had also flirted with the idea of removing Almond from the assignment in Japan to have him head the Joint Strategic Survey Committee, but demurred to keep from angering MacArthur. Even though Almond was personally unknown to MacArthur at the time, Almond had been promised to him.[15]

Almond flew to Tokyo on June 6, 1946, and joined twelve other general officers awaiting assignments. Maj. Gen. Paul J. Mueller served as MacArthur's GHQ chief of staff, supervising two staffs, each with its own deputy chief of staff: the SCAP (Supreme Commander, Allied Powers) staff and the AFPAC staff. Mueller assigned Almond to the AFPAC staff as the assistant deputy chief of staff for personnel (G1). Almond had never worked in personnel before, but he quickly managed to make himself extremely useful to MacArthur. He managed the myriad personnel requirements throughout the Far East, rotating people back to the States, coordinating their replacements, and arranging for transportation and quartering of dependents. The command included all US Army units in Japan and Okinawa, Korea, Guam, and the Philippines.[16]

General Headquarters, Tokyo, was a foreign world in more than just locale. As Supreme Commander, Allied Powers, General of the Army Douglas MacArthur reigned as a virtual shogun in Japan. The Joint Chiefs of Staff (JCS) gave MacArthur dual responsibilities in the theater. As SCAP, MacArthur headed all American, Australian, British, Indian, New Zealand, and Canadian forces conducting occupation duties in Japan, Korea, and the formerly Japanese-held islands. In this capacity he also had broad authority to establish occupation policies. As commander in chief, AFPAC, MacArthur commanded all US Army forces in the Pacific. He did not generally like having "outsiders" assisting him, and famously distrusted officers who had not served with him in the Pacific, particularly those who had served in Europe. Despite this, Almond quickly became one of MacArthur's most trusted lieutenants. The two had similar personalities, and MacArthur came to recognize and value Almond's absolute loyalty. Almond served as G1 from June to November 1946. When Maj. Gen. Percy Clarkson, AFPAC deputy chief of staff, returned to the States, Almond replaced him. Almond assumed the position just in time to supervise the transition of AFPAC into the new Far East Command (FECOM). The JCS had created a new Unified Command Plan in 1946, designed both to eliminate squabbles in the Pacific between the Army and the Navy and to assign areas of responsibility in the rest of the world. FECOM activated on January 1, 1947, with the Army chief of staff as executive agent, making it an "Army theater."[17]

Once Almond arrived in Tokyo, he surrounded himself with men he considered capable, as did many senior officers of that era, and ensured they reached positions of responsibility. The first of his former officers that Almond recalled was Lt. Col. Ed Rowny, then at Yale in an international relations and engineering graduate program. He and Almond had stayed in touch, and Rowny offered his services to Almond after graduating. Almond requested that the US Army G1 send Rowny to Japan as soon as possible. Almond had also identified several officers in the 2nd Infantry Division whom he respected, and he worked to get them to Japan as well. Col. P. D. Ginder came to Tokyo in 1947 as the executive officer of the G3 section, and the following year he became the deputy G3. Col. John Chiles had left the division one year after Almond went to Tokyo, and attended the Armed Forces Staff College. Immediately after his graduation, Almond brought him to Tokyo as secretary of the General Staff. Lt. Col. Donald P. Christensen (G1) also soon found himself again under Almond's command, and more would follow.[18]

Racial integration was not the only major upheaval to rock the Army in the years after World War II. As early as 1944 the government had explored the possibility of combining the services into one unified department. With the war over, President Truman accelerated the pace of this unification. The National Security Act of 1947 (NSA 1947) created a new National Military Establishment (NME). Under the act, the War Department became the Department of the Army, and the Army Air Forces moved to the newly created Department of the Air Force. Two years later, an amendment to NSA 1947 created the Department of Defense (DoD) and mandated that DoD headquarters supervise these two departments, Army and Air Force, and the Department of the Navy. The secretary of defense replaced the secretary of war in the cabinet, and the service secretaries were reduced to subcabinet rank. NSA 1947 also solidified the position of the chairman of the Joint Chiefs of Staff, who represented the service chiefs on the National Security Council. The Air Force gained a chief of staff as a full member of the Joint Chiefs, but the Marines remained subordinate to the Navy. The commandant of the Marine Corps attended meetings of the Joint Chiefs only when Marine Corps matters were under discussion.[19]

As the Army and Navy, and to a lesser extent the new Air Force, wrangled over declining budgets, each service worked to secure its future through defining increased missions. The growing cold war with the Soviet Union shifted the strategic emphasis toward Air Force–dominated nuclear war. President Harry S. Truman imposed austerity measures on DoD to save money, and all signs seemed to point to adoption of a strategy based on the US Air Force winning the next war without the use of large numbers of troops or ships. On July 26, 1947, President Truman issued Executive Order 9877, giving responsibility to the Army for airborne and joint amphibious operations. This rankled the Marine Corps, which considered amphibious operations its exclusive mission. Secretary of Defense James V. Forrestal met with the JCS in March 1948 in Key West, Florida, to identify specific roles and missions for each service, which resulted in the so-called Key West Agreement. President Truman revoked EO 9877 on April 21, 1948, and published the agreement as "Functions of the Armed Forces and the Joint Chiefs of Staff." The agreement left control of joint airborne operations to the Army but gave joint amphibious missions to the Marine Corps. Each service was allowed to develop its specific capabilities but would subordinate its operations to the controlling service in joint operations.[20]

While NSA 1947 specified that the Army would provide logistical support to the Air Force for the first two years, Almond feared it would become a permanent mission. He was especially troubled that without UMT and with the diversion of personnel to support services for the Air Force, Army manning would suffer. He believed the Army would have difficulty amassing large forces in the event of another major war. He asked Gen. J. Lawton "Lightning Joe" Collins, US Army deputy chief of staff, for details on how the separation of the forces would work, especially in AFPAC. Collins confirmed that the Army would provide support services but vowed that it would not be "solely a service installation for the Air Force."[21]

Shortly after Almond arrived in Tokyo, he wrote to his friend Col.

William McCaffrey, then serving at the Pentagon, that his family would be joining him shortly. Almond was especially anxious to see his grandson, Tommy: "I think they will be happy and where we will have a good chance to develop Tommy in his younger years. He is a great little fellow, smart and alert and very observing. He is much like his father and in later years we hope to develop those many fine characteristics which his father possessed." Almond's wife Margaret, daughter Margaret (Peggy) Galloway, and grandson Tommy Galloway arrived in August 1946 and settled down in a plush villa in Tokyo. After Ned Jr.'s death, little Tommy had become Almond's surrogate son.[22]

In May 1947, Peggy married Captain Charles Fergusson, a cavalry officer assigned to the 1st Cavalry Division in Tokyo and a West Point classmate of her late husband. Peggy's remarriage pleased Almond, and Charles adopted three-year-old Tommy, but Almond continued to dote on his grandson. After the wedding, Charles, Peggy, and Tommy moved to a small apartment close to Almond's villa. Almond came home every day and picked up Tommy for lunch, and then drove him back to his mother's house. The Fergussons left Japan in July 1948 for Princeton University, where Charles entered graduate school in preparation for a West Point teaching assignment. Almond found his grandson's absence painful, and he wrote to the boy regularly for the remainder of his service in the Far East.[23]

After World War II, the War Department gave families of soldiers buried in overseas cemeteries the option of having their loved ones' remains returned to the United States. Almond consulted with the Galloway family, and together they decided to have the remains of Ned Jr. and Tommy Galloway Sr. disinterred and reburied in Arlington National Cemetery. The bodies arrived in the United States in late 1948, and Almond arranged with the quartermaster general to store the bodies after their arrival. He asked the US Army chief of chaplains to provide both a priest for Tommy, who had been Catholic, and a Protestant chaplain for Ned Jr. Almond returned to the States with Margaret for the funeral, and he wanted Tommy Jr. to be involved because he would be old enough to remember it. Thomas T. Galloway and Edward M. Almond Jr. were buried side by side in Section 2, Arlington National Cemetery, in January 1949.[24]

In February 1949, Maj. Gen. Paul Mueller returned to the States, and Almond became the FECOM chief of staff. CINCFE was a unified rather than a pure joint command, which meant that MacArthur commanded the theater through the senior commanders of the other services.[25] As Commander in Chief, Far East (CINCFE) MacArthur's subordinate US commands included US Eighth Army; Headquarters and Service Group, GHQ; Ryukyus Command (RYCOM); Marianas-Bonins Command (MARBO); US Thirteenth Air Force; US Naval Forces Far East (NAVFE), and US Far East Air Forces (FEAF). The Joint Chiefs expected MacArthur to support US policies in the areas he controlled, and to prepare to meet a general emergency at any time.

Despite the reorganization and new name, the staffs and their functions remained essentially the same. The reorganization applied primarily to the major units and responsibilities assigned to the command. Almond's replacement as deputy chief of staff was Maj. Gen. Doyle O. Hickey, a fifty-five-year-old artilleryman who had commanded the 3rd Armored Division for the last months of the last war, after that unit's commander, Maj. Gen. Maurice Rose, was killed in action. Hickey arrived in Tokyo in January 1949, having previously been assigned as assistant chief for developments, Army Field Forces. Maj. Gen. Alonzo P. Fox, who had arrived with Almond in 1946 as the executive for economic and industrial affairs, became the deputy chief of staff for SCAP, Hickey's counterpart on the government side.[26]

Almond usually arrived at work ninety minutes before MacArthur and read everything requiring his chief's attention that had come in overnight. MacArthur kept very odd hours, usually arriving about 10:30. After MacArthur settled in, Almond met with him to bring him up to date on various projects and staff actions. MacArthur then went home for lunch and a nap, returned to work about 4:30 or 5:00 p.m., and worked late into the evening, sometimes as late as midnight, seven days a week. After meeting with MacArthur, Almond took his guidance and instruction to the rest of the staff. This insulated MacArthur from the staff, and made Almond indispensable to him. This is the job of any chief of staff, but MacArthur preferred to deal directly with very few people. Almond was, by his own admission, a tough taskmaster. "My thought was that I could estimate about the time it would take to do a job, and I gave them adequate time," Almond later recalled. "But I was impatient, I'm sure, with those who didn't deliver what I wanted in a time that I thought it was necessary and adequate to complete the task." Thus he continued the habit of underestimating the amount of time required for any task. While this often pushed staff and commanders to excellence, it just as often disrupted operations and bred anger and resentment among subordinates who failed to meet sometimes unrealistic expectations. MacArthur also delegated to the chief of staff the delivery of bad news, so disapprovals appeared over Almond's signature. This often proved a point of friction with subordinate commanders.[27]

Almond refused to leave the office until MacArthur did, and his close-range, daily view of MacArthur provided insights into his chief's character. MacArthur once commented on his strange schedule and told Almond he need not keep the same. Almond should leave one staff officer in each section, he said, and go home whenever he chose. Almond refused, and told MacArthur that nothing he could do would disturb him. "Why is that?" MacArthur asked. "Because once I commanded the 92nd Infantry Division," Almond replied, and MacArthur laughed and walked away. This lighthearted banter indicates the casual, institutional racism in the Army of the day, and it also reveals the scars Almond still carried from his time in Italy.[28]

The chief of staff position carried an additional social responsibility. General MacArthur occasionally hosted visiting dignitaries for a brief luncheon at the embassy, but he did not conduct or participate in any evening social activities. MacArthur chose to limit his social interactions so as to maintain the prestige of the command. When Mueller returned to the States, this duty fell to Almond, and he and Margaret enjoyed hosting frequent dinner parties and entertaining guests.[29]

Despite an increasingly close relationship with MacArthur, Almond faced competition for his favor with Maj. Gen. Courtney Whitney and Maj. Gen. Charles A. Willoughby. Whitney and Willoughby were the last remnants of MacArthur's "Bataan Gang": those officers who had been with MacArthur in the Philippines during the last war. No other member of his staff was closer to MacArthur, not even Almond. Whitney, MacArthur's fifty-three-year-old chief of the Government Section of the SCAP staff, was charged with dealing with the Japanese and forming the democratic system of government. His primary role, however, was to function as MacArthur's chief confidant. After initial service as a Signal Corps officer, Whitney resigned his commission and moved to the Philippines to open a private law practice, where he first encountered MacArthur. Whitney returned to active duty in 1940 as an attorney, and three years later MacArthur had him moved to his Southwest Pacific Area (SWPA) staff.[30]

Whitney alone among all the staff could simply walk into MacArthur's office, sit down, and talk to MacArthur without an appointment. Almond and Whitney disliked each other intensely, their antipathy doubtless driven by mutual jealousy. Almond later recalled, "Whitney was a smart, ruthless, and incisive lawyer. He realized early in his career, I'm sure, the advantage of being a satellite to MacArthur. He made it his business to be agreeable with MacArthur. He would go to great lengths to obtain his purposes. He had a thick-skin attitude toward delicate matters, such as sitting in MacArthur's presence when he should have withdrawn. For example, when I'd go in to see MacArthur on matters, Whitney would be there, even though it didn't pertain to him."[31]

Almond could as easily have been describing himself in relation to being MacArthur's disciple, and he clearly did not like the competition from Whitney. Whitney used MacArthur's desire for information on the Japanese to leverage MacArthur. He would go out and talk to the Japanese, and then spend hours in MacArthur's office relating the information, and maintaining access. Senior American officers regarded occupation duty as relatively unimportant, and wanted to get back to the States to "prominent, worthwhile" positions. Whitney used this to his advantage, since alternate legal talent of the same caliber was not available to MacArthur. Almond rarely acknowledged MacArthur's weaknesses, but he said that that the general remained too loyal to men who had served with him previously, especially Whitney.[32]

Almond's relationship with Willoughby was less contentious, but he still competed with Willoughby for MacArthur's favor. Born Charles Adolph Weidenbach in Germany in 1892, Willoughby later emigrated to the United States to join his mother's family, and then enlisted in the US Army. After serving for three years, he left the Army to complete a bachelor's degree at Pennsylvania College (now Gettysburg College), then obtained a commission as a US Army officer just before World War I.[33]

Like Almond, Willoughby had commanded African American troops; he commanded a battalion of the 24th Infantry Regiment in 1919–1920 in New Mexico. Willoughby attended service and branch schools during the interwar years, and he also served as a military attaché in Venezuela, Colombia, and Ecuador and worked in the Military Intelligence Division of the War Department General Staff. In 1940, Willoughby was ordered to the Philippines, where he joined MacArthur's SWPA staff. MacArthur charged him first with organizing the defenses of Bataan, and then assigned him as his intelligence officer, a position he retained throughout World War II.[34] When Almond arrived in Tokyo, Willoughby continued as MacArthur's intelligence officer, retaining the position of GHQ G2 and occupying intelligence positions on both the FECOM and SCAP staffs. He thought highly of Almond, calling him a "high grade professional."[35]

The feeling was mutual, as Almond found Willoughby a "highly intelligent individual," though he found him excitable and prone to dismiss people's opinions when they ran counter to his own. Almond's two-year course at CGSS in 1928–1930 had overlapped with Willoughby's, but they evidently did not become close friends. Despite his generally friendly relationship with Willoughby, which Almond maintained until the latter's death, he resented Willoughby's ability to bypass him and go directly to MacArthur. Almond's later writings and interviews indicate a certain self-awareness, but he failed to note that the negative traits he found in both Whitney and Willoughby were those he shared with them.[36]

Despite those challenges, Almond supervised an excellent GHQ staff, which contained a mixture of MacArthur cronies and new blood. The end of World War II had found MacArthur surrounded by acolytes, but the passage of time had thinned their ranks. MacArthur preferred having his "own" people, Pacific veterans, on his staff, but he also made converts of those who joined the staff later. Brig. Gen. Edwin K. "Pinky" Wright was the FECOM G3 and led the Joint Strategic Plans and Operations Group (JSPOG), which was MacArthur's joint planning agency. Wright kept FECOM priorities in line with the Joint Chiefs of Staff, which saw maintaining bases in Asia, including those in Japan, as ultimately risky. Wright, a very capable officer and a favorite of Gen. Omar N. Bradley, had served under Bradley in the 12th Army Group, and Bradley had taken him with him to the new Veterans Administration. Bradley had then seconded Wright to the nascent Central Intelligence Agency in 1946. When Wright came to Tokyo in 1949, his expertise and experience in national intelligence made him a MacArthur favorite. Wright was a calming influence on the staff to counter Almond's volatility. Yet he and Maj. Gen. William A. Beiderlinden (G1-Personnel) and Maj. Gen. George L. Eberle (G4-Logistics) worked well with Hickey and Almond.[37]

In addition to the military staff, Almond's personal staff in Tokyo included an aide-de-camp who would go on to great renown himself. Alexander M. Haig was a twenty-six-year-old lieutenant, three years out of West Point, in his first Army assignment. Haig had been born into minor privilege living on Philadelphia's Main Line in Bala Cynwyd. His father, Alexander Sr., had served in World War I, and Haig spent his early youth playing with his father's Army uniform. He credited that experience with setting him on the path to his own career. Any early advantages Haig may have gained as the son of a prominent Philadelphia lawyer evaporated when his father passed away shortly after Haig's ninth birthday. He spent the remainder of his youth in a hardscrabble existence, aided at key points by a prominent uncle, who assisted him first with admission to Notre Dame, where he spent one year, and finally with a congressional appointment to the US Military Academy.[38]

Haig entered West Point in 1944, the last of the war-shortened three-year classes. He was a good student, but he showed no affinity for mathematics or science at an institution renowned for engineering. His cadet career was also marred by numerous disciplinary infractions, and he finished 214th out of 310. At graduation in 1947, Haig received a commission as an armor officer and assignment to Tokyo. After spending about a year as a platoon leader in the 1st Cavalry Division, Haig was selected as a general's aide-de-camp at AFPAC headquarters, where he had the good fortune to serve among many senior officers and observe operations at a very high level. The relationship between a general and his aide-de-camp is a close one; no one sees the general more often, even key staff officers. Aides often find the position a leadership laboratory, and many aides go on to flag rank themselves. These officers can become closer than family to their generals, especially in combat, and come to know their boss's personality intimately. Haig's close-range observations of Almond are valuable in that they represent those of a junior officer thrust into a challenging position, but filtered through his own four decades of experience and high command. While at headquarters, Haig also sometimes worked for Maj. Gen. Alonzo P. Fox, whose daughter Patricia quickly made an impression on the lieutenant. A courtship followed, and they were married on May 24, 1950, with Maj. Gen. and Mrs. Almond in attendance.[39]

FECOM's huge 265,000 square miles included Japan, the Ryukyu Islands, the Philippines, the Mariana Islands, the Volcano Islands, and the Bonin Islands, but not Korea. Though Korea was outside the US "defensive perimeter" in 1950, it would soon become the most important area in the world. The US government had occupied half of Korea since the end of World War II. JCS interest in Korea waxed and waned after World War II, and the entire region never climbed very high in American strategic priorities. Joint staff planners grappled with steeply declining budgets as they first addressed problems in Europe and the Middle East before turning to Asia. Within Asia, several issues ranked ahead of Korea on the scale of strategic problems, including the security of Japan, the Chinese threat to Formosa, a war in French Indochina, a new alliance between China and the USSR, and the possibility of war between China and India.

Lt. Gen. John R. Hodge commanded the XXIV Corps, dubbed US Army Forces in Korea (USAFIK), occupying South Korea (south of the

38th Parallel) as a bulwark against the Soviet influence in North Korea. Maj. Gen. Archibald V. Arnold, commanding the 7th Infantry Division, also headed the US Army Military Government in Korea (USAMGIK). Given the confusion over US intent, MacArthur argued that he could not occupy Korea with the forces available. He sent Almond to the Pentagon in 1947 to advocate strengthening the US occupation forces in Korea by bringing the depleted XXIV Corps to wartime strength, reasoning that without this the State Department might as well take on Korea as a diplomatic issue. Almond later remembered the mission as one of presenting an alternative to the decision the JCS had already reached.[40]

Almond had presented MacArthur's views to the State-Army-Navy-Air Force Coordinating Committee, arguing that the occupation forces were too small to be effective. The JCS argued that Korea held little strategic interest. The US had also excluded Korea from its defense perimeter, and the JCS had recommended removing the 45,000 troops occupying Korea for use elsewhere. The JCS believed that, in the event of war in the Far East, holding ground troops in Korea would only be a hindrance to prosecuting a war elsewhere. The defense establishment's newfound faith in airpower led to the belief that if an enemy were to invest Korea with bases, US airpower could easily destroy them. The Defense Department felt it could not spare any more troops and eventually did pass along the "Korean problem" to the State Department, which then turned it over to the United Nations as an international issue. Notably, MacArthur relinquished all but logistics and emergency evacuation responsibility for Korea, with USAFIK reporting directly to the Department of the Army. Despite the potential backlash from the Soviets, the American occupiers began creating a South Korean army from the existing constabulary. The first units were modeled on American formations, and USAFIK sent advisors to each one to train the Koreans.[41]

In May 1948 the Republic of Korea's first true election saw Syngman Rhee elected president. When he assumed office on August 15, the United States officially ended the occupation and dissolved the USAMGIK. John J. Muccio arrived as the US envoy to Korea on August 27, and Maj. Gen. John Hodge transferred control of the new government to Rhee and his officials. Hodge began moving soldiers out of Korea the following month; all four understrength divisions had moved to Japan by January 1949. The XXIV Corps headquarters departed as well and deactivated in Japan, leaving one understrength combat team in Korea. That unit moved to Japan on July 1, 1949. The fledgling South Korean government was not yet ready for full independence, however, so the few remaining US forces became the Provisional Military Advisory Group (PMAG), later re-designated the Korean Military Advisory Group (KMAG).[42]

As occupation duties in Korea wound down, the American units in Japan turned toward more realistic training. When Lt. Gen. Walton H. "Johnny" Walker arrived in Japan in September 1948 to command the US Eighth Army (dubbed EUSA), he found significant readiness problems. The Eighth Army's four understrength divisions—1st Cavalry (organized as an infantry division), 7th Infantry, 24th Infantry, and 25th Infantry Divisions—reported directly to Walker, because XXIV Corps headquarters had been deactivated. Walker instituted a training plan aimed at making all four divisions combat ready by the end of 1950. He faced significant obstacles, including the lack of adequate training space in Japan, insufficient training funds and supplies, and a constant personnel turnover.[43]

Walker, a gruff sixty-one-year old protégé of General George S. Patton, had commanded XX Corps in Patton's legendary Third Army during World War II. Walker was three years older than Almond, but the early years of their careers had roughly paralleled each other. During World War I, Almond had commanded a machine gun company, and briefly the 12th Machine Gun Battalion, in the 4th Division, while Walker had briefly commanded the 13th Machine Gun Battalion in the 5th Division. Walker taught at West Point during the same years that Almond served as an instructor at Fort Benning. Walker later served as executive officer of the 5th Infantry Brigade, 3rd Infantry Division, earning the respect of his commander, then-Col. George C. Marshall. The beginning of World War II found Walker in the War Plans Division of the War Department General Staff, but he was quickly promoted and assigned command of the 3rd Armored Division. In August 1942, Walker assumed command of IV Armored Corps, a training unit for Army Ground Forces. The following year, the unit was redesignated XX Corps and assigned to Patton's Third Army.[44]

The relationship between Almond and Walker has become infamous, but the two men were not always at odds. When Walker arrived in Far East Command, Almond greeted him warmly. They had met as young officers in 1933 when their families returned to the United States from the Far East on the same ship—Almond from the Philippines, Walker from China—and in their letters they renewed their friendship and recalled their sons playing together as small boys. That old friendship soured after Walker arrived in Japan.[45]

Walker's association with the flamboyant Patton did not endear him to MacArthur; he did not command the sort of respect at headquarters that Almond did. Almond realized this, and treated Walker with a cavalier lack of respect. As the chief of staff, Almond jealously guarded access to MacArthur, with Whitney and Willoughby being the notable exceptions. Almond attempted to restrict Walker's access as well, violating the Army tradition that permitted subordinate commanders to go directly to the senior commander. Wright believed that this was the main problem between Almond and Walker. He recalled, "Almond resented the fact that Walker could come up and see General MacArthur anytime he wanted to." He went through Almond only for courtesy, but it was a condemned relationship. Walker's experience as a corps commander in World War II and now commander of a field army doubtless fed Almond's insecurity.[46]

The Far East Command, and specifically Walker's Eighth US Army, encountered a problem that Almond found familiar: poorly trained soldiers with low intelligence, though this time the soldiers were white. The command had reported to the National Military Establishment in April 1949 that 43 percent of the enlisted men assigned were Categories IV and V on the Army General Classification Test, and all had received incomplete basic training before going to the Far East. These challenges led to discipline and administrative problems, and affected readiness. Almond later recalled that routine occupation duties had prevented commanders from doing any meaningful training until those duties ended in the fall of 1949.[47]

The EUSA's NCOs were an even greater concern, with 35 percent of corporals and 23 percent of sergeants also testing in the two lowest AGCT categories. Rapid demobilization after World War II and reduced military budgets had resulted in abbreviated basic training. The Army reduced the standard thirteen-week training period to eight weeks and required units in the field to remedy the deficiencies found in each batch of conscripts. This imposed an unrealistic burden on the EUSA, whose units were widely scattered all over Japan. A constant turnover in personnel, which only filled the units to peacetime strength (60 percent of wartime), with shorter enlistments and conscript periods, made adequate training difficult. By 1949, 50 percent of new soldiers arriving in the Far East were under twenty years of age, and this resulted in reduced maturity levels and caused discipline problems.[48]

The US Army inspector general reviewed the EUSA in the spring of 1949, and found all these problems and more. The IG also faulted the Eighth Army's leadership, having discovered tensions between Regular Army and US Army Reserve officers, a feeling of abandonment because of the occupation stations, and lack of urgency or interest in training. He also found many service units completely untrained. Almond, fearing the report would reflect poorly on MacArthur, wrote a preemptive letter of rebuttal to Lt. Gen. Harold R. "Pink" Bull, US Army G3. Almond defended the Eighth Army, blaming its shortcomings solely on the soldiers' AGCT scores. Almond's shortsighted view of the problem, and his failure to credit the plans Walker had in place for correcting it, made Almond look small and doubtless angered Walker.[49]

Given the Army's World War II amphibious experience, and despite the Key West Agreement that gave proponency to the Marine Corps, the Army leadership believed the need for an amphibious capability still existed even in the new atomic age. JCS planners recognized the utility of potential amphibious operations, perhaps to mount a counterattack in Europe, and conducted several large, joint amphibious operations in 1948 and 1949. MacArthur ordered the GHQ staff to plan regimental-sized exercises, and then a division-sized landing in Okinawa beginning in May 1950. The plan, code-named Bluehearts, followed a study called SL-17 and had been approved and distributed in early June 1950.[50]

Almond took an active role as chief of staff in planning these amphibious operations, working to find adequate shipping when the Navy was unable to provide enough landing craft.[51] GHQ established an amphibious training center at Camp McGill, seventy-five miles southwest of Tokyo, and Army officers with World War II amphibious experience went there to help set up training. Marine Col. Edward H. Forney brought Mobile Training Team Able from Camp Pendleton, California, to assist in this effort. Training began on June 1, 1950. The 35th Infantry Regiment, 24th Infantry Division, arrived for training on April 29 at Camp McGill, followed in May by the 5th Cavalry Regiment, 1st Cavalry Division. That training was both valuable and prescient, but it would soon be overcome by other events.[52]

The close of the 1940s found Ned Almond's career thriving in Japan. After another brief but frustrating command, he found success as a staff officer and trusted agent to one of the Army's most powerful and legendary officers. In a little more than two and a half years, Almond had moved from unknown outsider to ultimate insider. His appointment as chief of staff cemented his idolatrous relationship with MacArthur, which he maintained until the latter's death. Basking in the light of MacArthur's favor, he could put the shame he felt over the 92nd Division's collapse in Italy behind him. The Army had begun to change, however, taking its first small steps toward desegregation and universal service. Assignment to Japan had insulated Almond from those changes and placed him in a separate world. The US Army was, in effect, divided between soldiers in the States and those on occupation duty, especially those in MacArthur's command. That separation became all too evident when war came to Korea.

11

Planning for War

1950

On June 25, 1950, Lt. Col. Ed Rowny and Lt. Alexander Haig had the Sunday duty at General Headquarters, Far East Command. Shortly after 10:30 a.m., a message came in from Seoul alerting GHQ that the North Korean People's Army (NKPA) had attacked in force across the 38th Parallel separating North Korea from the Republic of Korea (ROK), its neighbor to the south (see map 11.1). Ambassador John J. Muccio said the attack included large formations of infantry and aircraft, and asserted "this is not a false alarm." Haig's and Rowny's recollections of the event differ slightly in the details, but both remembered trepidation in notifying the volcanic Almond, because of the large number of false alarms in the previous year. Haig regarded Almond as "brilliant, but irascible," and dreaded calling him with this news. After Haig assured Almond that Muccio regarded the invasion as genuine, Almond called MacArthur. MacArthur later noted in his memoirs that the receipt of such stunning news made him feel like he must be dreaming. "But then came the crisp, cool voice of my fine chief of staff, General Ned Almond," MacArthur recalled. "'Any orders, General?'"[1]

What orders, indeed. When war came in 1950, Almond was fifty-seven years old, four-and-a-fraction years from mandatory retirement. He stood 5'8" tall, with a slightly stooped posture despite his always correct military bearing. Almond's close-cropped gray hair was not unusual for men of his age, but visitors often found his piercing blue eyes distinctive with a hint of skepticism. He spoke with an unmistakable yet soft Virginia drawl, somewhat high-pitched and urgent. Haig remembered that "you had to prove yourself to him every day." Despite his age, Almond possessed the "athletic physique of a soldier who kept himself in shape for any duty he might be called upon to perform."[2]

At the time of the invasion, there were comparatively few forces in the ROK positioned to defend South Korea. The ROK Army mustered a mere eight divisions, only three of which contained more than 9,000 of

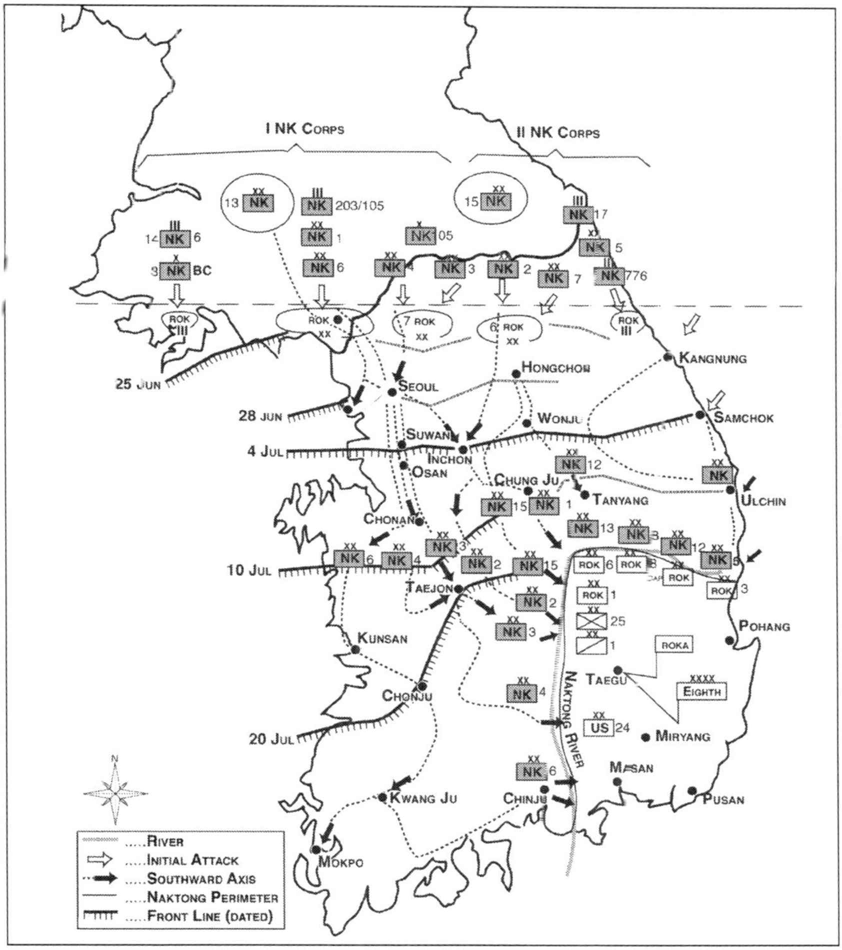

11.1. North Korean Attacks, June 25, 1950

their authorized 10,000 soldiers. Four divisions held positions along the 38th Parallel, and one regiment of the Capital Division, with the remainder of that division in Seoul. The other units were located in the southern portion of the peninsula. The initial attack devastated the ROK Army. From a divisional combat strength of about 65,000 soldiers at the time of the attack (see table 11.1), only about 40,000 remained two weeks later. The losses in personnel and equipment were so great that the ROK Army was forced to inactivate three divisions, and the five divisions it retained had a strength of fewer than 8,000 soldiers each.[3] The basic organization of the ROK division was the same as an American division, but it lacked much of the firepower of its US counterpart. The ROK division had few heavy weapons, limited primarily to .50 caliber machine guns, and only one artillery (105 mm) battalion. The United States began to try to build up the ROK Army quickly, but these deficiencies would last throughout much of the first year of the war.[4]

Table 11.1. Strength of the ROK Army as of June 25, 1950

Unit	Authorized	Present	Percent
Capital Division	10,000	7.061	71
1st Division	10,000	9,715	97
2nd Division	10,000	7,910	79
3rd Division	10,000	7,059	71
5th Division	10,000	7,276	73
6th Division	10,000	9,112	91
7th Division	10,000	9,698	97
8th Division	10,000	6,866	69
TOTAL	80,000	64,697	81

Source: Appleman, *South to the Naktong, North to the Yalu,* 15, table 1.

The sole American military unit in Korea, the Korean Military Advisory Group, included fewer than five hundred officers and enlisted men. The KMAG remained simply to assist the South Korean government in developing its security forces. In nearby Japan, MacArthur had only the four understrength, undertrained divisions assigned to the US Eighth Army (see table 11.2). Korea remained outside the FECOM area of responsibility, and MacArthur had no mandate to do anything in Korea except support the American Embassy and its ambassador, John J. Muccio. Nevertheless, on June 26 Almond ordered Brig. Gen. Edwin K. Wright to begin planning for Korean contingencies with the JSPOG.[5]

MacArthur immediately requested permission from the Joint Chiefs of Staff to send forces to Korea and to increase his units in Japan to full strength. When the JCS authorized MacArthur to take charge of all military activities in Korea, he sent a small group of officers to assess the situation. Brig. Gen. John Church led this GHQ Advance Command and Liaison Group (ADCOM) to Korea on June 27. ADCOM found the ROK Army fleeing south and Seoul in danger of falling to the North

Table 11.2. US Army Divisions in Japan

Unit	Authorized	Present	Percent
1st Calvary Division	18,900	12,340	65
7th nfantry Division	18,900	12,907	63
24th Infantry Division	18,900	12,197	65
25th Infantry Division	18,900	15,018	79
TOTAL	75,600	52,462	69

Source: Appleman, *South to the Naktong, North to the Yalu,* 50n2

Koreans. Church worked with KMAG and ROK officers to try to stabilize the line, and then notified MacArthur.[6]

At Almond's urging, MacArthur visited Korea to examine the situation personally, flying into Suwon Airfield thirty miles south of Seoul on June 29. Almond, Willoughby, Wright, Far East Air Forces commander Lt. Gen. George Stratemeyer, and several staff officers accompanied MacArthur. After three hours of briefings from General Church and his staff, MacArthur asked to see the battle area for himself. Almond and MacArthur rode together to Yongdungpo, on the south bank of the Han River near Seoul. The ROK Army had destroyed the bridges over the river, but the NKPA had already captured the South Korean capital. MacArthur remained silent for most of the trip, mentioning only one thing: all the ROK soldiers they passed on the road retreating were armed, fully supplied with ammunition, smiling, and showing no evidence of wounds. That convinced him that the ROK Army was not fighting, and that the United States needed to commit significant forces to the Korean Peninsula.[7]

The JCS authorized MacArthur to send one American regiment to Korea immediately and, after initial hesitation, cleared him to send more formations to stabilize the ROK Army. MacArthur began ferrying troops from Japan to the southeast Korean port of Pusan. He also designated Walker as the ground commander in Korea pending the deployment of EUSA. Almond recommended deploying one stripped-down infantry battalion and one artillery battery to Korea as quickly as possible. A shortage of transportation forced the Eighth Army to deploy to South Korea in piecemeal fashion, and proximity dictated that the 24th Infantry Division units should go first. After dispatching the 1st Battalion, 21st Infantry (later designated Task Force Smith after its commander, Lt. Col. Brad

Smith), on July 1, Walker began stripping other units from the Eighth Army to bring the 24th Infantry Division up to full strength.[8]

MacArthur had contemplated relieving Walker when the Korean conflict began, but instead left him in place and remained in Tokyo. MacArthur was not alone in his sentiments; Chairman of the Joint Chiefs Gen. Omar N. Bradley believed the job called for a "younger, more vigorous man—a Van Fleet or a Ridgway." When President Truman sent Averill Harriman to Korea on a fact-finding mission in early August, he also recommended relieving Walker and replacing him with Ridgway. Army Chief of Staff General J. Lawton "Joe" Collins demurred, however, because he planned to elevate Ridgway to deputy chief of staff the following year.[9]

The remainder of the 24th Infantry Division landed in Korea by July 6, 1950, and the 25th Infantry Division began boarding ships in Japan on July 8. Walker established his command post at Taegu in the southeast corner of South Korea on July 13 and began organizing the divisions into a defense as they arrived, christening his forces the Eighth US Army in Korea (EUSAK). The hastily organized and deployed units, however, were unable to mount a solid defense. By July 26, Walker had made plans to withdraw to the Naktong River, and he called Almond in Tokyo to notify MacArthur. Almond agreed to pass along the information, but warned Walker that the retreat might have a deleterious effect on EUSAK morale. Almond then told MacArthur, and recommended that he visit Korea as soon as possible.[10]

MacArthur and Almond visited Walker at Taegu the next day, and MacArthur issued emphatic orders to hold the line. Taking Walker aside, MacArthur told him he could conduct reconnaissance and engineer preparations, but any decision to retreat would be MacArthur's alone. Almond later recalled that MacArthur told Walker, "There will be no . . . Dunkirk in this command. To retire to Pusan will be unacceptable." Walker must have considered this a dressing down, and one that stung all the more because of his attempts to ready the Eighth Army for war. Almond was the only other officer present, which doubtless embarrassed Walker. Almond and Walker already had a contentious relationship, and this could not have helped. Almond acknowledged Walker's fighting spirit, however, and recalled that Walker then stepped back in front of his staff and told them, "This army fights where it stands. There will be no retirement." Almond recalled that Walker's staff had been surprised by this, evidently hoping they would withdraw.[11]

Two days later, Walker began visiting the divisions, starting with the 25th Infantry. Walker recalled MacArthur's comments to him, as he exhorted his commanders, "There will be no Dunkirk, there will be no Bataan, a retreat to Pusan would be one of the greatest butcheries in history. We must fight until the end. Capture by these people is worse than death itself. We will fight as a team. If some of us must die, we will die fighting together." The speech gained notoriety as the "stand or die" order, and bred a certain amount of confusion as EUSAK continued to withdraw. During the first week of August 1950, Walker set up a defensive line along the Naktong River. The river formed a natural barrier running more than eighty miles from the vicinity of Hamchang south until the Naktong joined the Nam and flowed east. Walker's northern defense extended from Hamchang to a point near Yongdok. The terrain from Naktong-ri to Yongdok on the coast provided an anchor for the northern part of the defense. It became known as the Pusan Perimeter for the major seaport it protected.[12]

MacArthur conceived a daring plan to relieve pressure on the Pusan Perimeter. He envisioned an amphibious assault at Korea's second largest port, Inchon, in the middle of the peninsula's western coast, and a quick lunge east to recapture Seoul. On July 2, 1950, Almond ordered the FECOM Joint Strategic Plans and Operations Group (JSPOG) to begin staff studies for an amphibious operation to hit the North Koreans in the rear and cut their highway and rail lines and thus relieve pressure on the Naktong line. MacArthur envisioned a possible double envelopment, or pincer movement, at Inchon and Wonsan if sufficient forces were available. When war came, FECOM's amphibious training exercise already underway in Japan reflected the command's belief in the importance of amphibious operations.[13]

MacArthur set an aggressive timeline, with D-Day planned for July 18, but EUSAK had withdrawn too far by July 8 to make a landing at Inchon feasible. At the suggestion of Rear Adm. James H. Doyle, commander of the Navy's Amphibious Group One, MacArthur switched the planned landing to Pohang, a port on the southeast coast close to Pusan. The JSPOG staff continued to develop alternatives: plan 100-B envisioned a landing at Inchon, plan 100-C at Kunsan on the Korean west coast south of Inchon, and plan 100-D at Jumanjin on the east coast, with the alternate landing beaches at Jinnapon on the west coast and Wonsan on the east coast. This last landing option aimed a strike in the NKPA rear, diverting enemy attention and resources from the Pusan

Perimeter and allowing EUSAK there to launch a counterattack. The subsequent recapture of Seoul would produce a salubrious effect on American and South Korean morale (see map 10.2). Regardless of the options, MacArthur continued to prefer Inchon.[14]

The frenetic planning effort caused additional friction between Almond and Walker, especially after planning began in earnest for an amphibious landing. Relations between the FECOM staff and the EUSAK staff reflected the tensions between their chiefs. GHQ staff officers held the EUSAK staff in low regard. Walker staff viewed the FECOM staff as meddlesome and unhelpful. Neither staff was prepared for contingency war planning, and the urgency of the situation made for a chaotic environment. Miscommunication was inevitable, and only made matters worse. In early planning, for example, GHQ had earmarked the 1st Cavalry Division as part of the invasion force, but word of that decision failed to reach Walker. When an unknowing Walker ordered the division to Pusan, Almond became angry. The FECOM G3 explained the confusion and Almond calmed down, but the affair did not improve his relationship with Walker. The situation in Korea had become so desperate that MacArthur released the 1st Cavalry Division from planning for the main amphibious assault and ordered it to land at Pohang. The division landed in three lifts between July 18 and July 29.[15]

With amphibious operations in the planning stages, MacArthur requested additional forces through the JCS. He asked for a Marine regimental combat team, the amphibious-trained 2nd Infantry Division from Fort Lewis, Washington, an airborne infantry RCT, and several support units. He also requested two corps headquarters, since these had deactivated during the restructuring in 1949. MacArthur committed the Marine RCT and the 2nd Infantry Division and one of the corps headquarters to the Pusan Perimeter, but he earmarked the second corps headquarters to plan for the amphibious operation. He also designated the 7th Infantry Division, the one remaining division in Japan, as the attack force in the amphibious mission.[16]

Tactical air support concerned Almond early in the operation, though he praised the Air Force's efforts. Early air support missions using B-29 strategic bombers had been partially successful, but the infantry needed more than bombing runs. The bombers struck important targets beyond the Pusan Perimeter that slowed the North Korean advance, but the infantry needed the close air support that only tactical fighter-bombers could provide. Almond wrote Collins in mid-July describing operations in Korea and pointing out the need for better support for the infantry: "This application of even B-29s to the support of our ground forces where so sorely needed gives us hope that more effective methods based on experience will be developed. . . . I have nothing but praise for how air support has been rendered in present operations. My only desire, as I explained to you, is to apply more power in places which will relieve our sorely pressed infantrymen."[17]

Almond intended this letter to give Collins the information he needed to pressure the Air Force into increasing emphasis on tactical (close) air support. Almond noted that air ground control and use of spotter planes showed improvement, and the Army had "great faith in building greater efficiency in this system." EUSAK organized Tactical Air Control Parties early on that became very successful. Almond quoted a dispatch from Walker: "I think the air is learning methods to give us closer support." Almond conducted similar correspondence with Brig. Gen. William Colbern, the assistant commandant of the Artillery School, who had commanded Almond's artillery during War II. Colbern noted that the Artillery School had been developing the concept of a "forward air controller" based largely on the Rover Joe and Horsefly operations they had used during World War II, and he forwarded to Almond the latest doctrinal manuals. Tactical air support would remain one of Almond's interests for the rest of his career.[18]

On July 10, Almond's friend and fellow VMI graduate, Marine Lt. Gen. Lemuel C. Shepherd, commander of Fleet Marine Force, Pacific, came to visit MacArthur to suggest including more marines in the invasion force. Almond encouraged Shepherd to offer a full Marine division to MacArthur, though such forces were not readily available. MacArthur remembered his successful use of the 1st Marine Division during World War II and amended his earlier request for a Marine RCT to a full Marine division, with supporting air components.[19]

After talking with Shepherd, MacArthur began to visualize the landing force and its follow-on mission to capture Seoul. The deployment of the 24th Infantry, 25th Infantry, and 1st Cavalry Divisions left only the Army's badly understrength 7th Infantry Division in Japan, to be joined by the requested Marine division. At the end of July 1950, the 7th Infantry Division was 9,117 soldiers understrength, having lost them to fill vacancies in the other three divisions. In the days before the war the JSPOG may have been MacArthur's grudging acknowledgment of the need for joint planning, but once war came, it became the core of the FECOM planning effort.

While the command gathered additional forces, Almond began

assembling his team. Every commander likes to work with the best subordinates available. Almond selected as the corps chief of staff Maj. Gen. Clark L. "Nick" Ruffner, who had recently arrived in Japan. Almond did not know Ruffner, but MacArthur recommended him. Almond and Ruffner became fast friends, with Ruffner joining his chief's group of close confidants. He formed a small group of staff officers with Lt. Col. Rowny as one of his lead planners, designated them Force "X," and put them to work on a plan dubbed Operation Chromite. Almond lodged Force X in Building AP-1, an unused aircraft hangar in the FECOM motor pool. Almond earned opprobrium then and later for "cherry-picking" the FECOM staff to provide the best officers for the planning group, and Almond admitted he stripped MacArthur's GHQ of some of its ablest officers. Yet this was not an unrealistic practice. Planning for war had become the headquarters' most important function, and finding the best people to do that planning was reasonable.[20]

As good as that team was, it had no experience in planning or coordination for amphibious operations. On August 19, Almond attached Col. Edward H. Forney (USMC) and his twelve-member Mobile Training Team A, Troop Training Unit, Amphibious Training Command, to the Force X planning staff. Almond made Forney deputy chief of staff and divided the other officers among the staff sections according to their areas of expertise. In addition to amphibious operations, this gave Almond experts in fire support coordination, air operations, targeting, and naval gunfire.[21]

He experienced difficulty, however, in ordering supplies from the States. His requirements got snarled in military red tape. The supply system did not recognize Force X as a legitimate unit and rejected his requisitions as invalid. Almond finally brought the problem to MacArthur on August 10 and suggested that the planning group be designated as a corps headquarters in order to alleviate the supply bottleneck. Almond recommended that MacArthur call it X Corps, serving the twofold purpose of playing on the Force X name and recalling one of MacArthur's World War II corps, whose shoulder patch featured the Roman numeral X as its symbol. MacArthur readily agreed, and the Department of the Army authorized MacArthur to activate X Corps on August 26.[22]

With the matter of a unit designation settled, Almond asked who would command X Corps. MacArthur's answer shocked Almond: "You will be the landing force commander and I will accompany the landing force." Almond protested that he was the GHQ chief of staff and could not perform both roles. MacArthur responded, "Oh, we'll all be back in two weeks. You can turn your job over to Hickey and let him be acting chief of staff while you are in command of this force." MacArthur believed that after a quick strike at Inchon to break the enemy's back, he would turn over the "mopping up" operation to EUSAK. Almond believed that X Corps would join Walker's EUSAK after the landing. Almond later remembered, "I had no idea that I would have anything to do with the execution of the plan that might be devised."[23]

In one of the most controversial decisions of Almond's Korean experience, he issued orders as the GHQ chief of staff, creating X Corps as the GHQ Reserve, and assigning all units in Japan or en route there to X Corps. Almond then assumed command of X Corps. The decision had been MacArthur's, but Almond's signature on the orders convinced many that he had influenced his chief's judgment. It rankled even more those who already found Almond difficult. Almond himself later acknowledged the incongruity of the situation in a letter to his wife just after the Inchon landing: "It is a rarity indeed when one has the opportunity to plan his campaign as chief of staff in a high headquarters, then execute the plan."[24]

MacArthur enjoyed a great deal of public prestige and a legendary status among military officers. The Joint Chiefs of Staff, however, had grown weary of MacArthur's independence. They regarded him with a mixture of awe and suspicion, and monitored his actions closely. They were shocked when MacArthur announced Almond as X Corps commander. MacArthur's machinations surprised General Collins, who believed Shepherd would get the job. Adm. Forrest Sherman, the chief of naval operations, had already recommended to the JCS that Shepherd provide the headquarters and staff for the landing force from Fleet Marine Force, Pacific. MacArthur had presented his decision to strike Inchon as a fait accompli and expected the chiefs simply to endorse it; such arrogance angered many in the Army and the other services. Further, the JCS viewed Almond as MacArthur's man, which would remove X Corps even further from Washington's control.[25]

MacArthur's selection of Almond did not surprise everyone. Lt. Gen. Matthew B. Ridgway, the deputy chief of staff for administration (G3), believed that appointing Almond gave MacArthur someone he trusted to carry out his plans: "Almond was a highly capable officer and a fine Corps Commander. I think General MacArthur recognized his ability before he made him his Chief of Staff. . . . No doubt due in part to his feelings about Walker he did not want to place Almond under Walker's command because, I think more than anything else, MacArthur wanted to pull the strings from Tokyo. He wanted that corps under his direct command."[26]

Gen. Omar N. Bradley, chairman of the Joint Chiefs of Staff, clearly thought well of Almond as well, having known him since their days teaching together at Fort Benning. "He was a career officer of extraordinary ability," Bradley declared in his memoirs. "Almond was not the usual yes-man or sycophant that seemed to gravitate to MacArthur's staffs." Bradley expressed a minority opinion on the last point, but he clearly respected Almond's abilities.[27]

Almond later noted that MacArthur encountered a lot of opposition to his decision to land at Inchon. The Joint Chiefs became so alarmed that they sent a delegation of officers to Tokyo to try to persuade MacArthur not to go through with the operation. The JCS party consisted of Admiral Sherman, General Collins, General Shepherd, US Air Force deputy chief of staff Lt. Gen. Idwal H. Edwards, and Adm. Arthur W. Radford, commander of the US Pacific Fleet. They met with MacArthur and his staff on August 23. There were many good reasons not to land at Inchon, an unpredictable tide chief among them. At thirty-one feet, the tidal exchange in Inchon Harbor was the second highest in the world. Ships could reach the docks only at high tide, for low tide left mudflats a thousand yards wide off the beach. The operation would need to be timed perfectly, because the evening high tide was thirteen hours after the morning tide. Just before MacArthur walked into the briefing room, Almond stopped him and said, "They are here to talk you out of this. Don't let them." MacArthur smiled and passed on. MacArthur's GHQ staff talked for three hours, and then MacArthur made his pitch. The chiefs had been unmoved by the staff presentation, but MacArthur won them over.[28]

Before Collins departed, he asked Almond if there was anything else he could do to aid in the operation of the plan. Almond replied by handing Collins a list of thirty names of officers with whom he had served in Europe and the 2nd Infantry Division. "When I presented this to General Collins he almost had heart failure." Collins protested that these people, some of whom were generals, were in important positions such as the Pentagon staff. One of those names was Col. William J. McCaffrey, who Collins noted had just moved to a new position at the Infantry School. Almond argued that he particularly wanted McCaffrey and planned to make him his assistant chief of staff. Almond was able to get about a third of the officers he requested.[29]

After the JCS meeting, Almond turned over his chief of staff responsbilities to Hickey and focused on inspecting elements of X Corps. Retaining a habit from his World War II days, he traveled to see all of his units as they prepared to embark for Inchon. Time was short, but Almond managed to conduct a three-day field exercise with the fledgling X Corps headquarters during which he prepared staff officers for their required functions. He practiced moving the headquarters ten miles while maintaining control of notional units in combat operations.[30]

For the remaining positions Almond selected deputies and other officers recommended by their chiefs. With an eye toward leaving the GHQ and JSPOG staffs intact, Almond left "Pinky" Wright in place as the GHQ G3 and selected his secretary of the general staff, Col. Jack Chiles, whom he had brought from the 2nd Infantry Division, as corps G3. Lt. Col. Olinto M. Barsanti as corps G1 (Personnel), Col. William W. Quinn as corps G2 (Intelligence), and Col. Aubrey Smith as corps G4 (Logistics) rounded out the staff. Lt. Col. Frank Mildren, who had served as 2nd Division's G3 and had commanded the 23rd Infantry Regiment (alternating with Chiles), had recently taken a new job in the Pentagon when Almond's request came through. He would arrive later and become Chiles's deputy.[31]

Not all officers waited for the call from Tokyo. McCaffrey wrote Almond a letter on August 23 offering his services; Almond received the letter five days later and replied by message that he had already requested McCaffrey by name, directly through General Collins. Almond later called McCaffrey "one of the best young officers I have ever served with" and made him X Corps's assistant chief of staff. McCaffrey arrived just before the Inchon landing.[32]

One of the many junior officers swept up in the stateside push to quickly fill out FECOM requirements was thirty-two-year-old Lt. Col. Ellis Warren Williamson, a recent graduate of the US Army Command and General Staff College at Fort Leavenworth. Despite his youth, Williamson was a very experienced officer. He had enlisted in the North Carolina National Guard while still in high school and received a commission when that state's 30th Infantry Division was federalized for World War II. Williamson landed with the 120th Infantry Regiment at Normandy on D+5 and remained with the regiment throughout the war. After several promotions, he commanded 1st Battalion, 120th Infantry Regiment, in the Battle of the Bulge. Williamson integrated into the Regular Army after the war.

When Williamson arrived in Tokyo, he was initially assigned to JSPOG, and then became the assistant operations officer in X Corps G3.

Williamson reported that in the hectic days of planning for the Inchon landing, the headquarters often had difficulty requisitioning the proper supplies and equipment. The designation of X Corps headquarters had allowed the unit to requisition material from the States, but local supply depots in Japan often needed specific authorities under which the equipment was to be used. Invoking General MacArthur's name often was enough to break bureaucratic logjams, but the staff quickly developed a shorthand authority that seemed to work. They simply used the initials GASS, which stood for "General Almond Said So."[33]

Though the controversy about Almond's "dual-hatting" has dominated the historiography of his participation in the Korean War, in practice it did not amount to much after Inchon. Historian D. Clayton James is primarily responsible for establishing the legend of Almond as a dual-hatted chief of staff and corps commander. In a series of more than twenty interviews James conducted some twenty years later with key officers and senior commanders in Japan's occupation and the Korean War, he asked each a leading question: "Did you think it was strange that Almond was dual-hatted?" This question brought its share of disapproving responses, and there were negative aspects to the arrangement. In practice, however, Almond did not have time both to command X Corps and to function as MacArthur's chief of staff, and he quickly turned his responsibilities over to Hickey.[34]

From the staff perspective, the lines were clear. Wright, the GHQ G3, later remembered: "As far as [MacArthur] was concerned, his chief of staff was Doyle Hickey, no question about it. He never, for example, went around him and referred back to Almond on anything at all. But we felt a little strongly about it on the staff. We thought [dual-hatting] was wrong, and as far as we were concerned Doyle Hickey was the chief of staff."[35] For Almond's part, Wright contended, "During the time when he commanded X Corps, Ned Almond never exercised any of the functions of chief of staff. He was strictly the corps commander." Col. Frank Mildren recalled that Almond got very angry if anyone brought up the issue of dual-hatting, though he did occasionally use his clout with MacArthur to get what he needed. Despite all the concern over Almond's dual status, the practice has become commonplace in the years since. For his part, Almond never used the title Chief of Staff after August 26, 1950, in any of his official biographies for the remainder of his career. From that date forward, he is listed only as Commanding General, X Corps.[36]

The Joint Chiefs granted MacArthur's request for a Marine division and alerted the 1st Marine Division at Camp Pendleton, California. The 1st Marine Division organization mirrored that of an Army division, with three infantry regiments and support units. Marine regiments were larger than infantry regiments, and the division included a Marine air wing that Army divisions did not have, but it lacked the ground transportation necessary to move.

Marine Maj. Gen. Oliver P. Smith had been designated to command the 1st Marine Division on July 18, but he had not yet assumed his post when the JCS authorized the division to increase its personnel to war strength, with a directive to sail to Japan by August 15. Smith had received a commission in the US Marine Corps in 1917 after graduating from the University of California at Berkeley, but his first assignment found him at the Marine barracks in Guam rather than in France during World War I. After the war he held assignments attending Army schools and teaching in Marine Corps schools, as well as attaché positions in Haiti and France. He commanded the 1st Battalion, 6th Marines, from 1940 to 1942; however, the battalion deployed to Iceland and never saw combat. After two years at Headquarters, Marine Corps, Smith assumed command of the 5th Marine Regiment in the New Britain campaign. He received a promotion to brigadier general in April 1944 and was assigned as assistant division commander, 1st Marine Division, which captured Peleliu in September and October of that year.[37]

In a foreshadowing of his Korean War experience, Smith was next assigned as the deputy chief of staff, Tenth Army, commanded by Lt. Gen. Simon Bolivar Buckner. The Tenth Army consisted of an Army corps and a Marine amphibious corps. Buckner established a joint headquarters staff, with a deputy chief of staff from each service. Smith was known as a rising star in the Marine Corps and had been sent to Tenth Army as a gesture of goodwill during a period of tense Army–Marine Corps relations. Adm. Chester W. Nimitz, commander in chief, Pacific Ocean Areas, did not believe that the Tenth Army staff sufficiently understood the limitations necessary in amphibious operations. He directed Smith to work to reduce Army requirements in order to conform to the available shipping. As the senior marine on the Tenth Army staff, and with this specific guidance, Smith regarded himself as the savior sent to help the Army.[38]

Smith respected his Army peers and superiors, but his comments at the time reflected irritation with the Army way of doing business. The Tenth Army landed on Okinawa in April 1945 and secured the island two months later. Buckner was roundly criticized by senior Army officers for a plodding, risk-averse strategy that prolonged the operation and produced heavy casualties. Tellingly, Smith supported Buckner's risk-averse strategy. His own such predilections and irritation with Army procedures would later bring him into conflict with Almond.[39]

MacArthur's plan clearly relied on surprise and speed rather than combat power. Almond had few forces at his disposal for a large offensive operation: only the 1st Marine Division and the Army's 7th Infantry Division. GHQ began diverting all infantry and artillery replacements arriving in the theater to the 7th Division to fill critical shortages. MacArthur had approved these diversions to begin building combat power for an offensive operation, thereby risking a rupture in Walker's defensive lines. This decision further poisoned Almond's relationship with Walker, who desperately needed replacements to shore up the Pusan Perimeter.[40]

Beset by a grave manpower shortage, MacArthur appealed to the Korean government for augmentation by Korean citizens. The government readily agreed, and by mid-August thousands of recruits began arriving at EUSAK to help fill holes in the line. Some of those recruits, called Korean Augmentees to US Army (KATUSAs), went to Japan to join the 7th Infantry Division. The division received more than 8,600 KATUSAs before it embarked for Inchon, bringing its total strength up to 24,845. The KATUSA program was only moderately successful. The ROK government conscripted men right off the street and sent them to the US Army with no military training at all. The 7th Infantry Division integrated them throughout the command at the ratio of 100 per company or battery, and paired each KATUSA with a US soldier in a "buddy" system.[41]

EUSAK units formed KATUSAs and their buddies into separate platoons with American officers and NCOs. The lack of military training and the language barrier prevented the experiment from being successful, and the units dropped the buddy system as new American replacements arrived throughout the fall and winter. American officers and NCOs then organized the KATUSAs into squads and platoons with American leaders, and used them for security, limited patrolling, and labor details. The KATUSAs were more effective under these circumstances.[42]

Almond's selection to command X Corps, rather than Shepherd or Smith, had angered the Marines. Almond's G3, Colonel Chiles, ascribed the deterioration of the Almond-Smith relationship primarily to the latter's reluctance to serve under an Army commander, doubtless fueled by World War II experience. Chiles related that Almond and Smith hated each other by their second meeting, but he conceded that Almond was overbearing and abrasive. Smith's concerns about the extent and complexity of this mission were well founded, and he was particularly concerned about his division's capabilities, given its current structure.

When Smith arrived in Japan, the 1st Marine Division consisted only of the 1st Marine Provisional Brigade under the command of Brig. Gen. Edward A. Craig, which had deployed into Pusan on August 3. The brigade included the division's only active regiments: the 5th Marine Regiment (Infantry), 11th Marine Regiment (Artillery), and Marine Aircraft Group-33 (MAG-33). The 5th Marine Regiment, commanded by Lt. Col. Raymond L. Murray, remained with the Eighth Army in the Pusan Perimeter.

The 1st Marine Regiment, commanded by the already legendary Col. Lewis B. "Chesty" Puller, and the 7th Marine Regiment, commanded by Col. Homer D. Litzenburg, had both activated on August 7, 1950, and were still forming at Camp Pendleton. In the years after World War II, the Marine Corps had experienced the same budget pressures as the other services, but the push to reduce their structure had fallen particularly hard on the smallest of the services. In order to fill out the remaining two regiments, the commandant of the Marine Corps directed that the 2nd Marine Division at Camp Lejeune, North Carolina, be stripped to fill all available spaces in the 1st Marine Division. The commandant had also recalled individual current Marine reservists and reserve units, some of whom had already deployed with the provisional brigade. Security force units around the country were authorized to reduce to 50 percent manning in order to provide marines to deploy. Finally, the 3rd Battalion, 6th Marines, currently deployed in the Mediterranean, was re-flagged as 3rd Battalion, 7th Marines and ordered to move directly to Korea.[43]

Walker was hesitant to release Marine units for the landing because of concerns over morale within the perimeter. GHQ promised to pull out the 5th Marines to join the 1st Marines for the invasion, and replace them with an Army regiment. The 7th Marine Regiment was still assembling in California. Smith's mission analysis, however, did not address the 7th Infantry Division's parallel mission, and Smith did not appear to attach any importance to the 7th Division at all.[44]

Smith met Almond for the first time on August 22, 1950. He had come to the headquarters in Tokyo to meet MacArthur, but was irritated because neither MacArthur nor Almond was present when he arrived, and he had to wait for an hour and a half. His first impression of Almond was not good: "He was supercilious in manner. He discussed the forthcoming operation with me. I voiced objections. . . . With a wave of the hand, he said there was no organized enemy anyway, that our difficulties were purely mechanical, and that the date was fixed. Then he questioned me as to my command experience. He insisted upon calling me 'son '"[45]

Such apparent condescension was bound to irritate a man only ten months Almond's junior. Lt. Haig recognized the problems between Almond and Smith early on, and had ample opportunity to observe his chief closely. He did not believe that Almond intended to be condescending. "[Almond's] affection for his men was genuine and, again resembling MacArthur, fatherly: he called most soldiers and officers, including other generals, "son,' but he usually called me only Haig, possibly because I was too close to him for intimacy to work." Once again, however, Almond's unconscious linguistic paternalism served to irritate his subordinates and reduce his effectiveness.[46]

Almond went in to talk to MacArthur before bringing Smith in. Smith then described being "ushered into his presence" and being greeted warmly by MacArthur. Smith appreciated that Almond prepared MacArthur to talk to Smith. "It was apparent that Gen. Almond had briefed him on my objections." MacArthur then spent several minutes explaining the plan to Smith. He emphasized that the North Koreans were heavily engaged at the Pusan Perimeter, and therefore the landings would not be heavily opposed. MacArthur said he understood that the Marines always strove for perfection and that the Inchon landings would be somewhat helter-skelter. MacArthur tried to allay Smith's misgivings, telling him the war would be over in a month anyway.[47]

Almond's own comment, though tactless, was grounded in his vision of the landing as merely the first step in a larger campaign. He had less experience with the Marines than did MacArthur, but doubtless reflected MacArthur's confidence. He was conveying respect for the Marines' ability to accomplish the mission, rather than disrespect for its complexity, but at the same time subtly pointing out that the landing itself paled in comparison to the mission of capturing Seoul. The actual operation would prove Almond correct. To Smith and other Marine officers with experience in amphibious operations during World War II, however, this seemed foolhardy and reckless. Stuck with a corps commander whose competence he doubted, Smith's attitude toward Almond soured.

During a second briefing the following day with Almond and Maj. Gen. David Barr, CG, 7th Infantry Division, Smith brought up the possibility of doing the landing at a separate location: Posung-Myon. Relations with Almond became worse during this conference, because Smith felt that Almond arrogantly disregarded his thoughts. Almond rejected the second landing idea altogether, unless it were to be a subsidiary landing to Inchon. Smith believed Almond and other Army planners ignored the landing itself and focused on the follow-on mission to "cut the enemy line of communication." Almond's detractors perceived his stand as an example of his unblinking devotion to MacArthur, but the point obscures a larger issue. MacArthur's primary operational goal was to capture Seoul, and landing at Inchon provided the best opportunity for strategic surprise. Almond explained that the capture of Seoul was the primary objective, not just cutting the lines of communication. The next day Smith and several senior Navy officers met with the GHQ staff to air their concerns about the landing. It was clear from that meeting that the Navy had not understood, or not been properly briefed on, the major objective of the mission, which was to capture Seoul. After Smith understood that, he admitted that the secondary landing area at Posung-Myon was inappropriate and directed his staff to begin planning for the landing at Inchon.[48]

The friction between Almond and Smith stemmed more from a clash of service cultures than of strong individual personalities. Acknowledging that the Marines had fought heroically and been very successful in Korea, Haig said that Almond appreciated their sacrifices but could not understand Marine Corps tactical doctrines, "which most often seem to involve identifying the enemy strong point and overwhelming it by frontal assault." MacArthur's desire to use envelopment to overcome strong points was evident in the campaign to reduce Seoul. MacArthur's "island hopping campaign" in the Southwest Pacific during World War II is more properly described as "maneuver from the sea." While each island's campaign might have included frontal assault at a tactical level, MacArthur used a series of strategic envelopments and developments to continually try to turn the Japanese flank, cut lines of communication, and threaten support bases.[49]

The Marine Corps viewed amphibious operations as its key mission, requiring complex planning and coordination. The Navy–Marine Corps "Mid-Pacific doctrine" (a post–World War II term) called for removing the landing force shortly after securing the beachhead, and preparing for follow-on operations—a reflection of MacArthur's World War II operations. Army doctrine, however, followed the "European and Mediterranean" model, which held that the landing force assaulted the beach and then remained engaged for continental operations—the conquest of Europe. The landing was, therefore, a means to an end. The two concepts, as described, generalize the World War II European and Pacific experiences.[50]

The viability of a landing at Posung-Myon illustrated the Army–Marine Corps operational dichotomy. While Posung-Myon had a better beach profile than Inchon and would have been easier to capture, a reconnaissance team found the beach exits to be completely unsuitable for getting an American force inland. Moreover, Kunsan was too far south of Seoul to enable the landing force to capture the city. Almond later explained: "The real essence of the Inchon landing was not merely to land and form a beachhead but to drive across difficult terrain eighteen miles and capture a large city and thereafter properly outpost and protect that city and to furnish 'the anvil' upon which the Eighth Army would hammer the enemy which had been taken in reverse."[51]

Smith attended several briefings at GHQ headquarters, and his diary comments expose the haphazard and somewhat unrealistic planning process Smith found at FECOM. Smith assessed one briefing: "Correct as to form, but having nothing particular to do with reality. . . . I found, from this presentation, . . . [I was to] capture the Kimpo airfield, then cross the Han River, capture Seoul and the high ground North thereof, then fortify a line north of Seoul which was about 30 miles in extent, then when relieved (apparently by the 3rd Division still in the US), re-cross the Han River. . . prepared to attack in the direction of Inchon."[52] This tendency toward hyperbole, with an offended sense of persecution, reflected Smith's attitude throughout his service in Korea.

The plan called for the Marines to land on the island called Wolmi-do, a triangular outcropping of high ground that protected the approach to Inchon Harbor. The 7th Infantry Division would land in the harbor at the docks and advance on Inchon. The tide presented the greatest challenges to the landing. The first Marine unit ashore would land on the first high tide on September 15 and hold its ground until the remainder landed on the next high tide eleven hours later. The ships would arrive in the transport area off the mouth of the harbor at low tide at about 11:30 p.m. and would land at high tide, beginning about 5:00 a.m. The LCVPs (landing craft, vehicle, personnel) and the LVTs (landing vehicle tracked) required 23 feet of water, but the LSTs (landing ship, tank) required 29 feet.[53]

Though Smith was generally uncomplimentary toward Almond, he occasionally acknowledged brief instances in which Almond showed his support. In late August 1950 the Marines began unloading commercial shipping in Kobe, Japan, and reconfiguring and preparing for the landing at Inchon. The dock managers at Kobe, however, would not allow Smith to have any warehouses for use in unloading, reconfiguring, and reloading his troops and equipment. He asked Almond for help with that, and Almond directed his G4 to fly to Kobe immediately and sort out the situation. Despite Almond's alleged antipathy toward the Marine Corps, he took a paternal view of the Marines from the moment of their assignment as he did all of his Army units, perhaps having learned some harsh lessons from his World War II experience.[54]

Discussions that engaged Smith and the Navy and Marines on one side and Almond and the Army on the other side, in the days immediately preceding the landing, reflected large disconnects between Army and Navy concepts of the operation. Smith's most pressing problem continued to be getting the 5th Marines released from the Pusan Perimeter. In a heated discussion between Smith, Almond, Ruffner, and Seventh Fleet commander Vice Adm. Arthur Struble, Smith made it clear that without the 5th Marines present he would not be able to complete the landings as designed. Almond had offered the 32nd RCT from the 7th Infantry Division as a substitute, but Smith did not believe that the Army unit could easily adapt to the amphibious operations of the Marines. Smith argued that if he could not get the 5th Marines in time, he would modify the operation by eliminating one of the landings.[55]

Almond's ignorance of the details required for amphibious landing aside, he again underestimated the time required for all necessary operations. Even if he could have swapped the 32nd Infantry Regiment for the 5th Marine Regiment, the ships required to conduct the operation were already in Korea. Moving them back to Japan to pick up the 32nd Infantry Regiment and then back to Korea to download and pick up the 5th Marine Regiment would have made the planned assault on 15 September impossible. The Navy at last stepped forward to cut the Gordian knot, as Smith reported: "Adm. Struble suggested that one of the regiments of the 7th Division be embarked immediately, proceed to Pusan, act as a floating reserve for General Walker, and thus permit the release of the 5th Marines." Almond like this idea immediately and took it back to MacArthur, who readily agreed. Walker was ordered to release the 5th Marine Regiment at midnight on September 5.[56]

The 3rd Infantry Division, and other units in the States, faced problems similar to those of units already in the Far East. The immediate demand for replacements in Japan and Korea had decimated stateside units that were already understrength. Maj. Gen. Robert H. Soule had assumed command of the 3rd Infantry Division at Fort Benning, Georgia, in August 1950, shortly before the division was ordered to go to war strength and deploy. The Army had removed so many soldiers from the division to fill vacancies elsewhere that Soule reduced his 30th Infantry Regiment to cadre strength and placed all his remaining soldiers in the 15th Infantry Regiment. Soule's third regiment, the 7th Infantry Regiment, commanded by Col. John S. Guthrie, was stationed at Fort Devens, Massachusetts. It had already lost one battalion as a unit replacement for Korea.

As the 3rd Infantry Division and its two remaining regiments prepared to deploy, the Army staff assigned the 65th Infantry Regiment to round out the division for combat in Korea. When forty-three-year-old Col. William W. Harris received an alert to move his 65th Infantry Regiment from Puerto Rico to Korea, he had been in command for a little over a year. The 65th Infantry was a Regular Army regiment based in Puerto Rico. Under the custom of the time, most of the unit's officers were "continentals," while some of the junior officers and all the NCOs and enlisted soldiers were Puerto Rican. This unique unit was not immune to the ravages of the postwar drawdown, and in August 1950 it could muster only 92 officers and 1,895 enlisted of the 4,000 authorized. Only two of the three battalions authorized were active. The Army ordered the 3rd Battalion, 33rd Infantry, consisting largely of Puerto Rican soldiers, at Fort Kobbe, Panama Canal Zone, to provide the 65th Infantry's third battalion. To accelerate the deployment, the 65th Infantry Regiment moved directly to Korea, picked up that battalion as it passed through the Panama Canal Zone, and arrived before the rest of the division. The regiment lacked a tank company, so the Army deployed a tank company from Fort Meade, Maryland, to arrive separately. Unique among the regiments sent to Korea, the 65th deployed with its full complement of officers and soldiers, with a 10 percent overage. After arriving in Korea, the regiment was augmented with the 58th Armored Field Artillery Battalion, 999th Armored Field Artillery Battalion, and a tank company from Fort Lewis to form the RCT.[57]

While the JCS prepared to deploy these forces, MacArthur also began to receive assistance from other nations fulfilling their responsibilities under the United Nations Security Council Resolution 83 of July 7, 1950, which called on member nations to provide forces to "repel the armed attack and to restore international peace and security in the area." Great Britain placed all British naval forces in the region under MacArthur's control, and in mid-August the British War Office deployed the UK 27th and 29th Infantry Brigades from Hong Kong to Korea. Like the American units that these brigades reinforced, they were sorely understrength.[58]

By mid-September, Almond had most of the forces that he would need in place. The 7th Infantry Division had received most of the replacements from the States to fill up its regiments, and the conscription of Koreans had yielded more than 8,000 draftees; the division embarked 24,845 soldiers. The 1st Marine Division continued to build combat power, with two of its infantry regiments as well as its artillery regiment, 1st Marine Aircraft Wing, and supporting units in place. When the 7th Marine Regiment joined the division several days after the landing, the 1st Marine Division (Reinforced) included some 29,235 Marine and Navy personnel. Almond would command more Marine units in the following operations than had existed in the entire Fleet Marine Force when the war began. In total, X Corps would land at Inchon with almost 70,000 men. Almond had also received, to the detriment of EUSAK, the 5th Field Artillery Group, which boasted two artillery battalions (one self-propelled, one towed) with 155 mm howitzers. In order to allow Almond to operate independently until he linked up with Walker's EUSAK, MacArthur authorized additional service units and ordered Almond to establish a stockage of fifteen days' worth of supplies. EUSAK was prepared to assume logistical support of X Corps after the two forces joined.[59]

Operationally, Almond's unit was as ready as it could be, given the time allotted for formation. Tactically, he harbored doubts. In the last days of preparation before embarking, he had inspected as many units as possible. With the gunner's practiced eye, he noted deficiencies in some of the marines' familiarity with crew-served weapons, but his overall impression of the Marine units was favorable. Calling up combat-experienced reservists had helped the 1st Marine Division gel quickly. Almond's visits to the 7th Infantry Division had revealed potentially more serious problems. Several leaders lacked aggressiveness, an unforgivable trait for Almond. The large influx of replacements had filled the division's vacancies, but the brief time before embarkation had allowed little opportunity for collective training. Almond identified several unit tasks on his visits that required additional training. He admonished the 7th Infantry Division staff to maintain close liaison and coordination with the Marines throughout their operation. Nevertheless, Almond radiated confidence as he conducted a press conference aboard the USS *Mount McKinley* the night before the landing. He explained the X Corps mission to "seize and hold the Inchon-Seoul complex and provide the 'anvil' against which the 8th Army, the 'hammer,' would drive and destroy the enemy forces in South Korea."[60]

Almond graduated 3rd in his class from VMI in 1915. *Almond Family Photo, Edward M. Almond Photo Collection, US Army Heritage and Education Center.*

The Almond family enjoys a day of swimming during the time Ned commanded 3rd Battalion, 45th Infantry Regiment (Philippine Scouts)(1930-1932) at Fort McKinley, Philippines. Pictured left to right: Margaret Mallory Almond (b. 1920), Margaret Crook Almond, Edward M. "Ned" Almond, Edward M. Almond, Jr. (b. 1921). *Almond Family Photo, Edward M. Almond Photo Collection, US Army Heritage and Education Center.*

Officers were also subject to inspection, and Almond demanded high standards. On an early visit to Camp Robinson, Arkansas, Almond inspects the officers of the 371st Infantry Regiment along with commander Col. Sterling A. Wood (left). *Edward M. Almond Photo Collection, US Army Heritage and Education Center.*

While NCOs conducted most training for soldiers, here a lieutenant demonstrates the proper bayonet technique for three of his soldiers. As newly-commissioned black lieutenants replaced white officers, soldiers needed to see those officers in leadership roles. *US Army Signal Corps Photo, Edward M. Almond Photo Collection, US Army Heritage and Education Center.*

A combat patrol from the 92nd Division, having advanced 3 miles north of Lucca, takes cover on the slope while pinned down by machine gun. An Italian partisan guiding the patrol dashes across the road for cover. *US Army Signal Corps Photo, Edward M. Almond Photo Collection, US Army Heritage and Education Center.*

The crew of Battery B, 598th Field Artillery, 92nd Division, readies their 105 mm howitzer before to receiving a fire mission near the banks of the Arno River on 16 SEP 1945. *US Army Signal Corps Photo, Edward M. Almond Photo Collection, US Army Heritage and Education Center.*

(*Above*) (Original caption) There are no racial problems on the front lines in Italy. Tech. Sgt. Charles Jones (Somerville Georgia), a medic from 92nd Infantry Division, bandages the leg of a white buddy, PFC Thomas W. Skayhand, (Dorchester Massachusetts) of 1st Armored Division, a few hundred yards south of the walls of Lucca. *US Army Signal Corps Photo, Edward M. Almond Photo Collection, US Army Heritage and Education Center.* (*Below*) Men of Company C, 365th Infantry Regiment, 92nd Infantry Division troops, are pinned down by a sniper who infiltrated through division lines. The men are carrying ammunition to the assault companies in the Sommocolonia area Italy. January 10, 1945 *US Army Signal Corps Photo, Edward M. Almond Photo Collection, US Army Heritage and Education Center.*

Army Chief of Staff Gen. George C. Marshall visits the 92nd Infantry Division on February 14, 1945. Marshall ordered the reorganization of the 92nd Infantry Division during this visit. Officers pictured (left-right): Gen. George C. Marshall, Army Chief of Staff; Almond; Col. Ray Sherman, CO of 370th Infantry Regiment (facing Marshall); Lieut. Gen. Mark Clark, CG, 15th Army Group (obscured by Sherman; Master Sergeant Parks, senior NCO in the 92nd Infantry Division; Maj. Gen. Willis D. Crittenberger, CG IV Corps; Lt. Col. Thomas St. John Arnold, Ass't. Chief of Staff, G3, 92nd Inf. Div. *US Army Signal Corps Photo, Edward M. Almond Photo Collection, US Army Heritage and Education Center.*

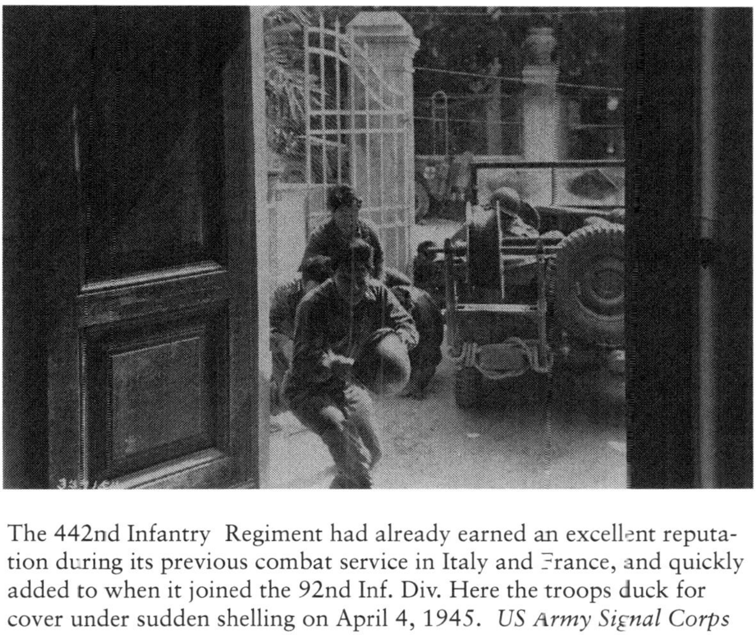

The 442nd Infantry Regiment had already earned an excellent reputation during its previous combat service in Italy and France, and quickly added to when it joined the 92nd Inf. Div. Here the troops duck for cover under sudden shelling on April 4, 1945. *US Army Signal Corps Photo, Edward M. Almond Photo Collection, US Army Heritage and Education Center.*

Almond drives his own jeep as the 92nd Infantry Division liberates Genoa, Italy on April 27, 1945. *Almond Family Photo, Edward M. Almond Photo Collection, US Army Heritage and Education Center.*

Soldiers from the 598th Field Artillery Battalion, 92nd Infantry Division, lead the procession returning the remains of Genoa's favorite son, Christopher Columbus, after the 92nd Infantry Division liberated the city. *US Army Signal Corps Photo, Edward M. Almond Photo Collection, US Army Heritage and Education Center.*

The 92nd Infantry Division's officers hosted a farewell dinner for Almond in Viareggio, Italy, in August 1945. These and other photos illustrate the division's fully integrated officer mess. The officers pictured a (L-R): Lt. Col. J.M. Hanley, Cdr, 370th Inf. Reg.; Lt. Col. Marcus Ray, Cdr., 600th FA Bn; Col. J.C. Horne; Col. J.D. Armstrong, Cdr, 365th Inf. Reg.; Col. R.G. Sherman, Chief of Staff; unidentified officer; Almond; Col. J. Notestein, Cdr., 371st Inf. Reg. Other photos from the event illustrate that all tables were integrated. *US Army Signal Corps Photo, Edward M. Almond Photo Collection, US Army Heritage and Education Center.*

Relations between Almond and Walker were not always bad. When Walker arrived in Tokyo in September 1948, they renewed their friendship. *Almond Family Photo, Edward M. Almond Photo Collection, US Army Heritage and Education Center.*

While in Tokyo, Almond made time every day to go home and have lunch with his grandson Tommy. *Almond Family Photo, Edward M. Almond Photo Collection, US Army Heritage and Education Center.*

Lt. Al Haig's wedding, May 24, 1950. Haig accorded Almond a position of honor on the groom's side, perhaps unconsciously, occupying the position of the father he had lost when he was nine. Pictured, L-R: Maj. Gen. & Mrs. Edward M. Almond; Lieut. Alexander Haig; Patricia Fox Haig; Mrs. Alonzo (Elizabeth) Fox, mother of the bride; Mrs. Douglas (Jean) MacArthur, representing the General; and Maj. Gen. Alonzo P. Fox, father of the bride. *Almond Family Photo, Edward M. Almond Photo Collection, US Army Heritage and Education Center.*

15 SEP 1950 Almond holds a press conference aboard the USS Mount McKinley, as the landing at Inchon, Korea, gets underway. *US Army Signal Corps Photo, Edward M. Almond Photo Collection, US Army Heritage and Education Center.*

(*Above*) Lieut. Gen. Lemuel C. Shepherd, CG, Fleet Marine Force-Pacific, confers with Almond as they go ashore at Inchon aboard a motor launch from the USS Mount McKinley, on September 16, 1950. *US Army Signal Corps Photo, Edward M. Almond Photo Collection, US Army Heritage and Education Center.* (*Below*) In a climatic meeting on Sep. 25, 1950, Almond explains the Corps scheme of maneuver to a doubting Maj. Gen. O. P. Smith, CG, 1st Marine Division. Pictured (L-R):Maj. Gen. David G. Barr, commanding 7th Infantry Division; Brig. Gen. Henry I. "Hank" Hodes, assistant Division Commander, 7th Inf. Div. Smith; Almond; unidentified officer. *US Army Signal Corps Photo, Edward M. Almond Photo Collection, US Army Heritage and Education Center.*

Almond explains the Han River crossing operation to VADM Arthur Struble, Sep. 23, 1950. Officers pictured, (L-R); Col. Edward L. Forney (USMC); unidentified (obscured); Almond; Struble; unidentified. *US Army Signal Corps Photo, Edward M. Almond Photo Collection, US Army Heritage and Education Center.*

Almond speaks with PFC James H. Gatewood while inspecting 2nd Battalion, 9th Inf. Reg. on 10 APR 1951. *US Army Signal Corps Photo, Edward M. Almond Photo Collection, US Army Heritage and Education Center.*

On one of his daily inspections, Almond visited the 31st Infantry Regiment on Nov. 12, 1950 at Untaek, North Korea. Col. Allan D. MacLean, C.O. 31st Infantry Regiment, does not appear to be happy with the guidance his corps commander is giving him as 2nd Infantry Division Commander Maj. Gen. David Barr looks on. Almond later awarded MacLean the Silver Star later that day. MacLean was killed in action at the Chosin Reservoir two weeks later. *US Army Signal Corps Photo, Edward M. Almond Photo Collection, US Army Heritage and Education Center.*

Almond prepares to fly out of Hagaru-ri on November 28, 1950, after visiting the 1st Marine Division and the 31st Infantry Regiment. Later that day he received orders to Tokyo, where General MacArthur ordered Almond and Lt. Gen. Walker to begin retreating in the face of the Chinese offensive. *US Army Signal Corps Photo, Edward M. Almond Photo Collection, US Army Heritage and Education Center.*

16 DEC 1950 No "Dunkirk" at Hungnam: Despite the pressure of daily Chinese attacks, Almond insisted on saving as much equipment as possible, to enable the corps to be comabt ready wehn it landed again in South Korea. Col. Edward H. Forney, USMC, planned and supervised the rapid but very organized withdrawal that saved 105,000 US and ROK soldiers, 98,000 civilian refugees, 17,500 vechicles, and 350,000 tons of bulk cargo. *US Army Signal Corps Photo, Edward M. Almond Photo Collection, US Army Heritage and Education Center.*

Feb 7, 1951 Col. Paul L. Freeman, Commanding 23rd RCT (with French Battalion attached), 2nd Inf. Div. and Maj. John Dumaine, S3, 23rd RCT, brief Almond on the situation at Chip Yong-Ni as Operation ROUNDUP begins. Place at a crucial point in the X Corps sector, the 23rd RCT would mount a legendary defense of Chip Yong-Ni under a withering Chinese counterattack one week later. *US Army Signal Corps Photo, Edward M. Almond Photo Collection, US Army Heritage and Education Center.*

12

Initial Success in Korea

September–November 1950

Maj. Gen. Ned Almond stepped into the chilly early morning air on the flag bridge of the USS *Mount McKinley* shortly before dawn on September 15, 1950. He joined General of the Army Douglas MacArthur, Brig. Gen. Edwin Wright, Maj. Gen. Courtney Whitney, Maj. Gen. Oliver P. Smith, Rear Adm. James H. Doyle, and other FECOM staff officers as they prepared to watch the landing at Inchon. The ships in the task force opened fire on predetermined positions at 5:45 a.m. Spotter planes circled the fleet and Wolmi-do to report the results of that opening preparation. After the landings began, these planes reported progress as marines moved ashore, and their reports were relayed over the loudspeaker to the flag bridge.[1]

The Marines launched Operation Chromite at 6:25 a.m. with one battalion of the 5th Marine Regiment landing at Green Beach on Wolmi-do (see map 12.1). They found the island lightly defended and secured it by 7:50 a.m. The 1st Marines assaulted Blue Beach, south of Inchon, while the remainder of the 5th Marines landed at Red Beach, north of Wolmi-do, on the next high tide just after 5:30 p.m. Despite the Marines' earlier misgivings, pre-assault intelligence estimates proved correct and Inchon fell quickly with few casualties. The 1st and 5th Marines made contact with each other east of Inchon a mere twenty-four hours after the landing began and moved east toward the next objective, Kimpo Airfield. Doctrinally, the operation would remain under the control of the amphibious commander, Admiral Doyle, until at least half of the landing force was ashore. Almond went ashore daily to watch operations and gauge progress. Admiral Doyle had given Almond and Smith a tour of the USS *Mount McKinley* a couple of days before the landing. Smith reported that Doyle liked to use the tour to impress Army officers with the complexity of amphibious operations and the difficulties involved with command, control, and communications. Smith reported that Almond was "duly impressed." Smith, still nursing a grudge concerning

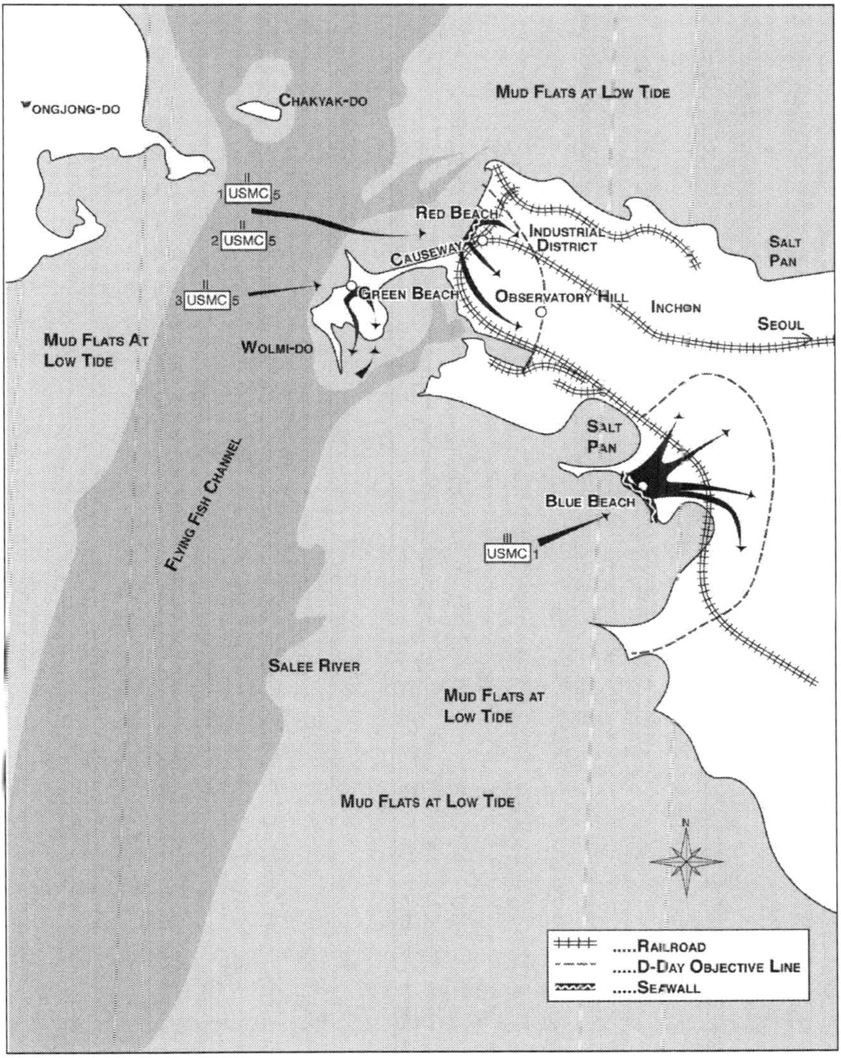

12.1. Inchon Landings, September 15–16, 1950

Almond's comment about a "mechanical operation," seemed mollified. Almond did not record his impressions of the tour, but Smith was probably correct. Almond had always been a great student of his profession, and he would doubtless soak up such information.[2]

Almond was a tough man to work for, and no one knew that better than his aides. When war came, Lieutenant Haig had begged to return to the 1st Cavalry Division as a platoon leader, but Almond turned him down and kept him as his aide. Haig took Almond's mobile command post ashore on September 16, landing about 6 p.m. on Blue Beach with the ninth wave of the 1st Marines, but two of the five jeeps he took had been lost overboard during a typhoon en route to Korea. Almond landed about fifteen minutes later and immediately demanded of Haig whether or not his mobile CP was ready. Almond's demands proved as unstinting in combat as they had been in peacetime. Haig got his first glimpses of war on the ground that day, and he recalled Almond's first order: "Make notes for the war journal!" Haig began writing down everything Almond saw, and Almond saw everything. Haig remembered that "no detail was so small as to escape his notice. This was only the beginning. Almond inspected everything: a Navy temporary hospital in a beached LST, every Marine and Army command post he could visit, a prisoner of war camp, the LSTs unloading supplies on the beaches."[3]

The 5th Marines captured Kimpo Airfield on September 18 without significant opposition. Lieutenant Colonel McCaffrey took the X Corps Advanced CP ashore the following day and co-located it with the 1st Marine Division. By September 22 all three Marine regiments and the 32nd RCT of the 7th Infantry Division were ashore and attacking toward Seoul. Almond activated his main corps CP and assumed control of the operation the following day. Almond moved X Corps headquarters into Ascom City, a warehouse area halfway between Inchon and Seoul, on September 23.[4]

The operation's initial success buoyed Almond's spirits. In the first of many letters he wrote to Margaret over the next ten months, Almond praised the Navy and Marines: "This has gone just as planned and at a little better speed. The cooperation of the Navy and the spirit of the Marines has been wonderful and I am sure that the 7th Division will do equally well when they are fully in it." After describing his visit to the recaptured Kimpo Airfield, Almond remarked, "The Marines are wonderful and a pleasure to command." Almond's opinion of the Marines remained high, despite his later strained relations with Maj. Gen. Oliver P. Smith. He also acknowledged his great debt to MacArthur for having given him the opportunity to command: "He is the only one who has given me such a chance and I will not forget it."[5]

MacArthur's breezy projections exceeded even Almond's general tendency to underestimate the time required for a given task. Seoul lay eighteen miles east of Inchon, on the eastern shore of the Han River.

MacArthur had told Almond before the landing that he expected him to be in Seoul in five days. That timeline was too aggressive, even for Almond. Almond told MacArthur that he could not capture Seoul in five days but he could do so within two weeks. Almond knew that MacArthur wanted to capture Seoul by September 25, the three-month anniversary of the beginning of the war. MacArthur believed that the liberation of Seoul on that date would have psychological resonance. Though many extolled MacArthur's genius in the wake of the spectacularly successful Inchon landing, Almond also earned his own accolades. US Army Deputy Chief of Staff Lt. Gen. Matthew B. Ridgway sent Almond a personal note that surely buoyed his spirits and calmed his insecurities.

> Dear Ned:
>
> The full fruits of brilliant planning, and courageous execution seem about to be gathered. In the flood tide of victory personal messages will count but little. Yet I do want you to know how deeply we all rejoice in current developments. You are about to inscribe another and unsurpassed chapter in our combat records.
>
> Congratulations.[6]

Seoul was not just the capital of South Korea, it was also the communications and supply center supporting the NKPA facing EUSAK. Its capture would turn the tables on the invaders. X Corps would have to both flank the city and cross the Han River under fire. While optimistic estimates for the capture of Inchon had been met, the capture of Seoul would be a different matter. NKPA troops occupied a series of hills protecting the western approach to Seoul. The Japanese had built fortifications on that high ground during World War II, and the South Korean Army had used them extensively for training. The NKPA 25th Brigade had begun moving its 2,500 soldiers from Chorwon south to Seoul on the day of the Inchon landing to reinforce the 78th Independent Regiment there. The brigade contained two infantry battalions, four heavy machine gun battalions, a 76 mm artillery battalion, and a 120 mm mortar battalion, which allowed it to present a formidable defense using prepared positions that included concrete caves.[7]

Despite Almond's difficult relations with Marine Maj. Gen. Oliver P. Smith, he found the Marines overall tactically sound. When visiting the 1st Marines, he liked the commander's aggressive spirit; his respect and admiration for Col. Lewis B. "Chesty" Puller began in the first days of the Inchon operation and continued until Puller's death. When Almond visited Puller's headquarters on September 20, Puller reported that he had encountered stiff opposition and requested permission to burn the town. Almond authorized it. Almond grew concerned, however, that while the Marines were advancing aggressively, they were not using artillery or mortar fire. Moreover, the supporting naval gunfire was missing critical targets and was largely ineffective.[8]

He found greater problems with the 7th Infantry Division, which began disembarking on September 19. Almond intended to use the 7th Infantry to protect the flanks and support the attack. But while Almond had high hopes, the division was not a very good unit in September 1950. The chaotic stripping, filling, and deployment had not allowed it to develop any unit cohesion or to conduct any meaningful unit training. The 1st Marine Division had experienced similar disruption, but it benefited from an initial infusion of trained reservists familiar with the division, and from large numbers of active-duty marines who had served together in the 2nd Marine Division. The Marine Corps also slotted all its replacements into the two new regiments before leaving the States, and then deployed those regiments as units. The 7th Infantry Division, by contrast, was filled largely by soldiers arriving in Japan as individual replacements. This lack of unit cohesion was to give Almond difficulties in the weeks to come.

After some training exercises, he notified the division's commander, Maj. Gen. David G. Barr, of his findings. Barr had left the Army Ground Forces G1 for China in 1948 and spent some eighteen months there as an advisor. He moved to Japan in May 1949 and took command of the 7th Infantry Division, which had just completed the move back to Japan as the Korean occupation ended. In addition to being understrength, the unit had been hampered by policies associated with the move. Rather than making a unit move as a whole to Japan, the Army made all moves individual ones. Many of the most experienced NCOs and officers, therefore, left Korea and moved on to their next duty stations instead of going to Japan with the unit. Moreover, inbound replacements were screened upon arrival, and those with higher test scores were diverted away from units into high-level staffs. Almond had intervened in early 1950 and put a stop to the practice, but it was too late to help the divisions in a meaningful way.[9]

Perhaps influenced by MacArthur's predilections, Almond designed a double envelopment of Seoul with a keen eye for the terrain. There were three main roads out of the city of Seoul that a defender could use to retreat. One stretched east briefly before turning south toward Chungju, presenting an avenue by which the North Korean forces could reinforce their units on the Eighth Army front. A second road led north out of the city toward Uijongbu, providing a means of escape for North Korean forces in the city. A third led northeast toward the east coast port city of Wonsan. South Mountain, on the southern edge of the city, overlooked and dominated the city center.[10]

Haig saw the relationship between Almond and Smith deteriorate rapidly after Inchon, especially with Almond's noted curtness. Haig believed that a showdown confrontation between the two men on September 24, 1950, exemplified the differences between Army and Marine Corps doctrine. The 5th Marines, with an attached battalion of ROK Marines, had begun its assault on September 22. The next day, Smith ordered the recently arrived 7th Marines to move up on the west side of Seoul and to cross the Han River behind the 5th Marines. Almond had presented a plan to Smith that he thought would allow the Marines to envelop the city of Seoul in twenty-four hours; if Smith did not, Almond intended to send in a regiment of the 7th Infantry Division. Almond believed that Smith had wanted the 1st Marine Division to capture Seoul single-handedly, but the Marine general did not possess the same sense of urgency as his corps commander. When Almond found the Marine attack on the western side of the city slowing, he suggested that the 7th Marines go around the enemy's southern flank. Smith refused to split his two regiments and instead chose to focus both in a concentrated attack against the city. Smith saw the plan as dividing his forces, while Almond saw it as a double envelopment. Smith ordered the 1st Marines to cross the Han at Yongdungpo on September 24, while the 7th Marines then attacked on the left flank of the 5th Marines (see map 12.2).[11]

As Almond feared, the 7th Marines ran behind schedule. He ordered the 32nd RCT and the 17th ROK Regiment to cross the Han River on the southeast side, capture South Mountain, and form the second arm of the pincer movement that would complete the double envelopment of the city. This move would also relieve pressure on the 1st and 5th Marines. Almond later reported, "General Smith liked this not at all," and Smith was outraged when Almond ordered him to send the amphibious tractor battalion to carry the 32nd RCT across the river. Most of the bridges on the Han had been destroyed during the evacuation. His clear disdain for the Army showing, Smith argued that the LVTs (landing vehicle, tracked) or "amtracks" were "Marine property." Such a specious argument was guaranteed to draw Almond's ire. As the two generals argued, Almond contending that they were government property, Smith counter-

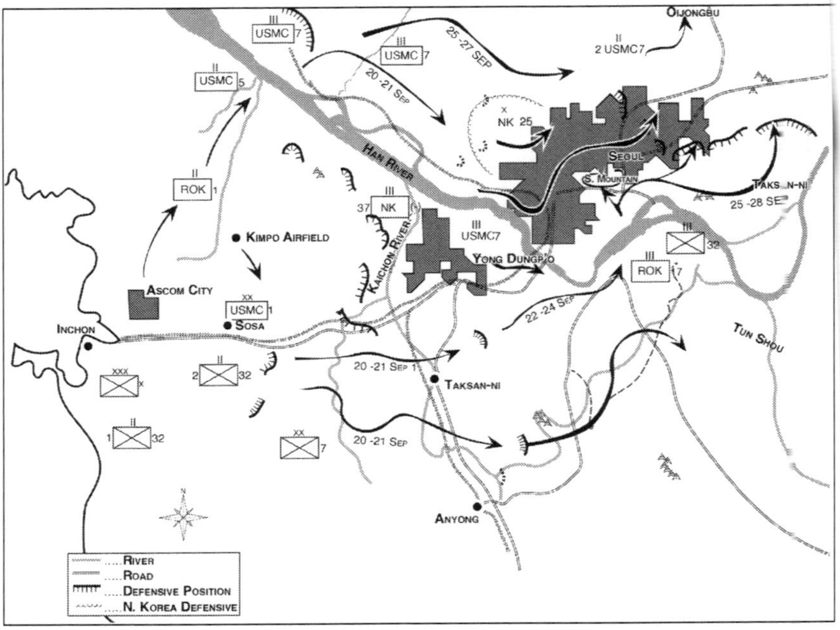

12.2. Capture of Seoul, September 20–28, 1950

ing that Army soldiers did not know how to use amtracks, one of Smith's own officers broke the impasse. The commander of the amtrack battalion himself spoke up and said that he could easily move the soldiers; they merely needed to be divided into small groups for boarding each amtrack. The Marine general's petulance in this instance further angered Almond and put additional strain on their relationship.[12]

Though Almond and Smith accomplished the mission, they harbored an intense hatred for each other. Almond later tried to extend an olive branch, telling Smith that the crossing of the Han on amphibious tractors was "the finest small unit action that he has ever seen." But the testy exchange between Almond and Smith amplified the competition between the Army and the Marines and further soured the relationship between the two men and their staffs.[13]

Almond's fears about the enemy's potential escape proved well founded. Aerial intelligence confirmed that North Korean forces had begun abandoning city, with large units moving to the north. Almond requested that the Far East Air Force begin attacking the withdrawing enemy column, and then ordered the Marines to attack as well. Though the Marines had performed better in general than had the Army units, even Smith knew that this order was perhaps beyond his unit's capabilities. "This order from Corps directed a night attack in an oriental city to a depth of about 3 miles, which is the limit of our objectives." The 1st and 5th Marines made the assault beginning at about 1:00 a.m. with a short artillery preparation. The Marines, unfamiliar with the city, had difficulty coordinating between the regiments, and when the North Koreans counterattacked, the Marines were unable to advance further. Smith concluded that "this episode did not tend to restore my confidence in the judgment of the Corps commander."[14]

With the plan in place, Almond went to observe the operation on September 25 along with Vice Adm. Arthur Struble, McCaffrey, Lt. Col. John Chiles, Haig, and other officers. Under the pressure of war, Haig noticed another of his chief's troubling traits: personal courage. "In combat situations, he exposed himself to mortal risk several times a day, and, if you happened to be his aide, he exposed you to the same risk with the same insouciance." Writing decades later, and with much more combat experience, Haig observed that he had occasionally seen other soldiers who not only mastered fear but appeared to be fearless, and Almond was one of them. "In regard to his own safety, Almond was the most reckless person I've ever known—and luckiest. As far as I can tell, he was utterly without fear."[15]

Almond selected a point on the forward slope of a hill on the west bank of the Han River from which he could view the river crossing and the city of Seoul. A couple of hours after the party arrived, a mortar round landed a hundred yards away from the observation point where the group stood. Everyone except Almond moved to a more covered position. Almond watched for a few more minutes, and then joined the group.[16]

Historians, and even Almond's contemporaries, have criticized him for his tendency to micromanage. He frequently skipped layers of the chain of command to issue orders directly to lower-level units. While this was a lifelong habit, seeing Almond's actions in context reveals that he often had good reason to step in in order to correct serious leadership or coordination mistakes. Upon arriving to watch the assault crossing of the Han River on September 25, Almond discovered a breakdown in communications between the commanders of 1st and 2nd Battalions, 32nd RCT. Almond and the party boarded an amtrack and crossed the river, where he found the 1st Battalion securing the high ground. The battalion, however, had stopped, pending coordination with the 2nd Battalion, which had preceded it in the river crossing, while the 2nd had stopped to await coordination with the 1st. Almond ordered the 2nd Battalion forward, but this kind of problem bedeviled Almond throughout the early weeks of the war.[17]

Things were no better when Almond visited the 31st RCT. Col. Richard P. Ovenshine briefed Almond on regimental operations and reported that a patrol en route to Osan had been stopped halfway by small-arms and automatic weapons fire. The battalion commander had requested his unit be withdrawn. This reflected the fear of green troops exposed to combat for the first time, but also the timidity of the commanders who similarly faced their first test. Almond expected his subordinate commanders to mirror his own aggressive nature, and he dealt harshly with those who did not. Almond impressed upon Ovenshine the necessity for aggressive action, and when General Barr arrived shortly after, Almond admonished him as well.[18]

This tendency strained already tense relations with Smith, who remonstrated with Almond early in the operation about giving orders directly to Smith's regimental commanders. Almond denied having given any orders directly to Marine regiments, though he mentioned that he had discussed the scheme of maneuver with Colonels Puller and Murray. Here Almond's natural tendency was magnified by military tradition: guidance imparted by a corps commander directly to a regimental commander might sound very much like an order. Almond promised that he would correct the impression with the regimental commanders that he was giving them orders directly. Smith, to his credit, noted parenthetically in his log that he had had no further report of Almond giving direct orders to the regimental commanders.[19]

Almond wrote to Margaret on September 24 that he hoped to send MacArthur a telegram the next day saying, "Seoul is ours, just three months after Korea was invaded." He did just that to mark the anniversary, and GHQ released a communiqué announcing that Seoul had been captured just ninety days after the original North Korean incursion. This angered Smith and the Marines, because there was still significant fighting in their sector. X Corps did not fully secure Seoul until September 28. MacArthur flew in the next day and ceremonially turned over the city to ROK president Syngman Rhee.[20]

MacArthur had told both Walker and Almond before Inchon that X Corps would revert to EUSAK control after the capture of Seoul, and that Almond would return to Tokyo to resume his duties as chief of staff. That time appeared to be near as Seoul fell. EUSAK had begun its counterattack out of the Pusan Perimeter on September 16 and made initial contact with X Corps on September 26 just south of Suwon. This contact symbolically linked the invasion force with the breakout force as Walker's EUSAK hammer landed on Almond's X Corps anvil, but it did not imply or result in a change to the command relationships. Other events beyond either Almond's or Walker's control were about to change the strategy of the war, and prewar plans became moot.[21]

As Almond was planning the ceremony at which MacArthur would hand over the city of Seoul to President Rhee, the JCS authorized MacArthur to launch offensive operations north of the 38th Parallel. This changed MacArthur's whole approach, and once again he called for a bold stroke. This plan also demonstrated MacArthur's fondness for the double envelopment. MacArthur directed Walker to attack northward to capture the North Korean capital of Pyongyang, while Almond's X Corps would simultaneously conduct an amphibious landing at Wonsan on Korea's east coast and attack westward toward Pyongyang. MacArthur chose Wonsan for "Operation Tailboard" because it was the second-best port on the east coast after Pusan, and because it lay in a nearly direct line across the peninsula from Pyongyang and was connected to that city by a good highway. The road from Wonsan to Pyongyang was an all-weather gravel road 23 to 25 feet in width. The Marines were to re-embark on their landing ships and sail straight for Wonsan, while the 7th Infantry Division would move overland to Pusan and await transport. After the naval vessels landed the Marine units at Wonsan, they would return to Pusan for the 7th Infantry Division. GHQ relieved X Corps of its tactical responsibilities on October 7, 1950, and Almond began preparations for the move to Wonsan. He flew to EUSAK HQ at Taegu to coordinate the action with General Walker that afternoon (see map 12.3).[22]

Theoretically, X Corps's retrograde movement to prepare for the Wonsan landing was essentially administrative in nature and relatively unopposed. In practice, it presented great difficulties for both the Eighth Army and X Corps staffs. A shift to Wonsan for the second landing was a complex operational move, but it was even more intricate logistically. MacArthur ordered Walker to give X Corps priority for outloading at both Inchon and Pusan. Doing so prevented the remainder of the Eighth Army's supplies from being unloaded through the same ports. MacArthur also directed that X Corps must leave with all supplies that had been shipped to it. For the first seventeen days of October, the port of Inchon was exclusively devoted to outloading the 1st Marine Division and its supplies. EUSAK could therefore not begin its attack toward Pyongyang

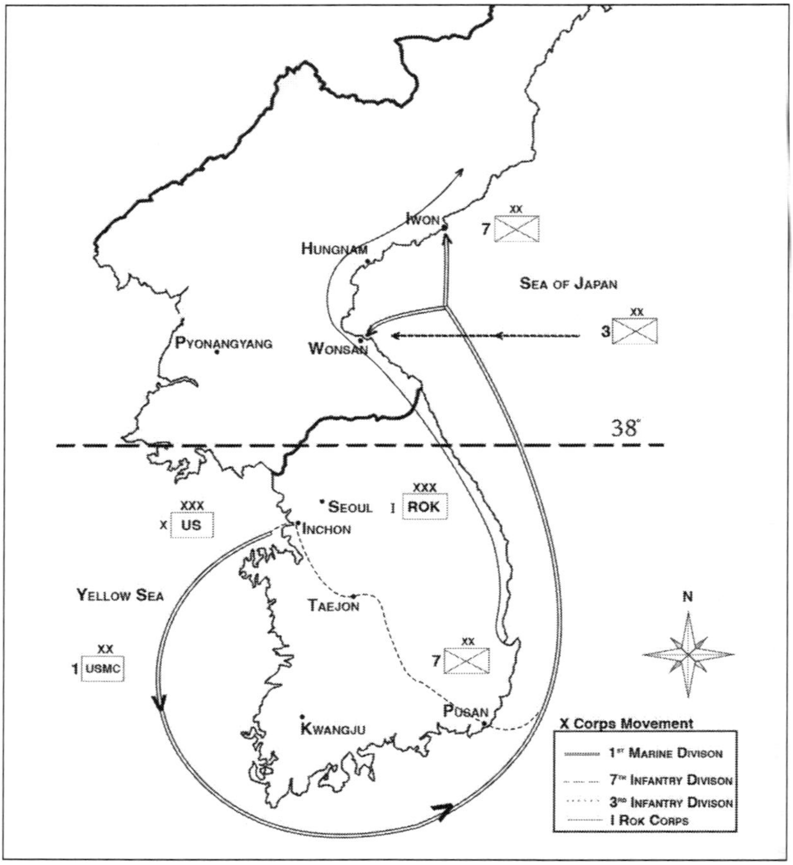

12.3. Wonsan-Iwon Landings, October 9–26, 1950

until it could consolidate all of its units and supplies to prepare for the move.[23]

MacArthur's initial plan was to use Almond's X Corps as the hammer, attacking from Wonsan to Pyongyang using the few serviceable east-west roads on the Korean Peninsula. The Wonsan-Seoul highway was the principal cross-peninsula road of Korea. It was also a gravel-surfaced all-weather road 23 to 25 feet wide. Walker would again provide the anvil with EUSAK, moving northwest from Seoul to capture Pyongyang. Walker had envisioned a similar plan, but using X Corps in a ground role rather than an amphibious assault. Wonsan had been considered during the planning for Inchon, and in fact MacArthur had planned a double envelopment if sufficient forces had existed. He saw the second amphibious landing at Wonsan much like his previous successful operations cutting the communication and supply lines, isolating enemy troops. Walker, for his part, thought the operations should have gone in reverse: X Corps to Pyongyang on land, then a strike across the peninsula from the rear. He never mentioned this to MacArthur, however.[24]

MacArthur's plan kept X Corps separate from EUSAK and only stoked the antipathy between Walker and Almond. MacArthur had a concept of unity of command that was similar to Walker's, yet broader. MacArthur had experienced his greatest successes during World War II in the New Guinea and Philippine Islands campaigns when he had command of all air, land, and sea forces, which he termed "triphibious warfare," a harbinger of future joint and combined operations.[25]

The differences between Walker and MacArthur went beyond personal animosity. They also reflected each man's experiences during World War II. Walker, of course, had commanded a corps in Gen. George C. Patton's Third Army, in an environment that prized unity of command. Having a separate corps operating in the same area was simply antithetical to everything Walker knew. MacArthur had operated differently in the Pacific. His entire strategy revolved around amphibious operations used to envelop the Japanese enemy, always avoiding large troop concentrations where possible, and aiming instead at supply lines and lines of communication in the rear. MacArthur in his memoirs explained his strategy:

> To successfully envelop the enemy called for the careful selection of key points as objectives and the choosing of the most opportune moment to strike. I accordingly applied my major efforts to the seizure of areas which were suitable for airfields and base development, but which were only lightly defended by the enemy. Thus, by daring forward strikes, by neutralizing and bypassing enemy centers of strength, and by the judicious use of my air forces to cover each movement, I intended to destroy Japanese power in New Guinea and adjacent islands, and to clear the way for a drive to the Philippines.[26]

He used the technique very effectively to first cut off some 80,000 Japanese troops in the Bismarck Archipelago, then another 40,000 as he made several enveloping amphibious landings on the north coast of New Guinea.

The conquest of the Philippines began with an amphibious landing at Leyte Gulf, a move designed to strike in the rear of Japanese troops on the island of Mindanao. MacArthur reported that in July 1944 in a conversation with President Franklin D. Roosevelt he had argued that the Philippines should be the next strategic objective rather than Formosa, he told Roosevelt, "Mr. President, my losses would not be heavy, any more than they have been in the past. The days of the frontal attack should be over. Modern infantry weapons are too deadly, and frontal assault is only for mediocre commanders. Good commanders do not turn in heavy losses." He argued that, after retaking the Philippines, he could then assault the Japanese-held Dutch East Indies from the rear.[27]

Some of the early conflicts between EUSAK and X Corps grew out of supply problems and soured the Almond-Walker relationship further. EUSAK was assigned to provide all the support to the UN forces in Korea. MacArthur's earlier directive to Almond to establish fifteen days of supply was expanded to thirty in preparation for the next phase of the operation, making the logistics burden on EUSAK even greater. After X Corps linked up with the Eighth Army at Osan, Walker attempted to have X Corps support the 1st Cavalry Division, since it was furthest from the base of supply at Taegu. By that time, however, Almond had received orders to redirect the corps toward Wonsan. X Corps received orders from FECOM not to supply 1st Cavalry Division except for emergency issues. This did not sit well with General Walker.[28]

Almond's dual-hatting did cause confusion in one respect. The X Corps staff continued to request supplies directly through GHQ G4 even after the Inchon landing. This became increasingly frustrating for all concerned, because GHQ G4 had no means of resupplying a deployed corps. Almond's X Corps G4, Col. Aubrey D. Smith, later argued that inserting EUSAK into the supply chain actually made his job more difficult. "Through direct contact of X Corps staff with JLCOM [Japan Logistical Command] agencies, detailed supply plans had been completed to meet expected difficulties in unloading. The introduction of Eighth Army into channels interrupted these arrangements at a critical time." Almond held a conference in his headquarters on October 4 with Maj. Gen. Walter L. Weible, commander of JLCOM, and made clear his requirements. MacArthur would eventually order Almond to send his supply requests directly to the Japan Logistical Command, which could supply them directly from Japan to the east coast of Korea.[29]

The formation of logistical support units to sustain first the defense of the Pusan Perimeter and then the counterattack at Inchon was at least as rushed and as haphazard as the development of the combat units. The Japan Logistical Command was formed by combining existing logistical and medical commands from all over Japan. It was neither designed nor organized to deploy tactically, so the Pusan Base Section was redesignated as the 2nd Logistical Command to support the Eighth Army. It too was a provisional command, not designed to go forward, and so the 3rd Logistical Command was established in September 1950 to support the X Corps landing at Inchon. When the X Corps mission changed to go to Wonsan, however, the 3rd Logistical Command was left behind and absorbed by the Eighth Army.[30]

While X Corps headquarters and the 1st Marine Division moved out for Inchon, the 7th Infantry Division moved south toward Pusan, where it would reload aboard ship for the transit to Wonsan. When MacArthur had ordered Almond to split his two divisions to go by different routes in order to mount a second amphibious operation, he had also ordered Walker to consolidate the Eighth Army north of Seoul to prepare for the assault on Pyongyang. The Korean National Railway system had been turned over to UN forces and was operated by Korean civilians under the supervision of US Army railway operating battalions, but it had sustained heavy damage during the initial fighting and the defense of the Pusan Perimeter. Almond was fortunate that the so-called Main Line running between Pusan and Seoul was double tracked, the only such line in South Korea. He was able to move all of his tracked and heavy engineer vehicles by rail. Light wheeled vehicles and most soldiers moved by road. Given the rudimentary road network of the time, the 7th Infantry Division and the 2nd Infantry Division were each moving across the country using the same road. The condition of the unimproved road damaged vehicles and caused bottlenecks as the two columns attempted to pass each other.[31]

This demonstrated one of the key problems with MacArthur attempting to be the ground commander while remaining in Tokyo, despite the success he had enjoyed in the Southwest Pacific during World War II. Had he simply reassigned the 7th Infantry Division to EUSAK, and Walker's 2nd Infantry Division to X Corps, many of these difficulties could have been avoided. EUSAK could have been ready to continue the northern attack toward Pyongyang earlier. Assigning the 2nd Infantry Division to X Corps and directing it immediately to outload at Pusan would also have accelerated Almond's preparations. Almond and Walker, however, as the commanders on the ground, bear greater responsibility for the confusion and congestion after Inchon. Neither made these recommendations to MacArthur, probably out of jealousy of each other. Walker had believed that X Corps would join EUSAK immediately after Seoul was captured, and was angered when it did not. Almond viewed the 7th Division as part of "his" corps, and at this early stage of the war was not prepared to "lose" his divisions.[32]

Moreover, while the move was largely unopposed, it was not completely so. The 7th Infantry Division suffered several casualties in guerrilla attacks and sporadic artillery fire. As was his habit, Almond became angry when the 7th Infantry Division did not move as quickly as he thought it should. He ordered Lt. Col. Warner Williamson to go down to the 7th Infantry Division headquarters and try to get things sorted out and get them moving faster. Williamson spent about thirty-six hours trying to help untangle a traffic jam that had stopped movement in both directions.[33]

The complexity of the move increased when the fleet arrived at Wonsan to find the harbor filled with Russian-built mines. The Navy needed two weeks to clear away these obstructions, by which time the Marines could have pushed to Wonsan overland. While the Taebaek Mountains had few east-west routes to enable an army to cross, the road from Seoul to Wonsan lay in a broad lowland area between the north and south Taebaek ranges.

The pause while the Navy cleared the mines at Wonsan allowed Almond to focus his attention on the 7th Infantry Division as it waited in the Pusan Perimeter. Ever the trainer, he identified numerous problems with the division. These were not surprising, given the division's reduced manning when the war began followed by the chaotic arrival of untrained KATUSAs and an influx of undertrained replacements from the States. Almond noted on September 28 after another visit to the 31st RCT and a meeting with Colonel Ovenshine that "this regiment is inexperienced and lacks the aggressive spirit of combat trained units. I remained with this regiment during the initial phase of the attack and discussed sound Battalion tactics in attack by infantry and tanks." Almond relieved Ovenshine shortly thereafter. This would not be the last instance in which Almond would feel compelled to make corrections due to inadequate training or leadership.[34]

Almond acknowledged the difficulties under which the unit had formed, but he identified shortfalls in fire control, tank-infantry coordination, command, and communications that he expected Barr to fix quickly. Almond demanded immediate action, but the problems he identified were critical to the unit's success and mission accomplishment. The collective skills the division needed required time, training, and practice. Understanding the need for more time, and perhaps because of their previous friendly association, Almond did not relieve Barr, but he did continue to push Barr and his subordinate commanders to improve their performance.[35]

With the recapture of Inchon and Seoul, MacArthur and his subordinate commanders began to sense that the end of the conflict was near, believing that Wonsan would be the last push of the war. Attention turned to postwar operations even as planning and preparation for the Wonsan landing were under way. With an eye toward the civil government of North Korea, MacArthur began planning pacification activities and designated X Corps as the postwar occupation force headquarters, with EUSAK to return to Japan. Almond noted again that the war was over "except for a few small bands but we have the job of Civil Organization and duties similar to those found in Japan in 1945." The JCS demanded that two of the divisions then in Korea prepare to redeploy elsewhere as soon as the conflict ended. UN forces were not to hand over control of North Korea to the ROK government, but to maintain civil government until elections could be held. When a new government was in place, all non-Korean UN forces would depart.[36]

Almond advocated leaving one Marine RCT, three Marine fighter squadrons, and appropriate amphibious lift in Japan after the war, "so that our amphibious training and modest lift may be retained in the Far East Command." Admiral Struble and Admiral Doyle supported the idea, and these discussions focused on basing rather than availability. Maj. Gen. Oliver P. Smith found the situation distracting and later recalled that this information contributed to a "let down" among the troops, who thought the war was over. "However," Smith related, "it was only a matter of days until the operations at Kojo brought home to us forcefully the fact that the war was not over. Talk of redeployment was never heard again."[37]

Despite the frenzy of operations, Almond found time to write to his grandson Tommy, and he never failed to update his friends on Tommy's activities. Even after a new grandchild was born and named Edward Mallory "Ned" Almond Fergusson, Tommy remained Almond's favorite. Throughout Almond's time in Korea, he kept in contact with his family and especially little Tommy. Almond had written to Tommy as he began to advance toward North Korea that "the war is over in this area and now we're looking for new fields to conquer." All of Almond's letters to Tommy showed his interest in his grandson's life and activities, but he also told the boy what he had been doing. One letter included photos with MacArthur and X Corps patches for Tommy and little Ned.[38]

Almond's letters to his son-in-law, Capt. Charles M. "Fergy" Fergusson, revealed more personal thoughts. "I am enjoying this job greatly," he admitted, "since it fulfills several desires which were never realized by me in WWII (The Command of a corps and the Command of White troops)." He clearly felt, despite the failure, that his World War II command experience had failed to show his true potential. He noted after Inchon that the Marines had been excellent up to that point, and he was satisfied with the speed with which the enemy collapsed, "in spite of Eighth Army claims that they 'had the enemy licked on 6 Sept.'"[39]

Each of Almond's letters included his news from the war and indicated whether he or X Corps would be in the press. He kept the letters he had received from Tommy and commented on what each member of the family was doing. Almond might have been a vain and ambitious man, but that did not diminish his love and concern for his family. He rarely wrote a letter to any other senior officer in which he did not include notes on how Margaret, Peggy, Fergy, and Tommy were doing.

Almond had revealed his own insecurities only to his wife, but they came to the surface occasionally. Press coverage of X Corps angered Almond because he believed that the media ignored his headquarters and focused only on his individual divisions. The *Stars and Stripes* newspaper, for instance, placed a reporter in each division and the 187th Airborne Regimental Combat Team, but none at Almond's headquarters. Almond felt this was a waste of personnel, since the corps planned operations and could tell reporters where the next important action would be. He was further incensed when the media ignored his seven press releases on actions throughout the corps. He took quiet pleasure, however, when *Time* magazine featured him on its October 23, 1950, cover under the bold headline "COMMAND: Sic 'Em Almond." The article provided a succinct picture of the man:

> Almond (pronounced All-mond) is a whip-cracking officer. He never compromises with discipline, drives himself hard and his subordinates only a shade less hard. To some he seems an insufferable martinet. Those who know him best say his professional manner, at times as tough as armor plate, is only the protective covering for a courtly, convivial, even sentimental off-duty personality.

> During the Inchon campaign, Almond toured his front lines indefatigably. As early as 4 a.m., he would leave his 2½-ton trailer CP (equipped with refrigerator and alfresco shower) to drive his own jeep to some jumping-off point. He got to know by name every X Corps battalion commander, talked to several score men in the ranks daily. One G.I. gave him this passing mark: "The soldiers here may not like him, but they sure as hell admire him. That's one general who sticks his neck out just like we have to."
>
> But he insists on speed in paperwork. An operational order, once given, must be written, stenciled and back on his desk in 20 minutes. And it must not be longer than one foolscap page. "Then," he says, "maybe someone will read it."[40]

The article contained a short description of his family, whom Almond no doubt mentioned to the reporter. Despite his obvious pride, however, he made little reference to the article. He wrote to Fergy and Tommy just before the Wonsan landing, and told Tommy to watch for *Time* and *Life* magazines to see what he and his corps were doing in Korea. He then turned immediately to encouraging the boy's studies and urging him to join the Cub Scouts. His letter to Margaret the same day was even more brief, asking her only to save six copies of that issue of *Time* for him. He never mentioned the article again except to thank friends who wrote to congratulate him.[41]

Almond's reactions to this article and various other stories about him, as well as his irritation at the lack of press coverage of his headquarters, reflect a deep insecurity. He had faith in his own considerable tactical ability and rarely doubted his decisions, yet had little patience for others whose perceived tactical acumen did not match his own. His desire for recognition is natural, but having received that approbation, he appears to have been uncomfortable with it. His failure to mention the article again indicates that he merely sought recognition of his victories to reduce the sting of failure that he evidently still felt from World War II.

President Syngman Rhee had given command of all armed forces of the Republic of Korea to MacArthur on July 7, 1950, and the bulk of the forces remaining intact after the invasion had helped defend the Pusan Perimeter with EUSAK. While most ROK units moved north in concert with EUSAK, the I ROK Corps moved up the coast road out of Pusan. This corps consisted of the Capital Division and the 3rd ROK Division, and it cleared the east coast of NKPA forces north over the border and past Wonsan toward Hamhung by October 15, negating the need for an assault landing.[42]

The need for a second landing at Wonsan has been debated, and many leaders later saw another amphibious landing as foolhardy. But MacArthur unified command at his level, and he was comfortable sending separate task forces to perform widely separate missions, as his operations in the Southwest Pacific demonstrated. In all of these amphibious operations, the land forces were fully supported by naval aviation and gunfire, and at times by land-based aviation. The operations were daring but not foolhardy, and MacArthur's plan had few detractors at the time. Inchon's tremendous success had created a morale boost that made everyone believe in MacArthur's infallibility. Oliver Smith later remembered, "People figured that MacArthur had gotten away with it at Inchon, maybe he would get away with this too—but he didn't." McCaffrey later argued that, unlike Inchon, the Wonsan landing was unnecessary. "Inchon was brilliant, but it was lucky," McCaffrey said, believing the enemy could have sunk the entire fleet off Wolmi-do. "We could have driven to Wonsan. We didn't have to load out at Inchon and load out at Pusan." Rowny also believed that the Wonsan gambit was a mistake: 'It would have made more sense to stay here and worked this way, but to go around that other side [to Wonsan] and the run into the mines, you know. . . . The idea was that the North Koreans would be weak up there and we could shoot up to the Yalu, which we did."[43]

On October 14 Almond had sent McCaffrey to the Wonsan Airport with an advanced corps CP to prepare for the arrival of X Corps units, but the mines continued to prevent any ships from landing troops. The operation that had begun as a second bold masterstroke devolved into Operation "Yo-Yo," as the soldiers, marines, and sailors in the task force began referring to their repeated trips up and down the coast while waiting to land. The campaign took a comedic turn on October 25, as Bob Hope landed at the Wonsan Airport and put on a show for those soldiers who had been able to get ashore.[44]

Walker captured Pyongyang on October 19, and MacArthur's priorities changed. MacArthur directed Almond to take command of all UN forces in northeast Korea and to turn north and move quickly to the Yalu River, the border with China. MacArthur's plan for a final offensive to end the war envisioned EUSAK attacking north out of Pyongyang toward the Yalu, with X Corps mounting a supporting attack northwestward out of the Hamhung-Hungnam area to cut off retreating North Korean forces. The ROK Army was also moving faster than expected toward the northeast, and MacArthur doubtless felt the need to assert control over it.[45] Almond moved to Wonsan on October 20 and assumed control of the ROK I Corps and its two divisions, the 3rd and Capital Divisions. Haig later recalled that Almond had given him the "honor" of being the first staff member from the X Corps to land at Wonsan on October 25. Unfortunately, the boat taking him to shore capsized, and Haig and the coxswain were thrown into deep water. Haig was only able to save Almond's bedroll, and Almond chewed him out in typical fashion.

Rather than joining with EUSAK, X Corps would remain independent. This caused concern at the time and has dominated the historiography since the war, but MacArthur, as the ground commander, based the employment of his forces both on terrain and on the perceived ability of his commanders. MacArthur had enjoyed great success in the Pacific during World War II, and his Korean operations reflected his experience and inclinations. He was hampered somewhat by his physical distance from battlefield, but that also reflected his specific experiences. His headquarters always remained at some distance from the front line. This, too, reflected a mode of operation now considered common. The Korean Peninsula is dominated by the northern and southern Taebaek mountain range, which is a continuation of the mountains of southern Manchuria and runs the length of the country. The mountains range from 4,500 to 8,000 feet high, with steep and rugged slopes that would make cross-country movement extremely difficult. The few roads were susceptible to washouts after rains, and the valleys featured winding streams and rice fields that restricted movement in any direction. Both Almond and MacArthur were well aware of the terrain, having received updated information from the Army G2.[46]

With the two ROK divisions operating along the coast, Almond intended to employ the 1st Marine Division on the corps's left flank after its arrival at Wonsan, with the 7th Infantry Division in the center between the Marines and the ROK. The speed of the ROK advance, however, meant that the 7th Infantry Division would actually land south of its intended operating area. Almond proposed to Admirals Doyle and Struble that the Navy put the 7th Infantry Division ashore at Iwon, eighty miles north of Wonsan on the coast. The admirals protested at first, citing the possibility of mines in Iwon Harbor, but Almond believed that Iwon was less likely to be mined than Wonsan. The admirals agreed to send minesweepers to Iwon, and if they found it clear, they would land the 7th Infantry Division there.[47]

Almond saw the operation as an opportunity to prove himself to his boss, but his tactical deployment demonstrated his inexperience. Some of Almond's staff were uneasy about the attack, but they realized that Almond would never buck MacArthur. Besides, the feeling of inevitable success growing out of the Inchon operation continued to pervade the corps headquarters. Almond's scheme of maneuver assigned the ROK Capital Division to continue up the coast road toward the short (eleven-mile) Russian border, while the 3rd ROK Division would move north from Hamhung toward Manchuria. The 1st Marine Division would follow the route of the 3rd ROK Division northward from Hamhung to the Chosin Reservoir area, with the route beyond that point to the border subject to the tactical situation. The 7th Infantry Division would attack north out of its port of Iwon on the left flank of the ROK Capital Division.[48]

Almond flew to the Chosin Reservoir on October 30 when he learned that some soldiers of the Chinese Communist Forces (CCF) had been captured. He interrogated them and determined that they were from the CCF 124th Division. Colonel Mildren accompanied Almond, and Almond considered the Chinese the sloppiest soldiers he had ever seen. "They are the most decrepit looking bunch you've ever run into. Some of them didn't even have shoes. They had gunny sacks wrapped around their feet." Almond tried to give them close order drill through an interpreter, but Mildren recalled they looked, "like a mob." Mildren said this convinced the staff, and even the corps G2, Col. William Quinn, that there were no large Chinese units in the area.

On November 1, 1950, Chinese troops that had infiltrated into North Korea throughout October suddenly attacked both EUSAK and X Corps. Intelligence estimates from the FECOM G2, Maj. Gen. Charles Willoughby, and from Almond's X Corps G2, Colonel Quinn, differed in strength and numbers. Willoughby identified elements of four CCF armies, totaling some 16,500 troops in North Korea. Quinn believed that Willoughby underestimated the strength of CCF units in Korea because he mistrusted the source from which it came. Willoughby relied on human intelligence gathered from nationalist Chinese infiltrated into Communist Chinese formations, but he deliberately discounted their information because he believed them to be self-serving. By November 3 the strength of the CCF attack was clear. Willoughby estimated that some 316,000 regular Chinese soldiers and 274,000 security forces were in southern Manchuria, poised to cross the Yalu into North Korea. In reality, many of these had already done so. Willoughby put the Chinese troops in North Korea at no more than 16,500, but there were in fact more than 300,000, with 120,000 deployed in front of Almond's X Corps. Six Chinese divisions managed to surround the corps at the Changjin Reservoir, a large lake made by damming the Changjin River and called on American maps (drawing on Japanese terminology) the Chosin Reservoir.[49]

November saw the piecemeal arrival of the 3rd (US) Infantry Division. The 3rd Infantry Division headquarters and two remaining regiments, the 7th RCT and 15th RCT, had arrived in Japan on September 16. Like the other units, the 3rd Infantry Division had arrived critically short of personnel, and its two regiments required 8,500 KATUSAs to bring them up to strength. They had spent the intervening two months training and operating as GHQ reserve. Despite the shortages, the time to conduct cohesive unit training with at least two of the regiments made a difference. The 3rd Infantry Division would fare much better in its initial combat experience than had the 7th Infantry Division, which had been unable to do any unit training at all. After landing on November 13, division commander Maj. Gen. Robert H. Soule gained the 65th RCT, recently detached from EUSAK, and the 26th ROK Regiment, detached from the 3rd ROK Division. The division's two organic regiments completed disembarking on November 21.[50]

The 65th RCT had arrived and begun unloading at Wonsan on November 5. Almond went to the port to observe the unloading, and regimental commander Col. William W. Harris quickly got his first mission. He was to deploy thirty-five miles northwest to Yonghung to interdict enemy forces coming from the north, with a follow-on mission to move seventy miles west and make contact with EUSAK. Almond attached the 65th RCT to the 1st Marine Division for this mission, but his predilection for skipping over subordinate commanders once again rankled General Smith. Almond hosted Smith and Harris for dinner on the evening of Harris's arrival in Wonsan, and gave both specific instructions.[51]

Having been assigned a mission directly by the corps commander, Colonel Harris set out to impress his new boss with his aggressiveness. Rushing to get his units out quickly, Harris failed to ensure that the units took a complete basic load of ammunition, and he allowed his lead battalion to deploy without its mortar section. In his zeal to get quickly under way, Harris also "captured" a communications truck he found in the dock area; he later learned that this was the truck that Almond used to communicate with GHQ in Tokyo. Almond provided trucks to move the 65th RCT, and got one infantry battalion into position by the evening of November 6. Harris accompanied his lead battalion, losing contact with and control of his remaining battalions. Harris later learned that Almond had briefly attached the other two battalions to the Marines for a different mission.

Harris settled his battalion in on good high ground for the night, but he failed to establish a perimeter with an adjacent artillery battalion. The North Korean 11th Regiment, 5th Division, attacked both battalions during the night, briefly forcing Harris to surrender some ground and producing casualties. Harris requested an immediate resupply of ammunition, and X Corps made an airdrop of ammunition the next morning. Almond himself arrived at Harris's CP shortly afterward and gave him specific instructions as how to defend his ground. Almond did not record the conversation, but he would doubtless have told Harris that while his aggressiveness was admirable, his lack of attention to detail had been deadly. Almond demanded both. The episode humbled Harris, but it also demonstrated Almond's nature: aggressive to the point of rashness and impulsive, yet always eager to see things at the front for himself and ready to lend assistance. Harris quickly learned that Almond expected rapid and decisive movement at all times.

After the regiment recovered from its initial trial by fire, Almond pushed Harris to speed up the movement of a battalion to the west to link up with EUSAK. On Almond's next visit to the regiment on November 10, Harris reported that his lead battalion was moving slowly due to reports of a breach in the route to the west. Almond then flew along the entire route to the X Corps boundary with EUSAK and returned to 65th RCT headquarters to report that the road was clear. He demanded that Harris move the battalion immediately to a prearranged point to establish a defense and send daily patrols to a contact point with EUSAK.[52]

Soule, as soon as he arrived, also received ample evidence of Almond's sometimes unrealistic expectations. Almond assigned Soule a threefold mission: establish contact with EUSAK, protect X Corps's left flank, and protect the Wonsan and Hamhung area. Even with the addition of the ROK Regiment, this mission gave the 3rd Infantry more ground than it could adequately cover. The division already lacked sufficient transportation to move units, and the 65th RCT had relied upon X Corps trucks to move to its first position. The newly strengthened X Corps was essentially a small field army; comprising three US divisions (1st Marine, 3rd Infantry, 7th Infantry), two ROK divisions (3rd ROK, Capital), and the 26th ROK Regiment, it totaled some 83,000 soldiers, nearly 62 percent the size of EUSAK.[53]

Almond's by-name requests for his former subordinates continued to yield results, as Lt. Col. Frank T. Mildren, Almond's former G3 from the 2nd Infantry Division, arrived at the headquarters just before the Wonsan landing. After a couple days in a replacement depot in Japan, Mildren had gotten a ride on a troopship headed for Pusan, where he was left to his own devices. He managed to catch a flight into Wonsan and joined the X Corps advanced CP as forces flowed in. The corps had not yet landed, and the advanced HQ consisted only of Almond, McCaffrey, corps G3 Col. Jack Chiles, and a few other officers. Mildren was assigned as the deputy G3.[54]

Almond had arranged with Walker to run patrols between their two commands, both to stay in contact and to gather intelligence. These patrols found few large enemy forces, but they did discover small pockets of Chinese soldiers. Almond later recalled that both he and Walker thought that there was one Chinese division operating in the gap between EUSAK and X Corps, but this did not alarm either of them. Neither they nor MacArthur gave the Chinese any credence. The two generals were more concerned with beating each other to the Yalu than with any Chinese threat. McCaffrey later remembered, "General Almond was always trying to be farther north than Eighth Army. In any given day, he wanted X Corps's front line north of wherever Eighth Army was. It was a childish competition."[55]

General Walker planned to renew his Eighth Army attack to the north beginning on November 15, with his three corps arranged from west to east: US I Corps holding his western flank, US IX Corps in the center, and II ROK Corps holding his eastern flank. MacArthur ordered Almond to do everything possible to support EUSAK, which was the UN main effort. While Walker delayed the beginning of his assault in order to get his logistical operations set, Almond exchanged letters with Wright and the JSPOG on how best to achieve MacArthur's intent. The JSPOG believed that Almond should reorient his northward attack to the northwest, in order to protect EUSAK's eastern flank. Intelligence estimates at the time indicated the presence of large Chinese Communist forces, but the specifics of those forces were unknown either to EUSAK or to X Corps. General Willoughby had provided MacArthur with some estimates, and MacArthur chose to launch the attack to further develop the situation.[56]

Tactical air support of infantry troops had been one of Almond's early concerns, dating back to the weeks right after the invasion. By November the need was critical. Almond sent a message to Lt. Gen. George E Stratemeyer, CG, Far East Air Forces, headed "operational immediate."

He requested that thirty-four additional Tactical Air Control Parties be furnished as soon as possible to X Corps. He requested the TACPs on the basis of one per infantry battalion, one per infantry regiment, one per division, and one for the X Corps headquarters. "Current inadequate number of TACP's seriously hampers present operations in mountain terrain which compartments already widely separated units. Most critical TACPs shortages existing 3rd US Inf. Div., 3rd ROK Div., and Cap Div with only 3, 3 and 4 TACPs respectively including 4 TACPs recently furnished by FEAF." The message reflected his growing concern with the dispersion of his units because of the terrain, but also his frustration with managing air support.[57]

The abrupt changes in mission had some unintended consequences. The GHQ order that had sent Almond to Wonsan and launched Walker toward Pyongyang also authorized Almond to keep thirty days of all classes of supply, while Eighth Army units had been limited to fifteen days of supply. Walker needed to issue the remainder of the supplies as well as winter clothing for all 40,000 US troops in X Corps. This not only consumed the quartermaster section of 2nd Logistical Command for several days, it also depleted all stocks of winter clothing in the depots. Almond's abrasive manner tended to make things worse; in this case, he issued an administrative order directly to a depot commander in the 2nd Logistical Command who did not know he was supporting the X Corps. The matter was resolved, but it did not improve relations between Eighth Army and X Corps. Moreover, because Almond's original mission had been to attack across the peninsula to Pyongyang in order to link up with EUSAK, he did not need to bring all of his support units on the landing. Those were designated to follow the Eighth Army and rejoin X Corps after it made linkup with EUSAK. The change of mission left all of Almond's maintenance units far to the rear, and his vehicle readiness would suffer throughout the campaign.[58]

EUSAK found supporting X Corps units from Inchon impossible, and it was difficult even from Pusan. The few available rail lines were not located in areas useful for Army support, and those north of the 38th Parallel were largely inoperative due to disrepair before the war. The road network was primitive, and airdrop could not be used to handle the large quantities required. The mountainous terrain that impeded troop movement made normal supply routes impossible. EUSAK eventually began resupplying X Corps by water, with 2nd Logistical Command sending resupply ships up the coast. Even this became confused, as in one instance the 2nd Logistical Command directed a ship coming from the United States to divert to support X Corps directly, with the result that its cargo arrived unsorted and unprioritized. Almond was also angered when he discovered that some requisitions were being reduced at EUSAK headquarters without his knowledge, because of the disparity in allowable stockpiles. In late October, when Almond received permission to request supplies from Japan Logistical Command which then flowed through Wonsan, most of the problems were alleviated, but those items not available in Japan such as tents, stoves, and winter clothing were still supplied by the 2nd Logistical Command in Pusan.[59]

The attack into North Korea appeared initially to have succeeded. The North Korean force had retreated under the dual hammer blows of EUSAK in the west and X Corps in the east. Almond's deployment in North Korea did not go as well as the Inchon landing and capture of Seoul, but he was not entirely to blame. MacArthur's plan for invading North Korea was ill conceived, perhaps counting on the incompetence of the NKPA and assuming no Chinese intervention. He doubtless expected that X Corps could quickly destroy the remnants of the NKPA. MacArthur's forces would remain separated both to serve his emphasis on the double envelopment and because of the Taebaek Range. This troop displacement close to the Chinese border unnerved some observers, but having chased the NKPA to the Yalu River, most senior leaders sensed victory in the air—including Almond. The movement scattered the entire Corps along a four-hundred-mile front, and Almond had no connection to the Eighth Army. He acknowledged this was excessive and left the units vulnerable to concentrated attack, but he felt that the terrain and the mission dictated this deployment (see map 12.4).[60]

With the gift of hindsight, Col. Frank Mildren, X Corps deputy G3, later argued that US forces should never have gone to the Yalu in the first place. He estimated the distance between them to be at least a hundred miles; "it was just like another theater. It was a no man's land in between and included the terrible mountain jungle range." Mildren thought if EUSAK and X Corps had formed the line from Wonsan to Pyongyang, then issued a statement that UN forces were not going any further north, the Chinese might not have intervened. This "waistline" was the shortest frontage to defend. Instead, the corps could not effectively hold the large area it occupied. Almond spread out his divisions in such a way as to cover more ground, but this made his line vulnerable. No one thought that of the time, however, and Mildren acknowledges that the Chinese might still have come in while UN forces held Wonsan and Pyongyang.[61]

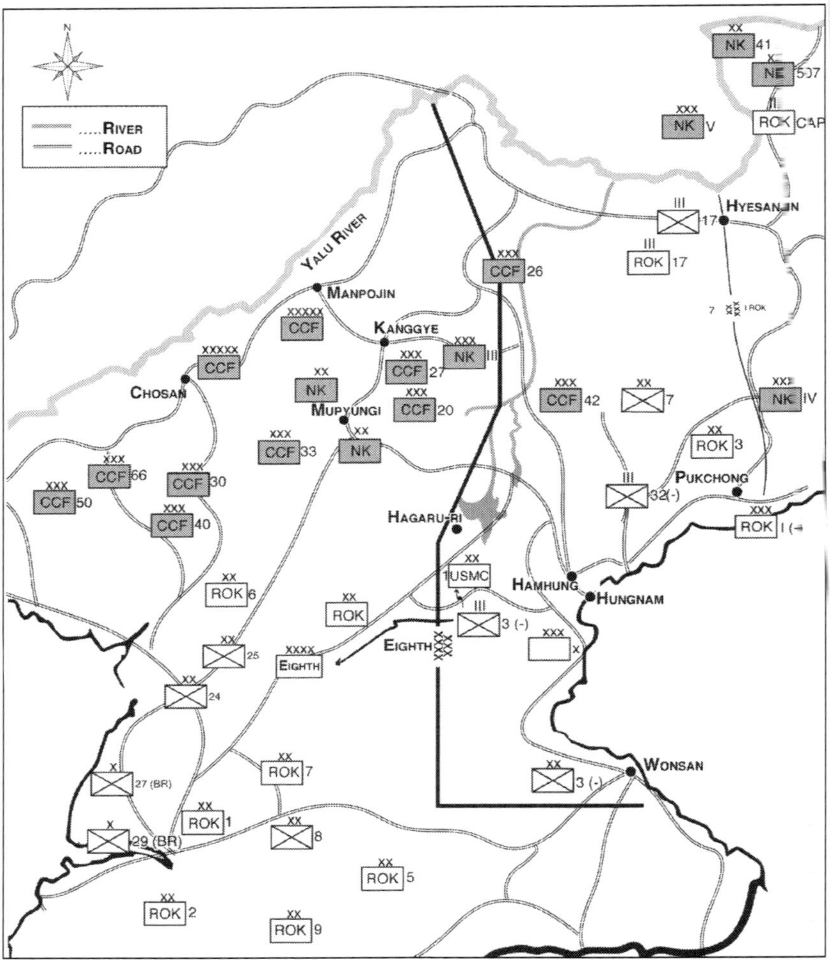

12.4. X Corps Deployment in North Korea, October–December 1950

Haig saw Almond as a tough boss, but he also saw qualities that Almond's superiors perhaps saw as well. "Almond was blessed with an intuitive gift for understanding the possibilities of terrain. He could glance at the battlefield and know at once where to place his troops and guns, how to maneuver them, how to take advantage of the mistakes that he seemed to know in advance the enemy would make. He took this talent for granted and was annoyed when others could not perceive through earnest study what he saw, as a great painter must see a picture he has not yet painted, by means of inborn genius."[62]

These statements are difficult to reconcile with Almond's initial deployment in North Korea. The US units were largely road bound, and the few roads in the area left lots of open space the Chinese used to move between units. The CCF consisted primarily of infantry, with very little support, and could therefore move overland more quickly and easily than could US units with all their vehicles and equipment. After the attack came, American units discovered that several Chinese units had been bypassed, and those units infiltrated behind US lines.[63]

With Almond's corps now composed of three US divisions and two ROK divisions, Almond seemed to demonstrate none of the "intuitive" grasp of terrain that his aide believed he had. Almond was indeed very tactically proficient, more so than many of his subordinate commanders. But he tended to focus on small-unit actions, which blinded him to the big picture. Indeed, he experienced some of the same growing pains in handling a corps as did some of his division commanders in handling their regiments. Almond's micromanagement and lack of expertise in handling larger formations, combined with inaccurate and poorly analyzed intelligence, nearly spelled disaster for X Corps. The two months his corps spent in North Korea provided painful lessons for him in shifting his view to the broader perspective of a corps commander. He lost, or likely never had, the operational view that would have revealed the inadequate disposition of his corps.

13

Winter of Discontent

1951

Almond's dash to the Yalu had scattered his divisions widely. Thanksgiving week, 1950, found the X Corps spread across North Korea from the Manchurian border to the Sea of Japan, to the Changjin Reservoir (Chosin Reservoir to the Americans), to Wonsan. The initial corps movement north out of Wonsan toward the Yalu had been orderly, with normal operational control measures. After the North Korean opposition collapsed, the operational scheme became a pursuit. US forces were forbidden to go near the Siberian border, so the I ROK Corps and its two divisions ranged widely in that area along the coast. The 7th Infantry Division's movements had scattered it widely, with the 32nd Infantry Regiment well to the east, close to the coast, while the 31st Infantry Regiment remained northeast of the Chosin Reservoir and the 17th Infantry Regiment reached the Yalu near Hyesanjin on November 21. Almond flew to Hyesanjin the day before and spent the night at the 17th RCT CP, then followed the lead company to the river the next day. He congratulated the soldiers on being the first American unit to reach the river, the northernmost point of the US advance.[1]

The 1st Marine Division made its headquarters at Hagaru-ri, at the southern tip of the Chosin Reservoir, and occupied positions on the west, east, and south sides of the reservoir. This disposition alarmed Maj. Gen. Oliver Smith, and he asked Almond to realign the Army units so that he could consolidate his Marine regiments on the west side of the reservoir. The 3rd Infantry Division, recently landed, occupied the corps rear with the mission of securing the line of communication (LOC) to the forward units, but Smith found the division deficient and used his own 1st Marine Regiment to secure the LOC.[2]

General Walker began moving the Eighth Army north on November 24, the first steps of what was to be a general UN offensive. Almond planned a supporting attack to begin on the morning of November 27. He ordered the 1st Marine Division to attack northwest to seize the town of Mupyong and then continue to advance to the Yalu River and destroy the enemy in the zone of advance. In order to allow the Marine regiments to consolidate on the west side of the reservoir, Almond ordered Lt. Col. Don C. Faith's 1st Battalion, 32nd Infantry, then en route from Kujung-ni to Pukchong to become corps reserve, to divert north to the Chosin Reservoir in the vicinity of Hagaru-ri. There it would relieve in place the 5th Marine Regiment on the east side of the reservoir, allowing the 5th Marines to rejoin the rest of the 1st Marine Division on the west side. Faith's battalion was to be attached to the 1st Marine Division upon arrival. Almond also ordered 7th Infantry Division commander Maj. Gen. David G. Barr to send a regiment to assist Faith in taking over the 5th Marines position. Barr sent the 31st RCT, commanded by Col. Allan D. MacLean. MacLean took two battalions of his own 31st Infantry Regiment with supporting artillery. In all, what historians later called Task Force MacLean numbered about 3,200 men, including 700 ROK soldiers (see map 13.1).[3]

The two US Army divisions faced much more challenging tasks. Almond ordered the 7th Infantry Division to attack from the Chosin Reservoir and advance to the Yalu River, destroying any enemy in zone while coordinating operations with I ROK Corps, which was to maintain its positions in northeast North Korea. The division's three widely separated regiments could in no way mount a coordinated attack. The 3rd Infantry Division had a complex set of tasks. Almond ordered Maj. Gen. Robert Soule to gain and maintain contact with the Eighth Army right flank; protect the west flank of X Corps; support the 1st Marine Division as the corps's main effort; protect the airfield and harbor facilities in the Wonsan area, and destroy enemy guerrilla forces in zone. The 3rd Infantry Division was separated by more than a hundred air miles from the EUSAK flank, and that space included the rugged Taebaek range. Wonsan was also nearly a hundred miles from the 1st Marine Division's lead elements at Yudam-ni, so Soule would have been hard pressed to continue to guard Wonsan while also protecting the X Corps west flank.[4]

Almond's time at the Air Corps Tactical School had given him a deep appreciation for the use and versatility of the airplane, but he had first become interested and completed his first flights while assigned to the Philippines. He also used airplanes during training in the States to visit his widely scattered units, and in Italy during World War II. He saw the airplane as a critical tool for the ground commander, and that ground-focused view informed his attitude toward the use of airpower in a combat role. Almond made aerial reconnaissance a vital part of his own

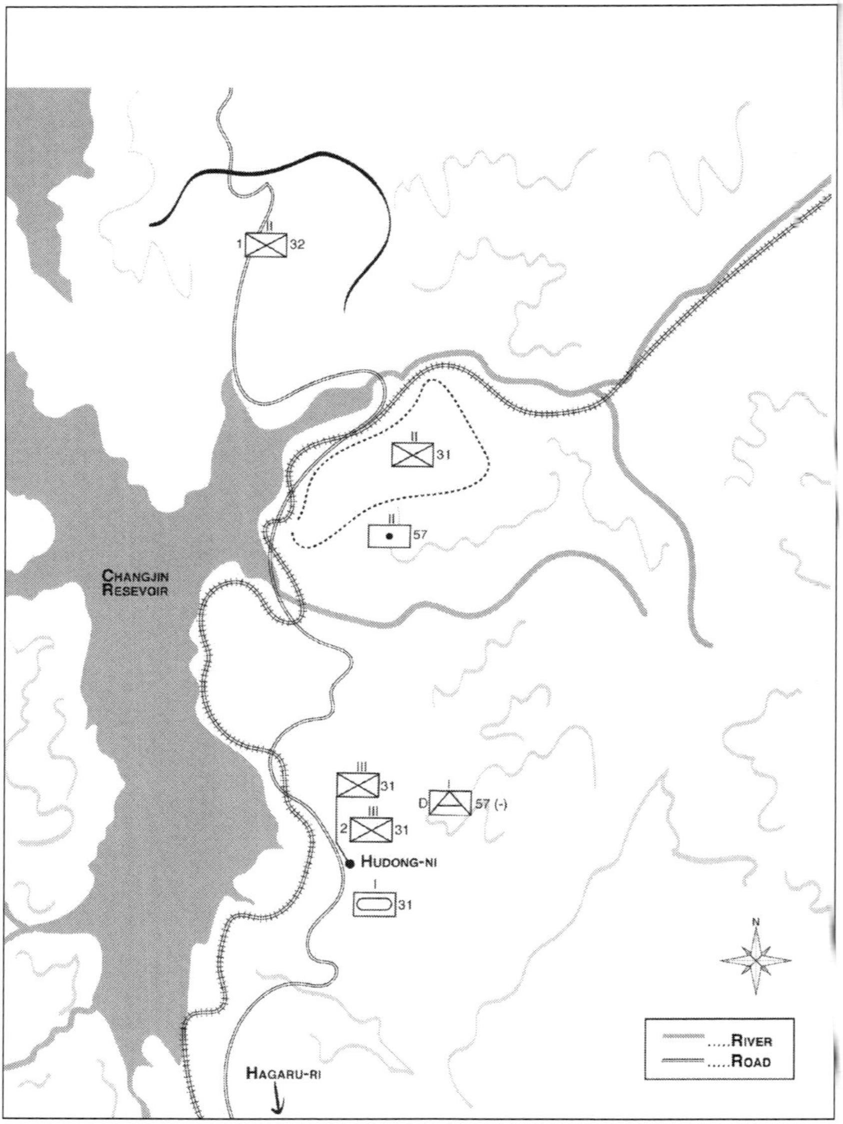

13.1. Task Force MacLean/Faith, November 27–December 2, 1950

inspection of the battlefield, and his frequent use of the airplane allowed him to stay in touch with his forward troops every day. He required each regiment to construct a landing strip adjacent to its headquarters whenever it moved so that he could fly in and inspect the position. Moreover, he simply loved to fly. A visiting newspaper reporter noted that Almond "won't drive two miles if he can fly." His X Corps air section included eleven aircraft of three different types, all generally used for artillery spotting and personnel transportation. They included four L-4 Grasshoppers, the military version of the two-seat Piper Cub J3; five L-5 Sentinel two-seaters; and two L-17 Navions, which carried a pilot and three passengers. He would later gain a Bell H-13B Sioux helicopter, the two-seat version used for observation and casualty evacuation.[5]

Almond favored one particular L-5, which came to be called the Blue Goose. When the war began, the plane had just come out of the maintenance shop for an overhaul and had the engine and skin replaced. With little time before the invasion, the plane was placed aboard the aircraft carrier USS *Baedong Strait* with its shiny aluminum skin unpainted. With no olive drab paint available aboard the ship, mechanic Sgt. Eldon E. Brasel painted it navy blue, spawning the name. Almond's primary pilot, Capt. Charles Keleman, flew the plane off the aircraft carrier on September 16, bound for Kimpo Airfield. The field had not yet been captured, however, so he turned back, then staged what is believed to be the only landing of an army airplane on an aircraft carrier during the Korean War.[6]

Almond's mission would have been difficult under any circumstances, but then the Chinese People's Volunteer Army (CPVA) initiated a large counteroffensive against the entire UN line on November 25 that changed all UN plans. The CPVA XIII Army Group, numbering nearly 200,000 soldiers, weighted its attack on the II ROK Corps on the EUSAK right flank. The CPVA IX Army Group (120,000) launched a large attack around the Chosin Reservoir. Five divisions attacked southward down each side of the reservoir, hitting both the Marine and army units. Frank Mildren believed that the North Korean soldier was a better fighter than the Chinese soldier. The only Chinese advantage was their practice of operating en masse. He found it easy to overwhelm them in the defense with massed artillery and airpower. "The North Koreans are more persistent and better, and they stay right there and die." In the offense, he would rather be attacked by the North Koreans than the Chinese, however, because the Chinese simply launched massive attacks designed to overwhelm the defenses by sheer numbers, infiltrate around the units, smother the Americans with people.[7]

Almond very succinctly described the situation in North Korea in a letter to his friend Lt. Gen. Alfred Gruenther, whose son Almond had recently promoted to captain. He very kindly sent a photo of young Dick Gruenther being promoted, and then gave Gruenther an appraisal of the situation:

> You are aware of what we face here. Try to imagine a winter campaign in the Canadian Rockies without benefit of a single first-class road and you about have it. The logistics of maneuver problems are tremendous but are being solved as rapidly as our resources permit. It was a genuine lifesaver to get the 3rd Division. While it is concentrating for future employment, I'm currently using it to clean up the southern end of my zone where the guerrillas have been a real menace. By throwing them across the escape avenues, we hope to throttle the bothersome infiltration of North Korean remnants, while at the same time providing that division with valuable training in the terrain conditions that prevail in this area. Later, of course, they will be used for more important tasks.[8]

Besides the gap with the Eighth Army, there were large gaps between the units, primarily within the 7th Infantry Division. The 1st Marine Division kept its regiments much closer together, and the Chinese were not able to infiltrate between the regiments, but 31st RCT (Task Force MacLean) was nearly destroyed. Mildren recalled: "The 1st Marine Division wrapped up in a ball by regiments and slowly pulled back on the west side of the Chosin reservoir to the southern tip of it. We could not get the 31st out. . . . The parts of the 7th that got out were further north than the 31st. . . . the 17th got out in pretty good shape, but it was way to the East."[9]

The Chinese tended to launch mass attacks at night, against units already demoralized by crippling cold and cut off from other units. Col. Allan MacLean experienced this firsthand just after midnight on the night of November 27. Mildren recalled that the Marines suffered more than 3,000 casualties, mostly from frostbite because of the cold. "I remember up around the Chosin it was 40 degrees below zero." The 7th Infantry Division did not have as many cold-weather casualties as the 1st Marine Division, because of their stationing at the time. The bulk of the cold-weather casualties came from 31st RCT at the Chosin Reservoir. The 17th Infantry Regiment and the two ROK divisions suffered fewer because they were along the east coast, which was considerably warmer than the mountainous area around the Chosin Reservoir. The 32nd Infantry Regiment was X Corps reserve and living in tents, so suffered comparatively little. All those units were able to use fires and stoves unavailable to the Marines and 31st RCT.[10]

Gen. Matthew B. Ridgway, US Army deputy chief of staff for administration, monitored Almond's situation from the Pentagon. "Certainly he had that Corps of his scattered from 'hell to breakfast.' It was very poor tactical handling, but that in large part was MacArthur's fault, because MacArthur kept urging him, you know." Ridgway had much harsher words for MacArthur. In an interview twenty years after the war, Ridgway recalled that MacArthur had said in Senate testimony that had he known of the Chinese offensive in late November, he could not have disposed his troops better than they had been. Ridgway condemned MacArthur's disingenuous statement, and by association also condemned Almond's troop deployment. "Well, that was such a glaring falsehood. Absolute falsehood. Absolute falsehood. Anybody of MacArthur's genius at all knew it. It couldn't have been a worse disposition of his troops, as a matter of fact."[11]

On November 28, Almond visited the 1st Marine Division in the morning and received a briefing from Smith on the previous evening's attack. Smith had sustained heavy casualties in an attack that began about three hours before the attack on the 31st RCT. Smith reported that the attack came initially from the south, and then from the west, and his main supply route to the south had been cut by the enemy. Almond flew to the 31st RCT in the afternoon and received briefings on the situation from both MacLean and Faith. The RCT still did not have its regiments consolidated, owing to heavy traffic on the few serviceable roads, but Almond assured MacLean that the Chinese who had attacked the night before were merely stragglers, and the 31st should be able to continue its attack as soon as the remaining units arrived. Almond awarded the Silver Star to Faith, who tried to protest the award and later reportedly threw it away, but Almond insisted. Almond had asked if there were any other soldiers who deserve to be decorated, and Faith selected a soldier seemingly at random. Faith and other junior commanders resented Almond's periodic inspections and impromptu award ceremonies, but their resentment overlooks the genuine concern that their corps commander exhibited.[12]

Despite Almond's reputation during World War II, he believed in recognizing and decorating soldiers immediately after a worthy action.

Almond rarely missed an opportunity to present combat decorations, and most of his unit inspections included award ceremonies. After awarding Silver Star medals to 31st RCT commander MacLean and the commander of his 3rd Battalion, Lt. Col. William R. Reilly, Almond returned to his headquarters. A couple of days later, Almond forwarded the completed citation to MacLean with a letter. His attention to detail ever present, Almond mentioned that he had worked on the citation with General Barr on the way back on his airplane to ensure that it was accurate, and he asked MacLean to correct any inaccuracies that might persist. He used the letter to impart his philosophy of awards:

> My purpose in awarding the citations to commanders in the field at the time of the action for which the recognition is offered is that of informing all concerned of an event at the time of its occurrence and not at a much later date. In previous combat experiences I have been greatly impressed with the dereliction of senior commanders in their failures toward indications of valor in a high degree of leadership at the time of the event. My [having] awarded this citation to you and to Lieut. Col. Riley [*sic*] is designed to further my conviction that worthwhile effort by combat leaders should be immediately recognized.[13]

Almond was also concerned with the fairness of awards. In a later visit to the 9th Infantry Regiment, he decorated eight officers and two noncommissioned officers. After the ceremony, however, he told the battalion adjutant that the next time he held a decoration ceremony, there should be more lower-ranking enlisted soldiers honored.[14]

The mission had begun as a large reconnaissance in force, designed to determine the strength of the enemy and uncover its intentions. Almond later said that his visit to the 7th Marines on November 27 and his visit to the 31st RCT the following day made clear to him just how precarious was his situation. Debate has ensued in the intervening years about whether or not Almond understood the strength of the force facing him at that point.[15]

MacArthur realized the grave threat that the Chinese now posed to all of his forces in Korea. He recalled both Walker and Almond to Tokyo for an immediate conference on the evening of November 28. After the two generals described their situation to MacArthur, he ordered both to begin pulling back from their forward positions. He ordered Almond to consolidate his forces around the Hamhung area. MacArthur believed that EUSAK was in greater danger than X Corps, and asked Almond what he could do to help Walker. Almond replied that he would need to get X Corps consolidated before he could do anything, reflecting his understanding of his precarious situation. Several options were discussed, but Walker and Almond left Tokyo before any final decisions were made. Their first task was to get their units out of danger.[16]

Almond flew back to his headquarters on November 29 and directed his staff to begin preparation of a new operations order, which would discontinue the attack to the northwest and begin the concentration of all X Corps units around Hamhung and Hungnam. Recognizing the danger to both the 1st Marine Division, isolated on the west side of the reservoir, and the scattered forces of the 7th Infantry Division, Almond attached all 7th Infantry Division units at or north of Hagaru-ri to the 1st Marine Division. X Corps assumed control of all elements south of Koto-ri to coordinate their movement toward Hamhung. Almond ordered Barr to begin assembling the 7th Infantry Division immediately and to establish blocking positions on the route north to Koto-ri along which the 1st Marine Division would have to pass (see map 13.2).[17]

On December 1, Almond met with 3rd Infantry Division commander General Soule and ordered him to form a task force of infantry, artillery, and engineers, commanded by a general officer, to deploy and act as a covering force to the 1st Marine Division withdrawal. The covering force was designed to protect the withdrawing unit by delaying and disrupting the enemy. Soule directed his assistant division commander, Brig. Gen. Armistead Mead, to form Task Force Dog, based around 3rd Battalion, 7th Infantry Regiment, and the 92nd Field Artillery Battalion. After working out the details with Soule, Almond sent McCaffrey to brief the plan to General Smith at the 1st Marine Division.[18]

On December 4 as the situation grew more critical, Almond flew into Hagaru-ri to check on the Marines. For all Almond's antipathy toward Smith, he still maintained a fierce loyalty to his subordinate. The corps commander's abrasive manner could also not always hide his emotions. Smith later related his surprise at Almond's demeanor at Chosin. "He came to see me. He gave me the Distinguished Service Cross. I never could figure out whether it was the cold or his emotions, but he was weeping when he came up to see me." Smith and Almond remembered Almond's instructions for evacuation quite differently. Smith later claimed that Almond told him to burn everything and get out, but Smith replied his Marines were going to fight it out there and needed all their equipment to do that. Almond, however, later recalled that he had told

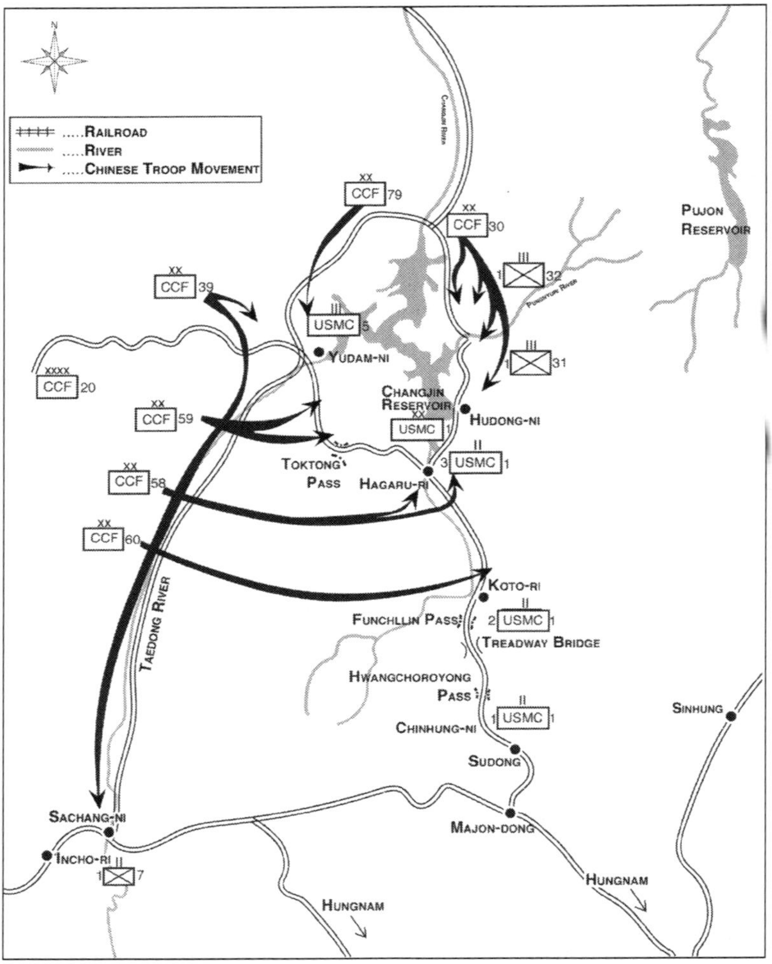

13.2. Retreat from Chosin Reservoir, November 27–December 1, 1950

Smith to "bring out such equipment as he could but not to sacrifice manpower for the sake of equipment. I ordered him to withdraw such equipment as the enemy would permit but if necessary to destroy it rather than trying to protect it at the cost of further casualties." Almond had realized the seriousness of the situation, and his comment to Smith was intended to demonstrate his support of the subordinate commander. Smith's frustration with the situation prevented him from according Almond any measure of credit or goodwill.[19]

With the situation worsening, MacArthur ordered Almond on December 8 to "evacuate all UN forces from the northeast zone of Korea as soon as an orderly withdrawal could be effected." MacArthur also notified Walker that "current planning calls for withdrawal in successive positions, if necessary to the Pusan area. Eighth Army will hold the Seoul area for the maximum time possible short of entailing such envelopment as would prevent its withdrawal to the South."[20]

As the X Corps deputy G3 and later G3, Mildren also had the opportunity to observe the relationship between Almond and Smith firsthand. By the time Mildren arrived in the corps, relations had deteriorated to the point that Smith refused any order from Almond unless it was in writing. Mildren saw Smith's irascible personality as the problem, and also that Smith did not like how Almond operated. "General Almond really wanted things done in a hurry, and Marines are very methodical and very slow. And, they were so used to amphibious operations that they didn't want to go beyond one side, you know."[21]

The evacuation plan called for establishing a perimeter around the port of Hungnam and slowly collapsing the defense as units embarked. Almond's attitude turned glum as he realized how much the circumstances had changed. He wrote to Col. Ray Sherman, his 370th Infantry Regiment commander during World War II, that "we have had to pull in our horns quite a bit," and "we are now engaged in activities which aim at cohesiveness rather than exploitation. . . . We are so vastly outnumbered that we are faced with constant improvisation." Almond even allowed a note of sadness to creep into a note to his grandson Tommy. He told the boy that times had changed in Korea, and he could ask his father to explain that to him. He told him not to worry, but added, "It is a bit disappointing though for us to have succeeded in the beginning!" Almond must have felt a twinge of disappointment, regardless of the fact that MacArthur had ordered the evacuation. He no doubt remembered being present when MacArthur had lectured Walker in relation to preparations for pulling back or evacuation from Pusan the previous summer.[22]

Almond issued X Corps Operations Order 10 on December 11, listing the priorities for withdrawal. This was not to be a Dunkirk-style evacuation, because all units were expected to bring out all equipment and supplies. The 3rd Infantry Division would form the western portion of a defensive perimeter around Hamhung and the port city of Hungnam, with the 7th Infantry Division forming the northeastern portion and the I ROK Corps divisions forming the eastern portion (see map 13.3). The 1st Marine Division, still fighting at Chosin, would then break

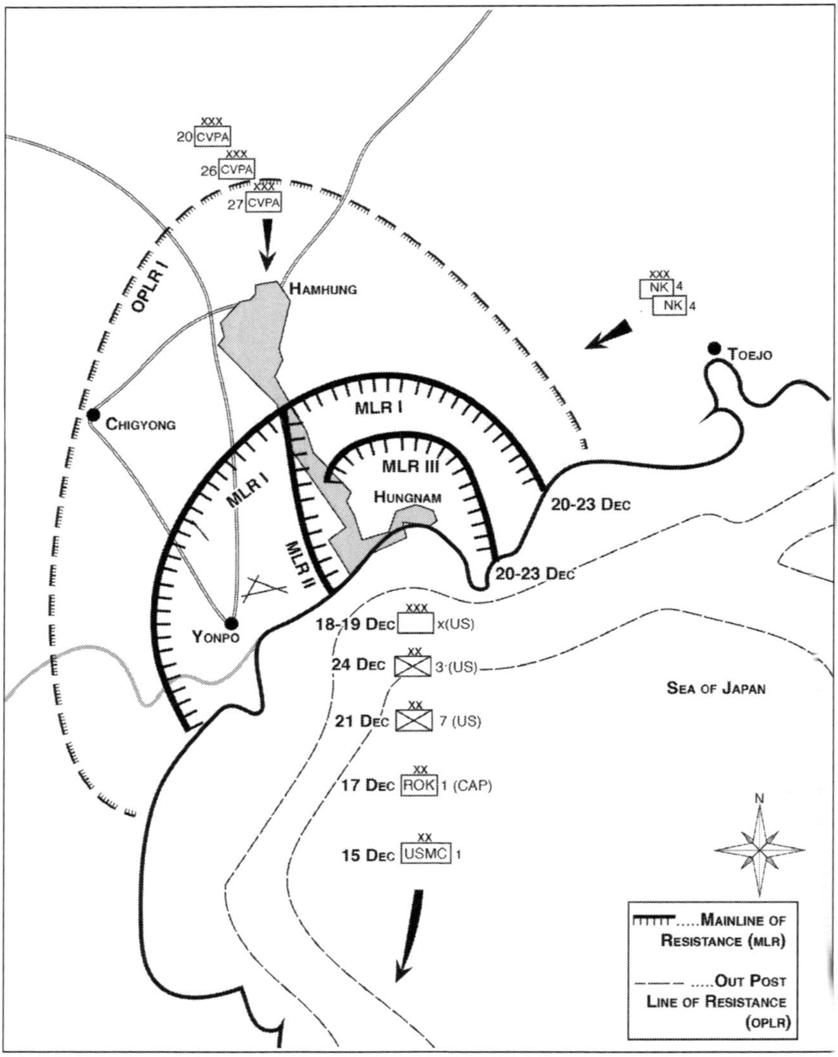

13.3. Hungnam Evacuation, December 10–24, 1950

contact and move to Hungnam and embark immediately. Remnants of Task Force MacLean and the remainder of the 7th Infantry Division would follow the 1st Marine Division. As units entered the perimeter and embarked, those battalions holding back the Chinese would withdraw gradually toward the port, steadily contracting the defensive line. The 3rd Infantry Division and the two ROK divisions would leave last, with X Corps headquarters troops and support units interspersed throughout the embarkation.[23]

Mildren remembered that lack of transportation ironically helped the Marines escape from the Chosin Reservoir quicker, because the roads were not as clogged. "Every time we moved the 1st Marine Division it took every vehicle we had in X Corps. That was to their advantage given the situation around the Chosin reservoir." Almond assured Smith on every visit that he was focusing all possible resources from the corps on supporting the extraction of the Marines. Any request that Smith made, Almond immediately gave orders to staff to fulfill it. One such order came without a request: Almond gave control of all artillery in the Hagaru-ri area, including X Corps's own and the artillery from the other two divisions, to Smith.[24]

Almond met with Maj. Gen. Field Harris, commanding general of the 1st Marine Aircraft Wing, and several Air Force officers on December 5 to discuss tactical air support. The need for US Navy, Marine Corps, and Air Force aircraft to support the troops on the ground was paramount during the evacuation. Almond noted in his log that when the subject turned to who should command supporting air units, "My statement was that *the Ground Commander should have operational control of supporting air units*." Almond underscored the last part to indicate his emphasis on this requirement; he would continue his vehement support of the ground commander controlling air support for the remainder of his career. Three days after this meeting, Almond reiterated his urgent requirement of the TACPs. General Harris also had good reason to ensure that the ground forces had adequate air support: his son, Lt. Col. William Harris, was commanding the 3rd Battalion, 7th Marines, then providing the rearguard action as the 1st Marine Division moved south toward Hagaru-ri.[25]

MacArthur visited X Corps briefly on December 11, and Almond explained the plans for defending Hungnam and evacuating his units. He also provided MacArthur with an estimate of the time and equipment required to complete the move. MacArthur told Almond that his corps would report to EUSAK after the evacuation. Almond noted in a letter to Margaret that he met privately with MacArthur, who revealed he had recommended him for promotion to lieutenant general based on his service as a corps commander. Almond said cryptically, "He advised me what to do pending my promotion, then he would take the proper steps. This in the long run will be best and in the meantime no possible harm can ensue."[26]

Despite the obvious dangers, the evacuation proceeded well. The combination of the Marine Aircraft Wing bombing and strafing, naval gunfire, and all of X Corps artillery being concentrated on the perimeter ensured that the Chinese were unable to impede operations. Eventually the Chinese dropped all opposition. After the Marines evacuated the area, the Chinese took over the power plant at the Chosin Reservoir and turned off power to the port, which made loading at night more difficult. By December 17 the Chinese had yet to launch a coordinated attack on the X Corps perimeter, but Almond began to receive indications that such an attack might be forthcoming. As the perimeter contracted, Almond believed the likelihood of attack increased. Early evacuations had included flights out of the airport at Yonpo, but Almond then contracted the perimeter and excluded the airfield. The CCF launched its heaviest attacks on December 18 and 19, but the attacks were easily repulsed with artillery fire, naval gunfire, and limited counterattacks. These were the last significant attacks against the Hungnam perimeter, though the enemy continued probing attacks daily until X Corps was completely embarked. The lack of meaningful opposition made the evacuation easier, because the docks could accommodate several ships at a time.[27]

Despite the urgency of the situation, the evacuation was a very organized and deliberate operation. Almond assigned the 2nd Engineer Special Brigade to organize and supervise the loading of the ships. Almond ordered his staff to maintain a balance between combat and service troops in the loading, in order to ensure that he had enough troops to maintain the perimeter, and also that he had enough logistical support of embarking units. While X Corps units moved from Hamhung to Hungnam to embark, thousands of Korean refugees clogged the roadways. The operations order directed that there be "no movement of civilians into or out of X Corps Def. areas. Permit no refugees to enter outpost area." Almond directed his provost marshal to keep the route clear of civilians. Chasing refugees off the main road pushed them out into the fields and other roads, but did not stop them from going to Hungnam. The refugees crowded the port and clamored to be evacuated as well, and neither Almond nor his officers could ignore their plight.[28]

Col. Edward H. Forney, who had so ably directed the Inchon planning, now masterfully integrated the entire corps evacuation plan. Forney devised a plan to evacuate refugees, placing them on, in, and around the cargo after it was loaded, which avoided the displacement of soldiers or equipment. Almond's officers also used refugees to help load the ships with the cargo piling up on the docks. Rowny remembered that Forney's impassioned pleas moved Almond to permit these arrangements.[29] Almond later espoused a humanitarian yet pragmatic view: "I decided that this humanitarian attitude towards the evacuation of refugees would in no way interfere with the operations plan of X Corps troop movements. For that reason, I thought we should take a kind and humanitarian attitude toward the refugees in return for the staunch support we could get from these people in the future war operations."[30] Whatever the reason, Almond evacuated more than 98,000 civilians (not including babies) in addition to saving his entire corps and all of its equipment. Almond awarded Forney the Legion of Merit for his efforts. MacArthur had not authorized the humanitarian move, but appeared pleased with Almond's actions.[31]

Almond sent his CP aboard the USS *Mount McKinley* on December 19, but he continued to go ashore daily to observe loading operations. He finally embarked for the last time at 11:15 a.m. on December 24. As with the Inchon landing, Admiral Doyle commanded the amphibious operation. Almond watched as the last battalion of the 3rd Infantry Division still on shore destroyed the Hungnam docks with explosives before embarking. The *Mount McKinley* then sailed for Ulsan, a port north of Pusan on Korea's southeast coast. Almond breathed a great sigh of relief and went to bed right after dinner, too tired to remember that it was Christmas Eve. He later remembered waking about midmorning on Christmas Day, having apparently missed a scheduled breakfast with Admiral Doyle. Almond and Maj. Gen. Clark Ruffner went ashore about 3:00 p.m. to inspect unloading areas, and then had dinner that night at Admiral Doyle's home at the base at Ulsan.[32]

Almond had successfully evacuated from North Korea three American divisions, two ROK divisions, and his corps support troops totaling some 105,000 soldiers. In keeping with his requirement that units evacuate all possible equipment in order to be combat ready upon landing in South Korea, the evacuation included 17,500 vehicles and 350,000 tons of bulk cargo, including 8,635 tons of ammunition. As the units disembarked, they moved to various places in the EUSAK operational area to refit. Almond established X Corps headquarters at Chungju, southeast of Seoul, to prepare for its next mission.[33]

Smith gave his corps commander no credit at all, even when pressed, for the Hungnam evacuation, crediting Admiral Doyle for the entire operation. Smith's G3, Col. Alpha Bowser, had more positive things to say. "General Almond was probably one of the most aggressive corps commanders I have ever seen in action," Bowser declared. "He was aggressive almost to a fault in my estimation. . . . He was what we referred to as a 'hard charger.'" But Bowser also saw another side of Almond. "I questioned his judgment on many occasions, and as a matter of fact . . . I think that General Almond pictured this in his mind's eye as a sweeping victory that was in his grasp. But he gambled and lost."[34] Brig. Gen. Edwin K. Wright believed that the 92nd Division's failures in Italy in World War II remained in Almond's mind as his corps retreated from North Korea: "I think Ned Almond was one of the [most] aggressive officers whom I have ever known. He was very positive in his opinions. I think he bore a rather heavy load on his mind over the World War II problems that he confronted with his division command. I think he felt that maybe we could have done better under the circumstances. . . . But I do have the feeling that maybe this was a corpse to him."[35]

That "corpse" became evident anytime MacArthur visited, prompting Almond to report to his wife everything MacArthur said. Almond hungered for praise from MacArthur, though he was clearly already his favorite lieutenant.

Despite successfully evacuating X Corps and the refugees, Almond doubtless felt the sting of failure from the retreat. What had seemed to be a total, righteous destruction of a fleeing enemy and the liberation of a nation had turned into a much wider war with a more numerous and dangerous foe. Only a couple of months before, Almond had basked in the glow of the successful Inchon landing. His photo on the cover of *Time* magazine seemed to confirm his accomplishment, and perhaps banished forever the lingering feeling of failure from his 92nd Division experience. Now, he could not ignore the failure of his latest mission, however successful the evacuation may have been. The brief comments from MacArthur boosted Almond's sagging self-esteem, as did his selection for promotion, but his fragile ego required continued stroking. Margaret probably felt it too, as she wrote just before Christmas to complain about South Korean president Syngman Rhee decorating General Walker with the Korean Order of Military Merit, Korea's highest decoration for foreigners, and not bestowing the same honor on her husband. Almond told her this would come later, if at all, and he was not concerned either way. When Rhee surprised him with the award in February, however, he wrote four pages to Margaret about it, clearly very pleased. More than simple vanity, this demonstrates his insecurity and need to feel recognized.[36]

EUSAK was changing in more than just its composition. General Walker died in a jeep accident on December 23, 1950, and the JCS quickly named Lt. Gen. Matthew B. Ridgway to replace him. Though Almond and Walker (and their wives) had been antagonists, Walker's sudden death shocked Almond. He wrote to Margaret on Christmas Day, sounding wistful about the soured relationship: "Small differences are made 'smaller' by such events and it was a tragic loss and it seems to me to be very uncalled for. Much like Patton's death." Almond was hopeful about Ridgway, however, saying, "I think Ridgway's selection was a good one and I am sure he is a brilliant leader. . . . I hope that with us combined with the EUSAK we can do something effective, and more effective than in the recent past to destroy this avalanche of yellow fiends." His use of an ethnic slur indicated his feelings toward the Chinese, but many others shared his attitude, and this language was common.[37]

Two days after Christmas, Almond wrote to his friend Brig. Gen. Hal Eastwood, the First Army chief of staff, who had served on MacArthur's staff during World War II. Almond commented briefly on the successful evacuation at Hungnam, assuring Eastwood that most of the press reports in the States had been wrong, and there was little loss of life or equipment. As for X Corps's future, he added, "We are now here in south Korea ready for another go in another direction and in concert with the remainder of EUSAK, of which we are now part as you know." He commented on the "great shock" of Walker's death in a needless accident, and assured Eastwood that he always drove his own jeep. "In that way I can think for myself and if anything happens it is my own fault." Almond's peers would have chuckled at the irony of this comment. One observer noted that the only man who had an easy job in Almond's headquarters was his driver. "When he does go in a Jeep, he does the driving while the Sgt. driver hangs on for dear life." On an early visit to the 1st Marine Division, Almond drove the jeep, with General MacArthur in the front and Generals Smith and Wright in the back. Smith recorded a humorous element of the episode in his log: "He is a very fast driver. On one stretch of road he drove a truck off the road and it turned over. Fortunately, no one was hurt. At the end of the trip General Wright asked General Almond if he had a driver's license."[38]

The Hungnam evacuation was a great success, and the X Corps had successfully brought out most of the equipment not lost in the initial CCF attacks. The urgency of loading out at Hungnam, however, prioritized speed over organization. EUSAK established assembly areas around Pusan in order to allow X Corps to reorganize for combat. The integration of X Corps into EUSAK assisted both organizations. As a separate command, X Corps had enjoyed the use of the 1st Marine Aircraft Wing as well as several extra support units, especially signal units, that EUSAK lacked. General Ridgway immediately began redistributing these units to better support the entire EUSAK. Almond was also relieved of the responsibility of planning support for his own units, passing that to EUSAK. The official EUSAK history noted that "as an independent command, X Corps wrestled with problems beyond its organizational capabilities. It was performing Army type functions with a corps-sized staff."[39]

Almond looked forward to Ridgway's arrival. "I have just heard over the radio that Ridgeway [*sic*] has just arrived. . . . He is a most able officer and I am sure that his choice was a happy one. It will, I trust, bring us a streak of luck which combined with our resolution to give these yellow bastards what is coming to them, will make a winning combination." Almond had identified the various routes to follow into North Korea, not MacArthur. MacArthur knew about the corps's brittle situation, but he never second-guessed his protégé. Secretary of State George C. Marshall questioned the disposition of forces, but General Bradley defended the move, explaining that MacArthur was attempting to occupy all of North Korea in preparation for holding elections. Bradley acknowledged that moving the defensive perimeter further south would be more sound militarily, but moving forces backward would affect the UN's prestige and degrade the South Koreans' morale.[40]

When Ridgway arrived in Korea to assume command, he immediately began to assess the Eighth Army's condition. Ridgway was a breath of fresh air to the Eighth, but he found it in poor shape, with a defeatist attitude and in the middle of one of the longest retreats in US Army history. He needed not only to stop the withdrawal and reinvigorate EUSAK but also to prepare for a large CCF attack building just north of Seoul. He immediately set out to meet with his corps commanders, two of whom presented him with plans to withdraw to Pusan. He found IX Corps commander Maj. Gen. John B. Coulter to be a defeatist, and resolved to relieve him as quickly as possible. I Corps commander Lt. Gen. Frank W. "Shrimp" Milburn was slow and lacked initiative, but he was an old friend, and Ridgway hesitated to relieve him. Almond was the only commander who wanted to attack, and his corps staff had been working on the plans. Ridgway met with Almond on December 28, 1950, for about a half an hour. Almond later remembered: "General Ridgway greeted me very pleasantly and wholeheartedly and when I reported to him, he outlined to me his intentions to 'fight cohesively and to kill as many CCF as possible.' Those words were my guidelines and I flew that night to Taegu to spend that night there with the Eighth Army staff." If Ridgway bore Almond any ill will, Almond did not repeat it to his wife. Almond found those officers to be pessimistic and defeatist, but he told them Ridgway intended to fight.[41]

Almond's initial tactical failings and personality clashes aside, Ridgway knew he had found what he needed—a forceful corps commander. Ridgway found dispirited commanders and staff officers everywhere he went, but Ned Almond was ready to attack and to do so immediately. Almond's pugnacious nature remained unchanged when X Corps joined the Eighth Army. Mildren later recalled a conference with all the corps commanders and Ridgway, during which Coulter and Milburn announced plans to withdraw all the way back to Pusan. In order to infuse the Eighth Army with a fighting spirit, Ridgway announced upon assuming command "that the American Army was fighting for the honor and prestige of the United States in the Far East and throughout the world and that there would be no withdrawal from Korea." Almond reiterated that message as he visited his units daily.[42]

Maj. Gen. Smith was not impressed with US Army operations in general, and he despised Almond in particular, but even he was moved to render a somewhat positive judgment on Almond in comparison with his peers. Some years after the war, Smith began compiling his notes from his Korean War diary and his notebook with an eye toward publishing a memoir. He gave Almond his due, albeit grudgingly. "Certainly, no one could accuse General Almond, the Corps commander, of defeatism. My objections throughout had been to his grandiose concepts which often had little regard for time and space factors, logistical considerations, and the integrity of units."[43]

Ridgway believed an enemy attack was imminent. EUSAK held a line across the waist of Korea, at the 38th Parallel. The I Corps (consisting of a tank brigade, the 25th Infantry Division, 1st ROK Division, and the United Kingdom's 29th Brigade) occupied a sector from the Yellow Sea on the west to Uijongbu, which straddled the Seoul-Wonsan corridor. US I Corps joined US IX Corps (6th ROK Division, 24th Infantry Division, 1st Cavalry Division, and 27th UK Brigade) at Uijongbu. III ROK Corps defended a large sector in the center of the peninsula with the ROK 2nd, 5th, and 8th Divisions in line and the 7th ROK Division in reserve. II ROK Corps contained only one division, the 3rd ROK, defending a small sector between the Soyang River and Route 24. The final sector between

Route 24 and the Sea of Japan belonged to I ROK Corps, consisting of the ROK 9th and Capital Divisions. This left Ridgway with US X Corps as EUSAK's only reserve.

Ridgway initially planned to leave the three American divisions in X Corps and replace the loss of the ROK divisions with the 2nd Infantry Division. After meeting with Almond, however, Ridgway realized that the X Corps divisions would need more time to prepare. He sent the 1st Marine Division, which had been mauled so badly at the Chosin Reservoir, and the 3rd Infantry Division, which was the last to evacuate and therefore the last to unload at Ulsan, into EUSAK reserve. Several other UN forces were arriving or due to arrive but were not yet combat ready. The newly reorganized X Corps consisted of the 2nd and 7th Infantry Divisions, the 187th Airborne Regimental Combat Team, and the 5th and 8th ROK Divisions. Almond used the brief pause at the end of December to begin command inspections of all battalions of· the 7th Infantry Division, and then began inspecting battalions of the 2nd Infantry Division at the front in January. With his noted eye for detail, no aspect of operations, training, or logistics escaped his notice.[44]

On December 30, Ridgway ordered Almond to move immediately forward to Wonju, taking whichever division was ready to go, in order to counter potential attacks by the North Korean II and V Corps. Ridgway saw Wonju and Chipyong-ni as essential to the defense of his line. From Almond's base at Chungju twenty-five miles south, X Corps was to replace the III ROK Corps, which moved east into a narrower sector and allowed the I ROK Corps to narrow its sector as well. One regiment of the 7th Infantry Division was ready to move, and Almond transported it to Chechon, twenty miles south of Wonju, with the other regiments to follow. He also ordered the 2nd Infantry Division, now reinforced with one battalion each from France and the Netherlands, to move and secure Wonju.[45]

Ridgway's plan called for the 3rd Infantry Division to follow the 2nd and 7th into line at Wonju, with the 1st Marine Division staging initially at Pohang, to follow along the same axis. General Smith did not like this plan either, and blamed Almond for a plan devised by Ridgway: "I thought the Corps would've been sobered by its recent experiences, but there was the same lack of realism, the same disregard for time and space, and same disregard for the integrity of units." Because the 1st Marine Division had only recently arrived in the area, perhaps Smith may be forgiven his disregard for the grave nature of the Eighth Army situation. His comments, however, reflected a continuing disagreement with almost all US Army orders.[46]

Almond's chronic micromanagement caused problems within X Corps, but his energetic attitude mirrored Ridgway's own. The new Eighth Army commander issued orders shortly after his arrival that "division commanders [were] to be up with their forward battalions, and . . . corps commanders up with the regiment that was in the hottest action." Almond did not need to be told this, because that was his daily routine.[47]

While historians have judged Almond harshly for his tendency to micromanage, an examination of the facts shows that he often had good reason. Maj. Gen. Robert B. McClure, commanding general of the 2nd Infantry Division, exemplified the leadership problems Almond detested. McClure had replaced Lawrence B. "Dutch" Keiser when General Walker relieved the latter in November 1950. After the 2nd Infantry Division moved to X Corps in December, Almond sized up McClure as weak and ineffective, with a well-known drinking problem. McClure had commanded a division in combat during World War II, but he had admitted to Col. S. L. A. Marshall, the famed Army historian, that he was no longer up to the challenges and needed alcohol to brace himself. At their first meeting on December 31, 1950, Almond, McCaffrey, and Chiles met with McClure and his staff to discuss future operations. Almond later added handwritten notes to his diary: "2d Div was in a disheartened spirit. It had just come down from Kunuri and a terrific beating. McClure was *none too sure* as to what they could do in combat." That did not bode well for McClure.[48]

Almond visited the 2nd Infantry Division repeatedly over the next two weeks, logging six visits with McClure himself and four more with his subordinate commanders. The more he visited, the more things he found wrong. Each visit brought admonishments from Almond to McClure, pointing out deficiencies that needed to be corrected. Each day without a visit brought a phone call from McClure citing his fears of an open flank, or requesting to blow up ammunition that could not be carried. Almond authorized McClure to withdraw from the town of Wonju if necessary, but to occupy the high ground immediately south of it in order to control the town.

At 2:00 a.m. on January 8, McClure sent a message to Almond notifying him that he had withdrawn the division eight to twelve miles south of Wonju, much further than Almond intended. McClure emplaced his troops on the hills south of the town but failed to secure the town adequately. Almond's aides did not record his exact reaction, but it was surely volcanic. Almond immediately ordered McClure to send a battalion to recapture the airstrip at Wonju. Almond flew in himself to look over the situation and calm McClure's nerves, and then flew to Taegu to brief General Ridgway on the loss of the town that Ridgway had designated the key location in the Eighth Army sector. The following day, Almond went again to the 2nd Infantry Division CP to watch it attack toward Wonju. His aides recalled in detail the difficulties that Almond encountered:

> 1200—Arrived 23rd Inf. Regt CP, NICHON. Briefed on situation by S-3, Maj. Dumain. Directed that Brig. Gen. Haynes, Division Artillery Commander, and Gen. Choi Yung Hi, CG 8th ROK Division, come forward; Haynes to control artillery fire. Departed for front lines by Jeep. Dismounted at 81 mm mortar positions and proceeded on foot some 1500 yards to OP of 2nd Battalion, 23rd Inf. Regt talked Col. Freeman, CO 23rd Inf and Lt. Col. Edwards, Battalion CO. Deficiencies noted:
>
> (1) Artillery pieces not manned by gun crews. No apparent local security in numerous artillery and other areas.
> (2) Division Artillery Commander not present in area.
> (3) 2 rounds of artillery fell short in right company sector of 2nd Battalion 23rd infantry.
> (4) Attack being coordinated by Senior Battalion Commander instead of regimental staff.
> (5) Battalion Commander had not organized forward CP and companies not up to date in staff operations.[49]

Almond later found Maj. Gen. McClure and Brig. Gen. Loyal Haynes and angrily told them what they needed to correct. Almond had determined that the 2nd Infantry Division had leadership problems, but he needed to inspect the entire division to find out for himself the extent of the problem. McCaffrey believed that Almond was too hesitant to fire people, despite his impatience with poor performance. "Almond did a lot of yelling and shouting and he didn't relieve people quick enough."[50]

As the temperature dipped to -13° on January 13, Almond visited the 38th Infantry Regiment, where Col. George Peploe told him that most of his recent battle casualties came from trench foot and frozen feet. Peploe told Almond that the regiment had recently received 2,700 pairs of socks to alleviate a shortage, but Almond lectured all officers on the need for regular inspections by company, battalion, and even the regimental leaders to ensure that soldiers were changing their socks daily to avoid such injuries. These were not small issues: Almond knew that most of the noncombat injuries from the Chosin Reservoir had been related to trench foot and frostbite and other cold-weather injuries. The winter injuries from northeast Korea continue to weigh heavily on his mind, and he advised all regimental commanders to establish a sock laundry and exchange program to prevent trench foot for their soldiers. The 2nd Infantry Division had not experienced the crippling cold of the Chosin as the 1st Marine Division in the 7th Infantry Division had, and it was destined to suffer greatly over the next two months. The division would log nearly 3,000 cases of trench foot, frostbite, and immersion foot in the months of January and February.[51]

Almond then visited the 23rd Infantry Regiment, where he discussed the problem of getting hot food to units and control of foot injuries with Col. Paul Freeman. Though Almond asked for details, he focused on processes and systems. He did not ask the soldier if he liked the chow, he ordered the mess officer to bring him the last six menus so that he could determine whether or not the unit's basic systems were functioning properly. These were small details for a corps commander, but the difficulties the units were experiencing indicated leadership problems at the lower levels. Almond wanted his attention to detail to push the lower-level commanders to pay attention to these basic troop-leading procedures. Haig recalled vividly Almond's attention to detail and the methods he used to train his subordinate commanders: "Often these interviews were conducted while standing up in the open beside white-faced commanding officers while small arms fire crackled around their heads and mortar rounds burst at their feet; goodbye salutes were usually fervent."[52]

Almond then announced his intention to visit every frontline battalion that day. With the 9th Regiment in reserve, Almond visited two battalions of the 23rd and two battalions of the 38th, as well as the French Battalion and the Netherlands Battalion. What he saw both angered and embarrassed him. Throughout the US battalions, he saw foxholes that were poorly prepared, positions poorly dug-in, inadequate fields of fire, disorganized feeding of hot food, and general lack of proper leadership. On inspecting the French and Dutch battalions, he found high morale, well-organized and dug-in positions, and good organized leadership. He lost confidence in the division artillery commander, Brig. Gen. Haynes, when Haynes's estimate of the requirements for burning a nearby village fell well short of what Almond was able to easily demonstrate. While at the Dutch battalion, Almond requested a fire mission on a village located to the battalion's front. He was impressed that the fires were delivered quickly and accurately, and started the town burning. Almond expected all officers to be masters of their craft, especially general officers.[53]

Having inspected the entire division on the front line, Almond decided to relieve McClure. He wanted do so immediately, but he was concerned that McClure's friendship with US Army Chief of Staff Gen. Joe Collins complicated the issue. Almond went to Ridgway and recommended he relieve McClure. Ridgway concurred, and Almond chose Maj. Gen. Clark L. "Nick" Ruffner, his chief of staff, to replace McClure. The 2nd Infantry Division chief of staff, Col. Gerald Epley, believed that Almond fired officers simply to put his own people in command, but the evidence does not support this. In a handwritten note in the war diary two years after the event, Almond noted, "On this date (1–13–51) division commander 2nd Inf. Div. (Gen. Robt McClure) was relieved for poor leadership of his division. CG EUSAK designated Maj. Gen. Clark Ruffner by Chief of Staff as the new CG 2nd Infantry Division (on my recommendation). A wiser move, I never made."[54]

Two days later, Army Chief of Staff Gen. Joe Collins visited Korea and met Almond at X Corps headquarters. Almond did not mention discussing McClure's relief with Collins in the official copy of his diary, but years later he made handwritten notes: "Gen. Collins seemed quite concerned about the 'relief from command' of Gen. McClure. [He] asked me, 'Had McClure been drinking?' My reply: 'That was not in my written report to Gen. MacArthur. [H]e had made so many failures in other respects that I never got to the matter of his (McC's) sobriety.' (All commanders know that to try to prove that an officer 'is drunk' is a most difficult task)."[55]

Ruffner was one of many Almond subordinates placed in command after a relief or a rotation, but those subordinates also knew what to expect from Almond. He set high standards and demanded that they meet them. To replace Ruffner, Almond selected Col. John S. Guthrie, commander of the 3rd Infantry Division's 7th Infantry Regiment.[56]

In late January, Almond described his plans to deny sanctuary to the enemy through aggressive "power patrols" using combined-arms task forces. Ridgway asked Almond to share his plan with General Milburn's IX Corps, but these task forces also had negative effects. Creating small task forces for multiple missions around the battlefield answered Almond's need for more vigorous, responsive units, but it also destroyed cohesiveness and control. Since many of the units, especially in the 7th Infantry Division, had not worked together very long, breaking them out for these kinds of missions made their tasks even more difficult .[57]

Another issue that drew Almond's immediate concern was tactical air support, an issue beyond the control of regimental commanders. Almond immediately dashed off a message directly to Ridgway, stating the inadequacy of the air support the frontline units were receiving and describing in detail what they needed. Though Almond might often micromanage, he also never failed to give or request the support that his subordinate commanders required. Almond requested that the Eighth Army provide additional Tactical Air Control Parties for the 7th Infantry Division "due to the division's present situation requiring many independent actions by battalions which cannot always be adequately supported of artillery in view of the nature of the terrain." Almond then ordered Ruffner to create a TACP in each of his battalions, consisting of one officer, one radio operator, plus a Jeep and driver.[58]

Almond had conducted comparatively little coordination with the Eighth Army before Hungnam, but after X Corps joined it, Almond remained in near constant contact with Ridgway, the Eighth Army staff, and I and IX Corps. He met several times each week to coordinate X Corps operations as part of an Eighth Army offensive to be started either in late January or in early February.

Almond's need to please MacArthur and his inexperience at controlling large formations had blinded him to certain battlefield realities. The man's aggressive nature worked against him in the mission in northeast Korea, especially at the Chosin Reservoir. In Italy, mountainous terrain had dictated that Almond deploy the 92nd Infantry Division in small units over a large area, and he tended to do the same later with X Corps. While he could not avoid a certain amount of dispersion in either case, he tended to spread his units too thin. His tendency to micromanage inhibited the perspective that a corps commander required.

While Almond had used aircraft very effectively to conduct reconnaissance, maintain contact with his front lines, and assess conditions on the front, they also distorted his view of the battlefield. Moving by air from one unit to another in a few minutes, he failed to recognize that the dispersion of his troops was much greater on the ground that it appeared to him when flying between units. Almond failed to appreciate the difficulties of those units maneuvering over the same ground. Almond had again placed unrealistic expectations on his subordinate commanders.

14

Tragedy and Redemption

Spring 1951

After the initial problems and tactical disasters of the fall, Almond's tactical control of the corps seemed to improve as he gained experience and as new leadership improved the units. His subordinates grew more proficient at their jobs, too. In late January, Ridgway began working with the Department of the Army to "rotate" corps and division commanders to correct some problems. General Collins set up a rotational policy to allow division commanders to be eased out, and also give more general officers the opportunity to command. This process replaced Maj. Gen. David G. Barr of the 7th Infantry Division with Maj. Gen. Claude B. "Buddy" Ferenbaugh in January 1951.[1]

Ferenbaugh had graduated from West Point with the war-shortened Class of 1920, in November 1918. After early service on the West Coast, in Hawaii, and in the Philippines, Ferenbaugh graduated from the Army War College in 1940 and joined the War Department General Staff, where he spent the first three years of the war. In January 1944, Ferenbaugh reported to the 83rd Infantry Division as assistant commander, and he remained with the division throughout the rest of the war. After the war, Ferenbaugh returned to the War Department General Staff and then assumed command of the Military District of Washington in 1946. Ferenbaugh served as chief of staff for Operation Sandstone, the atomic bomb tests from October 1947 to June 1948, then commanded Schofield Barracks, Hawaii, for two years. In 1950, he had just reported to Third Army headquarters when he received orders to Korea.

Almond and Ferenbaugh began housecleaning and relieved several regimental commanders. One of the first decisions Ferenbaugh made was to move Col. Herb Powell out of the 17th RCT to be the 7th Division's chief of staff. He asked Almond to release Col. William W. Quinn, the X Corps G2, to command the 17th RCT. Almond hated losing key staff members whom he trusted, but he did support their advancement.

He also knew that he needed to support his new division commander. On Quinn's advice, Almond requested Col. James H. Polk as Quinn's replacement. Then on station in Tokyo, Polk was Willoughby's deputy in FECOM G2 and had already earned Almond's respect. McCaffrey also greatly respected Polk, and indeed believed Polk was better than the Eighth Army G-2, Lt. Col. James C. Tarkenton. McCaffrey argued that Polk focused on determining the enemy's intentions, while Tarkenton looked for capabilities.[2]

Having stabilized the line, Ridgway was almost ready to begin offensive operations with the Eighth Army. First, however, he needed to develop the enemy situation and determine its strength. He ordered a reconnaissance in force, using one division each from I and X Corps. On January 23, Ridgway issued an order for Operation Thunderbolt, the first of a series of campaigns designed to gain the initiative for the Eighth Army. The X Corps mission was to protect the right flank of the IX Corps main effort and be prepared to exploit the success of Operation Thunderbolt to the north. Ridgway directed the 2nd Infantry Division to conduct armored and infantry patrols to the front. This was to be a feint designed to distract attention from the main effort to the west. Units from the 2nd Infantry Division began patrolling ahead of the front line the following day.[3] On January 22, Almond returned to headquarters to find a congratulatory note from Ridgway and a pair of three-star insignia, indicating that the Senate had approved his promotion. Almond was touched by Ridgway's kindness, and wrote Ridgway a warm note of thanks. Ridgway launched Operation Thunderbolt on January 25, and five days later he converted the reconnaissance in force to a deliberate attack. As he pushed I and IX Corps forward to consolidate ground that their reconnaissance had gained, he ordered Almond to begin planning with III ROK Corps for operations in the east paralleling the other two corps. Almond designed X Corps's Operation Roundup to support Operation Thunderbolt, in which X Corps and III ROK Corps would move forward in parallel with I and IX Corps. Almond gathered the commanders of the 2nd Infantry Division, 7th Infantry Division, 187th RCT, and ROK 2nd, 5th, and 8th Divisions and III ROK Corps at X Corps headquarters to discuss plans for Operation Roundup (see map 14.1).[4]

After conducting an aerial reconnaissance of the entire X Corps front on January 27, Almond met with IX Corps commander Maj. Gen. John B. Coulter. Coulter remained concerned about the security of his right flank, particularly a gap that existed between the Han River and the X

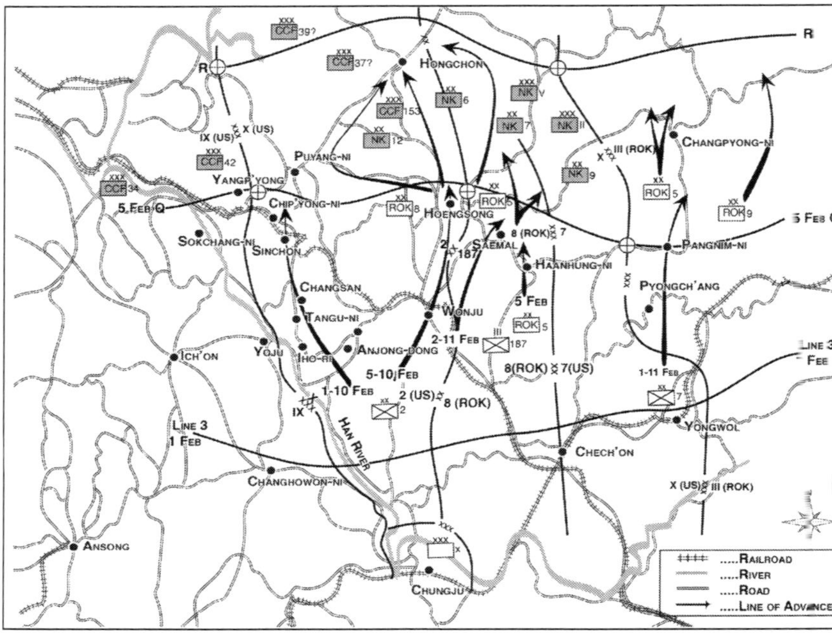

14.1. Operation Roundup, February 5–11, 1951

Corps boundary. Almond agreed to help cover the gap with patrols, and immediately ordered the 2nd Infantry Division to begin coordination with IX Corps.[5]

Almond visited Ferenbaugh on January 30 and strongly warned him to maintain control of his northern patrols and not to allow them to move so far forward that they would get cut off. This specific guidance and close mentoring of a new subordinate commander indicated that he had learned his lesson about dispersion of troops after the disasters in northeast Korea. Moreover, while Almond certainly was aggressive he adapted to the operational plan that he was given. His operations in North Korea reflected MacArthur's plan, while his operations in the Eighth Army reflected Ridgway's.

Almond's Operation Roundup envisioned an envelopment of the enemy forces that were then building up in the Hongchon area north of the center of the X Corps front, with a coordinated attack by X Corps and the ROK I and III Corps. Almond convened a special planning conference to coordinate with all commanders and to get Ridgway's approval. The operation would begin on February 5 with X Corps advancing from the

Q-Q line (Sokchang-ni–Hoengsong–Pangnim-ni) to the R-R line (Yangpyong–Hongchon–Pungnam-ni), and after reaching that line X Corps would execute a double envelopment of the enemy at Hongchon with the I and III ROK Corps on the east of X Corps. Planning called for the 5th and 8th ROK Divisions to pass through US units and to spearhead the attack. Almond directed 2nd and 7th Infantry Divisions to provide task forces with artillery, armor, and infantry units to strengthen the ROK divisions. Almond spent the next four days traveling all over the Corps sector, ensuring that all commanders were making adequate preparation and coordination.[6]

Almond visited the 8th ROK Division on February 6 and discovered that the attached American infantry company was not properly prepared for combat. Ever the teacher, Almond directed the company commander to get all the officers and NCOs together so that he could lecture them on the "necessity for each individual soldier being battle ready and for supervision of orders given by junior officers to ensure compliance." Almond told him that "a unit that takes care of its equipment properly will fight properly and give a good account of itself when called on to do so."[7]

The X Corps main effort in Operation Roundup was to be in the left (west) sector, in the vicinity of Hongchon, which Almond also believed was the enemy main effort down the Hongchon-Yoju axis. Almond placed the 2nd Infantry Division on the extreme left flank of the X Corps line (vicinity Chipyong-ni), the 187th Airborne RCT in the center (vicinity Hoengsong), and the 7th Infantry Division on the right, with one RCT on the right flank (vicinity Pyongchang) to support the advance of III ROK Corps.[8]

Almond launched Operation Roundup on February 5, with the 5th and 8th ROK Divisions spearheading the movement. Initial enemy resistance against the ROK divisions was generally light, and the 7th Infantry Division advanced slowly and against light resistance in order to support the III ROK Corps. Intelligence reports indicated that the weight of the Chinese counteroffensive would fall on X Corps's sector. While I Corps on the west and IX Corps in the center occupied natural defensive terrain, the X Corps sector contained a serious flaw. The Han River flowed east to west across the IX Corps sector, thus providing a defensive barrier, but it ran northward along the seam between IX Corps and X Corps. A joint patrol between the 2nd and 24th Infantry Divisions advancing along the seam between IX Corps and X Corps encountered twin railroad tunnels at a small town called Chipyong-ni (see map 14.2). The heaviest enemy pressure developed early in the operation in the western

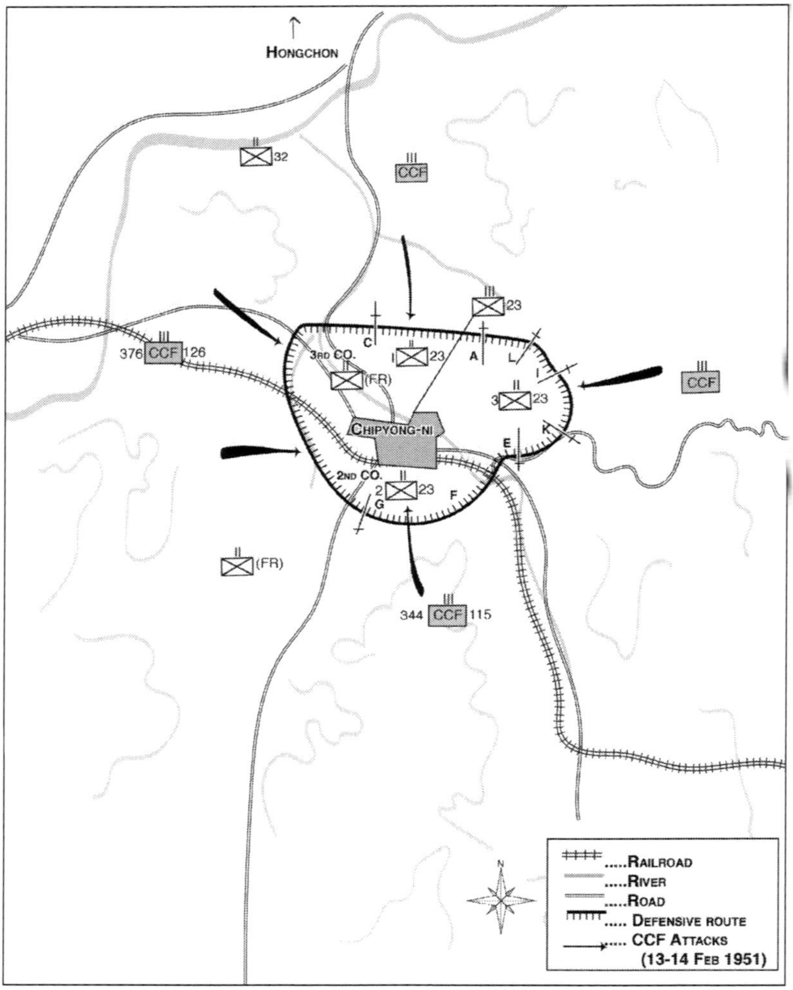

14.2. Battle of Chipyong-ni, February 13–15, 1951

portion of the X Corps sector where Col. Paul Freeman commanded the 23rd RCT (with the French battalion attached), 2nd Infantry Division, which held the town.[9]

The 23rd RCT needed to hold Chipyong-ni, an important road junction, to protect the northeast shoulder of IX Corps's right flank. Chipyong-ni sat at the far western edge of the X Corps sector, some twenty miles west of Wonju. Ridgway later remembered, "I went along with Almond when he proposed [the regiment's movement] as a series of probing attacks. Good initiative, good originality, boldness, and all that; but they were not mutually supporting each other in this, and this is where they got caught."[10]

Almond visited the 23rd RCT and the French battalion at Chipyong-ni on February 7 and the 5th ROK Division on February 8, and while inspecting its forward elements, he called in fire from the supporting US artillery unit. He then called the X Corps artillery commander, Col. William P. Ennis, and the commander of the supporting battalion forward and directed them to "take action to correct errors being made by the fire direction center, and to speed up the delivery of fire by the battalions." Enemy attacks increased from February 8 to 11, and reports indicated the enemy now included CCF as well as NKPA forces. Almond began adjusting units to meet these threats, and he ordered Maj. Gen. Ferenbaugh to prepare a plan to use the 32nd Infantry Regiment on blocking positions in the Yoju area.[11]

After a conference with Ridgway on February 8, Almond gained operational control of the 3rd ROK Division and placed it in line on the right flank of the 8th ROK Division. Almond wanted the 8th ROK to move to the west and relieve the enemy pressure against the advance of the 23rd RCT north of Chipyong-ni. It would also support the envelopment of the enemy that Almond planned. Almond received numerous reports of a large CCF buildup around Hongchon–Piryong-ni on the X Corps left flank. As the enemy resistance grew stronger, Almond was able to better define the enemy composition. CCF units attacked on the left flank of the X Corps zone, but elements of the North Korean II and V Corps faced the center and eastern portions of Almond's line.[12]

The enemy launched its main attack on X Corps on the night of February 11–12, with the NK II and V Corps attacking the eastern X Corps sector and the III ROK Corps sector, while three CCF divisions converged from the northwest and attacked along the Changbong-ni–Hoengsong Road, with a fourth CCF division attacking southward. The 23rd RCT encountered the strongest enemy resistance north of Chipyong-ni. The ROK 3rd, 5th, and 8th Divisions bore the brunt of the attacks in the eastern X Corps sector.[13]

The 8th ROK Division became completely disorganized and could not mount a cohesive defense, while the 3rd and 5th ROK Divisions were falling back rapidly before the enemy onslaught. The US artillery-armor-infantry task forces supporting the ROK divisions found their positions untenable, and these forces suffered heavy casualties while withdrawing.[14]

Almond visited the 8th ROK Division on February 12 and directed the commander to regain control of his regiments. General Ridgway arrived at the X Corps tactical CP later that day, and after Almond briefed him on the situation, Ridgway released the 187th Airborne RCT to Almond's operational control. Ridgway also gave Almond the I ROK Corps to control the 3rd and 5th ROK Divisions. Almond ordered the 23rd RCT with its attached French battalion to remain in place and directed a readjustment of positions to a closed perimeter at Chipyong-ni. He also released all US artillery-infantry-armored teams to control of their parent units. Almond then directed the 3rd and 5th ROK Divisions to begin reorganization to meet the continuing enemy attack and moved the 8th ROK Division to X Corps reserve.[15]

The results of the attack and counterattack were eerily similar to the situation at the Chosin Reservoir. The 8th ROK Division was cut off and destroyed, leaving the remainder of the corps exposed. When Almond realized that Chipyong-ni was about to be cut off, he notified Ridgway that he intended to pull the 23rd RCT back into the X Corps line, and Ridgway agreed. MacArthur did not want to give up the line of the Han River, however, and countermanded the order. By nightfall the following day, CCF forces had surrounded Chipyong-ni. During the ensuing battle, Colonel Freeman was wounded and Almond relieved him, replacing him with his own G3, Col. John Chiles. Freeman believed this was merely another attempt to get one of "Almond's boys" into command slots, and assumed it was because Almond did not like him. Almond's War Diary, however, reveals the idea came from Ruffner. After a conference at X Corps headquarters on February 14, Ruffner asked Almond for Chiles to replace Freeman at 23rd RCT, because Freeman had been wounded but refused evacuation. Almond released him immediately. Almond presented the Silver Star to Freeman before he was evacuated to the States. When Chiles left to command the 23rd RCT, Almond promoted his deputy G3, Col. Frank T. Mildren, to X Corps G3.[16]

Almond's losses during the Chinese offensive from February 11 to 13 were devastating. He found evidence that the 8th ROK division had been attacked by at least four divisions. Casualty estimates totaled more than 18,000 soldiers, with most of these coming from the ROK 3rd, 5th, and 8th divisions. The 8th ROK Division had dissolved, losing more than half its strength, and was no longer combat effective. The matériel losses were also severe. The 2nd Infantry Division began to evacuate toward Wonju, but intense enemy pressure forced the abandonment of twenty artillery pieces, six tanks, and nearly two hundred trucks. The 8th ROK Division had lost most of its vehicles, weapons, and organizational equipment, and the Korean units had lost a total of twenty-seven artillery pieces.[17] When Ridgway heard that several howitzers had been lost as the 2nd Infantry Division withdrew under the weight of the attack, he was furious and ordered an investigation into the loss of equipment.

> Dear Ned,
>
> While there is nothing sacrosanct about a piece of artillery compared to the loss of lives of men, I don't expect to hear again of such loss as reported to me this morning of five 155 Hows of Battery A, 503. It is prima facie indication of faulty leadership of serious import in some echelon. I am sending a senior officer of my G3 section to you this morning to discuss with you certain matters, which, from my operations map, give me concern: major units intact—delay—use of terrain. Please send back your reactions by him. Have ordered the howitzers replaced soonest.
>
> Faithfully, Matt
>
> Let me know if there is any help I can give.[18]

Though Almond's diary makes no mention, this attack occurred exactly six years after the disastrous attacks of February 8–11, 1945, in the Serchio Valley in Italy. He could not have failed to remark the eerie coincidence as he once again wrote a note explaining terrible losses to his commander. He surely felt the corpse of that early failure visiting him once again.

As the enemy launched its second-phase offensive on February 14, Ridgway arrived at X Corps headquarters for a briefing. Ridgway gave Almond his full support and directed that Almond should send immediate relief to the 23rd RCT at Chipyong-ni. His directives were:

1. The Chinese attack appears to be on about a 20-mile front. I want to be sure shoulders are held.
2. Major units should be maintained intact.
3. 8th Army is assuming responsibility for the III ROK Corps.
4. No equipment is to be abandoned.
5. Wonju must be held, and intact checked in that area.
6. The highest priority is the opening of the MSR with the 2nd Infantry Division employing the 23rd RCT for this purpose.
7. All echelons must be impressed with the importance of every hour. Many times one small group, by determined action, can influence the entire situation.

8. I expect the 1st RCT of the Marine Division to close this area in about 72 hours.
9. Corps commanders are given complete responsibility for the control of civilians within their areas.
10. We will do everything we can to assist you in stemming this attack.[19]

Ridgway and Almond also met with Brig. Gen. Lewis B. Puller, new assistant division commander of the 1st Marine Division, to brief him on Marine requirements.[20]

Almond directed that I ROK Corps become operational, and placed the 8th ROK Division under the control of Gen. Kim Pak Il. Almond asked Ridgway to employ elements of IX Corps to apply pressure from the west to prevent further enemy penetration in his sector between Yoju and the Han River corridor. Ridgway also attached the UK 27th Brigade and 6th ROK Division to X Corps, and Almond further attached them both to the 2nd Infantry Division. Almond also conducted a conference with Brig. Gen. Frank S. Bowen, CG, 187th Airborne RCT; Maj Gen. Yu, CG, I ROK Corps; and Ruffner and the X Corps primary staff. Later in the afternoon, Almond flew over the Chipyong-ni area and saw airstrikes in operation.[21]

Ridgway's anger from the previous couple of days dissipated quickly, and he returned to the X Corps CP at Chungju on February 15 to promote Almond to lieutenant general. That afternoon, Almond flew to the 7th Infantry Division CP and pinned a second star on division commander Buddy Ferenbaugh, and promoted assistant division commander Robert F. Sink to brigadier general. While visiting, Almond learned that Ferenbaugh had recently requested airstrikes on an enemy column that was moving toward his sector, but the airstrikes had been denied. Almond immediately called the X Corps G3, Colonel Mildren, to investigate why. He then flew back to his headquarters and met with Maj. Gen. Earle Partridge, CG, Fifth Air Force, to discuss his growing concern about air support to his forces.[22]

The enemy made one final attack on the corps's left sector at Chipyong-ni on February 15. The I ROK Corps and the 7th Infantry Division met and stopped the attack, after which the enemy's main effort shifted to the east, employing the North Korean II and V Corps in an attempt to reach the key communications and supply center of Chechon. The successful stand of the 23rd RCT at Chipyong-ni played a key role in halting the CCF advance. Despite terrible losses, the defense prevented the enemy from enveloping the corps's left flank. The enemy had employed an estimated five CCF divisions against the 23rd RCT position and suffered more than 5,000 casualties in unsuccessful attacks. By February 16 the enemy offensive had been contained, and the 2nd Infantry Division began aggressive patrolling to prevent the enemy from consolidating gains.[23]

The last series of attacks had overextended the enemy's supply lines. Ridgway briefed Almond on February 17 on his plan to shift the corps to the east to meet a new threat coming from that direction. Operation Killer would use IX and X Corps in a double envelopment to entrap the bulk of the enemy on the right of the X Corps front (see map 14.3). Ridgway narrowed the X Corps zone to the east of Wonju. Almond's X Corps was assigned to attack north on Route 60 in the eastern portion of the Eighth Army sector. Ridgway shifted the 1st Marine Division (IX Corps) to cover the 2nd Infantry Division sector, and Almond withdrew the 2nd Infantry Division to reorganize and refit and be prepared to attack to the north. Almond's main effort would be the 7th Infantry Division and the 3rd ROK Division, followed by the 2nd Infantry Division. He moved the 5th ROK Division to protect the corps MSR, and released the 8th ROK Division to ROK Army control.[24]

As was his habit, MacArthur arrived for a visit the night before the operation began and spent most of his time at X Corps. Once the operation got under way on February 21, the enemy quickly retreated to avoid the double envelopment that Ridgway planned. He then expanded the X Corps boundary to the west, and Almond redeployed his corps over a wider front. The 3rd ROK Division and elements of the 2nd Infantry Division assumed control of the 1st Marine Division sector, and Almond assigned wider zones to other X Corps elements.[25]

Almond's repeated visits to units helped him identify weak performers. Given his experience with weak regimental commanders, Almond watched them all carefully. Once he had identified a potentially weak commander, he watched him even more closely. Almond had a conference with Deputy Corps Commander Col. Larry K. Ladue on February 25, concerning the placement of artillery supporting the 9th RCT. He also asked Colonel Ladue to "pay particular attention to movements of the 31st RCT of the 7th Infantry Division."[26]

As part of Ridgway's policy of rotating officers, he was also trying to invigorate the units by changing out regimental commanders who were either too old or unsuitable. Lt. Col. Bill McCaffrey, Almond's deputy chief of staff, had been identified as one who clearly had the qualifica-

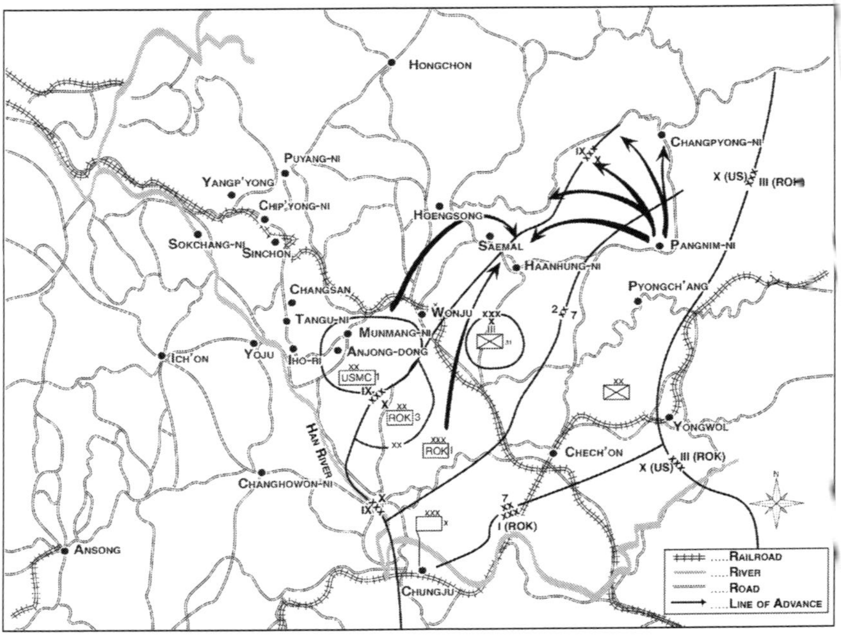

14.3. Operation Killer, February 20–March 6, 1951

tions for regimental command. In late February 1951, McCaffrey was offered command of the 24th Infantry Regiment, one of the few black units in Korea. McCaffrey readily accepted, saying that he had plenty of experience commanding black troops, and he wanted to command a regiment. When he told Almond, however, Almond had other ideas. Almond was concerned about the 31st Infantry Regiment commander, Col. John A. Gavin. Almond had not been happy with Gavin's performance thus far, and Ferenbaugh had asked him about Gavin. Ferenbaugh reportedly said, "he is primarily a staff officer and I don't think he is happy in his work." McCaffrey assumed command of the 31st Infantry Regiment the following day.[27]

By the end of the month, enemy resistance south of the Han River had collapsed. In Almond's command report after Operations Roundup and Killer, he estimated that X Corps had inflicted more than 50,000 casualties on the enemy. He attributed that to superior airpower and overwhelming firepower, with his artillery having fired more than 138,000 rounds into enemy ranks and positions. Having spent a good portion of his professional career teaching, Almond always sought to gather lessons from the combat actions in which his units participated. After the actions at Hoengsong during Operation Roundup, 5–12 February, Almond ordered the staff to collect lessons and insights from that battle. Almond then flew to each of the US divisions in turn and presented the findings. He began with a complete summary of the action, and then outlined the errors and prescribed corrections for the future.[28] Almond collected those lessons that he thought most valuable coming from the two operations and published them for his subordinate commanders:

1. Aggressive leadership and determination, coupled with the full employment of friendly superiority and firepower, can successfully contain the enemy's mast offensive thrusts.
2. Positions vital to the integrity of the friendly lines can be held against numerically superior forces by proper employment of the principles of perimeter defense (e.g. 23rd RCT at Chipyong-ni).
3. Operations involving joint US-ROK forces require close coordination and strong operational control of the ROK elements, utilizing where possible experienced ROK staffs.
4. In Operations involving use of special task organizations, it is essential that a clear and definite channel of command be established.
5. Higher headquarters be kept fully informed of enemy strength and apparent capabilities at all times. This is particularly important during periods of enemy offensive action in order to meet each new enemy move for the prompt disposition of friendly forces.
6. Adjacent dominating terrain must be secured before any attempt is made to move motorized forces. In addition, in the movement of such forces, adequate provision must be made for the prompt removal of disabled vehicles enroute.
7. Adequate provision must be made for the protection of friendly artillery positions at all times. When the enemy overruns artillery, friendly capacity to contain the enemy's numerical superiority is seriously impaired.
8. In a double envelopment of the enemy, the holding attack must not be so strong or aggressive as to force the enemy to withdraw from the trap.[29]

Ridgway's efforts were building momentum for the Eighth Army, and he began a series of offensives in which Almond's X Corps would a play key role. The Eighth Army's Operation Ripper objective was to defeat enemy forces south of the 38th Parallel and phase line Idaho. After Oper-

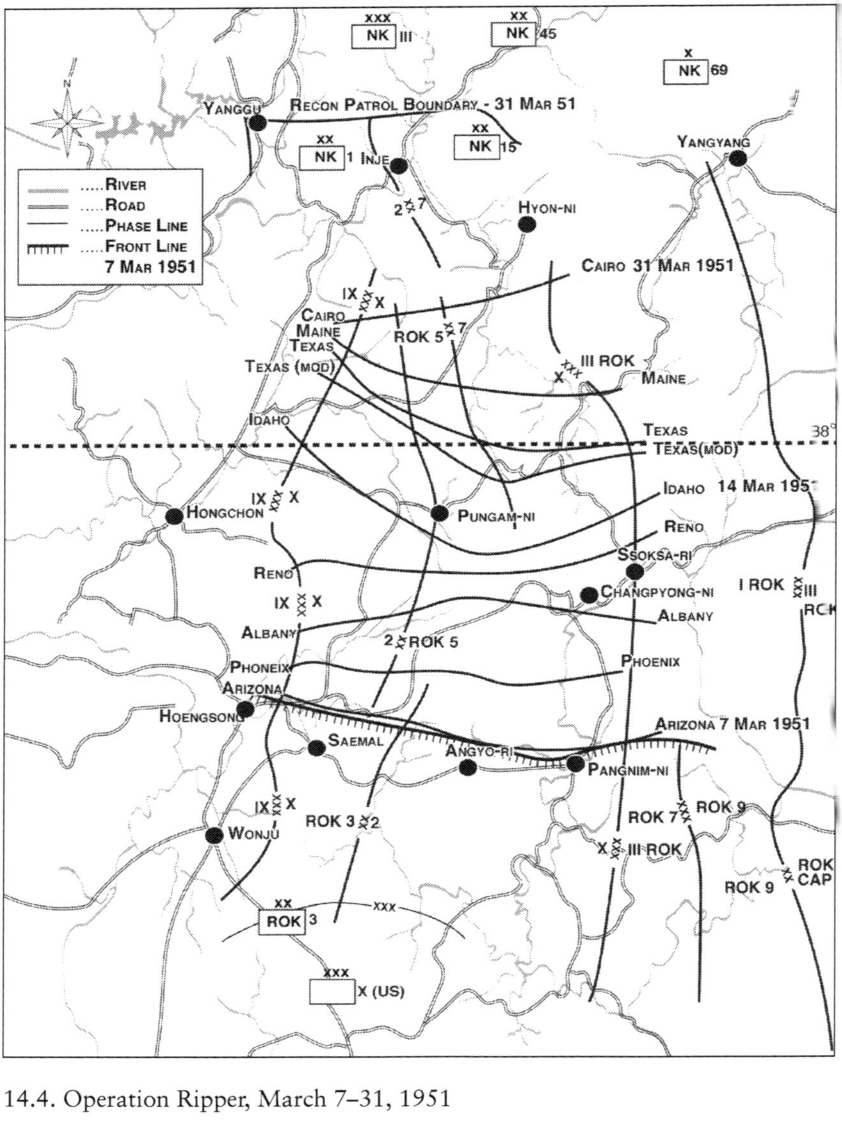

14.4. Operation Ripper, March 7–31, 1951

ations Roundup and Killer, X Corps had gained momentum. Almond used that energy as Operation Ripper got under way on March 7, with X Corps controlling III ROK Corps (ROK 7th and 9th Divisions) in addition to the 2nd and 7th Infantry Divisions (see map 14.4).

The two US divisions, with the 5th ROK Division between them, held the left and center of the X Corps line, while the III ROK Corps held the right flank. The III ROK Corps experienced trouble immediately, and Almond flew to its headquarters repeatedly to urge the commander to hold that front which threatened the entire right flank of X Corps. Two days into the offensive, Almond realized that the III ROK Corps was not holding, and this failure endangered the rest of X Corps. He flew to 7th Infantry Division headquarters at Pyongchang and discussed options for strengthening the III ROK Corps. Finally, Almond ordered the 32nd Infantry Regiment to move forward onto higher terrain, which would force the III ROK Corps to move beyond the 7th Infantry Division zone. Almond next flew to the 32nd RCT CP and impressed upon new commander Col. Charles E. Beauchamp the necessity for aggressive action. He then asked General Ruffner to send a company-size task force immediately to establish contact with the 1st Marine Division (IX Corps). Almond did not exempt his favorites from this critical eye: He observed one of Chiles's battalions executing an excellent attack "with maximum small arms and artillery support against enemy forces which were well dug in." Almond commented that the movement was too slow. While X Corps met its objectives during Operation Ripper, Communist forces began to withdraw by the middle of the month, leaving only a screening force behind. As a result, X Corps did not meet full enemy resistance. Almond remained concerned about air support. He visited the 7th Infantry Division and observed enemy troop concentrations in the vicinity. He told Ferenbaugh to request air strikes on the location through X Corps headquarters. Since the divisions had previously been denied air strikes, Almond wanted to bring pressure on the Fifth Air Force by routing the request through corps headquarters.[30]

Ridgway intended UN operations to continue forward with few pauses, and on April 3 he launched Operation Rugged, designed to push the Eighth Army offensive north of the 38th Parallel, After getting the X Corps attack under way, Almond placed Maj. Gen. Ruffner in temporary command of the corps and flew to Tokyo for a one-week leave. When he returned on April 9, Almond began a program of formal command inspections of units down to battalion and separate company level. He selected one battalion per day, generally when it was out of the line. At each inspection, he first assembled all of the officers for a presentation on leadership, command responsibility, and supply discipline. He then conducted an in-ranks inspection of the battalion. While this can be seen as micromanagement, Almond's message to his officers and leaders was clear: discipline matters in all things.[31]

Critics and his subordinate commanders bemoaned his attention to detail, but it was detail that caused many of his units' difficulties. He believed that if the corps commander showed interest, everyone else would as well. Previous visits had shown Almond that supply problems plagued his units at various levels, so he devoted particular attention to it. He was also concerned about the proper orientation of replacements. Visiting the 7th Infantry Division Replacement Company, he spoke to the newly arrived troops and their chain of command on discipline, including proper wearing of the uniform; the necessity of knowing their jobs; caring for their equipment; and battle lessons learned in Korea. He echoed these same themes on all of his unit visits.[32]

Shortly after Almond returned to Korea, he received shocking news. On April 11, 1951, President Truman relieved MacArthur and replaced him with Ridgway. Word of the relief reached Almond over the radio while he was inspecting 1st Battalion, 9th Regiment. He was not only shocked but angered, and did not at first believe his aide when he was told. He wrote to both MacArthur and Margaret the next day to express his dismay. He assured MacArthur that he would "always be among his great admirers" and that he stood "ready to render any assistance you may think I can perform." Calling his time with MacArthur the "pinnacle" of his service, he closed with a line sure to please his deposed chief: "My sincere hope is that this dismissal will meet the contempt of the American people it so richly deserves." MacArthur evidently did not reply by letter, but he did so to Margaret in person.[33]

Margaret later provided a detailed account of the MacArthur family's departure from Tokyo on April 16. She recalled that General and Mrs. MacArthur moved slowly down a long line of officers and diplomats gathered at Haneda Airport to say farewell, greeting each one. The MacArthurs then turned to the group of wives from the headquarters, and greeted them as well. When the general reached Margaret, she recalled, "Then he came to me and took my hand[.] I couldn't speak for my tears. He looked at me and there were tears in his eyes and he said clearly, 'Give my love to Ned.' I inclined my head and he went on to Mrs. Hickey, saying, 'good-bye.' He did not say good-bye to me. He just said, 'Give my love to Ned.'"[34]

This clearly made Margaret feel special, and MacArthur's kindness toward Ned deepened her own devotion to MacArthur. She continued: "I wish you could have gone with him. He is simply magnificent. I awakened at the three this morning, and the cocks were crowing all over Tokyo. There were enough for each betrayer; for each who have denied him." This messianic view of MacArthur helped taint Margaret's view of many other senior Army officers, especially Army Chief of Staff Gen. J. Lawton Collins. Whitney and Willoughby, the last remaining members of the Bataan Gang, quickly followed their chief into retirement.[35]

Two days after MacArthur's departure, Ridgway wrote Almond a personal letter to inquire into his preference for his next job. Ridgway asked, "Do you wish to stay on indefinitely in the command of your splendid Corps, go home at some definite future time, or at an early date[?]"Almond chose to remain with X Corps, and Ridgway removed him from the chief of staff's job. Almond's decision must have pleased his commander, as Ridgway later told historian Roy Appleman that he considered Almond "his best Corps Commander." The fact that Ridgway gave Almond a choice indicates his respect for Almond's abilities. Almond later reported that he was entirely satisfied with relinquishing the chief of staff title and had no desire to do anything other than to command X Corps. This reflects his personal feelings, despite the controversy in the decades since. Ridgway evidently considered the change a minor affair, as he failed to mention it in either of his two books, one a memoir, the other focused on the Korean War as a whole.[36]

Lt. Gen. James A. Van Fleet replaced Ridgway in command of the Eighth Army. Though he and Almond did not know each other well, they shared similar career trajectories. Both had commanded machine-gun battalions in World War I, suffered wounds, been decorated for bravery, and later taught tactics at Fort Benning. They quickly developed a strong rapport in Korea, and Van Fleet saw Almond as a strong leader.[37]

Ridgway knew that the Chinese were preparing for an attack, but intelligence experts in the Eighth Army were divided on the potential target. Most believed that the weight of the attack would fall on I Corps in the west, down the Seoul corridor. With Operation Rugged well under way, the Chinese People's Volunteer Army launched its "Fifth phase offensive" on April 22, 1951, with three field armies totaling 700,000 soldiers against the entire Eighth Army front. As predicted, the initial CCF main effort went against I Corps in the west, but the weight of the North Korean attack in the east soon fell on X Corps on April 24 (see map 14.5). The NK 12th Division targeted the 5th ROK Division on the X Corps right flank. Almond directed that the defense in the 5th ROK Division be stabilized along phase line Kansas north of the town of Inje and all efforts be directed toward it. He met with his staff and commanders on April 25 and made plans for closing off the North Korean penetration. Almond asked the commanding general of III ROK Corps to release

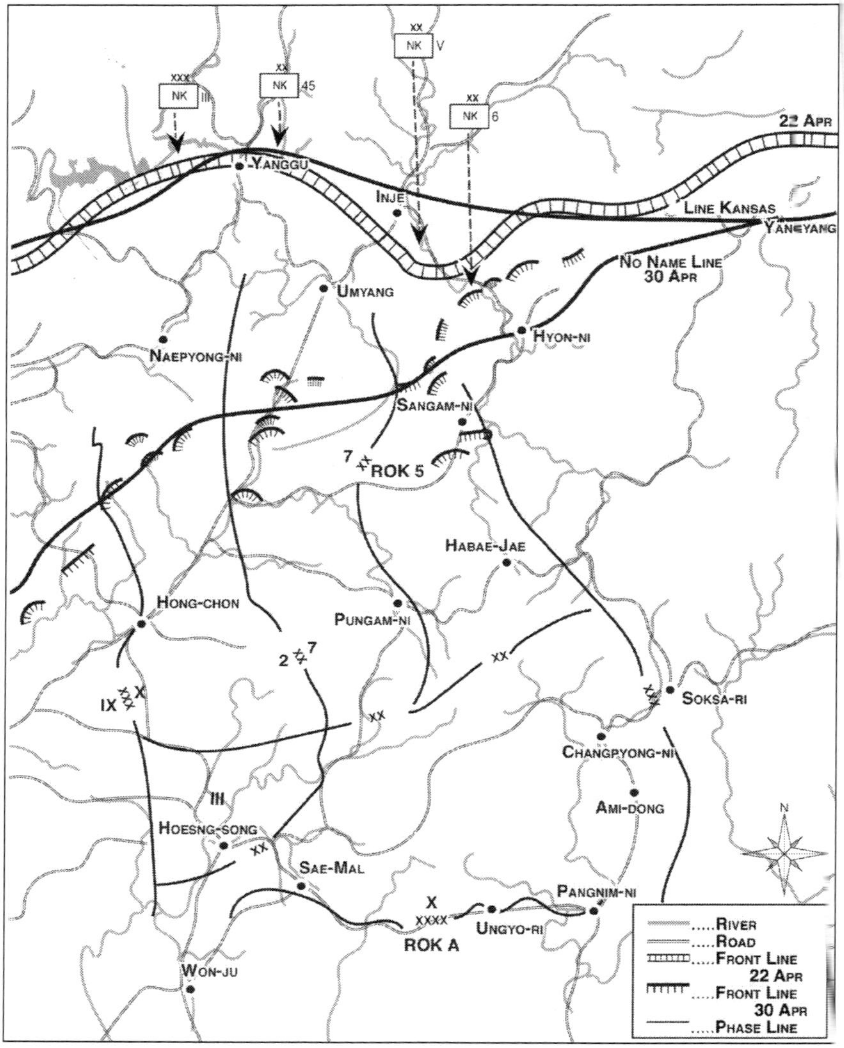

14.5. Operation Rugged, April 3–30, 1951

a regiment from the 3rd ROK Division to attack along the base of penetration, and directed the 7th Infantry Division to provide its Ranger company to protect that regiment's flank.[38]

General Van Fleet visited Almond at the X Corps CP on April 26 and reported that conditions in the west were much worse than in the east. He directed Almond and IX Corps commander Maj. Gen. William Hoge to withdraw southward to a line fifteen miles south of the town of Inje. Almond later reported that he asked his G3 the name of the new defensive line. The Eighth Army had not yet assigned a name, perhaps because of the fluidity of the situation, or perhaps because the Eighth Army staff had not yet meshed with its new commander. Almond told his G3 to call it the No Name line. When X Corps reported its positions back, the Eighth Army staff appropriated Almond's name for the line. Almond had left his deputy corps commander, Colonel Ladue, at the 5th ROK Division to continue to guide and prod that division in his defense. Following Van Fleet's conference, Almond visited Ladue and 5th ROK Division and found the situation considerably improved.[39]

The beginning of May saw changes in the X Corps force structure, as Van Fleet realigned the divisions to meet the most likely enemy avenues of attack. Almond lost the 7th Infantry Division, reassigned to IX Corps, but gained the 1st Marine Division, now commanded by Maj. Gen. Gerald C. Thomas. Almond's relations with Thomas were very good from the beginning, unlike his relations with Thomas's predecessor, Maj. Gen. Oliver P. Smith. Frank Mildren reported that things were completely different under Thomas. The two commanders got along well; Thomas invited Almond, Mildren, and the chief of staff to his CP for dinner, and Almond reciprocated. After the losses during the April offensive, the Eighth Army had consolidated along the No Name line, and Almond and the other corps commanders were conducting aggressive patrolling to their front to determine the enemy's intentions.[40]

During the first ten days of May, Almond established four RCT-sized patrol bases in the left and center of the X Corps zone. The 5th ROK and 7th Divisions launched limited-objective attacks on the right, and coordinated with the advance of elements of the III ROK Corps. The patrols encountered only light resistance, but intelligence reports indicated a strong enemy buildup in front of X Corps. Almond continued his daily visits to the frontline units, inspecting progress on defensive preparations along the No Name line. Almond always emphasized speed in the completion of defenses, and the importance of continuous and aggressive patrolling activities to determine the enemy's intentions. Almond inspected the line for efficiency, made notes for correction, and then referred them to the commander for corrective action.[41]

The X Corps G2, Col. James Polk, however, had developed his own intelligence sources, which told him the assault would concentrate on X Corps's sector. Polk recruited local Koreans as agents to "cross the line," gather intelligence, and bring it back. The process was time-consuming, but it worked. Radio intercept was useless: The Chinese did not use Western-style signal communications at regimental level and below, preferring bugle calls and verbal orders. Units above regiment used only landline communications. Unsurprisingly, Almond put more stock in his own G2's opinion than that of the Eighth Army G2. He sent Mildren up in a liaison/spotter airplane to do reconnaissance of the area where Polk expected the attack. Mildren found no Chinese at all, and in fact very few people. When he returned and reported to Almond, he told him that Polk must have been mistaken.[42]

Polk turned out to be correct, and on May 15, 1951, the CPVA launched the main effort concentrated on X Corps with the 15th, 60th, 20th, and 27th Chinese armies, totaling 137,000 Chinese and 38,000 North Korean soldiers attacking X Corps. Almond later discovered that the Chinese had stayed well away from the area and, camouflaged, began moving forward at dusk and attacked at midnight (see map 14.6). Based on Polk's information, Almond had tried to convince the Eighth Army that the attack was coming in the X Corps sector, but he was unsuccessful. The weight of the attack fell on the poorly trained 7th ROK Division, which consisted of conscripts with twenty-one days of military training. Almond must have been uncomfortably reminded of his experience in Italy, as both the 5th and 7th ROK Divisions dissolved under the assault, melting away to the rear. The 2nd Infantry Division held its ground, but with terrible losses. The 23rd RCT lost almost all of its equipment and vehicles, and Almond faulted the regimental leadership for having their vehicles too close to the line. The Chinese destroyed their vehicles but without wounding too many troops. Coming so soon after a large equipment loss that had earned him a stinging rebuke from Ridgway in February, and with his former G3, Chiles, now in command, it must have proved very bitter for Almond.[43]

The brunt of the attack in the 2nd Division sector, however, fell on the 38th RCT. The 1st and 2nd Battalions, each with 800-plus men, suffered more than 85 percent casualties. The 3rd Battalion had held a better position and was spared destruction, but the regiment was reduced to combat ineffectiveness by the end of the action. Almond relieved the commander of the 38th RCT and sent Mildren to take command, replacing him with his deputy, Lt. Col. Warner Williamson. Almond appreciated Mildren's sentimental attachment to the regiment, Mildren having commanded one of its battalions during the last war. Mildren needed to replace two of the three battalion commanders, most of the staff, and several of the com-

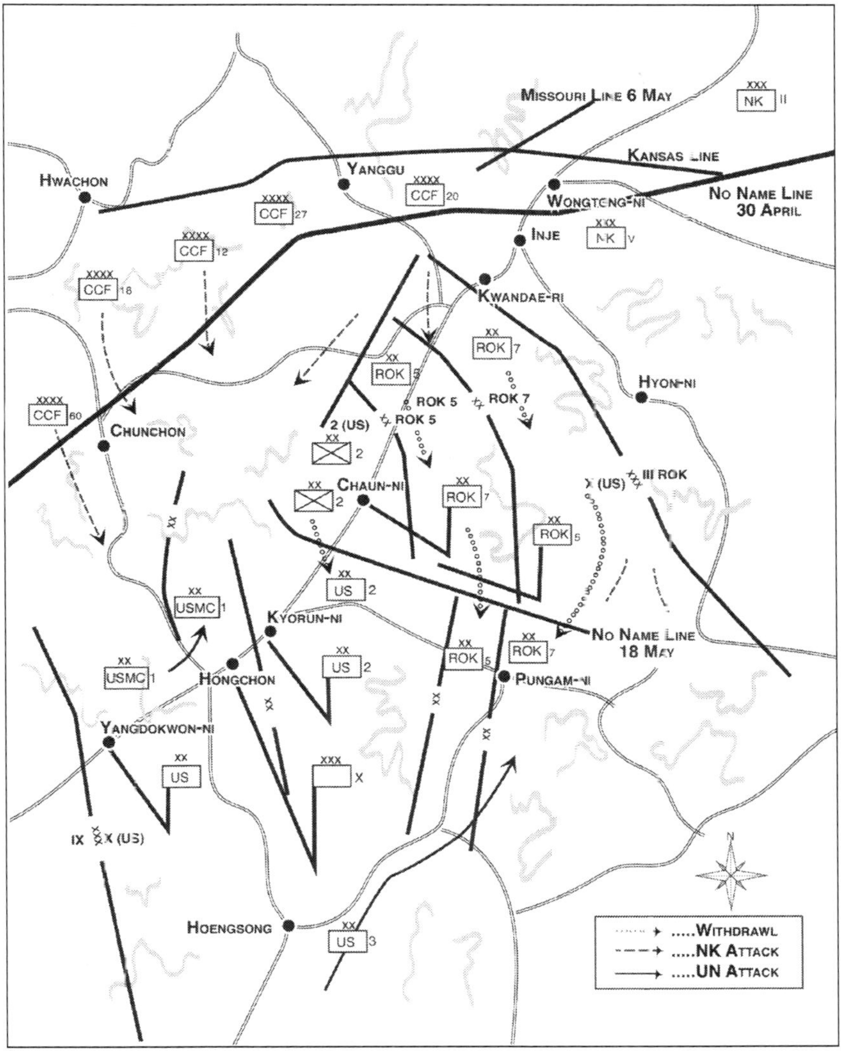

14.6. Battle of Soyang River, May 16–22, 1951

pany commanders in the regiment, and Almond allowed him his choice of officers from the corps headquarters for these replacements.[44]

Shortly after the attack began, Almond released the 23rd RCT, then in corps reserve, back to 2nd Infantry Division control. He also requested from Van Fleet that the 3rd Infantry Division be attached to the corps to strengthen the right flank where the 5th ROK Division was dissolving. On May 18, Almond began authorizing limited withdrawals, but he reiterated the necessity of killing the maximum number of enemy while withdrawing. The following day, Van Fleet arrived at the X Corps CP with Ridgway, who had been visiting from Tokyo. They asked Almond his opinion of the situation, and Almond replied that "the Chinese are flowing like water around my right flank." He warned that unless something drastic was done to reinforce that flank, both X Corps and EUSAK would lose their base of supplies. Van Fleet asked what Almond needed, Almond replied that he needed the 187th Airborne RCT, released from army reserve, for a corps reserve. He also needed the 3rd Infantry Division to arrive as soon as possible. He planned to use the three RCTs of the 3rd Infantry Division as "islands" to slow the advance of the Chinese armies on the right flank.[45]

Van Fleet immediately sent the 3rd Infantry Division and the 187th Airborne RCT to shore up the X Corps defense. The collapse of the ROK units had left a gap in the line. Almond stabilized the shoulders of that gap by May 16 and closed off the attack by May 22. He positioned the 3rd Infantry Division as a counterattack force to attack across the shoulders of the gap in order to cut off and destroy as many CCF units as possible. Almond credited the "unprecedented speed with which the elements of the 3rd US Division were deployed from the I and IX Corps zones to be committed on the Eastern flank of the X Corps was instrumental in the containment of the enemy offensive." He was disappointed by the hesitancy of some commanders to pursue the enemy, which slowed the start of the offensive. Almond launched a counterattack the same day, and though he captured or killed a large number of Chinese, many more had escaped through the gap. Polk had identified from intelligence reports several units that had not yet been seen at the front. Almond waited for the remainder of the uncommitted CCF armies to come through, but those units never appeared. Almond, always quick to identify mistakes and failures in others, did not spare himself when it came to criticism. He later lamented to Mildren that waiting too long to launch that counterattack was the biggest mistake of his life. Had he begun the attack two days sooner, he surely would have destroyed even more CCF capability than he did.[46]

On May 26, Almond initiated Operation Chopper, a rapid advance to seize and secure the vital Inje-Yanggu area, and a decisive thrust by a reinforced RCT to strike northeast to the coast at the port of Kansong (see map 14.7). The enemy withdrew rapidly, and the bulk of CCF

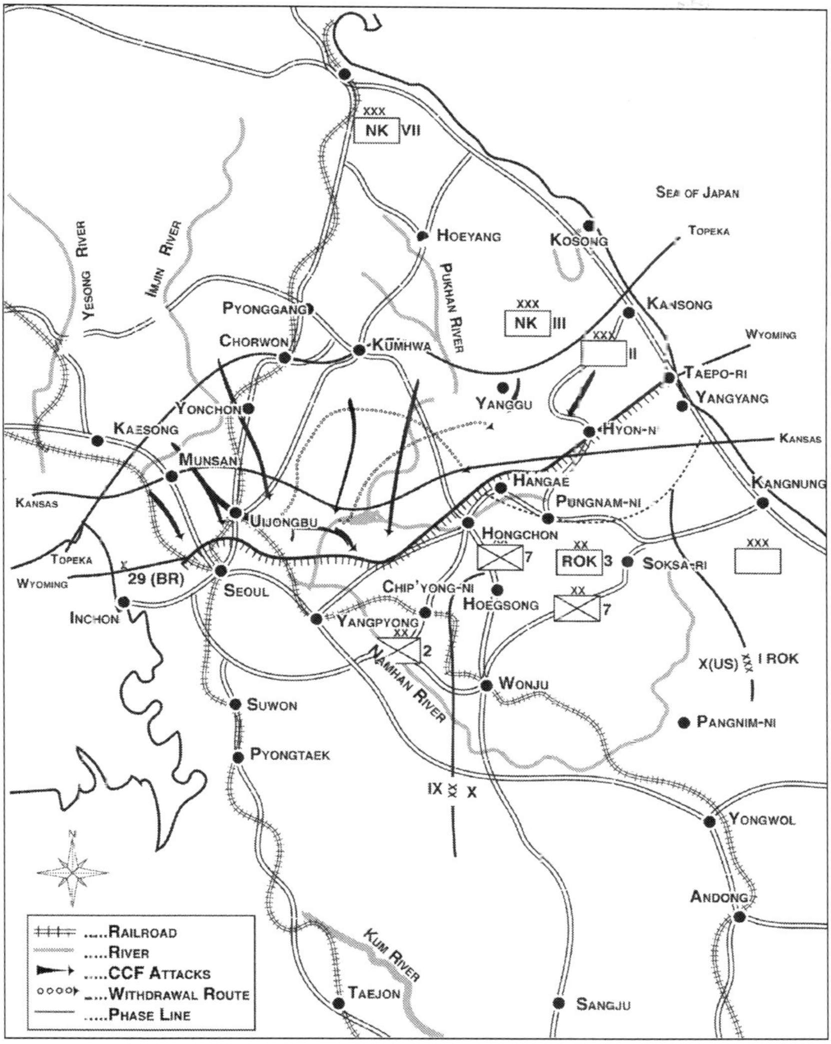

14.7. UN Advances, May–July 1951

forces managed to escape the trap, but they abandoned large quantities of war matériel. Despite the large number escaping, X Corps and other UN troops captured an unprecedented number of prisoners. Almond parlayed initial tactical defeats into a major UN victory, and he later estimated X Corps had destroyed the effectiveness of six corps and caused some 90,000 enemy casualties. That was the beginning of the end, because neither the Chinese nor the UN forces ever launched any more large-scale attacks. By June the military situation in Korea had reached the stalemate that would last until the signing of the armistice two years later. Meanwhile, X Corps maintained a defensive posture, with sustained probing action designed to keep the enemy confused and off balance.[47]

In the summer of 1951 the US Army instituted a rotation policy to bring home officers and soldiers based on their time abroad, similar to the post–World War II policy that had sent Almond to Japan. This time, however, Almond would benefit: he had spent five years overseas, longer than any other senior commander. General Ridgway offered Almond several choices for his next assignment, and Almond chose appointment as commandant of the Army War College. Visits from dignitaries filled the days before Almond's change of command in Korea. He entertained several notables, including Secretary of State George C. Marshall, New York governor and former Republican presidential candidate Thomas E. Dewey, US ambassador to Korea John J. Muccio, and Korean president Syngman Rhee. After Maj. Gen. Clovis Byers arrived in Korea to assume command of X Corps, Almond led him on a tour of the corps area prior to the change of command ceremony on July 13, 1951. Byers had been the US Army deputy chief of staff for personnel and had assisted Almond in getting his protégés Col. John H. Chiles and Col. William J. McCaffrey quick promotions.[48]

After a small official ceremony at X Corps headquarters, Almond received a unique honor: all the artillery batteries in the corps fired a simultaneous salute, with the reverberating sound carried throughout the corps area over open radio channels. General Van Fleet awarded Almond the Distinguished Service Medal. Shortly afterward, Almond departed for Tokyo.

Almond could feel justifiably proud of his accomplishments in Korea, especially during the last six months. He had integrated X Corps into the Eighth Army and quickly adapted his operational style to Ridgway's. When Secretary of Defense George C. Marshall visited Korea in May, he and General Ridgway had both expressed pleasure with the manner in which X Corps operations were being conducted. That was surely a boost to Almond's ego. Ridgway later remembered, "Almond was a very highly capable officer and a fine Corps commander. . . . Almond is one of the few corps commanders I've had that, instead of ever having to push at all, I would have to keep an eye on him unless he, maybe in his boldness, would have jeopardized his command or executed a risky operation."[49]

Almond was a tough boss, but a good mentor. He grew his subordinate leaders by pushing for faster and more effective action, and also by demanding and enforcing high standards. His inspections were designed not to identify temporary problems but to uncover systemic weaknesses, and then to correct those systems. Commanders should be judged not just on mistakes but on how they correct them and prevent recurrence. Almond made mistakes in the first months of the war, but he learned from them and corrected his troop deployments in the later months of the war.

The airplane and helicopter had come to define operations at a tactical level in the Korean War as never before, and Almond used them to great advantage. During the operations in North Korea, his use of an airplane may have given him a distorted view of the battlefield and obscured the units' difficulties in accomplishing their missions. But airplanes offered Almond unparalleled access to the battlefield, and daily use of them allowed to him to coordinate with his subordinate commanders' activities while remaining in touch with his higher and adjacent headquarters. From September 1950 to July 1951, Almond logged a total of 552 flight hours and some 52,951 miles in five different fixed-wing aircraft and one helicopter. He earned the Air Medal with 27 oak leaf clusters.[50]

Almond often alienated people with his abrupt manner, which caused them to view his every decision in a negative light. Almond's protégé Frank Mildren called his patron "probably one of the bravest men I've ever run into," but he realized that the general had problems dealing with people. "I used to feel he was without a doubt the cruelest man I've ever run into when dealing with human beings," Mildren recalled.[51] Ridgway also saw all sides of his irascible yet trusted subordinate. "Almond was apt to be pretty rough on other people's sensibilities, and he could really could be cutting and intolerant. Well, again, I don't want to detract from his ability; his overall abilities are very high. I would rate him as a superior Corps commander, not the top level but superior."[52]

Despite Almond's reputation for placing his own men in command, and thus creating a "command nursery," he actually hated losing his primary staff officers who were so critical in his headquarters. He allowed them to go to commands, and certainly shepherded the careers of more than a few, but in most cases of regimental commanders who came from his staff, they were actions requested either by the officer himself or by another general. While this reinforced Almond's reputation for looking out for his staff, each of these officers proved to be an excellent leader who benefited the unit he commanded. All of them became generals. With the exception of Chiles, who had replaced Freeman only after the latter's injury, each of Almond's new subordinate commanders proved a much better leader than the man he supplanted. It is a measure of Almond's success in both selecting and grooming officers that every single X Corps primary staff officer (with the exception of the Corps G4, who was murdered while on leave in Tokyo) and all their deputies, as well as every officer assigned to G3, was later selected for flag rank.[53]

15

A Final Assignment

Back to School, 1951–1953

After five years overseas and another war, Almond was going home. Having said his goodbyes all around at Eighth Army headquarters, he flew to Tokyo, where Margaret met his plane. He spent a week getting his affairs in order and preparing to move. He and Margaret, and his aide Capt. Ray Barrett, boarded a passenger ship in Yokohama for San Francisco, and then a train to New York and finally to West Point to visit Tommy and his family. Almond's son-in-law Charles, who had left Japan to attend graduate school, was then teaching at the US Military Academy.[1]

Almond felt uniquely prepared to head the recently reopened Army War College, having graduated from all the senior service schools. The War College had closed in 1940 at Washington Barracks, District of Columbia, due to the officer shortage caused by America's hurried efforts to mobilize for World War II. In 1949 the commandant of the US Army Command and General Staff College, Lt. Gen. Manton S. Eddy, had chaired a committee that studied the need for reopening the AWC. That report also found that "there is no true university approach and at no time in the Army education of an officer is he given this graduate student approach." The AWC reopened in 1950 at Fort Leavenworth, Kansas, a temporary home until moving to a more permanent location. With little to use as a guide, the War College course that first year became merely an extension of the CGSC. AWC commandant Lt. Gen. Joseph M. Swing began trying to change the curriculum, substituting a lecture program with distinguished speakers and student group discussions. In the Army War College's early redevelopment in the 1950s, the college faculty enjoyed wide latitude in choosing course materials. The college had no dean, and the small faculty largely developed their own courses, with input from the commandant and assistant commandant. The first class was limited to one hundred students; the AWC had its pick of the best colonels in the US Army for staff and faculty.[2]

Swing ran the college for academic year 1950–51 and then departed to command the Sixth Army in San Francisco. Meanwhile, Deputy Commandant Maj. Gen. Arthur G. Trudeau worked to find a new location and move the school. Trudeau had been the Army's director of training during World War II and remembered Carlisle Barracks, Pennsylvania, as the home of the Medical Field Service School. That school had outgrown the post and moved to Fort Sam Houston, Texas, after the war, and several smaller schools took its place. Trudeau thought that Carlisle Barracks would be the perfect location for a small college. He saw it as "far enough from Washington, where you couldn't be bothered by the Pentagon every day, but near enough that you could go there for whatever you wanted to do." It also gave easy access to other big cities from which guest lecturers could come. Senator Lister Hill of Alabama lobbied to move the AWC near the new Air War College at Montgomery, but Trudeau enlisted the help of Pennsylvania governor James H. "Red" Duff and other politicians and got the AWC moved to Carlisle. Trudeau began the move after the Class of 1951 graduated.[3]

Amid the time-consuming move to Carlisle and the logistical difficulties of setting up the college, the AWC faculty assessed the curriculum after the class of 1951 graduated. That evaluation resulted in some classes being eliminated. The Department of the Army also granted a request to lengthen the program by one week, so these changes yielded an "extra" three weeks for course development. Trudeau, whom Almond later remembered as a "brilliant" officer, had never met Almond before he arrived in Carlisle as commandant, but they had corresponded when Trudeau worked in Army G1 and Almond requested officers for the Far East Command. Almond had offered Trudeau a job in Japan if he came overseas. Trudeau never went to Japan, but the connection paved the way for a good relationship, and they got along well during their time together at the AWC. Trudeau provided continuity between Swing at Fort Leavenworth and Almond at Carlisle Barracks. Almond approved the faculty that Trudeau and Swing had recruited and brought from Fort Leavenworth.[4]

Those instructors included Lt. Col. William C. Westmoreland, future US Army chief of staff, whom Swing had recruited from the CGSC faculty for the AWC in 1950. Westmoreland later recalled that he "had cognizance over airborne operations, airmobile operations, and the use of helicopters" while teaching at the AWC. Westmoreland arranged to bring some early helicopters to Carlisle to introduce the students to this new technology. Almond liked to surround himself with officers he considered competent and quickly began assembling his old favorites. He requested

Col. William J. McCaffrey, then commanding the 31st Infantry Regiment in Korea. When McCaffrey arrived in December 1951, Almond installed him as his executive officer. Col. John Chiles also arrived from Korea, to be a member of the class of 1952. Almond trusted Chiles and McCaffrey and assigned them special projects such as reviewing the course work, retaining Chiles after graduation to replace McCaffrey, who then joined the class of 1953. Almond also kept five of the best officers from the class of 1952, and four more from the following class, for the faculty. Almond identified and groomed good officers, and his mentorship doubtless helped them achieve career success. Of the nine officers he selected, six later became general officers.[5]

Gen. Mark W. Clark, chief of Army Field Forces, provided specific guidance on the commandant's responsibilities as soon as Almond arrived. Clark clearly explained Almond's mandate: "As head of the senior school in our Army Education System, I hold you responsible for insuring the teaching of coordinated doctrine in the schools making up our Army schools educational system. . . . I may also ask you to conduct studies pertaining to changes in doctrine which may result from new weapons or equipment, or from changed military concepts or requirements."[6] Almond replied that he planned to continue the current policies and that he considered studies of current issues very important. Almond evidently saw this guidance as his license to pursue an interest he deemed important: interservice or "joint" cooperation.[7]

Almond's tenure at Carlisle Barracks commenced shortly before the class of 1952 opened, and he initially found the curriculum satisfactory. Since he was not one to accept the status quo, however, he quickly began identifying "deficiencies" as he saw them. Almond saw his AWC assignment as an opportunity to impart to future senior leaders the wisdom and experience he had gained from thirty-six years in the Army, specifically his exposure to high-level command in Korea. When he arrived at Carlisle, he knew that without a promotion or special arrangement, he had only about eighteen months remaining before then-current mandatory retirement at age sixty, and he wanted to focus his efforts. Almond's Korean experiences drove his interest in interservice operations. Principally, Almond believed that US Army senior officers "had failed to gain an appreciation for the true value of cooperation with the other Armed Services, particularly with the Air Force and the Navy." He established a joint exercise at Southern Pines, North Carolina, with the Air Corps Tactical School, to foster better understanding of the joint Army–Air Force mission. In another bow to jointness, the class included three US Air Force officers, two Marine officers, and a US Navy officer. The newly expanded class (150, up from the previous 100) also contained one National Guard and two Army Reserve officers.[8]

Almond effected a somewhat paternal tone when he addressed the AWC class for the first time as commandant on September 1, 1951. He encouraged each student to study the curriculum's problems "in a studious manner, as a mature officer, charged with perhaps execution of the plan you endorse." He then warned against arguing with invited speakers, and to consider their presentations thoughtfully. He left them with one final admonition, "Don't try to do it all yourself." He related a story from his own War College year, in which one officer had chaired a student committee and failed to delegate responsibilities. The same officer later had a "mental breakdown" and went to the hospital, and his team suffered. Almond used this as a warning to the officers to "share the load" so they would all profit from the course. Throughout the Army War College's history, its commandants have ranged from compliant caretakers to driven activists. Almond proved to be an active commandant.[9]

Almond and Trudeau agreed on most issues regarding improving the course curriculum. During Almond's year as a War College student, Commandant Maj. Gen. George Simonds had altered the lecture scheme to make learning interactive, giving the students pre-readings and making the lecture more of an exchange of ideas on a graduate level. Almond remembered that and wanted to bring back that environment for the new curriculum. They created a Civilian Advisory Group (CAG), which visited Carlisle in January 1952. The group included Professor Royden Dangerfield of the University of Illinois, Louisiana State University president Lt. Gen. (Ret.) Troy H. Middleton, and Julius Ochs Adler, publisher of the *New York Times*. After briefly studying the AWC curriculum, the group offered several recommendations, and Almond set about immediately implementing their conclusions.[10]

The committee first suggested that the faculty reduce the number of lectures and assign more extensive reading to help the students gain a deeper understanding of the topics. Almond reduced the lectures by 30 percent and changed the format, requiring the guest speakers to remain after the presentation to interact with the students. He also reduced the number of officers attending each lecture, to create a more intimate and collegial setting. Almond used the lectures very effectively, however, to focus the AWC course toward the ideas he thought most important. By selecting the lecturers and their topics, he could directly influence the course more than if he had been present during its development. Reflecting the graduate school approach, the college used the seminar, or "committee" format, that Almond had experienced as a student. Reducing the number of student committees and narrowing the students' research focus would also benefit the students, the advisory group reported. The CAG called for greater faculty involvement and for enlarging the faculty to provide students with closer attention. The Army had planned annual class size increases up to the 300 mark, but the CAG advised limiting each class to 200 while increasing the percentage of students from other services. The decision on class size rested with the US Army leadership rather than with Almond, but he lobbied the chief of staff to advocate for the change.[11]

The committee's most important recommendations concerned the college's basic mission statement. In the absence of the Army War College, the National War College, founded in 1946, had assumed prominence as the "senior" service college. In the new Department of Defense, the "joint" focus enjoyed greater support than a single service's parochial views. Almond and the senior Army leadership saw the AWC as the pinnacle of the officers' education, not a stepping-stone to the National War College, and the CAG recommended the AWC mission be clarified to avoid overlapping with the NWC mission. Almond used the committee's findings to rewrite his AWC mission. Almond believed the previous mission statement used since 1949 had been too limiting, given the Army chief of staff's desire to have the AWC be the "apex" of the Army education system: "To prepare officers for duty as commanders and general staff officers within the headquarters of army group and corresponding communications zone activities, the theater army, the theater, the zone of the interior army, and the Department of the Army, with emphasis on the Department of the Army."[12]

Almond did not believe that statement reflected the "breadth of the curriculum and the academic maturity" the college had attained over the previous two years and thought that the higher-level commander required formal education to ensure that he understood the political, economic, and social contexts of military employment. He proposed a change to the mission statement: "To provide a graduate course of study designed to broaden the education of selected officers with respect to national policy, national security organization, strategic planning, and employment of the Armed Forces, in order to assist in fitting them for high command and important staff assignments in the military service, with emphasis on the Army."[13]

Prescient though Almond may have been, General Clark did not agree with him. He believed that the AWC existed simply to "prepare officers for duty as commanders and General Staff officers at the highest United States Army levels." Clark still took the parochial view that Army schools should focus exclusively on Army subjects. US Army Vice Chief of Staff Gen. John Hull agreed with Clark and ordered the old mission statement retained. Despite this setback, Almond worked to shape the curriculum as he saw fit.[14]

The curriculum retained a military focus, but with a gradual increase in international affairs study. Almond had concluded that the curriculum should devote more time to studying other nations, particularly the Soviet Union. The class during Almond's first year featured eleven presentations on Soviet politics, strategy, economics, and tactical operations; the class of 1953 received twelve such briefings. Almond addressed this by instituting a weeklong class trip to New York City to visit the United Nations. The class was very fortunate to have opening presentations from Nobel Peace Prize laureate Dr. Ralph J. Bunche, director of the Department of Trusteeship and Information from Non-Self-Governing Territories, and Eleanor Roosevelt, the US representative on the Committee on Human Rights of the Economic and Social Council. The class then had opportunities to speak with senior representatives from the UN Permanent Missions from Egypt, Pakistan, Turkey, and Yugoslavia, and from the Special Assistant for Korea. Several senior American diplomats presented information on the United States mission to the UN, including its role in the Security Council, and the General Assembly. Lt. Gen. Willis D. Crittenberger, Almond's former boss during World War II, headed the US delegation to the UN Military Staff Committee, and he and his staff discussed his committee's functions as well as the US Military Advisory Group to the UN. The trip offered the students a broad view of international and military affairs. The tour for the following year's class enjoyed much the same itinerary, with minor variations.[15]

Almond complemented the New York trips with two days in Washington, visiting both the State Department and the Pentagon. The time in the capital would be limited, however, so Almond and the faculty scheduled a series of presentations to prepare students for their visit. Almond got some assistance in broadening the curriculum from the Army War College's first civilian faculty member, Frank S. Hopkins, from the State Department. Hopkins delivered an overview of the State Department's postwar organization, and provided an invaluable connection to the State Department. The eminent political scientist Hans Morgenthau, from the University of Chicago, opened the pre-Washington series of presentations with "Background and Basis for the Changes in US Foreign Policy." State Department officials then presented a series of six programs that explored American foreign policy problems in Western Europe, Eastern Europe, the Eastern Mediterranean, the Middle East, the Far East, and Southeast Asia. Other diplomats examined the "Relationship Between Foreign Economic Aid Programs and National Security" and additional subjects. The postwar development of new political alliances received attention as well, with orientations on the recently-formed North Atlantic Treaty Organization (NATO) and the Organization of American States. At the State Department, Assistant Secretary of State for Far Eastern Affairs Dean Rusk addressed the class on American foreign policy, and then Assistant Secretary of State for Public Affairs Edward Barrett spoke on the State Department's Overseas Information Program. The class received a briefing on the world situation, and then split into several groups for lectures exploring the "International Information and Educational Exchange Program," and "Intelligence Organization of the State Department."[16]

The course had already conducted several classes on all aspects of the Army staff, so the Pentagon portion of the trip focused on the Office of the Secretary of Defense (OSD) and the Joint Staff. Almond arranged for Secretary of Defense Robert A. Lovett to welcome and speak to the class, and then other officials from OSD lectured on the organization and operations of the department. The class also received detailed presentations on the National Security Council and the various functions of the Joint Staff before returning to Carlisle. The following year, Almond invited his former Army War College classmate, General of the Army Omar N. Bradley, to address the class while at the Pentagon. Bradley, then serving as the chairman of the Joint Chiefs of Staff, gave a brief welcome and then discussed the role of the Joint Chiefs. The classes each year also received presentations from each of the service chiefs.[17]

In addition to the foreign policy and military aspects of the AWC course, Almond introduced students to the roles of other federal agencies. Each class during his tenure benefited from presentations by the director of the Central Intelligence Agency, the director of the Federal Bureau of Investigation, the secretary of the Treasury, and congressmen, senators, or their staffs. The classes were also afforded an international perspective by luminaries such as Field Marshal Viscount Bernard Law Montgomery, the Deputy Supreme Allied Commander in Europe; the British chief of the Imperial General Staff, Field Marshal William J. Slim; and the Hon. Brooke Claxton, minister of National Defence, Canada.[18]

Almond's own War College class in 1934 had studied war plans for several different possible international scenarios, in order to remain current in military affairs. As commandant, Almond used lectures on the Korean War to keep students current in the same way. In October 1951, he brought in a staff officer from GHQ, FECOM, to present "The Far East Command," which set the stage for other lectures related to the war. The peace talks that had begun and broken down during the summer had resumed in late October, so Almond scheduled a briefing on the Korean situation in early November.

Almond then took the stage in January 1952 with "UN Operations in Korea," and subsequently brought in his friend Vice Adm. Arthur D. Struble, then commander of the US Navy's First Fleet in the western Pacific, who presented "Fleet Operations in Korean Waters." One week later Rear Adm. T. B. Brittain, commander of the Navy's Amphibious Group Two, presented "Amphibious Operations," with Inchon as the prime example. Almond also included updates on the latest technology and invited one of the nation's first helicopter test pilots, Joe Mashman from Bell Aircraft Corporation, whose topic was "Use of the Helicopter in Korea." The following year, Almond brought in the recently retired General Van Fleet; his own former corps G3, Maj. Gen. Edwin K. Wright; and Rear Adm. James H. Doyle, to present the Korean lectures. Almond also added presentations on logistics in Korea.[19]

Almond interpreted broadly Clark's guidance and launched several special studies, largely centered around his own experience. Typical of most senior officers, Almond believed his own knowledge and skills had served him well, and therefore junior officers would benefit from them. Many senior officers of Almond's era believed their battlefield successes should be shared with their subordinates to ensure their success as well. Almond directed McCaffrey to study whether or not tactical use of nuclear weapons would have provided any advantage to his forces in Korea. McCaffrey determined that X Corps never really had enough information on exact enemy positions to attack them in a timely manner. Despite that, Almond knew that nuclear weapons had become the dominant feature of the nation's military arsenal and scheduled appropriate lectures to discuss them. In October 1951, Almond brought in Brig. Gen. Herbert B. Loper from Army Operations (G3) to present "The Atomic Energy Commission." Two weeks later, Army G-3 sent a team of three generals to deliver "Military Characteristics, Capabilities, and Limitations of Atomic Weapons." In this case, Almond created three sections to enable the entire class to participate. Noted nuclear strategy theorist Bernard Brodie presented the final, capstone lecture in the series on the future of atomic power. The following year Almond added "Military Employment of Chemical, Radiological, and Biological Agents" to the nuclear lectures.[20]

The opportunity for study also allowed Almond to indulge his passion for history, especially of the units he commanded. He arranged to have one of his former officers, Maj. Paul Goodman, recalled to active duty with the office of the Chief of Military History to conduct a study of the 92nd Infantry Division's performance during World War II. Almond had maintained hundreds of official documents and copies of reports, and he sought out other material from his former subordinates. Goodman used these to complete the study in 1952 and later published a version of it as an official history of the division during the war.

Despite Almond's reputation for service parochialism in Korea, he worked to broaden the AWC curriculum to educate Army officers in the roles of the other services. In addition to the Korea-related naval briefings that had also addressed Marine Corps amphibious operations, Almond brought Vice Adm. Richard L. Conolly, president of the Naval War College, to lecture on sea power. The director of Naval Intelligence spoke on his area of expertise, and naval historian Fletcher Pratt presented "New Concepts of Sea Power." Almond asked his old friend Gen. Lem Shepherd, recently appointed commandant of the Marine Corps, to speak to the class about the past and future of his service.[21]

Of all the challenges Almond faced in Korea, tactical air support concerned him the most, so he scheduled nearly four times as many lectures on air power and related topics. Maj. Gen. William F. McKee, assistant vice chief of staff of the US Air Force, gave the first of these with a description of the Department of the Air Force, explaining the development and structure of that new service. Almond then asked Gen. John K. Cannon, commander of the Air Force's Tactical Air Command, to present "Tactical Air Support of Land Forces," and Maj. Gen. Glenn Barcus, recently named commander of the 5th Air Force, "Air-Ground Operations." Almond also invited the noted strategic airpower theorist Alexander de Seversky; Lt. Gen. Idwal Edwards, the president of the Air University; and Brig. Gen. James Selser from Strategic Air Command. All spoke on various aspects of strategic airpower. The remaining four Air Force lectures concerned logistics, intelligence, doctrine, and theater air operations.[22]

Almond's Korean experience informed his opinion of the US Air Force and led to lasting enmity between the two services. He believed he had received excellent, responsive support from the 1st Marine Aircraft Wing while in northeast Korea, but when the 1st Marine Division left X Corps, he lost his "X Corps Air Force." Almond felt he did not receive the same level of support from the Air Force. After being carved out of the Army as a separate service in 1947, the Air Force of the 1950s emphasized strategic bombing over tactical battlefield support. The clash of service cultures that Almond had first identified in Korea became clearer as time passed; the Air Force wished to be seen as the nation's "war-winning" arm, rather than as merely the Army's aerial auxiliary. Almond thought highly of his own grasp of airpower, both because he had attended ACTS and because he had used aircraft extensively to control actions on the ground. History judges Almond harshly because of his supposed antipathy toward the Marines, but he really saw Marine Corps air-ground teams as the model for how the Air Force should support the Army. Almond used his post as AWC commandant as a bully pulpit to identify weaknesses in air support to ground forces.[23]

While in Korea, Almond had vehemently disagreed with his former ACTS instructor, Lt. Gen. Earle Partridge, then the 5th Air Force commander, over the need for tactical air support. Almond argued for a Tactical Air Control Party with every battalion in combat, so that these units could call for immediate air support. Since Almond believed the Marines provided superior close air support, he lost no opportunity to needle the Air Force about it. In northeast Korea at the time of the Chosin Reservoir battle, the US Air Force had required requests for air support to be submitted twenty-four hours in advance. Almond had explained to Partridge that "unplanned" tactical requirements could not be known twenty-four hours in advance. Ground forces needed air support within 30–50 minutes of the request. When Partridge failed to respond as Almond had hoped, he broached the issue with Partridge's superior, Lt. Gen. George Stratemeyer, commander of the Far East Air Force. Almond also rubbed Stratemeyer the wrong way, and Stratemeyer confided to his diary: "General Almond is not a team player and is attempting to control, contrary to all written documents, the Air Force that supports him. His attitude ever since he has been appointed a commander has surprised me greatly. I should think that he would be grateful and would express his thanks for the communications and assistance which we have given the troops that have been placed under his control, but according to General Partridge, he has not done so."[24]

Successful air support in combat relied upon four critical measures: response time, or the time required to receive air support after calling for it; loiter time, or the time the aircraft could remain in the area to continue the support without returning to base: the number of missions, or sorties, available per day; and the distance from the front that aircraft had to cover. Almond knew that the US Air Force had provided fewer daily sorties in Korea than the Marines. The Marines had also typically arrived quicker and stayed longer in the combat area and engaged the enemy closer to the friendly troops than the Air Force did. The FECOM Operational Research Office provided information in 1951 that justified Almond's complaints (see table 15.1).

Table 15.1. Comparative USMC and USAF Air Support Response Times

	USAF	USMC
Response Time	45 minutes	10 minutes
Loiter Time	30 minutes	73 minutes
Sorties per Day	13	37
Distance from Front	3 miles	800–1600 yards

Source: Adapted from Crane, *American Airpower Strategy in Korea, 1950–1953,* 62.

Army complaints about Air Force support had reached the Pentagon even before Almond left Korea. Air Force Secretary Thomas K. Finletter had also ordered a civilian study in November 1950 of tactical support in the theater. Dr. Robert Starnes, president of the University of Colorado, completed this report in January 1951 and gave the US Air Force's close air support high marks. He noted, however, that joint doctrine and communications needed improvement, as did the quality of airborne antipersonnel weapons, and admitted weaknesses in night operations for close air support. Air Force Chief of Staff Gen. Hoyt S. Vandenberg had also ordered a study. His report in February 1951 "praised Air Force close air support and interdiction efforts and was very harsh in castigating those who denigrated them," though the report did agree with some of the Starnes report's findings.[25]

Response time needed to be short, while loiter time needed to be longer. Ground commanders also wanted as many sorties as possible available per day, and they needed the sorties as close as possible to the front of friendly troops. The Air Force collected all the reports, including the Army's input from FECOM, and determined "that there is no significant dispute among military professionals," which was patently false and allowed the Air Force to ignore the issue.[26]

Almond believed that the US Air Force had rejected the ground support role, and he used his position at the War College to continue the argument he had begun in Korea. He ordered a special study to find ways to make air-ground operations more responsive and forwarded it to General Clark and General Collins. Clark agreed with Almond's concerns about tactical air support, finding the analysis "a good contribution to the mass of evidence which points out a vital need for improvement."[27]

General Collins, however, argued that emerging US Air Force doctrine was addressing the issue. While this was a purely professional point, Almond's personal relationship with Collins soured even more after this. Vandenberg and Finletter probably suspected that Carl Vinson, chairman of the House Armed Services Committee, intended to wrest tactical air support and tactical aviation from the Air Force and shift it to the Navy and the Marines to give ground commanders more control over tactical air support. The Air Force's excessive focus on its strategic capabilities in the years after World War II threatened to jeopardize its tactical mission.[28]

To illustrate the problems and explain to Army officers the growing differences in Army and Air Force theories, Almond and his faculty compared the two doctrines. "Deviations Between US Army and US Air Force Doctrine," a faculty study completed shortly after he retired, attempted to give the students a better understanding of the problems affecting joint operations, with data taken directly from the two services' doctrinal publications.[29]

"Deviations" addressed sixteen conceptual areas: Nature of Conflict; Utilization of Forces; Objectives and Effects; Air Power and National Security; Command; Relativity of Forces; Nature of Operations; Objective; Employment of Forces; Control of the Air; Land Power, Air Power, and Strategy; Control of Theater Air Forces; Joint Command; Amphibious Operations; Command and Theater Forces; and Airborne Operations. The document clearly identified the fault lines between emerging Army and Air Force doctrine. Each service saw itself as the primary military arm. The Army believed that all other services existed to support the Army in defeating the enemy's ground forces, while the Air Force anchored its doctrine on precision bombing and air superiority ending the war before the Army became involved. While the document showed a clear Army bias, it also demonstrated that Air Force doctrine valued strategic bombing more than tactical air support.[30]

When Almond arrived at Carlisle Barracks, the post lacked sufficient housing and classrooms, and many of the students lived in surrounding communities. Some lived as far away as Gettysburg and York, each more than thirty miles from Carlisle. With the studies and curriculum changes under way, Almond continued the development of the housing and physical plant that Swing and Trudeau had begun. The summer of 1952 saw the beginning of student housing construction authorized under the Wherry Act, which had allotted money to build housing for military families in the years after World War II.[31]

Swing had received $5 million and "loose guidance" to move the college in the summer of 1951. He had spent $100,000 on rehabilitating Quarters 1, the commandant's quarters. This historical landmark from the Civil War era and the former home of the superintendent of the Carlisle Indian Industrial School (and the commandants of other schools at Carlisle Barracks) badly needed repairs "to bring it to a modern state of livability." When Almond arrived, the house's renovations did not satisfy him, and he ordered more work. The Truman administration had imposed austerity measures on the Department of Defense, however, and the press attacked the project, believing the Army sought to make the installation "plush." Military expenditures received close scrutiny in the election year of 1952. The Department of the Army inspector general investigated and determined that while neither Swing nor Almond had stolen the money, they had used poor judgment. This once again put Almond at odds with Gen. Joe Collins, who demanded that Almond explain the irregularities:[32]

> These alterations, costing $12,556.96 of appropriated funds, were appurtenances that seem unnecessary to the suitability of the public quarters to the purpose for which intended. Although there was no urgency in point of time to make the alterations, it appears that in violation of Army Regulation 420-10 you did not submit an individual project estimate until after the project was complete. Even then your word description of the project omitted mention of items which, under current operating conditions within the Army were neither necessary nor consonant with the stated policy of the Secretary of the Army with respect to economy.[33]

Collins ordered Almond to provide any further explanation or data, in writing, without delay. Almond, thoroughly chastened, responded with a detailed letter three days later:

> It was apparent that the quarters of the Commandant of the Army War College should be of substantial dignity and facili-

> ties should provide a suitable place in which, through the years, the many official guests could be appropriately received, entertained, and housed. All improvements ordered by me were ordered in good faith and in consonance with this belief. None were ordered solely for my personal needs and all remain as a valuable permanent improvement of this dignified house.[34]

While the house certainly required repair, Almond's tastes for comfortable living finally caught up with him. Almond acknowledged that his upgrades conflicted with the president's restrictions on expenses, but they had been approved before he arrived, and he believed the requirements justified the costs. McCaffrey believed Swing was as much at fault as Almond, both of them having badly underestimated the costs required to bring the historic home up to modern standards. Almond also explained that he believed that Headquarters, Second Army, had approved the improvements that Swing started and Almond finished. McCaffrey later remembered: "Joe Swing was not one to pay much attention to regulations under any circumstances and he treated the various restraints established as cavalierly as was his wont and, in honesty, to get the job done on time. Neither [Swing nor Almond] was sensitive to the changes in public opinion that had occurred with respect to the amenities that are appropriate. Simple improvements had resulted in tremendous costs."[35]

McCaffrey indicated that the antipathy between Almond and Collins might have hastened Almond's retirement. McCaffrey reasoned, "I am sure Joe Collins resented the position in which these lapses in good judgment by these two successful combat generals had placed him." It fell to McCaffrey to be present at another of the worst days in Almond's life. He had the unfortunate duty of delivering letters of reprimand to both Almond and Swing from the secretary of the Army, and a mandatory retirement letter to Almond. McCaffrey's description of that moment is eerily similar to the day Almond learned that his son had been killed. "One of my most enduring memories of General Almond was the way he handled himself when he received that retirement letter," McCaffrey recalled years later in a letter to historian Roy Appleman. "After the initial shock dissipated to some degree, General Almond regained his composure. He told me that when he was a young officer some older friend had advised him that whenever a new assignment was forthcoming it was best to undertake it with the mental attitude that the next assignment was going to be the best he had ever had. Ned told me that retirement was just another Army assignment."

Almond had known that he would have to retire at age sixty anyway, under then-current general officer age restrictions, but receiving this letter certainly injured his pride. It also ended any hope he may have had for promotion, and this disappointed him. McCaffrey believed that Almond and Margaret "felt that it was the political hierarchy that found him too difficult to control because of his dogged defense of General MacArthur." This sense of persecution may have had some basis in fact, due to MacArthur's long-running conflicts with other senior Army leaders and the Joint Chiefs of Staff, and Almond was inextricably linked to him. McCaffrey later said that he "regretted that General Almond could not view his career with more satisfaction and enjoy the peace and serenity his bravery and his ability and dedication so richly earned." As time went on, Margaret singled out General Collins as the cause of Almond's ouster.[36]

Almond maintained a deep loyalty to those with whom he had served during his remaining months in the Army, working to see that they received assignments that would ensure their future success. Almond especially cared about those whose work he respected, and he corresponded with them for decades after retirement. He took great pride in his former subordinates' accomplishments and followed their careers. Many, such as his most trusted friend, McCaffrey, became senior generals themselves. McCaffrey also later served as commandant of the Army War College before retiring with three stars. Almond's other favorite, Ed Rowny, likewise earned three stars, as did the former 473rd Infantry Regiment commander and War College faculty member William Yarborough. John Chiles retired with two stars, but his contemporary Frank Mildren reached four. Others who counted Almond as a mentor and reached the summit of their profession included Almond's senior aide in Korea, Alexander Haig, and William C. Westmoreland. Westmoreland later wrote to Almond just before the latter's retirement: "May I again state that it was a valuable experience serving on the Army War College faculty for two years. I feel very fortunate in having been on the scene during the building of this great institution." Despite Almond's pride in those with whom he served, seeing his old friend Clark "Nick" Ruffner receive a fourth star when he himself retired with three bothered him, and relations between the two cooled.[37]

Almond remained loyal to those friends who achieved great success, but he also corresponded regularly with those who did not become generals. He remained in contact with Joe Wood, Ray Sherman, and, perhaps surprisingly, Chap. (Lt. Col.) Louis J. Beasley, the former chaplain of the 92nd Infantry Division. Beasley wrote to Almond in September

1952, reporting his activities while assigned in Mannheim, Germany, and noting that he had kept up with Almond through the newspapers. Beasley planned to rotate to the States soon and hoped to be able to visit Almond in Carlisle. "I haven't been able to get an additional promotion since I served under you. Maybe I haven't been able to impress any one [*sic*] under whom I have served," Beasley lamented. "But be that as it may, I have always been most happy for the experience of serving under you and grateful for the encouragement and help you gave me." Almond responded cordially, explaining his pending retirement plans to return to Anniston, where Beasley would be welcome. "We shall be there from next February on and should you ever come in that direction," Almond said, "I assure you that we both will be delighted to see you." Almond clearly had warm feelings for the chaplain who had ministered to him in his greatest hour of need after his son's death.[38]

Almond did not limit his loyalty to combat officers. As his retirement approached, he worked to ensure that his trusted subordinates continued to receive career-building assignments. He wrote letters on behalf of several of his officers. Chap. (Col.) Frank A. Tobey had been Almond's chaplain in General Headquarters, FECOM, and Almond had taken him to X Corps. Tobey had moved to EUSAK in January 1951, but later reported to Carlisle as a student in the Army War College class of 1953. Almond wrote to the US Army chief of chaplains, Chap. (Maj. Gen.) Ivan L. Bennett, praising Tobey. Almond noted that Tobey had "demonstrated outstanding ability, leadership and moral courage." Almond concluded that Tobey's "inspirational religious services always are of a high caliber seldom found in or out of the Army." Almond then recommended that Tobey receive future assignments that would prepare him to be the chief of chaplains. Bennett agreed, and moved Tobey to Washington after he graduated from the AWC. One year later Tobey became the deputy chief, and he later served as chief from 1958 to 1962.[39]

Despite Almond's reputation for parochial squabbling, he did not hesitate to praise good officers from the other services. His choices indicated his skill at picking officers whom others would find talented. Almond wrote to Marine Corps commandant Gen. Clifton B. Cates to share his admiration for the leathernecks in Korea. "I regard most highly the esprit de corps and battle capabilities of the 1st Marine Division," Almond reported. "The officers and men were superb in their unfailing response to any command and wish that had to do with military operations." Almond's antipathy toward Marine Maj. Gen. O. P. Smith did not extend to all Marine officers. Almond praised the 1st Marine Division's second commander, Maj. Gen. Gerald C. Thomas, calling him a "superior tactician, a most cooperative leader, and a fine administrator and disciplinarian in all military associations that it was my privilege to have with him in both the battle area and the training area." The extent of Almond's influence on Cates is unknown, but Thomas later gained his third star and served as assistant commandant of the Marine Corps, retiring in 1955 as commandant of Marine Corps Schools.[40]

Almond also wrote to the commander of the Fifth Air Force, Lt. Gen. Glenn O. Barcus, to recommend another of his officers. Almond and Barcus held similar opinions about tactical air support, and Almond recommended that Barcus find a place as an air commander for Col. Einar A. Malmstrom, the senior US Air Force officer on the Army War College faculty. Malmstrom became deputy commander of the 407th Strategic Fighter Wing within a year of his departure from Carlisle.[41]

Some foreign officers had also gained Almond's respect. Before leaving X Corps, Almond had attempted to present a Silver Star to a French lieutenant attached to the corps, but US Army bureaucracy prevented the award from reaching the foreign soldier. This infuriated Almond, and he conducted a letter-writing campaign for more than a year, badgering EUSAK commander General Van Fleet and the US Army G1 to make the award. Finally, Van Fleet notified Almond in September 1952 that he had awarded the Silver Star to the French officer.[42]

Almond also worked to help the soldiers on his personal staff. He wrote to the commanding general, Caribbean Command, soliciting his assistance in getting three Puerto Rican soldiers assigned back home. Almond praised the soldiers who had helped to train non-English-speaking soldiers at Fort Indiantown Gap, Pennsylvania, near the AWC, claiming they would "render an excellent performance of duty in a training cadre assignment." He also wrote to the FECOM G1, Maj. Gen. Bryan Milburn, seeking an assignment for his Filipino cook and his wife, hoping to get them back to their native Philippines. Almond said that he would work with Army G1 to get the soldier assigned to FECOM and asked Milburn's help in getting him further assigned to the Philippines.[43]

Almond's final assignment proved rewarding, yet like some of his previous assignments, it ended in disappointment. His term at the Army War College set that institution on a firm footing, and his network of personal and professional contacts allowed him to establish a relationship with outside agencies that persisted after his retirement. The course of lectures and trips he developed for that first class continued the following year with few variations. General Clark had charged Almond to make the Army War College the "apex" of the US Army training system, and Almond did so by involving the senior leadership of the United Nations, Congress, Department of Defense, Joint Staff, other service staffs, and other government agencies in the curriculum. Involving these leaders personally with the course indicated the college's importance to the military educational program, and those leaders' willingness to return annually to speak to the class added to the Army War College's growing prominence. The Army War College curriculum retains much of Almond's original structure today.

16

Retirement and Epilogue

1953–1979

After appropriate ceremonies on the parade field at Carlisle Barracks and a reception in the Officers' Club, and one last address to the Army War College's current students, Almond retired to Anniston, Alabama, in 1953. His final assignment had proved especially rewarding. He left an indelible impression on the Army War College. Subsequent commandants have maintained and expanded many of his curriculum ideas, including a broader focus on international affairs and a joint perspective.

Retirement brought new activities, but Almond found himself unprepared for a changing world. One of his former battalion commanders in the 92nd Infantry Division, C. W. Daugette, owned an insurance company and offered Almond the position of Director of Military Programs, which changed several years later to Director of Public Relations. The job appears to have been little more than a sinecure, but a matter of prestige for the company, which could then boast a three-star general on its letterhead. It provided Almond with a title and stationery, but his correspondence indicates more work in his civic activities than in the insurance business. Almond believed in becoming active in the civilian community, and he joined several organizations and conservative causes, such as the American Security Council, which advocated for citizenship and the "American way of life," the American Conservative Union, Americans for Constitutional Actions, and the John Birch Society. Almond brought the same intensity to his civilian activities that he exhibited in the military.[1]

Almond wrote letters to the editor, editorials for local newspapers, and letters to elected officials from mayors to the president of the United States. He became president of the Gen. John H. Forney Historical Society at its first annual meeting on June 19, 1955. The society, named for the grandfather of Almond's friend Daugette, had organized earlier that year to promote patriotic, historical, and educational programs appealing to white southern sensibilities. Forney, an 1852 graduate of the United

States Military Academy, had served in the US Army on the western frontier from 1854 to 1859 and then in the tactical department at the USMA from 1860 to 1861. Forney resigned to join the Confederate Army when the Civil War began. The society placed historical markers all around Alabama, recognized distinguished civic leaders, and published historical papers on the Civil War. Almond brokered an agreement in 1962 with the USMA to establish the Gen. John H. Forney Award, presented annually to the best senior cadet in tactics.[2]

Clinging doggedly to the past and influenced by his Army experience, Almond fought school integration and became more intractably racist. His postretirement correspondence is replete with defenses of his command of the 92nd Division, disparaging statements about the fighting qualities of black soldiers, and his political activities. The civil rights movement also angered him, as he conflated that agitation with Communist infiltration of American society.[3]

Almond maintained a close association with the Virginia Military Institute for the remainder of his life and began to involve himself in VMI affairs as the class agent for the class of 1915. Almond and several other alumni became concerned about VMI after a cadet riot in November 1955 caused widespread damage to the campus. Though Almond did not serve on the committee, he did not hesitate to share his views with that body, and he gained renown in the alumni community for his opinions.[4]

The board retained as superintendent Maj. Gen. William H. Milton, but another controversial issue in early 1959 heralded both the end of Milton's career and the beginning of Almond's rise in influence. In February of that year, the *New York Times* published a petition supporting school integration signed by several college professors, including some VMI instructors. This infuriated Almond, and he sent a telegram to the Board of Visitors (BOV) president and vice president, the president of the Alumni Association, the superintendent, and the commandant: "As 1915 Class Agent I inquire why certain members of the VMI faculty of a privately supported institution should sign a petition as reported in the New York Times Feb. 8, 1959 demanding a free public school system even at the expense of integration? What action by VMI's authorities is being taken to remove such faculty members?"[5]

Almond then sent letters quoting the telegram to all other class agents and urged them to do the same. He found it "unthinkable" for VMI faculty to support such efforts and urged their dismissal. Almond then sent a petition to each of the class agents asking them to join in recommending removal of the superintendent, and presented the signed petition to the BOV. Almond's ploy enjoyed widespread support among the alumni. One of them, Jack V. Thompson, wrote immediately to Superintendent Milton. "We want no Ethiopian to enter the Washington Arch as a Cadet," Thompson said. "If you actually have any one on the Faculty who entertains such an idea of that sort of integration at the Institute, then do all you can to have him or them relieved, so that they may apply for a position on the staff at Howard University in Washington, DC." Many other alumni voiced the same opinion in their letters to Milton.[6]

While most of the class agents agreed with Almond, two argued vehemently against him. E. A. Whitehurst seemed especially offended. Almond's initial letter touched off a nasty correspondence between the two. Almond had evidently expressed "misgivings" about writing to Whitehurst at the University of Tennessee. This infuriated Whitehurst, who responded: "I presume that you feared that as a resident of East Tennessee, I might be a Republican, and that as a member of a university faculty I might be sufficiently intelligent not to be influenced by the mouthings of vociferous, rabble rousing bigots. To both of these indictments I cheerfully plead guilty." He compared Almond to Adolf Hitler, believing that both worked to silence those who disagreed with them. Ironically, however, he agreed with Almond's opinion: "I am opposed to any form of integration on social grounds. I am even more opposed to present efforts to force integration in the public schools on the grounds that I believe this is an area in which the Federal Government has no rightful authority. Regardless of my personal feelings, however, I am as nauseated by the rabid, irrational statements of 'professional Southerners' as by similar statements of the NAACP."[7]

Charles E. Kilbourne '94 also agreed with Almond on the integration issue. "Your views and mine on the matter seem to be the same," Kilbourne assured Almond. "I deplore the decision of the Supreme Court [*Brown v. Board of Education*, 1954] and its tragic consequences to the South as much as you or any man can." As a former VMI superintendent himself, however, Kilbourne deeply resented Almond's intrusion into the superintendent's affairs. He told Almond that college presidents "should not be subjected to arrogant demands from uninformed graduates." Moreover, Kilbourne argued that Almond had misrepresented to other alumni the facts of the original petition and assured him that the professors who had signed it had no intention of going against the constitution of Virginia or the "traditions of the Institute." He believed that Almond would not have gotten such widespread support from the alumni if he presented the facts correctly. The petition apparently did not explicitly address integration, but rather the state of Virginia's abandonment of compulsory school attendance to prevent integration.[8]

Despite these two negative reactions, Almond found broad alumni support. Superintendent Milton obviously felt threatened, as his personal correspondence indicated that Almond's letters to other alumni concerned him. When the embattled Milton finally resigned in September 1959, to become effective the following June, Almond led the alumni group charged with finding a new superintendent. He had clearly gained influence with the board, because it accepted his recommendation of Marine Brig. Gen. George R. E. Shell, then serving as the commanding general of the Parris Island Recruit Depot in South Carolina. Shell also enjoyed the full support of Almond's good friend and fellow VMI alumnus Gen. Lemuel C. Shepherd, commandant of the Marine Corps.[9]

As usual, Almond's headstrong, hard-charging nature had irritated some people, but it worked in his favor as he also impressed influential individuals. Virginia governor J. Lindsay Almond (no direct relation to the general) appointed Almond to an eight-year term on the VMI Board of Visitors in June 1960 as one of the first two out-of-state alumni to serve on the board. There is some indication that the "out of state" alumni position may have been specifically created in order to get Almond on the board. Almond doubtless knew the soft power he wielded. He wrote to Governor Almond shortly after attending the first meeting of the BOV, praising General Shell's performance as superintendent. Almond assured the governor that Shell "has restored the confidence of the Alumni and established a conviction in the Cadet Corps that The Institute will be run as it was always intended to be operated and in a manner which will produce the most effective results and retain the time honored customs and spirit of VMI."[10]

The letter signified the board's faith in the new superintendent, and helped solidify Almond's position of influence with the governor. Almond became an activist board member, not a silent partner. He cared deeply about VMI and took his position seriously. His correspondence indicated an untiring advocacy of various issues. For instance, Almond conceived the idea of creating a Hall of Valor at VMI in 1965 to honor graduates and to help cadets connect with their heritage. Almond donated some of his own medals and wrote letters to numerous fellow graduates asking that they do the same. He enjoyed hearty support from the BOV, the new superintendent, and the governor. Though new to the board, Almond used his status as a senior officer (and in fact the only general officer on that body) and his personal relationships with the governor and the superintendent to increase his influence.[11]

Almond's tenure on the board reached its peak at the board meeting on April 6, 1968. When Board president J. Randolph Tucker resigned to accept a judgeship, the board unanimously elected Almond to serve as president for the remainder of his term. This amounted only to an honorific position, as Almond's term expired at the end of June. Ironically, the VMI director of admissions reported to the BOV at that same meeting that the first successful African American applicants would arrive at VMI in the fall of 1968. The report indicated that the number of black applicants had grown from zero only a few years previously to four or five annually, all from out of state. None of these applicants had matriculated, either because of their failure to complete the application, or because they failed to qualify academically. The eleven candidates for the fall of 1968, however, included eight from Virginia, and with much better records than previous applicants. One of them had received a National Achievement Scholarship for Outstanding Negro Students, one of only fourteen awarded in the state. The director of admissions concluded that, while he could not determine exactly how many African American students would enroll in the fall, he expected at least two and possibly four. As it turned out, five black cadets entered VMI in August 1968. Four more entered the following year, and their numbers rose steadily after that.[12]

While the VMI Board of Visitors correspondence does not explicitly address the social issues and external pressures of the times, the board surely could not ignore the burgeoning civil rights movement. The state of Virginia had been unsuccessfully battling desegregation of public schools for years in the courts. The board meeting minutes, however, reflect no discussion of the admissions report. Moreover, the meeting took place only two days after the assassination of civil rights leader Dr. Martin Luther King, which triggered race riots across the country. Given the prevailing attitudes of the board members and VMI leadership, the lack of discussion probably reflects a grudging acknowledgment of enforced reality rather than willing acceptance. The board, however, had accepted as early as 1962 that black students would eventually enter the Institute. VMI drew significant financial support from the Ford Foundation, which demanded full integration for schools that received its support, rather than simple desegregation.[13]

Almond lived long enough to see the sons of many of his friends enter the services, and their letters to him are replete with reports of their sons' careers. His favorite grandson, Thomas Galloway Fergusson, graduated from West Point in 1965, and Almond remained devoted to him for the rest of his life, following Tommy's career wherever he went. William McCaffrey shared stories with Almond of his son Barry, one year ahead of Tommy at West Point. McCaffrey remained Almond's closest friend, and their correspondence continued until Almond's death.

Parochial views and an abrasive personality are part of Almond's legacy, but they may have also had positive effects. After retirement, Almond felt free to criticize Army leadership, and he astutely pointed out room for legitimate improvement. He remained staunchly opposed to Air Force tactical air support policy and wrote a stinging rebuke in an *Army Times* article, later picked up by the *Washington Post.* Almond charged that Gen. Joe Collins, the now-retired Army chief of staff, had "sold the Army short" in the Key West Agreement, which established the roles and missions of the services after the creation of the Department of Defense and separation of the Air Force from the Army. Almond also excoriated his old nemesis Gen. Earle E. Partridge, the Far East Air Force commander, charging "the Air Force knows nothing of the needs of the Army ground operations and cares less." He later argued that the Air Force improved its relationship with the Army primarily because of his consistent complaints, and this assertion may have some validity. Michael Lewis, a strategic planner at the US Air Force's School for Advanced Airpower Studies, analyzed the effect of Almond's work in 1997. Lewis determined that "Almond's emphasis on an improved CAS [Close Air Support] C2 [Command and Control] system, both during the Korean War and after, continued to increase attention on the subject, at least throughout the 1950s."[14]

Almond's experience as a student at VMI formed much of the basis for his subsequent life. He had excelled academically at VMI, and he never lost the thirst for knowledge he gained there. No cadet can attend VMI without being profoundly affected by that school's most famous professor—Thomas J. "Stonewall" Jackson. As a cadet and later as an officer, Almond took to heart Jackson's admonition: "You may be whatever you resolve to be." VMI nurtured Almond's can-do attitude, natural aggressiveness, ambition for advancement, demanding personality, and sometimes self-serving nature. These qualities later earned him the sobriquet "Sic 'em Ned," which stuck with him for the remainder of his career.

Almond learned important lessons about the value of training and leadership during his combat experiences in World War I. With the return of peace, Almond remained on active duty in a shrunken Army, and he performed well in a variety of assignments. He committed himself fully to any task, which helped him to excel. He gained a reputation for working hard and producing results, causing his superiors to mark him for further advancement. Almond considered himself a military scholar, and he welcomed opportunities for additional schooling. Attendance at advanced US Army schools, plus those of other services, left Almond especially qualified to handle joint operations. Almond believed this advanced education prepared him for future missions. Coupled with his experience as an instructor at the Infantry School, this educational bent developed him into the consummate troop trainer. These successes, however, bolstered the aggressive side of Almond's personality and filled him with unbounded faith in his own abilities and a lack of confidence in the skills of others. Almond's Type A personality would work both for and against him in the coming years.

When the United States entered World War II, Almond and other Army officers who had distinguished themselves in peacetime received quick promotions and key leadership positions. Gen. George C. Marshall, the US Army chief of staff, believed Almond possessed the "knack" required for training black soldiers and selected him to command one of the Army's two African American divisions. Contrary to expectations, he achieved moderate success in training his 92nd Infantry Division. His task was made all the more difficult by the educational limitations of his troops, the prevailing social environment, and growing pressure from the black community. Segregating units caused problems that the Army's white leadership failed to appreciate, but Almond made no move to address the social issues of segregation. He focused instead on getting his unit ready for combat. What began as a paternalist concern for soldier welfare hardened into overt racism during and after World War II. The War Department accepted local racist policies in the states where black soldiers trained under the guise of providing separate but equal facilities.

In addition to Stonewall Jackson's motto, Almond also endeavored to live by the military dictum "Units don't fail, leaders do." The 92nd Infantry Division's failure in combat and subsequent reorganization shook Almond's self-image as a competent commander. He convinced himself that he had provided proper leadership but his black soldiers had still fallen short. Privately, however, his role in the failure haunted him, and he never fully came to terms with this failure to live up to his own standards. Some historians have blamed white officers for the 92nd's combat problems, alleging that those officers wanted the black units to fail so as to discredit them.[15]

On the contrary, Almond had linked his own sense of honor and self-worth to the division's performance, and when it failed he felt disgraced. His reorganized division ultimately performed well when integrated at the regimental level, but Almond failed to grasp the full implications of his experiences with black troops. Neither he nor most of the Army's senior leadership saw benefits in integrating any further. Despite the 92nd's ultimate success after reorganization, Almond felt his honor had been stained. That conviction led to his issuing increasingly racist statements. Almond could only retain his self-esteem by dismissing the military capacity of an entire race, and the Jim Crow Army went along with this rationalization. These racial overtones have also prevented an objective assessment of the division's performance.

During the middle decades of the twentieth century, the American military's realization of its own complicity in the failure of African American soldiers came slowly, but it did come. When other officers began to change their attitudes, Almond clung to increasingly hidebound ideology that portrayed black men as innately incapable of becoming good soldiers. Almond continued to believe that black troops' shortcomings depended not on inferior educational opportunities or economic circumstances, but rather from something in their character that they could never overcome.

When the US Army demobilized after World War II, Almond remained in uniform. His transformation from an unwelcome addition to Gen. Douglas MacArthur's staff to one of the mercurial general's most trusted lieutenants testifies to both his personal charm and his military talents. Almond ingratiated himself with an initially skeptical MacArthur, impressing him with an indefatigable work ethic and sheer ability. MacArthur had used geographical distance and his own forbidding personality to insulate his command from the rest of the Army and the newly created Department of Defense. Although that separation maximized MacArthur's power and independence, it meant trouble when war came to Korea. MacArthur grew to trust Almond, and gave him a key command when the Korean War broke out. Almond must have regarded his assignment to X Corps as a chance to redeem his reputation. He still felt the shame of the 92nd Infantry Division's breakdown in Italy. Now he faced the challenge of commanding multiple divisions in major operations, and he certainly did not want to let down his doting patron, MacArthur.

Almond cultivated many loyal subordinates whom he found competent, yet he also alienated many others with his prickly personality. His abrasiveness has helped to color his historical image, as many of his contemporaries formed negative opinions of him even when he acted correctly. Those subordinates benefited from Almond's teaching experience and mentorship, but they also suffered from his wrath when they failed to meet his expectations. Some in Korea protested Almond's micromanagement, though the evidence shows that his reasons for doing so were often valid. The US Army had lost its edge since World War II, and this come-as-you-are war revealed all the Army's training and leadership deficiencies. Many of those who succeeded under Almond's leadership went on to flag rank and great renown themselves.

The controversy surrounding Almond's command in Korea largely overlooks his legitimate successes. He deserves criticism for his initial corps disposition in northeast Korea and inaccurate intelligence gathering. In the early months of this war, however, few other commanders possessed the requisite skills to adapt quickly to the fluid operational situation. Historians castigate Almond for his unflagging aggressiveness, but his contemporaries admired it. Lt. Gen. Matthew B. Ridgway, commander of EUSAK (Eighth US Army in Korea), later told historian Roy Appleman that he considered Almond "his best Corps Commander."[16].

Commanders must be judged, not just by their successes and failures, but how well or poorly they correct mistakes and recover from those failures. The success and relative ease of the Inchon landing and subsequent capture of Seoul gave Almond confidence but made him reckless. When MacArthur changed the operational plan to pursue the enemy into North Korea, Almond failed to adapt his tactical deployment to meet the conditions he faced. Almond's inexperience, lack of terrain appreciation, failure to anticipate the enemy, and an impossible mission almost spelled catastrophe for X Corps in northeast Korea. Despite the heavy losses, however, Almond was able to consolidate his forces and then safely evacuate them and their equipment, preserving their fighting strength. The disaster at the Chosin Reservoir certainly looms large in US Army and Marine Corps history, but Almond also deserves praise for preserving his corps and rescuing thousands of Korean refugees in the evacuation at Hungnam. Once X Corps joined the Eighth Army, Almond's tactical handling grew much better as he learned from previous mistakes and adapted to a new operational plan.

After leaving Korea in 1951, Almond's last assignment as commandant of the Army War College provided him with the opportunity to influence the Army in a profound way. He used the knowledge he had gained in the war colleges during the interwar years, his command experience, and his many years as a trainer to focus the AWC curriculum. Subsequent commandants have maintained and expanded many of his curricular ideas, which indicates that his thinking was generally correct. Almond also used his position and professional relationships to advance some of his theories about Air Force support for Army operations. Finally, Almond's legacy includes his efforts to foster interservice cooperation. His ideas about educating senior Army leaders on the roles of the other services and intergovernmental agencies have endured, despite his often acrimonious personal relationships with officers from other services.

Eighteen months after Almond retired from the Army, the US Supreme Court handed down the landmark *Brown v. Board of Education* decision that desegregated the schools across the country and overturned the "separate but equal" doctrine of *Plessy v. Ferguson.* The racial segregation of American society had been the law of the land for Almond's entire life, and the decision irritated him. Although Almond deserves condemnation for his bigoted views, especially for his comments and activities after retirement, many other white Americans shared his prejudiced beliefs. They belonged to a generation of Army officers raised in the Jim Crow era of the early twentieth century. Almond's Army embraced the racist taboos of the society that it defended. His sins were America's sins. He spent his youth in a racist, paternalist environment that shaped his values. The spotlight on the 92nd Infantry Division's problems in the existing historiography has tended to depict him as the lone racist in the World War II Army hierarchy, allowing his contemporaries to escape censure. He has come to symbolize a bygone era, and embodies an organization resistant to change.

While he had integrated his own officers' mess, he resented the federal mandate. Almond became more intractably racist over the years and fought school integration. The US Army did change, however, and Almond's entrenched beliefs made him a pariah in the eyes of most writers and historians. He is now viewed as a standard-bearer for hate. Almond became a convenient scapegoat for brother officers who privately shared his values but refrained from airing their prejudices so forthrightly in public.

Almond deserves to be viewed in the context of his time and environment. He was a man of prodigious abilities but intractable opinions and personal limitations. Almond earned the respect of his superiors with his diligence and aggressiveness. Indeed, one of Almond's contemporaries, Maurice H. Holden, possibly summed up Almond's personality best when he said, "When it paid to be aggressive, Almond was aggressive. When it paid to be cautious, Almond was aggressive."[17]

Almond died on June 11, 1979, from complications of a broken hip he had suffered some two weeks before.[18] His family buried him one week later in Arlington National Cemetery alongside his son and son-in-law, and his wife Margaret would join him in 1990. Lt. Gen. (Ret.) William McCaffrey wrote to historian Roy Appleman on the day of Almond's funeral: "He was a brave and energetic soldier. I knew him well and respected him greatly—I also liked him very much. He did have a full life and a good one but I know very well he had his share of disappointments and sorrows." It was a fitting epitaph for the man.[19]

Acknowledgments

I first want to thank my family for all their support: my wife Machele, daughters Catherine and Elizabeth, and son Joseph. They have endured Dad's near-permanent distraction from other events, vacations planned around research and writing, and Ned Almond accompanying us to basketball games, track and swim meets, and wrestling matches. I thank them for their patience, understanding, and support. Everyone contributed in some way, but I am especially proud that my daughter Elizabeth created all of the maps used in the book. My sister Kathy Browning and her family have also been very supportive.

I am extremely fortunate to work in the best military archive in the world. The depth and breadth of the collections at the US Army Heritage and Education Center (USAHEC), which includes the Military History Institute (MHI) and the Army War College Library in Carlisle, Pennsylvania, is a constant source of wonder to me, even after many years working there. The collections, however, would be useless without the talented and dedicated staff. I regret that my friend and mentor, Richard J. Sommers, passed away shortly before this book was published. Dick was a national treasure from whose expertise and knowledge I was privileged to benefit. Dave Keogh's prodigious memory and his understanding of the available primary sources made this work possible. Dave first introduced me to Almond through the rich collection of the general's papers at USAHEC. Marty Andresen, Louise Arnold-Friend, Rich Baker, LeAnn Fawver, Gary Johnson, and John Kurash helped me find sources or alerted me to related collections that enriched and expanded my work. I owe special thanks to Ross Webb, Pam Cheney, and Beth Shaffer, who expedited the security review that my command required. Conrad Crane has provided years of mentorship, and he granted me liberal leave to complete the project. Daily conversation with him strengthened my arguments.

My colleagues at the Army War College, John Bonin, Don Boose,

Henry Gole, Bill Johnsen, Doug Johnson, and Michael Matheny, supported me greatly by pointing out sources I had missed, sharpening my understanding of those I had found, and boosting my morale when necessary.

At the National Archives and Records Administration (NARA II), College Park, Maryland, Rich Boylan provided a graduate-level education in the relevant collections there.

In Lexington, Virginia, Mary Laura Kludy at the Virginia Military Institute Library and Archives introduced me to the VMI curricular archives and the Almond Alumni Collection, while Paul Barron and Jeffrey Kozak at the George C. Marshall Library and Archives not only assisted me in using the Marshall papers but alerted me to other valuable collections. Keith Gibson from the VMI Museum gave me a very rare copy of *The Bomb* from 1915, now donated to USAHEC.

At the Center of Military History at Ft. McNair in Washington, DC, I am very grateful to friends and colleagues Frank Shirer, who initially got me into the 92nd Infantry Division official records; Bryan Hockensmith, who tracked down CMH publications in digital form; and Bill Epley, who not only related his father's memories of Almond but pointed me to additional sources and served as a sounding board.

A good archivist often knows what a historian needs better than the historian himself, and Jim Zobel at the MacArthur Memorial Archives in Norfolk, Virginia, is one of the best. He met me at the door saying, "I know what you said you wanted to see, but here is what I think you need." It was one of the most productive of all my research days. The friendly staff at the Hoover Institution and Archives, Stanford University, assisted me in mining their valuable collections. The Tennessee State Library and Archives hold the Charles M. Fergusson family papers, and the staff there helped me access them efficiently and got me an expedited copy of the microfilm. Laura Shigemitsu, then the Hanashi Oral History Program manager at the Go For Broke National Education Center in Los Angeles, provided online access to those valuable collections, and Hanashi program volunteer Tim Yuge chased down critical information to properly cite the interviews. I spent many hours in Dickinson College's excellent library in Carlisle, Pennsylvania, where Ellen Kelly facilitated my research countless times.

Jim Ginther and his staff at the Archives Branch, History Division, Marine Corps Base Quantico, were extremely accommodating. I arrived on a day when the computer system was down, which can be disastrous when searching computerized archival catalog records. Steve

Coode, John Lyles, Alyson Mazzone, Sheila Phillips, and Nancy Whitfield worked hard to find what I needed and saved my research days.

The military history community is a warm and welcoming one, and I've been pleased and humbled by the acceptance I have received from noted historians who both lent encouragement and steered me to more sources. Rick Atkinson identified a valuable interview that I had overlooked, as did Kurt Piehler, and they along with Robert Citino, Brian Linn, and Michael Neiberg never failed to ask about my progress. Other historians doing research in related topics at USAHEC have generously shared their findings—Carolyn Johnston on her father, who commanded a company in the 92nd Infantry Division, and Krewasky Salter on African American officers.

Thomas Galloway Fergusson, Almond's grandson, has remained completely supportive of the project without attempting to guide it in any way. Tom, a historian himself, directed me to some family sources, and he arranged for me to speak briefly with his mother shortly before her death. Lt. Gen. (Ret.) Edward L. Rowny, then the only living member of Almond's staff, was very gracious in granting me an interview and quickly answering all of my questions. I regret that he passed away before this book was finished.

Finding the sources is one thing; understanding and interpreting them is another. A biography is more than history, and requires different skill sets. Mary Heck guided me through the language and science of psychology to better analyze Almond and his soldiers. Many historians and other friends have generously shared illuminating thoughts and comments. Bob Mages, Shane Reilly, Jessica Sheets, Jim Scudieri, Dave Wyche, and I discussed the project over gallons of coffee, while Dave Ulbrich lent a ready ear whenever I needed it. Many people have looked over early drafts of the manuscript, and their advice has been invaluable. Gregory J. W. Urwin gets special thanks for the sharp pen that made me a better writer. I'm also grateful to Roger Cirillo for his steady encouragement, and to the two anonymous reviewers for their insightful comments that made the manuscript much stronger.

At University Press of Kentucky, senior acquisitions editor Melissa Hammer introduced me to the publishing process and guided me through it to acceptance. Project editor Sarah Olson and editorial assistant Natalie O'Neal gently but firmly pushed me through the system. I formed an early alliance with copyeditor Ann Marlowe, and she provided expert guidance that made the manuscript much better and more readable. I am also grateful to Jackie Wilson and Mack McCormick and the marketing staff for their advice on how best to get this book into the reader's hands.

Finally, there is a core group of friends who helped all along the way. Some merely asked how the book was going and then politely endured the answer, some challenged me with specific questions, but all gave me moral support and steady encouragement when I needed it: Molly Baehr, Molly Bompane, Tom Buffenbarger, Steve Bye, Pete Crean, Rob Dalessandro, Matt Dawson, Michael Dolski, Anne Evans, Jessie Faller-Parrett, Shari Finkenbinder, Terry Foster, Rodney Foytik, Mary Gasper, Jack Giblin, Rick Harney, Stefanie Horvath, Geoff Mangelsdorf, Zach Matusheski, Sarah Pendleton, Judy Serach, Jenny Silkett, James Smith, Lindsay Strehl, Tim Sullivan, Bill Thompson, Mark Viney, and Karl Warner. Special thanks go to Jason Stamm, my computer doctor, who rescued my data when I had a catastrophic malfunction at a critical point during final editing.

No author ever writes a book alone, as these acknowledgments attest, and I am grateful for all the assistance I have received. All errors, however, are mine alone.

Appendix 1

Life and Career of Lt. Gen. Edward M. Almond

Table A1. Life and Career of Lt. Gen. Edward M. Almond

DATES	EVENT
December 12, 1892	Edward M. Almond born, Luray, Virginia
August 4, 1897	Margaret Crook born, Anniston, Alabama
September 1912 June 1915	Cadet, Virginia Military Institute
September 1915 November 1916	Teacher, French and Physics, Marion Military Institute, Marion, Alabama
November 30, 1916	Commissioned Second Lieutenant, Infantry
December 1916 April 1917	Student, Army Service School, Fort Leavenworth, Kansas
April 1917 June 1917	Company F, 4th Infantry Regiment, Fort Brown, Texas
June 1917 November 1917	Commander, Company M, 3rd Battalion, 58th Infantry Regiment, Gettysburg, Pennsylvania
August 4, 1917	Married Margaret Crook, Anniston, Alabama
November 1917 May 1918	Commander, Company A, 12th Machine Gun Battalion, 4th Infantry Division, Camp Greene, North Carolina
May 1918 August 1918	Commander, Company A, 12th Machine Gun Battalion, 4th Infantry Division, AEF, France
August 4, 1918	Wounded near Vesle River, France
August 1918 September 1918	Hospital/Convalescent Leave, Nevers, France
September 1918 November 1918	Commander, 12th Machine Gun Battalion, 4th Infantry Division, AEF, France
November 1918 July 1919	Commander, 12th Machine Gun Battalion, 4th Infantry Division, Army of Occupation, Remagen, Germany

September 1919 October 1923	Professor of Military Science and Tactics, Marion Military Institute, Marion, Alabama
September 1, 1920	Margaret M. Almond born, Marion, Alabama
December 7, 1921	Edward M. Almond Jr. born, Marion, Alabama
October 1923 June 1924	Student, Infantry School, Fort Benning, Georgia
June 1924 August 1928	Instructor, Tactics Department, Infantry School, Fort Benning, Georgia
August 1928 June 1930	Student, Command and General Staff School, Fort Leavenworth, Kansas
October 1930 June 1933	Commander, 3rd Battalion, 45th Infantry Regiment (Philippine Scouts), Fort McKinley, Philippine Islands
September 1933 June 1934	Student, US Army War College, Washington Barracks, District of Columbia
June 1934 August 1938	Desk Officer, Latin America, Military Intelligence Division, War Department General Staff, Washington, DC
August 1938 June 1939	Student, Air Corps Tactical School, Maxwell Field, Alabama
June 1939 June 1940	Student, Naval War College, Newport, Rhode Island
June 1940 January 1941	Desk Officer, Latin America, Military Intelligence Division, War Department General Staff, Washington, DC (temporary duty)
January 1941 January 1942	Assistant Chief of Staff, Operations and Training (G3), VI Army Corps, Providence, Rhode Island
January 1942 March 1942	Chief of Staff, VI Army Corps, Providence, Rhode Island
March 1942 August 1942	Assistant Division Commander, 93rd Infantry Division, Fort Huachuca, Arizona
August 1942 August 1945	Commanding General, 92nd Infantry Division, Fort McClellan, Alabama/Fort Huachuca, Arizona/Italy
July 24, 1944	Captain Thomas T. Galloway killed in action, France
March 19, 1945	Captain Edward M. Almond Jr. killed in action, France

September 1945 June 1946	Commanding General, 2nd Infantry Division, Camp Swift, Texas/Fort Lewis, Washington
June 1946 November 1946	Assistant Chief of Staff for Personnel (G1), Army Forces in the Pacific (AFPAC), Tokyo, Japan
November 1946 February 1949	Deputy Chief of Staff, Far East Command (FECOM), Tokyo, Japan
February 1949 April 1951	Chief of Staff, Far East Command (FECOM), Tokyo, Japan*
July 1950 April 1951	Chief of Staff, United Nations Command (UNC), Tokyo, Japan
August 1950 July 1951	Commanding General, X Corps, Japan/Korea
July 1951 December 1952	Commandant, US Army War College, Carlisle Barracks, Pennsylvania
January 1, 1953	Retired
June 1960 June 1968	Member, VMI Board of Visitors
June 11, 1979	Died, San Antonio, Texas

* Technically dual-hatted as chief of staff while commanding X Corps, in practice Almond never functioned as chief of staff after X Corps deployed to Korea.

Table A2. US Awards and Decorations

AWARD
Distinguished Service Cross w/ Oak Leaf Cluster
Distinguished Service Medal
Silver Star w/ Oak Leaf Cluster*
Legion of Merit
Distinguished Flying Cross w/ 2 Oak Leaf Clusters
Bronze Star w/ V device
Bronze Star w/ Oak Leaf Cluster
Purple Heart**
Air Medal w/ 15 Oak Leaf Clusters
Army Commendation Medal w/ 2 Oak Leaf Clusters

* Citation Star during World War I superseded by Silver Star, 1933
** Wound Chevron from World War I superseded by Purple Heart, 1932

Table A3. Foreign Awards and Decorations

AWARD	COUNTRY
Commander, Order of St. Maurice and Lazarus	Italy
Order of the Bath	Britain
Officer, Legion of Honor	France
Croix de Guerre w/ palm	France
Medalha de Guerra	Brazil
Estrella Abdon Calderon	Ecuador
Medal of Military Merit w/ Silver Star	Republic of Korea
Citizen of Genoa and Freedom of the City	Genoa, Italy

Table A4. Promotions

RANK	DATE OF APPOINTMENT
2nd Lieutenant	November 30, 1916
1st Lieutenant	November 30, 1916
Captain	July 25, 1917
Major	October 20, 1918 (temporary)
Captain	January 20, 1920*
Major	August 7, 1928 (permanent)
Lieutenant Colonel	September 1, 1938
Colonel	October 14, 1941 (temporary)
Brigadier General	March 13, 1942 (temporary)
Major General	September 10, 1942 (temporary)
Colonel	December 1, 1945 (permanent)
Major General	January 24, 1948 (permanent, retroactive to September 17, 1944)
Lieutenant General	February 13, 1951

* Reversion to permanent rank after World War I

Appendix 2

Task Organizations

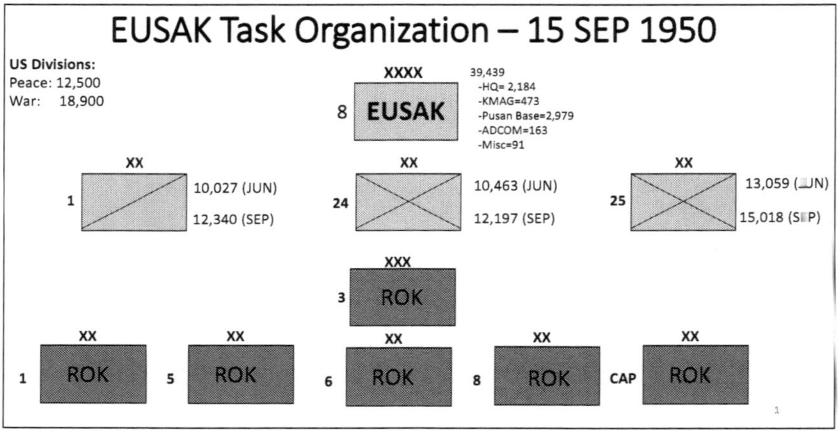

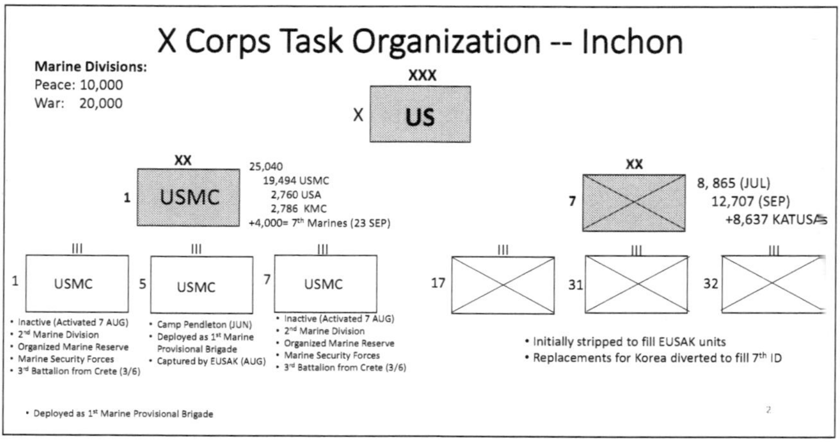

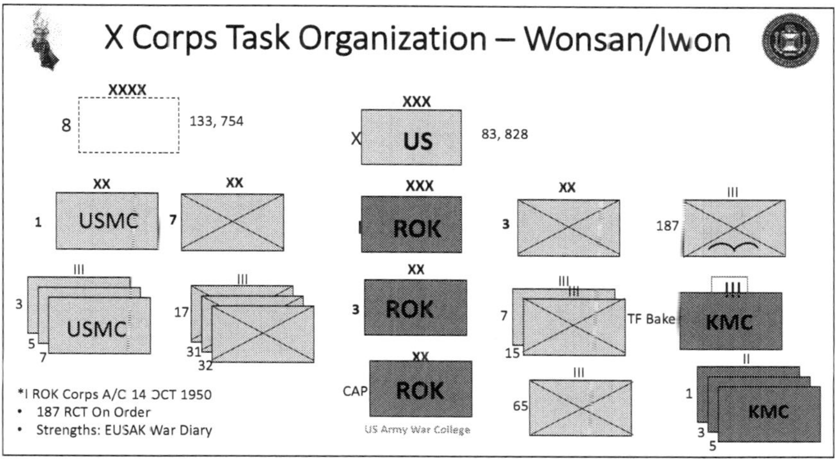
X Corps Task Organization – Wonsan/Iwon
XXXX
8
133, 754
XXX
X
US
83, 828
XX
1
USMC
XX
7
XXX
ROK
XX
3
III
187
III
3
5
7
USMC
III
17
31
32
XX
3
ROK
III
7
15
TF Baker
III
KMC
XX
CAP
ROK
III
65
II
1
3
5
KMC
*I ROK Corps A/C 14 OCT 1950
• 187 RCT On Order
• Strengths: EUSAK War Diary
US Army War College

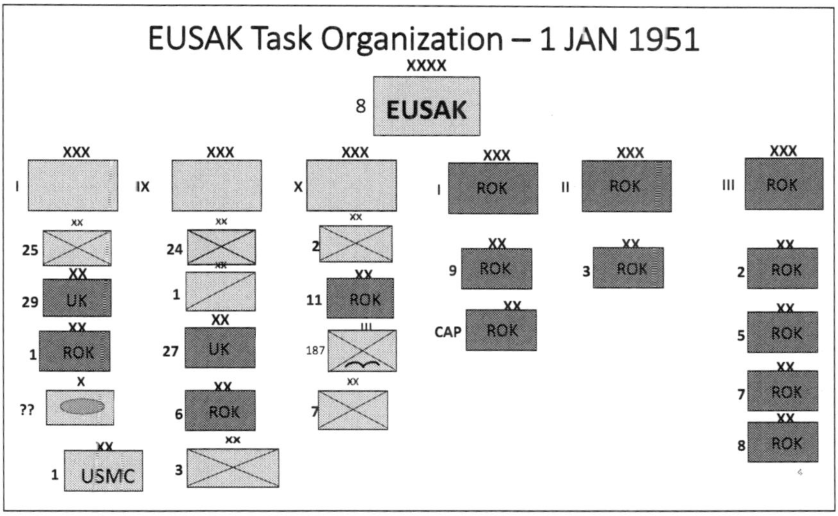
EUSAK Task Organization – 1 JAN 1951
XXXX
8
EUSAK
XXX
I
XX
25
XX
29
UK
XX
1
ROK
X
??
XX
1
USMC
XXX
IX
XX
24
1
XX
27
UK
XX
6
ROK
XX
3
XXX
X
XX
2
XX
11
ROK
III
187
XX
7
XXX
I
ROK
XX
9
ROK
XX
CAP
ROK
XXX
II
ROK
XX
3
ROK
XXX
III
ROK
XX
2
ROK
XX
5
ROK
XX
7
ROK
XX
8
ROK

Notes

Preface

1. See Ulbrich, *Preparing for Victory: Thomas Holcomb and the Making of the Modern Marine Corps;* Buell, *Master of Sea Power: A Biography of Fleet Admiral Ernest J. King;* Wyant, *Sandy Patch: A Biography.*

2. Fehrenbach, *This Kind of War: A Study in Unpreparedness,* 241.

1. Coming of Age

1. "Edward M. Almond," Virginia Military Institute (hereafter VMI) yearbook *The Bomb* 1915, page unnumbered.

2. Michael Miley, *Jackson Memorial Hall—Old,* photograph, 1910, Virginia Military Institute Archives (hereafter VMI Archives). See also Robertson, *Stonewall Jackson: The Man, the Soldier, the Legend,* 36; VMI yearbook *The Bomb* 1915, 47; Lt. Gen. Edward M. Almond, Senior Officer Oral History Program (hereafter SOOHP) interview by Capt. Thomas G. Fergusson, March 28–29, 1975 (hereafter Almond MHI interview), pt. I, 9.

3. Almond MHI interview, pt. I, 2–4, 10–11.

4. Winston, "The Relationship of the Whites to the Negroes," 321–22.

5. Brundage, *Lynching in the New South,* 140–41, 281, appendix A.

6. Brundage, *Lynching in the New South,* 151–53, 171.

7. Almond MHI interview, pt. I, 7; William R. Nalle to Mother, October 16, 1870, MS # 0042, MSS Collection, VMI Archives; "Gen. Wm. Nalle Dies Sunday Eve," *Culpeper Exponent,* August 4, 1911.

8. Almond MHI interview, pt. I, 19–21; Almond to General E. W. Nichols, March 12, 1912, Edward M. Almond Alumni Files, VMI Archives (hereafter Almond VMI Files); H. Wise, *Drawing Out the Man: The VMI Story,* 119–26; Couper, *One Hundred Years at VMI,* 4: 106–7, 210–12.

9. Almond MHI interview, pt. I, 12–19; T. W. Hendricks to Nichols, March 11, 1912, Almond VMI Files.

10. H. Wise, *Drawing Out the Man,* 390–91; Virginia Military Institute Reg-

ulations, 1911, 30, VMI Archives. See also J. Wise, *The Military History of the Virginia Military Institute from 1839 to 1865,* 10–11.

11. H. Wise, *Drawing Out the Man,* 391.

12. Almond MHI interview, pt. I, 24–25; H. Wise, *Drawing Out the Man,* 30–33, 71–74; Nye, "The United States Military Academy in an Era of Educational Reform, 1900–1925," 375, table 7.

13. Almond MHI interview, pt. I, 24; H. Wise, *Drawing Out the Man,* 70, 197.

14. Headquarters, VMI, General Order (hereafter GO) 63 [midterm exams], December 12, 1912, VMI Archives.

15. Headquarters, VMI, GO 143, June 23, 1915, Orders Book 1914–1915, VMI Archives; Almond MHI interview, pt. I, 28; "The Cadet Staff," *Cadet* (VMI), April 10, 1915, 4

16. Andrew, *Long Gray Lines: The Southern Military School Tradition, 1839–1915,* 47; Driver, *The 1st and 2nd Rockbridge Artillery,* 1–2; H. Wise, *Drawing Out the Man,* 21–22.

17. Headquarters, VMI, GO 4, September 8, 1914 [death of William T. Poague], VMI Archives.

18. Andrew, *Long Gray Lines,* 49; Headquarters, VMI, GO 4, September 8, 1914 [death of William T. Poague]; GO October 22, 1914 [death of Capt. E. E. Lee]; GO 146, May 29, 1913 [reburial of Richard Henry Lee], Orders Book 1912–1913, VMI Archives.

19. Almond MHI interview, pt. I, 20–21. See also "Stonewall Jackson Statue for VMI," *Cadet,* March 17, 1911; "New Market Statue Being Moved," *Cadet,* May 11, 1912; Poague, *Gunner with Stonewall: Reminiscences,* plate facing XIV. Headquarters, VMI, GO 89, March 25, 1915 [death of Mrs. T. J. Jackson], VMI Archives. See also Headquarters, VMI, GO 90, March 25, 1915 [resumption of schedule], VMI Archives.

20. Almond MHI interview, pt. I, 28; VMI yearbook *The Bomb* 1915, 47; VMI scrapbook 1915, Box 164, Edward M. Almond Papers, MHI (hereafter Almond Papers).

21. Almond MHI interview, pt. I, 29–31.

22. *Cadet,* September 16, 1914; Almond MHI interview, pt. I, 30–32; J. Wise, "Submarine, Blockade, and Neutral Rights," *Cadet,* May 15, 1915

23. Almond MHI interview, pt. I, 25–29, 34–35; Headquarters, VMI, GO 141, June 23, 1915, Orders Book 1914–1915, VMI Archives; *VMI Alumni Review* 70, no. 4 (Spring 1994): 16–21; Caplow, Hicks, and Wattenberg, *The First Measured Century,* 52–53. The Reserve Officer Training Corps (ROTC) concept originated after World War I.

24. Almond MHI interview, pt. I, 34–35; Marion Military Institute, "Marion Military Institute History."

25. Herring, "James Hay and the Preparedness Controversy," 383; Finnegan, "Military Preparedness in the Progressive Era, 1911–1917," 49–52.

26. J. G. Hiden to Almond, April 12, 1916, Box 9, Almond Papers.

27. United States Congress, *Biographical Directory,* 1221; Herring, "James Hay and the Preparedness Controversy," 385.

28. Herring, "James Hay and the Preparedness Controversy," 388–90.

29. Herring, "James Hay and the Preparedness Controversy," 385–88. See also Cooper, *Woodrow Wilson,* 310–12.

30. Herring, "James Hay and the Preparedness Controversy, 1915–1916," 388–402; Clifford, *Citizen Soldiers: The Plattsburg Training Camp Movement,* 117–29, 133–45; Finnegan, *Against the Specter of a Dragon: The Campaign for American Military Preparedness,* 155.

31. Adjutant General of the Army to Almond, "Subject: Result of Examination for Provisional Appointment as 2d Lieutenant," October 5, 1916; Secretary of War to Almond, November 30, 1916; Almond to Adjutant General, December 1, 1916, "Subject: Acceptance of Appointment as 2nd Lieut., US Army, all in Box 3, Almond Papers; Kreidberg and Henry, *History of Military Mobilization in the United States Army,* 221–22, 247.

32. Almond MHI interview, pt. I, 34–37.

33. Almond to Margaret Crook, n.d., Box 10, Almond Papers.

34. Almond MHI interview, pt. I, 34–37; Almond to Samuel Leander Crook, June 7, 1917; Crook to Almond, June 18, 1917, both Box 10, Almond Papers.

2. Introduction to Combat

1. Almond MHI interview, pt. I, 38; War Department, Special Orders 299, December 22, 1916, Box 3, Almond Papers.

2. Edward M. Almond to Margaret Crook, May 20, 1917, Box 11, Almond Papers.

3. Almond MHI interview, pt. I, 38–40; Headquarters, 4th Infantry Regiment, Special Order 56, Box 3, Almond Papers; Unrau, *Administrative History: Gettysburg National Military Park and National Cemetery,* 70–77, 116–18. The war in the Philippines in 1898 had created a similar emergency, and the War Department used the Chickamauga battlefield for large unit training.

4. Trask, *The AEF and Coalition Warmaking, 1917–1918,* 92; Weigley, *History of the United States Army,* 359–60, 386.

5. US Department of the Army, *United States Army in the World War, 1917–1919,* vol. 1, *Organization of the American Expeditionary Forces,* 342–44, tables 2, 4; Johnson and Hillman, *Soissons, 1918,* 19–23.

6. Unrau, *Administrative History,* 116–18; Morrow, *The Fifty-Eighth Infantry in the World War,* 9–11.

7. Almond MHI interview, pt. I, 41–44.

8. Almond MHI interview, pt. I, 35–36; Margaret Crook Almond to Mr. and Mrs. Samuel L. Crook, August 5, 1917; September 22, 1917, Box 11, Almond Papers.

9. Bach, *The Fourth Division, Its Services and Achievements in the World War* , 23–25.

10. Report of Operations, Camp Greene, NC, June 30, 1919, Installation History Collection, MHI; Bach, *Fourth Division,* 28–29.

11. Almond MHI interview, pt. I, 41; Bach, *Fourth Division,* 17–20, 281–86, appendix H; Morrow, *Fifty-Eighth Infantry,* 9, 14, 17–21.

12. Almond MHI interview, pt. I, 45–47; Bach, *Fourth Division,* appendix A, 283; Short, *Employment of Machine Guns,* 15–24.

13. Armstrong, *Bullets and Bureaucrats: The Machine Gun and the United States Army, 1861–1916,* 189–214; Almond MHI interview, pt. I, 69–70.

14. Margaret Crook Almond to Mr. and Mrs. Samuel L. Crook, April 27, 1918, Box 11, Almond Papers.

15. Margaret Crook Almond to Mr. and Mrs. Samuel L. Crook, April 30, 1918, Box 11, Almond Papers.

16. Morrow, *Fifty-Eighth Infantry,* 19; Bach, *Fourth Division,* 41.

17. Morrow, *Fifty-Eighth Infantry,* 20–21.

18. Morrow, *Fifty-Eighth Infantry,* 26–30; Bach, *Fourth Division,* 22–23, 56.

19. Almond MHI interview, pt. I, 48–49, 58–59; Almond World War I diary, Box 14, Almond Papers; Morrow, *Fifty-Eighth Infantry,* 23–24; Bach, *Fourth Division,* 48–49, 52–60.

20. Almond MHI interview, pt. I, 51–52.

21. Faulkner, *The School of Hard Knocks: Combat Leadership in the American Expeditionary Forces,* 76–77.

22. Smythe, *Pershing: General of the Armies,* 145; Trask, *AEF and Coalition Warmaking,* 77–79; United States, American Battle Monuments Commission, *American Armies and Battlefields in Europe,* 33–39.

23. United States, American Battle Monuments Commission, *4th Division, Summary of Operations in the World War,* 5–9; Bach, *Fourth Division,* 62–65; Almond MHI interview, pt. I, 47; Trask, *AEF and Coalition Warmaking,* 86.

24. Almond MHI interview, pt. I, 47.

25. Neiberg, *The Second Battle of the Marne,* 120–22.

26. Neiberg, *Second Battle of the Marne,* 120–22; Trask, *AEF and Coalition Warmaking,* 87–90; Morrow, *Fifty-Eighth Infantry,* 26–51; Bach, *Fourth Division,* 59, 66–90. French *groupements* were of unknown size but corresponded roughly to US regiments.

27. Almond MHI interview, pt. I, 60.

28. Almond MHI interview, pt. I, 62.

29. Bach, *Fourth Division,* 106–7; Morrow, *Fifty-Eighth Infantry,* 52–60.

30. Almond MHI interview, pt. I, 63–64.

31. Almond MHI interview, pt. I, 63–64, Almond WWI diary, Box 14 Almond Papers.

32. Headquarters, Fourth Infantry Division, GO 41, July 29, 1919, Box 9, Almond Papers.

33. Dethlefs, *History, 12th Machine Gun Battalion,* 28; Bach, *Fourth Division,* 128–39.

34. Smythe, *Pershing,* 172–78; Bach, *Fourth Division,* 128–39.

35. Smythe, *Pershing,* 179–89; Trask, *AEF and Coalition Warmaking,* 103–6.

36. Ferrell, *America's Deadliest Battle: Meuse-Argonne, 1918,* 40–42; Lengel, *To Conquer Hell: The Meuse-Argonne, 1918,* 61–62.

37. Lengel, *To Conquer Hell,* 61–62.

38. Almond MHI interview, pt. I, 65–68; E. E. Booth to President, Examination Board, March 31, 1919, Box 9, Almond Papers.

39. E. E. Booth to Almond, January 1, 1919, Box 9, Almond Papers; "Army and Navy: General Shift," *Time,* September 4, 1933.

40. Bach, *Fourth Division,* 164–66; Lengel, *To Conquer Hell,* 61–62; Dethlefs, *12th Machine Gun Battalion,* 28.

41. Bach, *Fourth Division,* 183–85, 201–4; Dethlefs, *12th Machine Gun Battalion,* 29–31.

42. Almond MHI interview, pt. I, 71.

43. Almond MHI interview, pt. I, 72; Bach, *Fourth Division,* 215–16, 226; Dethlefs, *12th Machine Gun Battalion,* 35–36.

44. Mark L. Hersey to Almond, July 22, 1919, Box 9, Almond Papers.

3. Soldier as Teacher

1. Almond World War I diary, Box 19, Almond Papers; Ruggles, *The Part the USS* Von Steuben *Played in the Great War,* 10; Kreidberg and Henry, *History of Military Mobilization,* 379, table 51.

2. E. E. Booth to President, Examination Board, March 31, 1919, Box 9, Almond Papers.

3. Application for Appointment in the Regular Army, February 8, 1919; Special Order 16–0, War Department, January 20, 1920, Box 3, Almond Papers; Almond MHI interview, pt. I, 6; E. E. Booth to Almond, March 16, 1919, Box 9, Almond Papers.

4. Almond MHI interview, pt. II, 14.

5. Almond MHI interview, pt. II, 7–9.

6. Almond MHI interview, pt. II, 25.

7. Almond MHI interview, pt. II, 25; Almond, "Let Machine Guns Support the Attack"; Almond, "Smoke: The Infantryman's Third Estate."

8. Marshall, "Profiting by War Experience"; the *Infantry Journal* articles included Switzer, "Concerning Machine Guns"; Best, "The Accompanying Gun"; Patch, "Machine-Gun Unit Organization"; Short, " Machine Guns of an Infantry Division"; Dravo, "Machine Guns"; Willoughby, "Machine Gun Known Distance Practice"; Doe, "Infantry Machine Guns—The Attack "

9. Almond, "Training for Citizenship," 126.

10. Almond, "Training for Citizenship," 127.

11. Almond, "Training for Citizenship," 128.

12. Almond, "Training for Citizenship," 128–29.

13. Bendersky, *The "Jewish Threat": Anti-Semitic Politics of the US Army,* 17. Bendersky's exhaustive study is the best such research on the racial attitudes of the officer corps of the 1920s and 1930s.

14. Bendersky, *The "Jewish Threat,"* 16.

15. Bendersky, *The "Jewish Threat,"* 25–26.

16. Almond to George C. Marshall, February 16, 1929, Box 23B, Almond Papers.

17. Ibid.; Almond MHI interview, pt. II, 9; Pogue, *George C. Marshall: Education of a General,* 256–57.

18. Almond MHI interview, pt. II, 29; memorandum for Assistant Commandant Infantry School, "Subject: Detail as Student to Command and General Staff School 1928–1929 Course," November 14, 1927, Box 3, Almond Papers; Muth, *Command Culture: Officer Education in the US Army and the German Armed Forces, 1901–1940,* 125.

19. War Department Special Orders 67, March 21, 1928; Adjutant General to Almond, August 10, 1928, "Subject: Promotion," both Box 3, Almond Papers; Almond MHI interview, pt. II, 29–34.

20. Almond MHI interview, pt. II, 38–39.

21. Linn, *Guardians of Empire: The U. S. Army and the Pacific, 1902–1940,* 124; Olson, *The Philippine Scouts,* 17.

22. Headquarters, Philippine Division, Special Orders 94, October 2, 1930, Box 3, Almond Papers; Olson, *The Philippine Scouts,* 17–20, 41–49; Linn, *Guardians of Empire,* 185, 291–92, n1; Urwin, *The United States Cavalry: An Illustrated History, 1776–1944,* 181–82.

23. Almond MHI interview, pt. II, 43; Linn, *Guardians of Empire,* 118, 200–201, 244.

24. Almond MHI interview, pt. II, 42–44.

25. "Methods of Crossing Unfordable Streams," December 20, 1932, Box 19, Almond Papers.

26. Almond, "Modern Methods in Stream Crossing"; Almond to Adjutant General, February 15, 1934; Almond to Office of the Chief of Infantry, February 18, 1934; memorandum, Almond to Adjutant General, November 2, 1933, "Subject: Methods of Stream Crossing by Combat Units"; memorandum, Adjutant General to Almond, December 4, 1933, "Subject: Methods of Stream Crossing by Combat Units," all in Box 23A, Almond Papers.

27. Paul B. Malone to Almond, April 25, 1933; Raymond C. Hamilton to Almond, August 26, 1936; Chief of Engineers Bulletin 4, June 1, 1933; Joe T. Green to Almond, June 7, 1940, all in Box 23A, Almond Papers.

28. Bendersky, *The "Jewish Threat,"* 28, 5.

29. Almond MHI interview, pt. II, 40–41.

30. Almond MHI interview, pt. II, 40–41; Olson, *The Philippine Scouts,* 5–7;

Linn, *Guardians of Empire,* 123; Almond to Mateo M. Capinpin, May 3, 1933, Box 18, Almond Papers.

31. Almond MHI interview, pt. II, 44–45; *Manila Daily Bulletin,* July 30, 1931, Box 18, Almond Papers.

32. Almond MHI interview, pt. II, 45–50.

33. Almond MHI interview, pt. II, 45–50; Almond to Mr. [Samuel] Crook and others, August 16, 1931, Box 23B, Almond Papers.

4. Education of a Senior Officer

1. AWC orientation lecture, quoted in Matheny, *Carrying War to the Enemy: American Operational Art to 1945,* 74; Almond MHI interview, pt. II, 51.

2. Army War College lectures, 1933–1934, G4 Course Box, File 404–8, 404A, US Army War College Curricular Archives (hereafter AWC Archives), MHI.

3. Gole, *The Road to Rainbow: Army Planning for Global War, 1934–1940,* 31–35, 156.

4. Report of Committee No. 7, Course at the Army War College, 1933–1934, File 401–7, AWC Archives.

5. Memorandum for Committee Chairman, Committee No. 2, "Subject: Negro Manpower in the Military Service," October 18, 1933, G1 Course Box, AWC Archives.

6. Ibid.; Humphreys, *Intensely Human: The Health of the Black Soldier in the American Civil War,* 142–45.

7. See note 5.

8. See note 5.

9. Kryder, *Divided Arsenal: Race and the American State during World War II,* 30.

10. See note 5.

11. Orientation, Lectures and Conference Committee Directives and Organization, G2 Course, 23–5, File 402–17, 1933–1934, G2 Course, AWC Archives; Matheny, *Carrying the War to the Enemy,* 66.

12. Matheny, *Carrying the War to the Enemy,* 66.

13. Kreidberg and Henry, *History of Military Mobilization,* 379, table 51; 433.

14. Conduct of War Course, Committee Orientation, Conduct of War Course Box, File 406–413; Preparation for War Course, Committee Orientation Directive, War Plans Course Directive, File 405–0, both in AWC Archives.

15. G4 Course Directive, File 404–1, AWC Course, G4 Course, AWC Archives.

16. Director, War Plans Division, to Assistant Commandant, US Army War College, April 3, 1934, "Subject: Suggested Subjects for Individual Studies," CSM Box, File 407–1 to 407–32, AWC Archives.

17. Individual Studies Course Directive, Subjects and Assignments of Students, AWC Archives.

18. J. Wilson, *Maneuver and Firepower: The Evolution of Divisions and Separate Brigades,* 117–21. See also Richardson, "Army Developments in Preparedness."

19. Memorandum for Assistant Commandant, May 5, 1934, CSM File 407–2, AWC Archives; Kreidberg and Henry, *History of Military Mobilization,* 441–49.

20. Gole, *Road to Rainbow,* appendix C, 164.

21. Almond MHI interview, pt. II, 53–54.

22. Almond MHI interview, pt. II, 56–57.

23. Gole, *Road to Rainbow,* 23; G2 Report, "Military Operations in the Chaco," Box 19, Almond Papers.

24. Almond to Chief of Infantry, October 14, 1937, Box 3, Almond Papers.

25. Almond MHI interview, pt. II, 66.

26. Almond MHI interview, pt. II, 66.

27. Almond MHI interview, pt. II, 66.

28. Almond MHI interview, pt. II, 68–72.

29. Kreidberg and Henry, *History of Military Mobilization,* 551–55.

30. Kreidberg and Henry, *History of Military Mobilization,* 575–80.

31. Almond to George V. Strong, June 23, 1940, Box 3, Almond Papers; John Magruder to Almond, June 25, 1940, Box 3, Almond Papers.

32. Gole, *Road to Rainbow,* 95.

33. Kreidberg and Henry, *History of Military Mobilization,* 555; National Guard Bureau, *Annual Report,* 1941.

34. Almond MHI interview, pt. II, 75.

5. Almond Takes Command

1. "Oral Reminisces of Lieutenant General Edward M. Almond, Interviewed by D. Clayton James, August 4, 1971, Anniston, Alabama," RG-49 (D. Clayton James Collection), MacArthur Memorial Library and Archives (hereafter Almond MMA RG-49 interview), 3; "Redskins Passes Top Eagles, 20–14," *New York Times,* December 8, 1941; Gabel, *The U. S. Army GHQ Maneuvers of 1941,* 137–41.

2. Palmer, Wiley, and Keast, *The Procurement and Training of Ground Combat Troops,* 434–35, 489–92.

3. Almond MHI interview, pt. I, 77–80; Almond MMA RG-49 interview, 2; Palmer, Wiley, and Keast, *Procurement and Training,* 439.

4. Palmer, Wiley, and Keast, *Procurement and Training,* 489–92; Stanton, *World War II Order of Battle,* endpapers.

5. U. Lee, *The Employment of Negro Troops,* 82–87.

6. Historical Section, 93rd Infantry Division, "Summary of Operations During World War II," Leonard R. Boyd Papers, Hoover Institution Archives, Stanford, CA; U. Lee, *Employment of Negro Troops,* 27–28. The 24th Infantry

Regiment, the other black Regular Army regiment, initially served as a school support unit at Fort Benning, and then deployed to the Pacific as an independent regiment. The 93rd Division during World War I had consisted of four regiments in two brigades: 369th and 370th Infantry Regiments (185th Brigade), and 371st and 372nd Infantry Regiments (186th Brigade).

7. U. Lee, *Employment of Negro Troops,* 127–28; Wilson, *Maneuver and Firepower,* 170; Matloff, "The 90-Division Gamble," 373–74; Palmer, Wiley, and Keast, *Procurement and Training,*434–5, 441, chart 1; Almond MHI interview, pt. II, 80–81.

8. Almond MHI interview, pt. II, 78.

9. War Department, Office of the Chief of Staff, memorandum to Commanding General, Services of Supply, "Subject: Professional Qualities of Officers Assigned to Negro Units," August 10, 1942, 92nd Infantry Division Special File, 1942–1944, Box 13695B, Record Group (hereafter RG) 407 (Records of the Adjutant General's Office, 1917–), NARA.

10. Ibid.

11. Ibid.

12. Almond MHI interview, pt. II, 79.

13. Almond MHI interview, pt. II, 79; "Charles Hall," Biography Files, MHI; "Memorandum for General McNair, October 22, 1942," quoted in Bland and Stevens, *Papers of George Catlett Marshall,* 3: 406–7 n3.

14. Bland and Stevens, *Papers of George Catlett Marshall,* vol. 3; Palmer, Wiley, and Keast, *Procurement and Training,* 441; Wade, *World War II Division Commanders,* 1–2.

15. Wade, *World War II Division Commanders,* 1–2; "Memorandum for Theater Commanders in Continental United States," January 16, 1942, in Bland and Stevens, *Papers of George Catlett Marshall,* 3: 67n1. See also Pogue, *George C. Marshall: Interviews and Reminiscences,* 476–78.

16. Wade, *World War II Division Commanders,* 3–4.

17. Wade, *World War II Division Commanders,* 4–6.

18. Wade, *World War II Division Commanders,* 4–6.

19. VMI, *Register of Former Cadets,* 158–60; US Military Academy, *Register of Graduates and Former Cadets,* 103–5; Wade, *World War II Division Commanders,* 3.

20. Memorandum, War Department to Each Officer Named, "Subject: Orders," July 3, 1942, Box 107 (General Correspondence, 1942–1948), RG 337 (Records of Headquarters, Army Ground Forces, 1916–1954), NARA; Wiley, "The Building and Training of Infantry Divisions,"434–35 (chart 1), 489–93.

21. US Army War College (hereafter AWC), Historical Section, *The Ninety-Second Division, 1917–1918: An Analytical Study,* 8.

22. Lt. Gen. William J. McCaffrey, SOOHP interview by Lt. Col. John E. Baggott, November 7–8 and December 9, 1996 (hereafter McCaffrey MHI interview), 10–20, 24.

23. Rowny, *Smokey Joe and the General: The Tale of Gen. John E. Wood and His Protégé Lt. Ed Rowny,* 68–70; US Army, *Historical and Pictorial Review, 41st Engineers,* 47.

24. Rowny, "Two Related Lives: Former Ambassador and LTG USA (Ret) Edward L. Rowny and BG John E. 'Smokey Joe' Wood," 39, 78–80.

25. McCaffrey MHI interview, 5, 26.

26. Rowny, *Smokey Joe and the General,* 32–33; McCaffrey MHI interview, 29; War Department Adjutant General's Office memorandum, "Subject: Orders," July 3, 1942, Box 13695A, RG 407, NARA; Stanton, *World War II Order of Battle,* 3; Rowny, "Two Related Lives," 22–24, 47–52.

27. Adjutant General to Named Officers, July 3, 1942, "Subject: Orders," Box 107, RG 337, NARA; "William H. Colbern," Biography Files, MHI; "Biography of Major General William Henry Colbern, US Army," Box 1, Robert J. Colbern Papers, MHI.

28. Goodman, *Fragment of Victory*2; Palmer, Wiley, and Keast, *Procurement and Training,* 434–36 and chart 1; HQ, 92nd Inf. Div. staff memorandum, "Subject: CG's Visit to Second Army Headquarters," September 19, 1942, Box 4148, RG 338 (Records of U. S. Army Operational, Tactical, and Support Organizations, World War II and Thereafter), NARA.

29. Brigadier General H. T. Mayberry, interview by Major Bell I. Wiley, Camp Shelby, Mississippi, July 6, 1945, Historical Section, Headquarters Army Ground Forces, Office of the Chief of Military History (hereafter OCMH), World War II Interviews, MHI.

30. AWC, *Ninety-Second Division, 1917–1918,* 1–2, 7–9, 11–13; Williams, *Torchbearers of Democracy: African American Soldiers in the World War I Era,* 81; Goodman, *Fragment of Victory,* 1–2, 190n1.

31. HQ, 92nd Inf. Div., staff memorandum, "Subject: Commander's Reconnaissance" (hereafter Command Reconnaissance), Fort McClellan Area, August 2, 1942, Box 4148, RG 338, NARA; AWC, *Ninety-Second Division, 1917–1918,* "Equipment and Clothing Shortages" annex; Command Reconnaissance, Fort McClellan Area, August 2, 1942.

32. Command Reconnaissance, Fort McClellan Area, August 2, 1942.

33. Stanton, *World War II Order of Battle,* appendix III, "Army Ground Forces Installations," 602; Command Reconnaissance, Camp Joseph T. Robinson, August 13, 1942.

34. "Handbook of Information, Replacement Training Centers, Camp Joseph T. Robinson, Arkansas," 26–27, 44, 46–47, Installation History Collection, USAMHI.

35. Command Reconnaissance, Camp Joseph T. Robinson, August 13, 1942.

36. Command Reconnaissance, Camp Atterbury, August 20, 1942. Place-names capitalized in the original.

37. Command Reconnaissance, Camp Breckinridge, Kentucky, August 22, 1942.

38. US Army, *Leadership and the Negro Soldier,* 55–56; *Plessy v. Ferguson* 163 US 537 (1896).

39. HQ, 92nd Inf. Div. staff memorandum, Subject: "Resume of Racial Laws of Alabama," October 30, 1942, Box 13695A, RG 407, NARA.

40. Goodman, *Fragment of Victory,* 3–4; Activation Address, Box 26, Almond Papers.

41. Almond MHI interview, pt. II, 80–81.

42. "Key Officers Rosters," Box 4148, RG 338, NARA; U. Lee, *Employment of Negro Troops,* 212–19.

43. Memorandum, CG, 92nd Inf. Div. to C. O. 370th Inf. Reg., "Subject: Assignment of Negro Officers," September 26, 1942; memorandum, Headquarters, 92nd Infantry Division, "Subject: Assignment of Negro Officers," October 8, 1942, both in Box 13695A, RG 407, NARA.

44. U. Lee, *Employment of Negro Troops,* 216–17; Jehu C. Hunter and Major Clark, "The Buffalo Division in World War II," Unit History Collection, MHI,13.

45. Memorandum, Headquarters, 92nd Infantry Division, "Subject: Efficiency of Officer Groups," November 14, 1942, Box 13695A, RG 407, NARA.

46. CO, 365th RCT to CG, 92nd Inf. Div., "Subject: Efficiency of Officer Groups.," November 20, 1942, Box 13695A, RG 407, NARA.

47. CO, 370th RCT to CG, 92nd Inf. Div., "Subject: Efficiency of Officer Groups," November 21, 1942; CO, 598th Field Artillery Battalion thru CO, 370th RCT to CG, 92nd Infantry Division, "Subject: Efficiency of Officer Groups," November 19, 1942, both in Box 13695A, RG 407, NARA.

48. CO, 371st RCT to CG, 92nd Inf. Div., "Subject: Efficiency of Officer Groups," November 25, 1942, Box 13695A, RG 407, NARA.

49. AWC, *Ninety-Second Division, 1917–1918,* 18.

50. Goodman, *Fragment of Victory,* 244, table 5, U. Lee, *Employment of Negro Troops,* 241–45; Palmer, Wiley, and Keast, *Procurement and Training,* 6.

51. "Training Notes," 5–6, Box 41, Almond Papers.

52. Jefferson, *Fighting for Hope; African-American Troops of the 93rd Infantry Division in World War II and Postwar America,* 52–54; "Training Notes," 15–18, Box 41, Almond Papers.

53. Palmer, Wiley, and Keast, *Procurement and Training,* 440–41; Goodman, *Fragment of Victory,* 4–12.

54. Goodman, *Fragment of Victory,* 4–5.

55. US Department of War, *Infantry Mobilization Training Program for Infantry Regiments at Unit Training Centers;* "G3 Data on Training Extensions Granted 92nd Division," Box 26B, Almond Papers.

56. Almond MHI interview, pt. II, 82; "G3 Data on Training Extensions Granted 92nd Division," Box 26B, Almond Papers.

57. "Thomas T. Galloway," Obituaries, *Assembly,* January 1949.

6. Trouble at Fort Huachuca

1. Historical Section, 93rd Infantry Division, "Short History of the 93rd Infantry Division," Leonard R. Boyd Papers, Hoover Institution Archives, Stanford, CA.

2. Almond MHI interview, pt. I, 81; "Training Notes," 4–5, Box 41, Almond Papers.

3. "Training Notes," 4–5, Box 41; "G3 Data on Training Extensions Granted 92nd Division," Box 26B; memorandum, "92nd Infantry Division Tactical School," Commanding General's Conference, May 13, 1943, Box 26B, all in Almond Papers.

4. McCaffrey MHI interview, 28.

5. McCaffrey MHI interview, 30.

6. Williams, *Torchbearers of Democracy: African American Soldiers in the World War I Era,* 346.

7. Williams, *Torchbearers of Democracy,* 348–49, Kryder, *Divided Arsenal,* 37, 248–52.

8. William Pickens, "FDR and His Negroes," *Kansas City Plaindealer,* April 14, 1933; Kryder, *Divided Arsenal,* 28; Eugene Davis, "Black Cabinet," *Kansas City Plaindealer,* April 4, 1934; "Negroes Profited with Roosevelt as President," *Kansas American,* October 16, 1936.

9. Fletcher, *America's First Black General: Benjamin O. Davis, Sr.*, 83–86; L. Baynard Whitney, "General Jim Crow," *Kansas City Plaindealer,* November 1, 1940; "Joe Louis Tells His People to Elect Willkie President," *Kansas City Plaindealer,* November 1, 1940; Kryder, *Divided Arsenal,* 31. "John L. Lewis, CIO Leader Calls On All of Our People to Vote for Wendell Willkie,"

10. *Cleveland Gazette,* November 2, 1940.

11. Ibid.; Fletcher, *America's First Black General,* 84–86.

12. Williams, *Torchbearers of Democracy,* 72–73; Kryder, *Divided Arsenal,* 34; Fletcher, *America's First Black General,* 94; MacGregor, *Integration of the Armed Forces, 1940–1965,* 19–20.

13. Fletcher, *America's First Black General,* 90.

14. Fletcher, *America's First Black General,* 93–94, 98, 106–7.

15. Fletcher, *America's First Black General,* 99–100.

16. Memorandum, Headquarters, Second Army to Commanding General, 92nd Infantry Division, "Subject: Cadres for 1943 Divisions," February 19, 1943, Box 13695A, RG 407, NARA.

17. U. Lee, *Employment of Negro Troops,* 333–35.

18. Urwin, *United States Cavalry,* 161; Kahn and McLemore, *Fighting Divisions: Histories of Each U. S. Army Combat Division in World War II,* 122; Johnston, *My Father's War: Fighting with the Buffalo Soldiers in World War II,* 45; Goodman, *Fragment of Victory,* 6. The 92nd Division in World War I con-

tained the 365th and 366th Infantry Regiments (183rd Brigade) and the 367th and 368th Infantry Regiments (184th Brigade).

19. Johnston, *My Father's War,* 45; Troy Johnson, World War II Veterans Survey Questionnaire, 92nd Infantry Division Collection, MHI;

20. "Training Notes," 5, Box 41, Almond Papers.

21. Humphreys, *Intensely Human,* 8–9, 11, table 1.1, 45, 77–79.

22. U. Lee, *Employment of Negro Troops,* 275–77.

23. Memorandum for the Inspector General, February 23, 1943, "Subject: Special Inspection of Colored Troops at Fort McClellan, Alabama," Box 17, Benjamin O. Davis Papers, MHI (hereafter Davis Papers).

24. U. Lee, *Employment of Negro Troops,* 170–71; "Judge William Hastie Resigns as Civilian Aide to Secretary of War," *Arkansas State Press,* January 22, 1943; "ANP Exposes Jim Crow at Fort Huachuca; Ala. General in Charge," *Kansas City Plaindealer,* September 10, 1943; Memorandum for Record, Headquarters, Army Ground Forces, June 21, 1943, Box 1228, RG 337, NARA; memorandum, Headquarters, Third Army, "Subject: Visit to 92nd Infantry Division," June 24, 1943, Box 1228, RG 337, NARA; memorandum, Acting Civilian Aide to the Secretary of War to Brig. Gen. Benjamin O. Davis, June 3, 1943, Box 3, Davis Papers.

25. Fletcher, *America's First Black General,* 101; "Report of Investigation at Fort Huachuca" (draft), n.d.; "Special Investigation of Colored Troops at Fort Huachuca," July 31, 1943, both Box 18, Davis Papers.

26. Memorandum, Headquarters, 92nd Infantry Division, Subject: "Study of Promotion of Colored Officers of 92nd Infantry Division," July 8, 1943, Box 18, Davis Papers.

27. U. Lee, *Employment of Negro Troops,* 218–20; MacGregor, *Integration of the Armed Forces,* 132–33.

28. "Visit to 92nd Infantry Division" (see note 24).

29. Jehu C. Hunter and Major Clark, "The Buffalo Division in World War II," Unit History Collection, MHI, 13. Major was Clark's first name rather than a rank.

30. Johnston, *My Father's War,* 23–34.

31. "Visit to 92nd Infantry Division" (see note 24); "Report of Investigation" (see note 25).

32. Benjamin O. Davis to Almond, September 13, 1943, Box 3, Davis Papers.

33. Commander, 371st Regimental Combat Team to Commanding General, 92nd Infantry Division, "Subject: Policy on Reclassification of Officers," November 15, 1942, Box 13695A, RG 407, NARA; "Visit to 92nd Infantry Division" (see note 24). For a discussion of the reclassification process, see Palmer, Wiley, and Keast, *Procurement and Training,* 124–30; Almond to Davis, September 8, 1943, Box 3, Davis Papers.

34. Fletcher, *America's First Black General,* 110.

35. "Report of Investigation" (see note 25).

36. "Report of Investigation" (see note 25).

37. Fletcher, *America's First Black General,* 109; "Report of Investigation" (see note 25); Benjamin O. Davis to the Inspector General, August 7, 1943, "Subject: Survey relative conditions affecting racial attitudes at Fort Huachuca, Arizona," Box 18, Davis Papers.

38. "Report of Investigation (see note 25).

39. U. Lee, *Employment of Negro Troops,* 334.

40. Fletcher, *America's First Black General,* 110.

41. Davis to the Inspector General, August 3, 1943, "Subject: Special Inspection of Colored Troops at Fort Huachuca, Arizona," Box 18, Davis Papers; "Report of Investigation" and "Special Investigation" (see note 25).

42. War Department staff memorandum for the Chief of Staff, "Subject: Policy on assignment and promotion of Negro officer personnel," December 20, 1943, Box 2, RG 165 (Records of the War Department General and Special Staffs), NARA.

43. War Department Policy Letter, AG 210.31, "Subject: Policy on Promotion and Assignment of Negro Officer Personnel," January 7, 1944, Box 13695A, RG 407, NARA.

44. Brig. Gen. William H. Colbern, interview by Major Bell I. Wiley, July 2, 1945, Historical Section, Headquarters, Army Ground Forces, OCMH World War II Interviews, MHI.

45. Interoffice reference sheet, Office of the Chief of Staff, 92nd Infantry Division, January 14, 1944, Box 13695A, RG 407, NARA; "Paratroop Volunteers Named," *Los Angeles Tribune,* January 17, 1944.

46. Moenk, *A History of Large-Scale Maneuvers in the United States, 1935–1964,* 102–3.

47. Ibid.

48. Dr. E. V. Davidson, interview by G. Kurt Piehler and Jason Bowen Veteran's Oral History Project, Center for the Study of War and Society, University of Tennessee, Knoxville, April 4, 2000, 39–40.

49. Moenk, *History of Large-Scale Maneuvers,* 103; McCaffrey MHI interview, 34–35, 43–44, 50.

50. Wilson, *Maneuver and Firepower,* 170; U. Lee, *Employment of Negro Troops,* 122–26; Stanton, *World War II Order of Battle*, 73, 170–72.

51. U. Lee, *Employment of Negro Troops,* 481–83; Bland and Stevens, *Papers of George Catlett Marshall,* 4: 151.

52. Kryder, *Divided Arsenal,* 207.

53. U. Lee, *Employment of Negro Troops,* 482; Dalfiume, *Desegregation of the U. S. Armed Forces: Fighting on Two Fronts, 1939–1953,* 97; Kryder, *Divided Arsenal,* 161; Fletcher, *America's First Black General,* 124.

54. Goodman, *Fragment of Victory,* 9; Almond MHI interview, pt. II, 83–84.

55. Quoted in U. Lee, *The Employment of Negro Troops,* 495.

56. U. Lee, *Employment of Negro Troops,* 536; Hargrove, *Buffalo Soldiers in*

Italy: Black Americans in World War II, 7; Houston, *Black Warriors: The Buffalo Soldiers of World War II,* 10–12; Goodman, *Fragment of Victory,* 9.

7. Initial Success in Italy

1. Houston, *Black Warriors,* 23–28.

2. Houston, *Black Warriors,* 1–8, 13; Almond MHI interview, pt. III, 7.

3. Atkinson, *The Day of Battle: The War in Sicily and Italy, 1943–1944,* xvii, 199–207.

4. Fisher, *Cassino to the Alps,* 227–28, 255–56, 269–70.

5. Fisher, *Cassino to the Alps,* 231–32.

6. Howe, *The Battle History of the 1st Armored Division, "Old Ironsides,,"* 362–66; Houston, *Black Warriors,* 29; McCaffrey MHI interview, 31–32.

7. Starr, *Fifth Army History,* annex 1A, "Operations Instruction 31," August 7, 1944, 8: 191–93; McGrath, *The Brigade: A History,* 48–49.

8. Starr, *Fifth Army History,* 7: 12–16, plate facing 17, 8: 1; Fisher, *Cassino to the Alps,* 286–87, 305–7, map X.

9. Vaughan et al., "Mud, Mountains, and Armor: The First Armored Division from Rome to the Alps,," 83–87; Fisher, *Cassino to the Alps,* 538–42; U. Lee, *Employment of Negro Troops,* 539.

10. Houston, *Black Warriors,* 36–37; "IV Corps History," typescript, 2: 287, Box 16, Willis D. Crittenberger Papers, MHI; M. Clark, *Calculated Risk,* 392; U. Lee, *Employment of Negro Troops,* 539; "Reported Missing in Action: Captain Charles F. Gandy," *Cleveland Gazette,* November 14, 1944.

11. Howe, *Battle History of the 1st Armored Division,* 382–83; Goodman, *Fragment of Victory,* 33–35.

12. U. Lee, *Employment of Negro Troops,* 542–44.

13. McCaffrey MHI interview, 32–33; Arnold, *Buffalo Soldiers: The 92nd Infantry Division and Reinforcements in World War II,* 31–33.

14. Arnold, *Buffalo Soldiers,* 35.

15. US Army, *Pictorial History, Three Hundred Sixty-Sixth Infantry, 1941,* 8; Fisher, *Cassino to the Alps,* 557–58; Arnold, *Buffalo Soldiers,* 60–63.

16. Hargrove, *Buffalo Soldiers in Italy,* 47–48. Hargrove became a historian after the war, and his book remains one of the best-known histories of the 92nd Infantry Division's experience.

17. Brooke, *Bridging the Divide,* 26, quoted in Johnston, *My Father's War,* 82; Houston, *Black Warriors,* 140.

18. Arnold, *Buffalo Soldiers,* 63.

19. Almond MHI interview, pt. III, 12; Arnold, *Buffalo Soldiers,* 63–64; Hargrove, *Buffalo Soldiers in Italy,* 47.

20. U. Lee, *Employment of Negro Troops,* 558–59; Arnold, *Buffalo Soldiers,* 63–64; Hargrove, *Buffalo Soldiers in Italy,* 48–49.

21. Rowny, *Smokey Joe and the General,* 139.

22. US Army, *Pictorial History, Three Hundred Sixty-Sixth Infantry,* 4–7, 15–19, 23–26, 30–37, 41–49, 51–59, 63–69, 73–77, 81–84.

23. Fisher, *Cassino to the Alps,* 559–60.

24. The Army's official histories disagree on whether this attack had Hitler's approval as a supporting attack or the timing was coincidental. U. Lee, *Employment of Negro Troops,* 562; Fisher, *Cassino to the Alps,* 410.

25. U. Lee, *Employment of Negro Troops,* 565; "IV Corps History," 2: 456, Box 16, Crittenberger Papers, MHI.

26. U. Lee, *Employment of Negro Troops,* 563–64; Arnold, *Buffalo Soldiers,* 75; Starr, *Fifth Army History,* annex 1A, Operations Instruction 37, December 23, 1944, 8: 101; Center of Military History, "Fox, John R.," Medal of Honor citation.

27. Colbern interview (see chap. 6, note 44), 10; Rowny, "Two Related Lives," 92; Gibran, *The 92nd Infantry Division and the Italian Campaign in World War II,* 132–34; Arnold, *Buffalo Soldiers,* 79; Goodman, *Fragment of Victory,* 69; Hargrove, *Buffalo Soldiers in Italy,* 64–65; U. Lee, *Employment of Negro Troops,* 564–65; Fisher, *Cassino to the Alps,* 409; "IV Corps History," 7: 457, Box 16, Crittenberger Papers, MHI; Houston, *Black Warriors,* 140.

28. Gibran, *92nd Infantry Division and the Italian Campaign,* 136–37, 169–76.

29. U. Lee, *Employment of Negro Troops,* 567; Almond MHI interview, pt. III, 12.

30. Goodman, *Fragment of Victory,* 72; Arnold, *Buffalo Soldiers,* 77–83; Almond MHI interview, pt. III, 18.

31. Fisher, *Cassino to the Alps,* 416–17; Arnold, *Buffalo Soldiers,* 68–70, 88; Goodman, *Fragment of Victory,* 80.

32. "Facts Concerning the Death of Captain Thomas T. Galloway, AC"; obituary, "Thomas Taylor Galloway," typescript, both Box 49, Almond Papers.

33. Edward M. Almond Jr. to Edward M. Almond Sr., January 22, 1945, Box 49, Almond Papers.

8. Winter of Discontent: 1945

1. Goodman, *Fragment of Victory,* 92–93, map III.

2. Headquarters, 92nd Infantry Division, Plan "Fourth Term," January 15, 1945, Box 34, Almond Papers; Goodman, *Fragment of Victory,* 85–89, map IV.

3. Plan "Fourth Term."

4. Memorandum, Commanding General (CG), IV Corps, Maj. Gen. Edward M. Almond, February 3, 1945, Box 35, Almond Papers.

5. Message, CG, Fifth Army, Personal For: CG, II Corps and CG, IV Corps, 03/804 (February 3, 1945 1804), Box 35, Almond Papers.

6. Plan "Fourth Term" (see note 2).

7. Report of Operations, 92nd Infantry Division in Italy, February 8–11

1945, Box 35, Almond Papers, 1–2; Goodman, *Fragment of Victory,* 86; Arnold, *Buffalo Soldiers,* 89–92; Plan "Fourth Term."

8. Report of Operations (see note 7), 1–2; Rowny, *Smokey Joe and the General,* 12–13; Goodman, *Fragment of Victory,* 86, 91, 97–98.

9. Goodman, *Fragment of Victory,* 86–87.

10. "Report on TF 1," quoted in Goodman, *Fragment of Victory,* 99; Hargrove, *Buffalo Soldiers in Italy,* 101–2.

11. "Report on TF 1," quoted in Arnold, *Buffalo Soldiers,* 104–5; Hargrove, *Buffalo Soldiers in Italy,* 103–5; Report of Operations of 3rd Battalion [366th Infantry], February 8–11, 1945, Box 35, Almond Papers; US Army, *Pictorial History, Three Hundred Sixty-Sixth Infantry,* 22, 81.

12. Operations of Task Force #1, annex #1, Box 35, Almond Papers; Arnold, *Buffalo Soldiers,* 106.

13. Report of Operations (see note 7).

14. Report of Operations (see note 7).

15. Houston, *Black Warriors,* 154–55.

16. McCaffrey MHI interview, 30–31.

17. U. Lee, *Employment of Negro Troops,* 568–71; Report of Operations (see note 7).

18. Report of Operations (see note 7), General Summary, 7.

19. U. Lee, *Employment of Negro Troops,* 568–71; Report of Operations (see note 7), 4–5; Operations of Task Force #1, annex #1, Box 35, Almond Papers.

20. Operations of Task Force #1, annex #1, Box 35, Almond Papers; Rowny, *Smokey Joe and the General,* 150.

21. Operations This Battalion [1st Battalion, 370th Infantry], February 8–11, 1945, inclusive, Box 35, Almond Papers; Report of Operations (see note 7); Houston, *Black Warriors,* 154–55.

22. "Jack F. Runyon," World War II Veterans Survey Questionnaire, 92nd Infantry Division Collection, MHI.

23. Almond MHI interview, pt. III, 21–22; Report of Operations (see note 7), General Summary, 6.

24. Report of Operations (see note 7), General Summary, 9; Goodman, *Fragment of Victory,* 96.

25. Report of Operations (see note 7), General Summary, 6, 9–11, 14; Goodman, *Fragment of Victory,* 9.

26. Report of Operations (see note 7).

27. Report of Operations (see note 7).

28. Wilson, *Maneuver and Firepower,* chart 15, 162.

29. Report of Operations (see note 7).

30. CG, 92nd Infantry Division to CG Fifth Army, February 11, 1945, Box 35, Almond Papers.

31. Ibid.; Hargrove, *Buffalo Soldiers in Italy,* 132–34; McCaffrey MHI interview, 50–51.

32. Kierein and Gold, "Pygmalion in Work Organizations.

33. Memorandum, CG, 92nd Infantry Division to CG, Fifth Army, February 11, 1945, Box 40, Almond Papers.

34. Headquarters, 92nd Infantry Division, "Subject: Approving Action of Commanding General, 92nd Infantry Division of Proceedings of Board of Review Appointed by Letter Orders Dated 23 June 1945 to Consider the Combat Effectiveness of Negro Officers and Enlisted Men," July 2, 1945, Box 40, Almond Papers.

35. Ibid.

36. Ibid.

37. Ibid.

38. D. Wilson, "Recipe for Failure: Major General Edward M. Almond and Preparation of the U. S. 92d Infantry Division for Combat in World War II," 474 481–86; Truscott, *Command Missions: A Personal Story,* 473; Heefner, *Dogface Soldier: The Life of General Lucian K. Truscott,* 229.

39. Edward L. Rowny, interview by author, October 9, 2009, Washington, DC.

9. Tragedy and Redemption

1. McCaffrey MHI interview, 80–81.

2. Almond MHI interview, pt. III, 23–24.

3. Gibson, *Knocking Down Barriers: My Fight for Black America,* 169–70.

4. U. Lee, *Employment of Negro Troops,* 553; Hargrove, *Buffalo Soldiers in Italy,* 146.

5. U. Lee, *Employment of Negro Troops,* 577.

6. Memorandum, Headquarters, 92nd Infantry Division, "Subject: Study of Promotion of Colored Officers of 92nd Infantry Division," July 8, 1943, Box 18, Benjamin O. Davis Papers, MHI; Gibson, *Knocking Down Barriers,* 170.

7. Hunter and Clark, "Buffalo Division in World War II," MHI, 35.

8. U. Lee, *Employment of Negro Troops,* 577; Gibson, *Knocking Down Barriers,* 171.

9. U. Lee, *Employment of Negro Troops,* 578; Gibson, *Knocking Down Barriers,* 173; "NAACP Votes Against Leadership of Gibson," *Arkansas Negro Star,* June 1, 1945.

10. U. Lee, *Employment of Negro Troops,* 578–79, n109.

11. US Army, *Leadership and the Negro Soldier,* 23–24, 65–66. Though US government publications generally do not list authors, the Office of the Chief of Military History later acknowledged historian Ulysses Lee as the author-editor of this manual. See also U. Lee, *Employment of Negro Troops,* viii; "Missing in Port Chicago Explosion," *Chicago Defender,* July 29, 1944; "Port Chicago 'Mutiny' Trial of 50 Becoming 'Hot Potato' for Navy," *Chicago Defender,* October 21, 1944; "J. C. Insults Strain Port Chicago Tars" *Afro-American,* May 5, 1945;

"President Roosevelt and the Philadelphia Transit Strike," *Chicago Defender*, August 17, 1944; "Detroit Officials Have Lessons; Can Prevent Future Race Riots," *Afro-American*, July 10, 1943; "Axis Propagandists Gloat over Detroit Race Riots," *Chicago Defender*, December 25, 1943.

12. CG, 92nd Infantry Division to CG, Fifth Army, "Subject: Plan for Reinforcement of the 92nd ID," February 18, 1945, Box 40, Almond Papers; CG, 92nd Infantry Division to CG, Fifth Army, "Subject: Fifth Army Operations in the Coastal Sector," March 3, 1945, Box 15, Lucian K. Truscott Papers, George C. Marshall Research Library (hereafter GCMRL), Lexington, VA; Goodman, *Fragment of Victory*, 110–11.

13. Goodman, *Fragment of Victory*, 110, 193n2; Houston, *Black Warriors*, 163; U. Lee, *Employment of Negro Troops*, 580.

14. Yenne, *Rising Sons: The Japanese American GIs Who Fought for the United States in World War II*, 40–47, 99–100.

15. Memorandum from Commanding General, Second Army to General Officers, Second Army, received September 26, 1942, Box 13695A, RG 407, NARA.

16. Yenne, *Rising Sons*, 43, 64–65; J. McCaffrey, *Going for Broke: Japanese American Soldiers in the War against Nazi Germany*, 57.

17. Yenne, *Rising Sons*, 67–68, 98, 100–101, 150–85, 188; Goodman, *Fragment of Victory*, 118–19, 129; Fisher, *Cassino to the Alps*, 459–60.

18. Arnold, *Buffalo Soldiers*, 113–17; "William P. Yarborough," Biography Files, MHI.

19. "Plan for Reinforcement" (see note 12); CG, Fifth Army to CG, 15th Army Group, "Subject: Plan for Increasing the Combat Value of the 92nd Infantry Division," February 19, 1945, Box 40, Almond Papers. The 336th Infantry Regiment was disbanded on March 28, 1945 and the soldiers remaining formed the 224th and 226th General Service Engineer Regiments.

20. Fisher, *Cassino to the Alps*, 448–54.

21. U. Lee, *Employment of Negro Troops*, 580; Fisher, *Cassino to the Alps*, 455–56.

22. Goodman, *Fragment of Victory*, 115; Fisher, *Cassino to the Alps*, 460; Starr, *Fifth Army History*, 9: 38; U. Lee, *Employment of Negro Troops*, 580.

23. Ben Doi, interview with Russell Nakaishi, October 18, 1999, videotape no. 5; Masaru Ishida, interview with Robert Horsting, June 29, 2002, videotape no. 3, both in Hanashi Oral History Program, Go For Broke National Education Center, Torrance, California, www.goforbroke.org (hereafter Hanashi Collection).

24. Robert Ichikawa, interview with Russell Nakaishi, February 25, 2001, videotape no. 4; Al Takahashi, interview with Stephanie Uchiwa, November 8, 1998, videotape no. 6, both in Hanashi Collection.

25. Center of Military History, "Daniel Inouye," Medal of Honor citation; Daniel K. Inouye, interview with Christine Sato, August 14, 2000, videotape no. 2, Hanashi Collection.

26. Starr, *Fifth Army History,* 9, map 3, plate facing 43; U. Lee, *Employment of Negro Troops,* 580.

27. "Jack F. Runyon," World War II Veterans Survey Questionnaire, 92nd Infantry Division Collection, MHI; Center of Military History, "Baker, Vernon," Medal of Honor citation.

28. Memorandum, Capt. J. F. Runyon to Commanding General, 92nd Infantry Division, 1 July 1945, "Subject: Report on Company C, 37th Infantry," 5–6 April 1945, quoted in Goodman, *Fragment of Victory,* 121–24; U. Lee, *Employment of Negro Troops,* 583–84; Baker, *Lasting Valor,* 179.

29. Baker, *Lasting Valor,* 204, 265.

30. Gibran, *92nd Infantry Division and the Italian Campaign,* 149–50.

31. Arnold, *Buffalo Soldiers,* 131–32; Starr, *Fifth Army History,* 9: 40–41; Fisher, *Cassino to the Alps,* 459–60.

32. Starr, *Fifth Army History,* 9: 39–40; Almond MHI interview, pt. III, 29.

33. Plt. Sgt. Frank Kimura, no rank indicated, interview with Steve Wasserman, March 5, 2004, videotape no. 5, Hanashi Collection; Yenne, *Rising Sons,* 272–73; Goodman, *Fragment of Victory,* 150. The Distinguished Unit Citation is now called the Presidential Unit Citation.

34. McCaffrey MHI interview, 70–73.

35. Margaret Almond to Edward M. Almond, April 3, 1945, Box 49, Almond Papers, MHI.

36. George C. Marshall to Margaret Almond, April 16, 1945, Box 12, Marshall Papers, GCMRL.

37. McCaffrey MHI interview, 46.

38. Edward M. Almond to Margaret Almond, April 13, 1945, Box 49, Almond Papers, MHI.

39. Edward M. Almond to Willis D. Crittenberger, April 13, 1945, Box 33, Almond Papers, MHI.

40. Louis J. Beasley to Margaret Almond, April 15, 1945, Box 49, Almond Papers, MHI.

41. Ibid.

42. McCaffrey MHI interview, 83.

43. Starr, *Fifth Army History,* 9:42–43; Fisher, *Cassino to the Alps,* 462, 483; Goodman, *Fragment of Victory,* 140–41.

44. U. Lee, *Employment of Negro Troops,* 586.

45. U. Lee, *Employment of Negro Troops,* 586–87.

46. Starr, *Fifth Army History,* 9: 40–41; Fisher, *Cassino to the Alps,* 459–61; U. Lee, *Employment of Negro Troops,* 586–87; Goodman, *Fragment of Victory,* 143–44.

47. Goodman, *Fragment of Victory,* 150–55; Fisher, *Cassino to the Alps,* 499–503.

48. Goodman, *Fragment of Victory,* 168; Arnold, *Buffalo Soldiers,* 185–93.

49. Arnold, *Buffalo Soldiers,* 193–94; Houston, *Black Warriors,* 189–90.

50. Rowny, *Smokey Joe and the General,* 171.

51. McCaffrey MHI interview, 76–77.

52. McCaffrey MHI interview, 76–77; Headquarters, Fifth Army, "Subject: Special Rating of General Officers (with 1st indorsement)," May 18, 1945, Box 15, Lucian K. Truscott Papers, GCMRL.

53. Lucian K. Truscott to Almond, August 31, 1945, Box 11, Almond Papers.

54. "92nd Division Is Vindicated," *Afro-American,* September 8, 1945.

10. New Challenges in Japan

1. Almond to Lucian K. Truscott, September 24, 1945, Box 52, Almond Papers.

2. Almond MHI interview, pt. III, 41; Almond MMA RG-49 interview, 5–6.

3. Sparrow, *History of Personnel Demobilization in the United States Army,* 64–75, 243, 326–27.

4. Gen. Frank T. Mildren, SOOHP interview by Lt. Col. James T. Scott, July 31, 1981 (hereafter Mildren MHI interview), 1, 149. "Maj. Gen. Philip D. Ginder" and "Maj. Gen. John Henry Chiles," Biography Files, MHI.

5. F. H. Boos to Almond, February 2, 1946, Box 52, Almond Papers.

6. CG, Fourth US Army to CG, 2nd Infantry Division, September 21, 1945, Box 52, Almond Papers.

7. Memorandum, Office of the Chief of Staff to Deputy Chief of Staff, "Subject: Utilization of Manpower in the Army of the United States," October 4, 1945, Report of War Department Special Board on Negro Manpower, Box 9, Alvan C. Gillem Papers, MHI (hereafter Gillem Board Report). Patterson had been appointed Secretary of War a few days previously upon the resignation of Henry L. Stimson.

8. George Collins, "Blames Gen. Almond, Army Policy for Record of 92nd," Now It Can Be Told, *Pittsburgh Courier,* November 10, 1945.

9. Roi Ottley, "92nd Had No Faith In Its Leadership," *Pittsburgh Courier,* December 21, 1946.

10. Gillem Board Report, Tab C.

11. Gillem Board Report, appendix Tab D, "List of Witnesses."

12. Gibson, *Knocking Down Barriers,* 221–23; MacGregor, *Integration of the Armed Forces,* 163n27.

13. Almond MHI interview, pt. III, 44; "Notes on Movement of Division from Camp Swift, Texas, to Fort Lewis, Washington," February 5, 1946, Box 53, Almond Papers.

14. Almond MHI interview, pt. III, 44–45; Lawrence W. H. Peyton to Almond, December 20, 1945, Box 52, Almond Papers.

15. Alfred M. Gruenther to Almond, September 17, 1947, Box 54A, Almond Papers.

16. Almond MHI interview, pt. III, 47–49.

17. Almond MHI interview, pt. III, 53–54.

18. Blair, *The Forgotten War: America in Korea,* 917; Edward L. Rowny to Almond, April 9, 1949; Almond to Rowny, April 18, 1945, both Box 55, Almond Papers. Blair called it a "command nursery," but that is an unfair characterization of a common practice among senior officers. Almond to D. Ginder, January 20, 1947; Almond to John H. Chiles, December 17, 1947; Almond to Donald Christensen, February 24, 1947; all Box 54A, Almond Papers; "Maj. Gen. John Henry Chiles," Biography Files, MHI.

19. National Security Act of 1947, Pub. L. 80–253, 61 Stat. 495 (1947); Hewes, *From Root to McNamara,* 271.

20. Boose, *Over the Beach: US Army Amphibious Operations in the Korean War,* 70–72; Executive Order No. 9950, Revoking Executive Order No. 9877 of July 26, 1947, Prescribing the Functions of the Armed Forces 13 FR 2191.

21. A. Cole et al., *Department of Defense: Documents on Establishment and Organization, 1944–1978,* 35; Almond to J. Lawton Collins, August 21, 1947; Collins to Almond, September 10, 1947; Almond to Collins, October 1, 1947, all Box 54B, Almond Papers. The position of Deputy Chief of Staff was elevated to a four-star position and renamed Vice Chief of Staff of the Army during Collins's tenure, and he was promoted to general.

22. Almond to William J. McCaffrey, July 12, 1946, Box 55, Almond Papers.

23. Almond to John Chiles, March 15, 1947, Box 54A; Almond to Clarence R. Huebner, April 22, 1947, Box 54A; Almond to John H. Chiles, December 13, 1947, Box 54A; Almond to Raymond G. Sherman, July 25, 1947, Box 55, Almond Papers. Almond abandoned his strict military bearing and rectitude only where Tommy was concerned; photos from the 1948 Army Day celebration in Tokyo show Almond sitting properly with other dignitaries, with Tommy on his lap; see Almond to Peggy Galloway Fergusson, July 9, 1948; Almond to Mrs. Charles M. Fergusson Sr., July 9, 1948, both Box 54A, Almond Papers.

24. Almond to Geoffrey Keyes, February 24, 1947; Almond to Joseph B. Galloway, September 4, 1947; December 18, 1948; December 20, 1948; November 1, 1948; Almond to Charles M. Fergusson, December 16, 1948, all Box 54A, Almond Papers.

25. General Headquarters, Southwest Pacific Area [*sic*], General Order 1, February 19, 1949, "Subject: Announcement of Staff," Box 56, Almond Papers; R. Cole et al., *The History of the Unified Command Plan, 1946–1993,* 11–14. MacArthur's staff used the acronym FECOM, but the Joint Staff in Washington used FEC. Contemporary sources use both. I have used FECOM throughout for clarity. Schnabel, *Policy and Direction: The First Year,* 48–49, n20.

26. Millett, *The War for Korea, 1950–1951: They Came from the North,* 70 "Maj. Gen. Alonzo P. Fox," Biography Files, MHI.

27. Almond MHI interview, pt. III, 68–71.

28. Almond MHI interview, pt. III, 68.

29. Almond MHI interview, pt. IV, 8.

30. "Charles A. Willoughby," Biography Files, MHI.

31. Almond MMA RG-49 interview, 23–27.

32. Almond MMA RG-49 interview, 26.

33. Knight, "'MacArthur's Eyes': Reassessing Military Intelligence Operations in the Forgotten War, June 1950–April 1951,," 40.

34. "Introduction to the Collection," RG-23 (Papers of Maj. Gen. Charles A. Willoughby, USA, 1947–1973), MMA.

35. "Oral Reminiscences of Maj. Gen. Charles A. Willoughby with D. Clayton James, July 30, 1971," RG-49, MMA, 7.

36. Almond MMA RG-49 interview, 23–24.

37. Millett, *They Came from the North,* 70.

38. Haig, *Inner Circles: How America Changed the World; A Memoir,* 5–12.

39. Haig, *Inner Circles,* 19.

40. Sawyer, *Military Advisers in Korea: KMAG in Peace and War,* 7.

41. Almond MHI interview, pt. III, 59–60; pt. IV, 10–12; Manchester, *American Caesar: Douglas MacArthur,* 541–42; Y. Lee, "The United States and the Formation of the Republic of Korea Army, 1945–1950," 125–27, 135–36, 160; R. Cole et al., *Unified Command Plan,* 11.

42. Millett, *The War for Korea, 1945–1950: A House Burning,* 235–36; Y. Lee, "Formation of the Republic of Korea Army," 138–50.

43. Walton H. Walker to Almond, August 11, 1948, Box 56, Almond Papers.

44. "Gen. Walton H. Walker," Biography Files, MHI.

45. Almond to Walker, July 24, 1948, Box 55; Walker to Almond, August 11, 1948, Box 56, Almond Papers.

46. Maj. Gen. Edwin K. Wright, interview with D. Clayton James, August 28, 1971, RG-49, MMA (hereafter Wright MMA interview), 16.

47. Schnabel, *Policy and Direction,* 56–57; Almond MHI interview, pt. IV, 16.

48. Hanson, *Combat Ready? The Eighth US Army on the Eve of the Korean War,* 20–28.

49. Hanson, *Combat Ready?*, 20–28, 29–30.

50. Boose, *Over the Beach,* 118.

51. Boose, *Over the Beach,* 81–82.

52. Boose, *Over the Beach,* 82–83, 115; Millett, *They Came from the North,* 74.

11. Planning for War

1. Haig, *Inner Circles: How America Changed the World, A Memoir,* 19–20; Edward L. Rowny, e-mail message to author, October 6, 2009; Rowny, *Smokey Joe and the General,* 207; MacArthur, *Reminiscences,* 327.

2. Haig, *Inner Circles,* 42.

3. EUSAK, *Special Problems in the Korean Conflict,* 9. The numbers of soldiers available before and after the invasion fluctuates among sources, owing to difficulties in accounting for soldiers with units in disarray.

4. EUSAK, *Special Problems,* 18.

5. Appleman, *South to the Naktong, North to the Yalu,* 13; Schnabel, *Policy and Direction,* 50; Boose, *Over the Beach,* 118.

6. Appleman, *South to the Naktong,* 42–44; Schnabel, *Policy and Direction,* 71–72.

7. Enclosure 3, "How Inchon Korea was selected for X Corps Amphibious Landing there on Sept. 15, 1950," to Lt. Gen. Edward M. Almond, interview by Col. J. Addison Hagan, January 20, 1967, RG-32 (MacArthur Memorial Oral History Collection), MacArthur Memorial Library and Archives, Norfolk, VA (hereafter, Almond MMA RG-32 interview); Almond MHI interview, pt. IV, 12–14.

8. Almond MHI interview, pt. IV, 18–19; Appleman, *South to the Naktong,* 60–61.

9. Bradley and Blair, *A General's Life: An Autobiography,* 539, 543–44; Gen. Matthew B. Ridgway, SOOHP interviews by Col. John M. Blair, November 24, 1971–March 24, 1972, MHI (hereafter Ridgway MHI interview) , 273.

10. Appleman, *South to the Naktong,* 206–7.

11. Almond MHI interview, pt. IV, 21–22; Appleman, *South to the Naktong,* 206–7. Almond remembered the date as "about 1 August."

12. Appleman, *South to the Naktong,* 207–8; Boose, *Over the Beach,* 117, 127.

13. Boose, *Over the Beach,* 81–82.

14. Boose, *Over the Beach,* 120–24, 157; enclosure 3, Almond MMA RG-32 interview; Boose, *Over the Beach,* 155–57.

15. Boose, *Over the Beach,* 120, 124–26.

16. Boose, *Over the Beach,* 157–58.

17. Almond to J. Lawton Collins, July 17, 1950, Box 54B, Almond Papers.

18. Almond to William J. McCaffrey, July 24, 1950, Box 71A; William H. Colbern to Almond, July 19, 1950, Box 54B, Almond Papers.

19. Enclosure 3 to Almond MMA RG-32 interview; Boose, *Over the Beach,* 155–56.

20. Almond MHI interview, pt. IV, 26–29.

21. Commanding General, X Corps to Commandant, U. S. Marine Corps, 11 November 1950, Box 54A, Almond papers.

22. Almond MHI interview, pt. IV, 29; GHQ, FECOM, GO 24, 26 August 1950, Box 62, Almond Papers.

23. Enclosure 3, Almond MMA RG-32 interview; Almond MMA RG-49 interview, 14–17; Almond MHI interview, pt. IV, 29–31, 58–59, 68–69.

24. GO 24 (see note 22); Headquarters, X Corps, GO 1, August 26, 1950, Box 62; Almond to Margaret Almond, September 18, 1950, Box 77, all in Almond Papers.

25. J. L. Collins, *Lightning Joe: An Autobiography,* 366; Almond MMA RG-49 interview, 18.

26. Ridgway MHI interview, 2: 75.

27. Bradley, *A General's Life,* 524.

28. Boose, *Over the Beach,* 160; Almond MHI interview, pt. IV, 41–42.

29. Almond MHI interview, pt. IV, 41–42.

30. Almond MHI interview, pt. IV, 41–42.

31. Gen. Frank T. Mildren, interview with D. Clayton James, May 24, 1971, RG-49, MMA (hereafter Mildren MMA interview), 1; Almond MHI interview, pt. IV, 27–28; "Maj. Gen. John H. Chiles," "Brig. Gen. Olinto M. Barsanti," "Lt. Gen. William W. Quinn," "Gen. Frank T. Mildren," Biography Files, MHI.

32. Almond MHI interview, pt. IV, 27–28; William J. McCaffrey to Almond, August 23, 1950; message, GHQ FECOM Chief of Staff to L. A. Diller, Career Management Division, Army G1, August 29, 1950, Box 55, Almond Papers; "Lt. Gen. William J. McCaffrey," Biography Files, MHI; McCaffrey MHI interview, 126–30; Almond MHI interview, pt. IV, 43.

33. E. Warner Williamson, "A Diary in Retrospect: The Fear of Failure Can Be Enhanced to Make It a Most Valuable Motivating Asset," unpublished memoir, Ellis Warner Williamson Papers, USAHEC, chap. 12, (unnumbered) p. 3.

34. Almond MHI interview, pt. IV, 41–42.

35. Wright MMA interview, 18.

36. Mildren MMA interview, 9. "Lieut. Gen. Edward M. Almond," Biography Files, MHI. Ironically, the position that Almond once held is now dual-hatted again. In 1992 the Combined Forces Command was separated from United Nations Command, and the commanding general, Eighth US Army, was also made chief of staff, Combined Forces Command.

37. Shisler, *For Country and Corps: The Life of General Oliver P. Smith,* 127–33.

38. Cunningham, "Command and Control of the US Tenth Army during the Battle of Okinawa," 46, 67–68. Marine Lt. Gen. Holland M. "Howlin Mad" Smith, CG of V Amphibious Corps, relieved Army Maj. Gen. Ralph Smith from command of the 27th Infantry Division for poor performance on Makin Island and on Saipan. A US Army board of inquiry determined that the relief was not warranted, and it caused considerable public and private bitterness between the Army and Marine Corps for years after the war.

39. Cunningham, "Battle of Okinawa," 46, 67–68.

40. Appleman, *South to the Naktong,* 491–92.

41. Appleman, *South to the Naktong,* 491–92.

42. Appleman, *South to the Naktong,* 386–89.

43. "Marine Corps Board Study: An Evaluation of the Influence of Marine Corps Forces on the Course of the Korean War (4 AUG 50–15 DEC 50)," vol. 1 of 2, Korean War Collection, Box 1, Archives Branch, Marine Corps History Division, Marine Corps Base Quantico, VA; Giusti, *The Mobilization of the Marine Corps Reserve in the Korean Conflict.*

44. Korean War diary, Oliver P. Smith Papers, Box 68A, Archives Branch,

Marine Corps History Division, Marine Corps Base Quantico, VA (hereafter Smith Korean War diary), August 23, 1950. References to Marine regiments typically omit the word "regiment," though unit designations such as battalion and division are always used. The 5th Marine Regiment, therefore, is generally always called the 5th Marines. I have continued to use the regimental designation where necessary to avoid confusion between 1st Marine Regiment, the "1st Marines," and its parent unit, the 1st Marine Division.

45. Smith Korean War diary, August 22, 1950. Smith left three sets of recollections as part of his papers. The first is his Korean War pocket notebook (September–December 1950) with his handwritten notes. The Korean War Log (August 1950–April 1951) is a fleshed-out, typewritten version of his notebook. I have used it most often here. Both are contemporaneous and have been very useful for research. The third collection is his unpublished aide-mémoire, undated but clearly written postwar. He based it on his typewritten log entries but added details not known then and opinions not noted at the time.

46. Haig, *Inner Circles,* 44.

47. Smith Korean War diary, August 22, 1951.

48. Smith Korean War diary, August 23, 1950; Heinl, *Victory at High Tide: The Inchon-Seoul Campaign,* 43.

49. Haig, *Inner Circles,* 40–41.

50. Boose, *Over the Beach,* 68–69, 161–62.

51. Boose, *Over the Beach,* 160–61, 206n22; Heinl, *Victory at High Tide,* 42–43, 54; Almond to R. D. Heinl, August 31, 1966, enclosure 2, "Questions for General Almond on Inchon Landing," Box 73, Almond Papers.

52. Smith Korean War diary, August 23, 1950.

53. Appleman, *South to the Naktong,* 499; Blair, *Forgotten War,* 223; Smith Korean War diary, August 24, 1950.

54. Smith Korean War diary, August 23, 1950.

55. Smith Korean War diary, September 1–3, 1950.

56. Smith Korean War diary, September 3, 1950.

57. Appleman, *Escaping the Trap: The U. S. Army X Corps in Northeast Korea, 1950,* 3–4; Almond MHI interview, pt. IV, 61–62; Almond to Margaret Almond, October 24, 1950, Box 77, Almond Papers; Villahermosa, *Honor and Fidelity: The 65th Infantry in Korea,* 17–25. The 65th Infantry Regiment was inactivated as a Regular Army unit in 1959 and subsequently reactivated in the Puerto Rico National Guard.

58. UN Security Council, Resolution 83 (1950) of 27 June 1950, www.refworld.org/docid/3b00f20a2c.html; Appleman, *South to the Naktong,* 48, 382–83.

59. Appleman, *South to the Naktong,* 492; Giusti, *Marine Corps Reserve in the Korean Conflict,* II-1, II-6; Schnabel, *Policy and Direction,* 171; EUSAK, *Special Problems,* 9.

60. "Personal Notes Covering Activities of Lieut. Gen. E. M. Almond During Military Operations in Korea 31 August 1950–15 July 1951," Almond Papers (hereafter Almond Korean War diary), August 31– September 14, 1950.

12. Initial Success in Korea

1. Almond Korean War diary (see chap. 11, note 60), September 15, 1950; Smith Korean War diary (see chap. 11, note 44), September 15, 1950.

2. Almond Korean War diary, September 16, 1950; Smith Korean War diary, September 14, 1950.

3. Haig, *Inner Circles,* 39–40.

4. Almond MHI interview, pt. IV, 44–50; Appleman, *South to the Naktong,* 386–89, 503–12, 519–24; Boose, *Over the Beach,* 190, 195–96.

5. Almond to Margaret Almond, September 18, 1950, Box 77, Almond Papers.

6. Lt. Gen. Matthew B. Ridgway to Almond, September 27, 1950, Box 71A, Almond Papers.

7. Almond MHI interview, pt. IV, 50–51; Appleman, *South to the Naktong,* 489–91, 523.

8. Almond Korean War diary, September 20, 1950.

9. Hanson, *Combat Ready?,* 62.

10. US Army, *Terrain Handbook 65: Seoul and Vicinity;* US Army, *Korea Handbook,* 30 ff.

11. Haig, *Inner Circles,* 41–42, 45; Appleman, *South to the Naktong,* 526.

12. Almond MHI interview, pt. IV, 53–54; Boose, *Over the Beach,* 198–99; General Oliver Smith, interview with D. Clayton James, August 25, 1971, RG-49, MMA (hereafter Smith MMA interview), 20.

13. Haig, *Inner Circles,* 45.

14. Smith Korean War diary, September 25, 1950.

15. Haig, *Inner Circles,* 44.

16. Haig, *Inner Circles,* 45–46; Almond Korean War diary, September 25, 1950.

17. Almond Korean War diary, September 25, 1950.

18. Almond Korean War diary, September 25, 1950.

19. Smith Korean War diary, September 24, 1950.

20. Appleman, *South to the Naktong,* 524; Almond to Margaret Almond, September 24, 1950, Box 77, Almond Papers; Appleman, *South to the Naktong,* 534; Smith Korean War diary, September 24, 1950.

21. Appleman, *South to the Naktong,* 544–45, 597.

22. Schnabel, *Policy and Direction,* 187–88; Operations Plan CINCFE no. 9–50, September 29, 1950, Box 67, Almond Papers; US Army, *Terrain Study No. 20: Central Korea Northeast Section,* X-1; Almond MHI interview, pt. IV, 61; Almond Korean War diary, October 7, 1950.

23. EUSAK, *Special Problems,* 43.

24. US Army, *Terrain Study No. 20,* X-1.

25. MacArthur, *Reminiscences,* 259.

26. MacArthur, *Reminiscences,* 169.

27. MacArthur, *Reminiscences,* 198.

28. EUSAK, *Special Problems,* 34, 36.

29. "Comments of Col. A. D. Smith," EUSAK, *Special Problems,* 37, 52; Almond Korean War diary, October 1950, passim; "X Corps Opn Plan No. 3," October 2, 1950; "Operations Instruction (OI) No. 9," October 3, 1950, both in Box 62, Almond Papers.

30. US Army, *Logistics in the Korean Operations,* vol. 1, chap. 6, pp. 20–23 (pages numbered within chapters).

31. US Army, *Logistics in the Korean Operations,* vol. 3, chap. 6, p. 10.

32. EUSAK, *Special Problems,* 37–39.

33. Williamson, "A Diary in Retrospect" (see chap. 11, note 33), chap. 12, (unnumbered) pp. 5–6.

34. Almond Korean War diary, September 28, 1950.

35. Almond Korean War diary, 1950 passim.

36. Almond to Margaret Almond, October 24, 1950, Box 77, Almond Papers; Schnabel, *Policy and Direction,* 222–25; Appleman, *South to the Naktong,* 685–686; Stanton, *America's Tenth Legion: X Corps in Korea,* 143–52.

37. Schnabel, *Policy and Direction,* 222–23, n.25.

38. Almond to Willis D. Crittenberger, June 29, 1948, Box 54A; Almond to Tommy Galloway Fergusson, August 7, 1950, Box 58, Almond Papers.

39. Almond to Charles M. Fergusson, October 16, 1950, Box 58, Almond Papers.

40. "COMMAND: Sic 'Em Almond." *Time,* October 23, 1950, 18–19.

41. Almond to Tommy Galloway Fergusson, October 16, 1950, Box 58; Edward M. Almond to Margaret Almond, October 16, 1950, Box 77, Almond Papers.

42. US Army, *The Far East Command, 1 January 1947–30 June 1957,* 16; Almond MHI interview, pt. IV, 58–59.

43. Appleman, *South to the Naktong,* 612–19; Smith MMA interview, 2; McCaffrey MHI interview, 147; Lt. Gen. Edward L. Rowny, interview by Clay Blair, Combat Leadership in Korea Project, n.d., Box 7, Clay Blair Papers, MHI, 20; MacArthur, *Reminiscences,* 180–91.

44. Haig, Inner *Circles,* 53–54; Almond Korean War diary, October 25, 1950.

45. Schnabel, *Policy and Direction,* 46–49, 192.

46. US Army, *Korea Handbook,* 15–16, figs. 9 and 10, 18–19.

47. Almond MHI interview, pt. III, 62–64.

48. Appleman, *East of Chosin: Entrapment and Breakout in Korea, 1950,* 10–11.

49. Gen. Charles D. Palmer, interview with D. Clayton James, June 14, 1971,

RG-49, MMA, 30; Knight, "MacArthur's Eyes," 244–45 (Knight provides the most recent scholarly analysis of the intelligence gathering operations in the Korean War, including recently declassified US, Chinese, and Korean documents); Blair, *Forgotten War,* 393–94; Schnabel, *Policy and Direction,* 241, 259n11.

50. Mildren MHI interview, 135; "Monthly Summary: 1 NOV 1950 to 30 NOV 1950," War Diary X Corps, Box 62, Almond Papers, 2.

51. Mossman, *Ebb and Flow: November 1950–July 1951,* 738–40; Villahermosa, *Honor and Fidelity,* 46; Almond Korean War diary, November 5, 1950; Smith Korean War diary, November 10, 1950.

52. Villahermosa, *Honor and Fidelity,* 47–51; Almond Korean War diary, November 8 and 10, 1950.

53. X Corps Operations Order 6 112400I Nov 50, and Operations Order 7, 252400I Nov 50, in "Monthly Summary (see note 50), 7; Almond MHI interview, pt. III, 71–72; Appleman, *South to the Naktong,* 685, n46.

54. Mildren MHI interview, 112–14.

55. Almond MHI interview, pt. IV, 68–69; McCaffrey MHI interview, 148–49.

56. EUSAK Operations Plan 14, November 6, 1950, quoted in Schnabel, *Policy and Direction,* 257; Edwin K. Wright to Almond, November 10, 1950; Almond to Wright, November 14, 1950, both in Box 62, Almond Papers; Knight, "MacArthur's Eyes," 323.

57. Message X 12449, CG, X Corps to CG, FEAF, November 14, 1950, Box 54A, Almond Papers.

58. EUSAK, *Special Problems,* 40–41,44.

59. EUSAK, *Logistical Problems and Their Solutions,* 49–51; EUSAK, *Special Problems,* 42–43.

60. Almond MHI interview, pt. IV, 72; Blair, *Forgotten War,* 367.

61. Mildren MHI interview, 115, 125–26.

62. Haig, Inner *Circles,* 43.

63. Mildren MHI interview, 118–19.

13. Winter of Discontent: 1951

1. Almond Korean War diary (see chap. 11, note 60), November 20, 1950.

2. Smith Korean War diary (see chap. 11, note 44), November 24, 1950.

3. Appleman, *East of Chosin,* 19, 42–43. Task Force MacLean consisted of the 2nd and 3rd Battalions, 31st Infantry (2/31 and 3/31); the 31st Tank Company; the 1st Battalion, 32nd Infantry (1/32), (attached); the 57th Field Artillery Battalion (105 mm howitzers); and a platoon of eight antiaircraft vehicles (M19s with dual 40 mm cannon and M16 quad-.50 halftracks) from D Battery, 15th Antiaircraft Artillery (Automatic Weapons) Battalion. After MacLean's death, Lt. Col. Don Faith assumed command of the renamed Task Force Faith.

4. Operations Order No. 7, 252400I Nov 50, in "Monthly Summary" (see chap. 12, note 50).

5. William C. Barnard, "10th Corps' Almond Is No GI's General," *Washington Post,* June 24, 1951; Smith Korean War diary, September 20, 1950; Almond to Tommy Fergusson, October 28, 1950, Box 54A, Almond Papers; Harding, *U. S. Army Aircraft since 1947,* 13, 209–11, 192–93, 252–53. L-4s and L-5s were replaced during the war by L-16s, L-18s, and L-19s. These were the same size aircraft but with improved flying characteristics.

6. Kenneth E. Lea, "Korea's Blue Goose," Box 54A, Almond Papers.

7. Mildren MHI interview, 127–28.

8. Almond to A. M. Gruenther, November 15, 1950, Box 54A, Almond Papers.

9. Mildren MHI interview, 116, 122.

10. Appleman, *East of Chosin,* 65–67; Mildren MHI interview, 119, 123, 133.

11. Ridgway MHI interview, 2: 74, 77.

12. Smith Korean War diary, November 28, 1950; Almond Korean War diary, November 27 and 28, 1950; Appleman, *East of Chosin,* 107–8.

13. Almond to Allan D. MacLean, November 14, 1950, Box 55, Almond Papers.

14. Almond Korean War diary, January 25, 1951.

15. Almond MHI interview, pt. IV, 10–12.

16. Almond Korean War diary, November 28 and 29, 1950; Almond MHI interview, pt. IV, 11–13.

17. Operations Order No. 8, 30 Nov 50, in "Monthly Summary" (see chap. 12, note 50).

18. Smith Korean War diary, December 1, 1950.

19. Smith MMA interview, 6; Almond MHI interview, pt. IV, 15–16; Smith Korean War diary, November 30, 1950; Almond Korean War diary, November 30, 1950. Smith saw no irony in the fact that he had issued identical orders to the remnants of the 31st RCT, which was then trying to make its way across the reservoir to join the 1st Marine Division.

20. Special Report on the Hungnam Evacuation, December 9–24, 1950, Box 75, Almond Papers; GHQ, UNC, Radio, CX 50635, "To all Commanders," December 7, 1950, Box 62, Almond Papers,.

21. Mildren MHI interview, 123–24.

22. Almond to Ray Sherman, December 4, 1950, Box 85; Almond to Tommy Galloway Fergusson, December 9, 1950, Box 58, Almond Papers.

23. Memorandum, CG, X Corps to CINCUNC, "Subject: Redeployment of X Corps in PUSAN—POHANG-DONG Area," December 11, 1950, Box 62; "Special Report on the Hungnam Evacuation, 9–24 December 1950," Box 75, Almond Papers.

24. Mildren MHI interview, 124–25.

25. Almond Korean War diary, December 5, 1950; Message X 13867, CG, X

Corps to CG, FEAF, November 14, 1950, Box 54A, Almond Papers. Harris was killed two days later while commanding his battalion.

26. HQ, X Corps, Special Report on the Hungnam Evacuation, Box 64; Almond to Margaret Almond, December 14, 1950, Box 77, Almond Papers.

27. HQ, X Corps, Special Report on the Hungnam Evacuation, Box 64, Almond Papers; Mildren MHI interview, 129–31.

28. HQ, X Corps, Special Report on the Hungnam Evacuation, Box 64; X Corps Operations Order number 10, December 11, 1950, Box 75, Almond Papers.

29. Rowny, *Smokey Joe and the General,* 250–51.

30. Almond MHI interview, pt. V, 24.

31. HQ, X Corps, Special Report on the Hungnam Evacuation, Box 64, Almond Papers; Almond MHI interview, pt. V, 22–30.

32. Almond Korean War diary, December 19–31, 1950.

33. HQ, X Corps, Special Report on the Hungnam Evacuation, Box 64, Almond Papers; Almond MHI interview, pt. V, 30–34; Almond Korean War diary, December 26, 1950.

34. Smith MMA interview, 7; Lt. Gen. Alpha Bowser, USMC, interview with D. Clayton James, September 3, 1971, RG-49, MMA (hereafter Bowser MMA interview), 20–21.

35. Bowser MMA interview, 12.

36. Almond to Margaret Almond, December 22, 1950, and February 7, 1951, Box 77, Almond Papers.

37. Almond to Margaret Almond, December 25, 1950, Box 77, Almond Papers.

38. Almond to Harold E. Eastwood, December 27, 1950, RG-22 (Harold E. Eastwood Papers), MMA; Barnard, "10th Corps' Almond Is No GI's General"; Smith Korean War diary, September 20, 1950.

39. EUSAK, *Special Problems,* 48–49.

40. Almond to Harold E. Eastwood, December 27, 1950, RG-22, MMA; Mildren MMA interview, 14–18; Bowser MMA interview, 20; Schnabel, *Policy and Direction,* 255.

41. Almond MHI interview, pt. V, 32; Almond to Margaret Almond, December 28 and 30, 1950, Box 77, Almond Papers. After Ridgway arrived, contemporary sources began using "Eighth Army" instead of "EUSAK."

42. Headquarters, X Corps, Command Report, January 1951, Box 75, Almond Papers.

43. "Aide-Memoire," Oliver P. Smith Papers, Archives Branch, Marine Corps History Division, Marine Corps Base Quantico, VA, 1271.

44. Mossman, *Ebb and Flow,* 180–82; Mildren MHI interview, 136; Command Report (see note 42), 7. The corps has no fixed structure and the units are attached or detached as necessary to complete specific missions.

45. Schnabel, *Policy and Direction,* 340; Mossman, *Ebb and Flow,* 184–86.

46. Smith Korean War diary, December 30, 1950.

47. Mossman, *Ebb and Flow,* 183.

48. Blair, *Forgotten War,* 499–500; Almond Korean War diary, December 31, 1950 (emphasis in original).

49. Almond Korean War diary, January 9, 1951.

50. McCaffrey MHI interview, 162.

51. Almond Korean War diary, January 16, 1951; Operations Research Office, *Evaluation of the Clothing and Personal Equipment of the Infantry Rifleman in the Korean Winter.*

52. Barnard, "10th Corps' Almond Is No GI's General"; Haig, *Inner Circles,* 44.

53. Almond Korean War diary, January 13, 1951.

54. Almond Korean War diary, January 13, 1951. Almond relieved the 2nd Division Artillery commander, Brig. Gen. Loyal Haynes, two days later (McCaffrey MHI interview, 162). Almond thought well of Epley, however, and recommended him for promotion to brigadier general.

55. Almond Korean War diary, January 15, 1951 (parenthesis in original).

56. Blair, *Forgotten War,* 616; Almond Korean War diary, January 15, 1951.

57. Mildren MMA interview, 22; Almond to Matthew B. Ridgway, January 25, 1951, Box 85; Almond to Frank W. Milburn, February 4, 1951, Box 62, Almond Papers; Blair, *Forgotten War,* 420–21.

58. Almond Korean War diary, January 16, 1951.

14. Tragedy and Redemption

1. Mossman, *Ebb and Flow,* 232–36.

2. "Lt. Gen. William W. Quinn," "Gen. James H. Polk," Biography Files, MHI; Quinn, *Buffalo Bill Remembers,* 299–301; Knight, "MacArthur's Eyes," 171n65, 361–62.

3. Almond Korean War diary (see chap. 11, note 60), January 23, 1951.

4. Almond Korean War diary, February 1, 1951.

5. Almond Korean War diary, January 27, 1951

6. Headquarters, X Corps, Command Report, February 1951, Box 75, Almond Papers (hereafter X Corps February Report), 3–5.

7. Almond Korean War diary, February 6, 1951.

8. X Corps February Report, 4.

9. X Corps February Report, 5; Mossman, *Ebb and Flow,* 248.

10. Blair, *Forgotten War,* 614–15; Ridgway MHI interview, 2: 76.

11. Almond Korean War diary, 7–8 February 1951; X Corps February Report, 6.

12. Almond Korean War diary, February 9, 1951; X Corps February Report, 5–6.

13. X Corps February Report, 6.

14. X Corps February Report, 6–7.

15. X Corps February Report, 8.

16. Schnabel, *Policy and Direction,* 284; Almond Korean War diary, February 14, 1951; Gen. Paul L. Freeman, SOOHP interview by Col. James N. Ellis, November 30, 1973, and April 16, 1974, pt. II, 4–5. Freeman did not mention dissatisfaction with Almond in his oral history interview, but he did so in later letters to author Clay Blair; see Blair, *The Forgotten War,* 699–701, 706.

17. MSG, CITE X 177SG, CG, X Corps to CG, Army Eight, Personal for General Ridgway from Almond, February 13, 1951, Box 76, Almond Papers.

18. Matthew B. Ridgway to Almond, February 13, 1951, Box 76, Almond Papers.

19. Matthew B. Ridgway to Almond, February 14, 1951, Box 76, Almond Papers.

20. Almond Korean War diary, February 14, 1951. Puller had been promoted to brigadier general on January 26.

21. Almond Korean War diary, February 14–15, 1951.

22. Almond to Matthew B. Ridgway; Almond to Margaret Almond, February 16, 1951, Box 62, Almond Papers; Almond Korean War diary, February 15, 1951; X Corps February Report, 18.

23. X Corps February Report, 8.

24. Almond Korean War diary, February 17, 1951; Mossman, *Ebb and Flow,* 232–36.

25. Almond Korean War diary, February 20, 1951.

26. Almond Korean War diary, February 25, 1951.

27. McCaffrey MHI interview, 170–73.

28. Almond Korean War diary, March 5, 1951.

29. X Corps February Report, 12.

30. Almond Korean War diary, March 7–10, 1951.

31. Almond Korean War diary, April 10, 1951.

32. Headquarters, X Corps, Command Report, March 1951, Box 67, Almond Papers, 4–5.

33. Almond Korean War diary, April 11, 1951; Almond to Margaret Almond, April 12, 1951; Almond to Douglas MacArthur, April 12, 1951, both in Box 77, Almond Papers, MHI.

34. Margaret Almond to Almond, April 16, 1951, Box 62, Almond Papers.

35. Ibid.; Knight, "MacArthur's Eyes," 372; C. Whitney, *MacArthur: His Rendezvous with Destiny,* 472.

36. Matthew B. Ridgway to Almond, April 14, 1951, Box 77, Almond Papers; Appleman, *Ridgway Duels for Korea,* 579; Almond MMA RG-49 interview, 19; Ridgway, *Soldier: The Memoirs of Matthew B. Ridgway,* and *The Korean War: How We Met the Challenge, How All-Out Asian War Was Averted, Why MacArthur Was Dismissed, Why Today's War Objectives Must Be Limited.*

37. Blair, *Forgotten War,* 813; Braim, *The Will to Win: The Life of General James A. Van Fleet,* 246.

38. Headquarters, X Corps, Command Report, April 1951, Box 67, Almond Papers, 6.

39. Headquarters, X Corps, Command Report, May 1951, Box 67, Almond Papers (hereafter X Corps May Report), 7; Almond MHI interview, pt. IV, 45.

40. Mildren MHI interview, 123–24; X Corps May Report, 1.

41. X Corps May Report, 1.

42. Knight, "MacArthur's Eyes," 171n65, 377–78.

43. Mildren MHI interview, 137–41; Almond MHI interview, pt. IV, 45–46.

44. Mildren MHI interview, 145–46.

45. Almond Korean War diary, 17–18 May 1951; Almond MHI interview, pt. IV, 46–48.

46. X Corps May Report, 3; Mildren MHI interview, 144–45.

47. X Corps May Report, 4–5; Headquarters, X Corps, Command Report, June 1951, Box 67, Almond Papers, 2; Mildren MHI interview, 140–46.

48. Almond MHI interview, pt. IV, 61–62; Almond to Clovis E. Byers, May 24, 1951, Box 14, Clovis E. Byers Papers, Hoover Institution Archives; Appleman, *Ridgway Duels for Korea,* 578–79.

49. Headquarters, X Corps, Command Report, June 1951, Box 67, Almond Papers, 4; Ridgway MHI interview, 2: 75–76.

50. Memorandum for Record, HQ, X Corps, 5th Light Aviation Section, Subj.: "Summary of Flying Done by Lt. Gen. Almond," Box 76, Almond Papers.

51. Mildren MMA interview, 7.

52. Ridgway MHI interview, 2: 75–76.

53. Stanton, *America's Tenth Legion: X Corps in Korea,* appendix 1; "John H. Chiles," "Paul Freeman," "William J. McCaffrey," "James H. Polk," "Edward L. Rowny," "William W. Quinn," Biography Files, MHI.

15. A Final Assignment

1. Almond MHI interview, pt. V, 61–62; Almond to Clovis E. Byers, May 24, 1951, Box 14, Clovis E. Byers Papers, Hoover Institution Archives; Appleman, *Ridgway Duels for Korea,* 578–79.

2. US Army Field Forces, Report of Board on Army Education System for Commissioned Officers, January 20, 1949, quoted in Pappas, *Prudens Futuri: The US Army War College, 1901–1967,* 152–55; Organizational Chart, December 10, 1953, Box 1953/1954, AWC Archives, MHI.

3. Arthur G. Trudeau, SOOHP interview by Col. Calvin J. Landau, January 13–July 13, 1971 (hereafter Trudeau MHI interview), Box 1, Arthur G. Trudeau Papers, MHI (hereafter Trudeau Papers), 2: 45.

4. Ball, *Of Responsible Command: A History of the US Army War College,* 295.

5. Almond to Arthur G. Trudeau, November 14, 1947; Trudeau to Almond, November 28, 1947, Box 26, Trudeau Papers; Almond MHI interview, pt. V, 67; Gen. William C. Westmoreland, SOOHP interview by Col. Duane G. Cameron and Lt. Col. Raymond E. Funderburk, 1978, 150–51; Trudeau MHI interview, 2: 46; Sorley, *Westmoreland: The General Who Lost Vietnam,* 26; McCaffrey MHI interview, 173–74, 184–85; Almond MHI interview, pt. V, 67; Directory of Staff, Faculty, and Graduates, 1950 to 1953, AWC Curriculum AY 1953–1954, Box 1953/1954–1, AWC Archives.

6. Mark W. Clark to Almond, August 28, 1951, Box 71A, Almond Papers.

7. Almond to Clark, September 5, 1951, Box 71A, Almond Papers.

8. Ball, *Of Responsible Command,* 295; Almond MHI interview, pt. V, 63–66.

9. Almond, "Remarks at Opening Exercises, 1 SEP 1951," Lectures AY 1951–1952; Course Book, Guest Speakers (Almond–Duff), 1 SEP 1951–19 JUN 1952, Box 1951/1952–1, AWC Archives.

10. Pappas, *Prudens Futuri,* 163.

11. Pappas, *Prudens Futuri,* 165–71; Ball, *Of Responsible Command,* 228–29.

12. Almond to Chief of Staff, Army, February 8, 1952, Box 26, Trudeau Papers; Trudeau MHI interview, 2: 56–57; Pappas, *Prudens Futuri,* 165; Ball, *Of Responsible Command,* 299.

13. Almond to Chief of Staff, Army, February 8, 1952, Box 26, Trudeau Papers; Almond MHI interview, pt. V, 65–66; Ball, *Of Responsible Command,* 299–301; Pappas, *Prudens Futuri,* 166.

14. Ball, *Of Responsible Command,* 300–301.

15. "Guest Speakers, Army War College School Year 1951–52," Box AY 1951/1952; "Guest Speakers, Army War College School Year 1952–53," Box AY 1952/1953–1, AWC Archives; Pappas, *Prudens Futuri,* 162.

16. Ball, *Of Responsible Command,* 296; Pappas, *Prudens Futuri,* 170–71; "Guest Speakers, 1951–52," AWC Archives.

17. "Guest Speakers, 1951–52"; "Guest Speakers, 1952–53," AWC Archives.

18. "Guest Speakers, 1951–52"; "Guest Speakers, 1952–53," AWC Archives.

19. "Guest Speakers, 1951–52"; "Guest Speakers, 1952–53," AWC Archives.

20. "Guest Speakers, 1951–52"; "Guest Speakers, 1952–53," AWC Archives; Ball, *Of Responsible Command,* 298; Trudeau MHI interview, 2: 56.

21. "Guest Speakers, 1951–52," AWC Archives.

22. "Guest Speakers, 1951–52," AWC Archives.

23. Y'Blood, ed., *The Three Wars of Lt. Gen. George E. Stratemeyer: His Korean War Diary,* 223, 317–18; Almond MHI interview, pt. V, 56–57.

24. Y'Blood, *Three Wars of Lt. Gen. George E. Stratemeyer,* 165, 259n.

25. Y'Blood, *Three Wars of Lt. Gen. George E. Stratemeyer,* 60–61.

26. Crane, *American Airpower Strategy in Korea, 1950–1953,* 62.

27. Ball, *Of Responsible Command,* 298; Mark W. Clark to Almond, October 26, 1951, Box 71A, Almond Papers.

28. Crane, *American Airpower Strategy in Korea,* 60–61.

29. "Deviations Between US Army and US Air Force Doctrine," Box AY 1954/1955–1, AWC Archives.

30. Ibid.

31. Almond MHI interview, pt. V, 64; Ball, *Of Responsible Command,* 297, 302.

32. William J. McCaffrey to Roy E. Appleman, July 20, 1979, Box 28, Roy E. Appleman Papers, MHI; Ball, *Of Responsible Command,* 297–98.

33. Memorandum, Chief of Staff, Army for Lt. Gen. Edward M. Almond, July 22, 1952, "Subject: Explanation of Irregularity," Box 61, Almond Papers.

34. Memorandum, Lt. Gen. Edward M. Almond, for Chief of Staff, United States Army, July 25, 1952, "Subject: Explanation of Alterations in Quarters 1," Box 61, Almond Papers.

35. William J. McCaffrey to Roy E. Appleman, July 20, 1979, Box 28, Appleman Papers.

36. Almond MHI interview, pt. V, 64–65; William J. McCaffrey to Roy E. Appleman, July 20, 1979, Box 28, Appleman Papers.

37. William C. Westmoreland to Almond, November 4, 1952, Box 70, Almond Papers; William J. McCaffrey to Roy E. Appleman, July 20, 1979, Box 28, Appleman Papers.

38. Louis J. Beasley to Almond, September 3, 1952; Almond to Beasley, October 4, 1952, Box 71B, Almond Papers.

39. Almond to Ivan L. Bennett, December 2, 1952, Box 71B, Almond Papers; Hewitt, *Principal Officials of the War Department of the Army, 1900–1963,* 404.

40. Almond to Clifton B. Cates, October 3, 1951, Box 71A; Gerald C. Thomas to Almond, August 11, 1955, Box 96, Almond Papers; Millett, ~I+Semper Fidelis: The History of the United States Marine Corps+I~, 524.

41. Almond to Glenn O. Barcus, December 3, 1952, Box 71B, Almond Papers.

42. James A. Van Fleet to Almond, September 3, 1952, Box 71B, Almond Papers.

43. Almond to Commanding General, Caribbean Command, December 5, 1952; Almond to Laurence B. Keiser, November 21, 1952; Almond to Bryan Milburn, November 20, 1952, all Box 71B, Almond Papers.

16. Retirement and Epilogue

1. Almond MHI interview, pt. VI, 2.

2. US Military Academy, *Register of the Officers and Graduates of the US Military Academy, 1852, Supplement 2010,* 1630.

3. Almond to Douglas MacArthur, September 5, 1963, Box 111, Almond Papers.

4. Memorandum, Bucher Committee, for [Board of Visitors] Reference, Sep-

tember 12, 1957, "Subject: Major General William H. Milton, Superintendent, Virginia Military Institute," Box 146, Almond Papers.

5. Telegram, Almond to William H. Milton, February 11, 1959, Edward M. Almond File, VMI Alumni Files, VMI Library and Archives (hereafter Almond VMI file).

6. Almond to Class Agents, February 17, 1959; Jack V. Thompson to William H. Milton, February 23, 1959, Almond VMI file.

7. E. A. Whitehurst to Almond, March 2, 1959, Box 146, Almond Papers.

8. Charles E. Kilbourne to Almond, March 7, 1959, Almond VMI file.

9. Harry A. deButts to Almond, February 17, 1959, Almond VMI file; memorandum, Almond to VMI Class Agents, "Subject: Nomination for Superintendent, V.M.I," October 5, 1959, Box 146, Almond Papers; H. Wise, *Drawing Out the Man,* 248–49, 255–56.

10. Almond to J. Leslie Almond, October 10, 1960, Chronological File, 1912–1965, Almond VMI file.

11. J. Lindsay Almond to Almond, June 15, 1960, Box 147, Almond Papers; Joseph D. Neikirk to Almond, June 21, 1960, Chronological File, 1912–1965, Almond VMI file.

12. H. Wise, *Drawing Out the Man,* 260, 287–89; Almond to Wallace M. Greene, May 29, 1967; VMI Board of Visitors Minutes, April 6, 1968, both in Chronological File, 1966–Current, Almond VMI file; memorandum, VMI Director of Admissions for Board of Visitors, April 5, 1968, Box 147, Almond Papers.

13. H. Wise, *Drawing Out the Man,* 287.

14. Almond MHI interview, pt. V, 56–57; Maj. Michael Lewis, "Lt. Gen. Ned Almond, USA: A Ground Commander's Conflicting View with Airmen over CAS Doctrine and Employment," MA thesis, School of Advanced Airpower Studies, Air University, Maxwell Air Force Base, Alabama, 76.

15. Edward L. Rowny, interview by author, October 9, 2009, Washington, DC; Dalfiume, *Desegregation of the US Armed Forces,* 97.

16. Appleman, *Ridgway Duels for Korea,* 579.

17. Quoted in Blair, *Forgotten War,* 32.

18. Memorandum, James C. Shepard to Military History Institute staff, June 13, 1979, "Subject: LTG Edward M. Almond, USA, Retired," Box 140, Almond Papers; email, Thomas G. Fergusson to author, November 5, 2013.

19. William J. McCaffrey to Roy E. Appleman, June 19, 1979, Box 28, Appleman Papers.

Select Bibliography

Before Edward M. Almond died in 1979, he donated all of his personal papers to the US Army Military History Institute, now part of the US Army Heritage and Education Center (USAHEC), in Carlisle, Pennsylvania. Almond's large collection includes not only his correspondence with family and friends but many official papers, diaries, and letters that reveal much about the man's background and personality. These materials have provided a firm foundation for this book. Apart from Almond's collection, USAHEC holds the personal papers of several senior officers who served with Almond, including Brig. Gen. Benjamin O. Davis, Lt. Gen. William McCaffrey, and Gen. Matthew B. Ridgway. Just as important, USAHEC contains the papers of historians Roy Appleman and Clay Blair, each of whom interviewed Almond and wrote significant books on the Korean War. These two collections offer additional views of Almond.

As this book went to press, USAHEC began a multiyear project to digitize all of its archival holdings. This will ultimately make USAHEC's rich and varied collections much more available, but accessibility will be temporarily reduced as the collections are prepared and digitized. Many collections, including Almond's, will undergo minor adjustments as part of digitization, so future scholars may note discrepancies between the location of a specific item indicated in the endnotes and its final location. All USAHEC source material remains available, however. Researchers preparing to work in any of the collections are advised to check with staff for availability and accessibility as the digitization process continues.

Several other institutions provided primary sources that filled in parts of Almond's life. The Virginia Military Institute (VMI) Archives contain materials on Almond from both ends of his life: the cadet records illustrate his early growth and development, while the records of the VMI Board of Visitors, on which Almond served after retirement, show him as the powerful, connected operator he became. The George C. Marshall Research Library, also at VMI, holds the papers of General Marshall and of Gen. James A. Van Fleet, both of which offer insights on Almond from among his superiors.

The MacArthur Memorial Archives in Norfolk, Virginia, yield a treasure trove of oral history interviews with Almond and other senior officers who served on MacArthur's staff during the Korean War. The National Archives and Records Administration (NARA) holds all the official records of the 92nd Division, plus official records from the War Department as a whole.

The Edwin H. Simmons Marine Corps History Center at Quantico, Virginia, is a rich source of Marine Corps history. It holds historical records and studies of US Marine combat operations, as well as the personal papers of senior US Marine Corps officers such as Maj. Gen. Oliver P. Smith.

Archival Sources

Duke University, Perkins Library, Durham, NC

Robert L. Eichelberger Papers

George C. Marshall Research Library, Lexington, VA

George C. Marshall Papers
Lucian K. Truscott Papers
James A. Van Fleet Papers
Walton H. Walker Papers

Go For Broke National Education Center, Hanashi Oral History Program, Torrance, CA

Ben Doi interview
Robert Ichikawa interview
Daniel K. Inouye interview
Masaru Ishida interview
Frank Kimura interview
Al Takahashi interview

MacArthur Memorial Archives (MMA), Norfolk, VA

Record Group 9: Collection of Messages (Radiograms), 1945–1951
Record Group 22: Papers of Brigadier General Harold E. Eastwood, USA, 1942–1953
Record Group 23: Papers of Major General Charles A. Willoughby, USA, 1947–1973

Record Group 32: Oral History Collection
Lt. Gen. Edward M. Almond interview (1967)
Record Group 38: Selected Papers of Lieutenant General Edward M. Almond, USA, 1946–1951
Record Group 49: D. Clayton James Collection
Lt. Gen. Edward M. Almond interview
Maj. Gen. William A. Beiderlinden interview
Lt. Gen. Alpha Bowser interview
Adm. Arleigh A. Burke interview
Maj. Gen. John H. Chiles interview
Lt. Gen. Edward A. Craig interview
Brig. Gen. LeGrande A. Diller interview
Gen. Frank T. Mildren interview
Gen. Charles D. Palmer interview
Gen. Oliver P. Smith interview
Lt. Gen. Joseph M. Swing interview
Maj. Gen. Charles A. Willoughby interview
Maj. Gen. Edwin K. Wright interview

Marine Corps History Division, Archives Branch, Edwin H. Simmons Marine Corps History Center, Quantico, VA

Korean War Collection
Oliver P. Smith Collection

National Archives and Records Administration, College Park, MD

Record Group 107: Records of the Office of the Secretary of War
Record Group 165: Records of War Department General Staffs and Special Staffs
Record Group 337: Records of Army Ground Forces Headquarters
Record Group 338: Records of U.S. Army Operational, Tactical, and Support Organizations, World War II and Thereafter
Record Group 407: Records of the Army Adjutant General

Stanford University, Hoover Institute of War, Revolution, and Peace, Palo Alto, CA

Leonard R. Boyd Papers
Clovis E. Byers Papers
Bonner F. Fellers Papers
Wade H. Haislip Papers
Charles Andrew Willoughby Papers

Tennessee State Library and Archives, Nashville, TN

Charles M. Fergusson Papers

University of Tennessee, Center for the Study of War and Society, Knoxville, TN

Oral History Collection
Dr. E. V. Davidson interview

US Army Heritage and Education Center, US Army Military History Institute (MHI), Carlisle Barracks, PA

Engineer Memoirs

Lt. Gen. Edward L. Rowny interview

Office of the Chief of Military History (OCMH), World War II Collection

World War II Interviews
Maj. Gen. William H. Colbern interview

Personal Papers Collections

Edward M. Almond Papers
Roy E. Appleman Papers
Clay and Joan Blair Papers
Charles Bolté Papers
Robert J. Colbern Papers
John B. Coulter Papers
Willis D. Crittenberger Papers
Benjamin O. Davis Sr. Papers
Alvan C. Gillem Jr. Papers
John P. Lucas Papers
William McCaffrey Papers
Frank T. Mildren Papers
James H. Polk Papers
William W. Quinn Papers
Matthew B. Ridgway Papers
Arthur G. Trudeau Papers
Walton H. Walker Papers
William C. Westmoreland Papers

Senior Officer Oral History Program (SOOHP) Interviews

Lt. Gen. Edward M. Almond interview
Gen. Paul L. Freeman interview
Lt. Gen. William J. McCaffrey interview
Gen. Frank T. Mildren interview

Maj. Gen. Arthur G. Trudeau interview
Gen. William C. Westmoreland interview

Specialized Collections

Authority Publications Collection
Biography Collection
Installation History Collection

Unit History Collection

Hunter, Jehu C., and Major Clark. "The Buffalo Division in World War II." 1985.

Jordan, Edward E. "The Operations of the 1st Battalion, 473rd Infantry Regiment (Separate) in the Attack up the Italian Coast, 8–15 April, 1945 (Po Valley Campaign)." Personal Experiences of a Heavy Weapons Company Executive Officer, Advanced Infantry Officers Course Monograph, 1949–1950.

Kashiwa, Genro, and Jun Yamato, eds. "Collection of Memoirs, Company L, 3rd Battalion, 442nd Regimental Combat Team." 6 vols. 1994–2000.

Oba, Ronald, ed. "The Men of Company F, 442nd Regimental Combat Team." 1989.

92nd Infantry Division History: G-2 periodic report, October 1944

Unpublished Memoirs

Williamson, E. Warner ."A Diary in Retrospect: The Fear of Failure Can Be Enhanced to Make It a Most Valuable Motivating Asset." N.d.

US Army War College Curricular Archives

Academic Years 1930–1931, 1931–1932, 1932–1933, 1933–1934
Academic Years 1950–1951, 1951–1952, 1952–1953, 1953–1954

World War II Veterans Surveys

92nd Division Surveys
93rd Division Surveys

Virginia Military Institute (VMI), Preston Library and Archives, Lexington, VA

Edward M. Almond Alumni Files
Thomas St. John Arnold Alumni Files
Record Group 1: Board of Visitors Records; Minutes, Board of Visitors
Record Group 2: Office of the Superintendent VMI General Orders
Record Group 6: Publications and Printed Material
Record Group 11: Registrar and Non-Current Student Records

Cadet (Virginia Military Institute). "The Cadet Staff." April 10, 1915. digitalcollections.vmi.edu/cdm/compoundobject/collection/p15821coll8/id/1666/rec/1.

———. "New Market Statue Being Moved," May 11, 1912.

———. "Stonewall Jackson Statue for VMI." March 17, 1911.

Caplow, Theodore, Louis Hicks, and Ben J. Wattenberg. *The First Measured Century: An Illustrated Guide to Trends in America, 1900–2000*. Washington, DC: AEI Press, 2001.

Center of Military History. "Baker, Vernon." Medal of Honor citation. https://history.army.mil/moh/wwII-a-f.html#BAKERV.

———. "Fox, John R." Medal of Honor citation. https://history.army.mil/moh/wwII-a-f.html#FOX.

———. "Inouye, Daniel." Medal of Honor citation. https://history.army.mil/moh/wwII-g-l.html#INOUYE.

Chicago Defender. "Axis Propagandists Gloat over Detroit Race Riots." December 25, 1943.

———. "Missing in Port Chicago Explosion." July 29, 1944.

———. "Port Chicago 'Mutiny' Trial of 50 Becoming 'Hot Potato' for Navy." October 21, 1944.

———. "President Roosevelt and the Philadelphia Transit Strike." August 17, 1944.

Clark, Mark W. *Calculated Risk*. New York: Harper, 1950.

Clark, Thomas D., ed. *The South since Reconstruction*. Indianapolis: Bobbs-Merrill, 1973.

Cleveland Gazette. "John L. Lewis, CIO Leader Calls On All of Our People to Vote for Wendell Willkie." November 2, 1940.

———. "Reported Missing in Action: Captain Charles F. Gandy." November 14, 1944.

Clifford, John Garry. *The Citizen Soldiers: The Plattsburg Training Camp Movement, 1913–1920*. Lexington: University Press of Kentucky, 1972.

Cole, Alice C., Alfred Goldberg, Samuel A. Tucker, and Rudolph A. Winnacker, eds. *Department of Defense: Documents on Establishment and Organization, 1944–1978*. Washington, DC: Office of the Secretary of Defense, Historical Office, 1978.

Cole, Ronald C., Walter S. Poole, James F. Schnabel, Robert J. Watson, and Willard J. Webb. *The History of the Unified Command Plan, 1946–1993*. Washington, DC: Joint History Office, Office of the Chairman of the Joint Chiefs of Staff, 1995.

Collins, George. "Blames Gen. Almond, Army Policy for Record of 92nd." Now It Can Be Told. *Pittsburgh Courier*, November 10, 1945.

Collins, J. Lawton. *Lightning Joe: An Autobiography*. Baton Rouge: Louisiana State University Press, 1979.

Cooper, John Milton, Jr. *Woodrow Wilson: A Biography*. New York: Alfred A. Knopf, 2009.

Couper, William. *One Hundred Years at V.M.I.* Richmond, VA: Garrett and Massie, 1939.

Cowart, Glenn C. *Miracle in Korea: The Evacuation of X Corps from the Hungnam Beachhead.* Columbia: University of South Carolina Press, 1992.

Crane, Conrad C. *American Airpower Strategy in Korea, 1950–1953.* Lawrence: University Press of Kansas, 2000.

Culpeper Exponent. "Gen. Wm. Nalle Dies Sunday Eve." August 4, 1911.

Cunningham, Paul E., II. "Command and Control of the US Tenth Army during the Battle of Okinawa." MMAS thesis, US Army Command and General Staff College, 2009.

Daily, Edward L. *MacArthur's X Corps in Korea: Inchon to the Yalu, 1950.* Paducah, KY: Turner, 1999.

Dalfiume, Richard M. *Desegregation of the U.S. Armed Forces: Fighting on Two Fronts, 1939–1953.* Columbia: University of Missouri Press, 1969.

Davis, Eugene. "Black Cabinet." *Kansas City Plaindealer*, April 4, 1934.

Dethlefs, Louis C. *History, 12th Machine Gun Battalion, 8th Infantry Brigade, Fourth Division, December 1917 to July 1919, Aisne-Marne-St. Mihiel, Meuse-Argonne, Army of Occupation.* Coblenz, Germany: Hartmann, 1919.

Doe, J. A. "Infantry Machine Guns—The Attack." *Infantry Journal* 17, no. 6 (December 1920): 546–55.

Dravo, C. A. "Machine Guns." *Infantry Journal* 17, no. 4 (October 1920): 319–29.

Driver, Robert J., Jr. *The 1st and 2nd Rockbridge Artillery.* Virginia Regimental Histories Series. Lynchburg, VA: H. E. Howard, 1987.

Eighth U.S. Army Korea (EUSAK). *Logistical Problems and Their Solutions.* Washington, DC: Office of the Chief of Military History, 1952.

———. *Special Problems in the Korean Conflict.* Washington, DC: Office of the Chief of Military History, 1952.

Faulkner, Richard S. *The School of Hard Knocks: Combat Leadership in the American Expeditionary Forces.* College Station: Texas A&M University Press, 2012.

Fehrenbach, T. R. *This Kind of War: A Study in Unpreparedness.* New York: Macmillan, 1963.

Ferrell, Robert H. *America's Deadliest Battle: Meuse-Argonne, 1918.* Lawrence: University Press of Kansas, 2007.

Finnegan, John Patrick. *Against the Specter of a Dragon: The Campaign for American Military Preparedness, 1914–1917.* Westport, CT: Greenwood, 1974.

———. "Military Preparedness in the Progressive Era, 1911–1917." PhD diss., University of Wisconsin, 1969.

Fisher, Ernest F., Jr. *Cassino to the Alps.* U.S. Army in World War II. Washington, DC: Center of Military History, Department of the Army, 1977.

Fletcher, Marvin E. *America's First Black General: Benjamin O. Davis, Sr., 1880–1970.* Lawrence: University Press of Kansas, 1989.

Franqui-Rivera, Harry. "Glory and Shame: The Ordeal of the Puerto Rican 65th U.S. Infantry Regiment During the Korean War, 1950–1953." MA thesis, Temple University, 2002.

Futrell, Robert Frank. *The United States Air Force in Korea, 1950–1953*. Rev. ed. Washington, DC: Office of Air Force History, 1983.

Gabel, Christopher R. *The U.S. Army GHQ Maneuvers of 1941*. Washington, DC: Center of Military History, 1991.

Gibran, Daniel K. *The 92nd Infantry Division and the Italian Campaign in World War II*. Jefferson, NC: McFarland, 2001.

Gibson, Truman K., Jr. *Knocking Down Barriers: My Fight for Black America*. With Steve Huntley. Evanston, IL: Northwestern University Press, 2005.

Giusti, Ernest H. *The Mobilization of the Marine Corps Reserve in the Korean Conflict*. Washington, DC: Headquarters, Marine Corps, 1953.

Gole, Henry G. *The Road to Rainbow: Army Planning for Global War, 1934–1940*. Annapolis, MD: Naval Institute Press, 2003.

Goodman, Paul. *A Fragment of Victory in Italy during World War II, 1942–45: A Special Study Concerned with the 92d Infantry Division and Its Principle Attachments, Including the 473d and 442d (Japanese-American) Infantry Regiments*. Carlisle Barracks, PA: U.S. Army War College, 1952.

Greenfield, Kent Roberts, ed. *Command Decisions*. 1958. Washington, DC: Center of Military History, 1987.

Greenfield, Kent Roberts, Robert R. Palmer, and Bell I. Wiley. *The Organization of Ground Combat Troops*. U.S. Army in World War II. Washington, DC: Historical Division, Department of the Army, 1947.

Haig, Alexander M., Jr. *Inner Circles: How America Changed the World; A Memoir*. With Charles McCarry. New York: Warner, 1992.

Hamburger, Kenneth E. *Leadership in the Crucible: The Korean War Battles of Twin Tunnels and Chipyong-Ni*. College Station: Texas A&M University Press, 2002.

Hanson, Thomas E. *Combat Ready? The Eighth U.S. Army on the Eve of the Korean War*. College Station: Texas A&M University Press, 2010.

Harding, Stephen. *U.S. Army Aircraft since 1947: An Illustrated Reference*. Atglen, PA: Schiffer, 1997.

Hargrove, Hondon B. *Buffalo Soldiers in Italy: Black Americans in World War II*. Jefferson, NC: McFarland, 1985.

Heefner, Wilson A. *Dogface Soldier: The Life of General Lucian K. Truscott Jr.* Columbia: University of Missouri Press, 2010.

———. *Patton's Bulldog: The Life and Service of General Walton H. Walker*. Shippensburg, PA: White Mane, 2001.

Heinl, Robert Debs, Jr. *Victory at High Tide: The Inchon-Seoul Campaign*. Philadelphia: Lippincott, 1968.

Herring, George C., Jr. "James Hay and the Preparedness Controversy, 1915–1916." *Journal of Southern History* 30, no. 4 (November 1964): 383.

Hewes, James E. *From Root to McNamara: Army Organization and Administration, 1900–1963*. Washington, DC: Center of Military History, US Army, 1975.

Hewitt, James E. *Principal Officials of the War Department of the Army, 1900–1963*. Washington, DC: U.S. Government Printing Office, 1983.

Hicks, James. "73rd Engineer Combat Bn. Cited for Working Miracle." *Afro-American*, July 7, 1951.

Houston, Ivan J. *Black Warriors: The Buffalo Soldiers of World War II*. With Gordon Cohn. Bloomington, IN: iUniverse, 2009.

Howe, George F. *The Battle History of the 1st Armored Division "Old Ironsides."* Washington, DC: Combat Forces Press, 1954.

Humphreys, Margaret. *Intensely Human: The Health of the Black Soldier in the American Civil War*. Baltimore: Johns Hopkins University Press, 2008.

James, D. Clayton. *Refighting the Last War: Command and Crisis in Korea, 1950–1953*. With Anne Sharp Wells. New York: Free Press, 1993.

Jefferson, Robert F. *Fighting for Hope: African American Troops of the 93rd Infantry Division in World War II and Postwar America*. Baltimore: Johns Hopkins University Press, 2008.

Johnson, Douglas V., II, and Rolfe L. Hillman Jr. *Soissons, 1918*. College Station: Texas A&M University Press, 1999.

Johnston, Carolyn Ross. *My Father's War: Fighting with the Buffalo Soldiers in World War II*. Tuscaloosa: University of Alabama Press, 2012.

Kahn, E. J., Jr., and Henry McLemore. *Fighting Divisions: Histories of Each U.S. Army Combat Division in World War II*. Washington, DC Infantry Journal Press, 1946.

Kansas American. "Negroes Profited with Roosevelt as President." October 16, 1936.

Kansas City Plaindealer. "ANP Exposes Jim Crow at Fort Huachuca; Ala. General in Charge." September 10, 1943.

———. "Joe Louis Tells His People to Elect Willkie President." November 1, 1940

Kierein, Nicole M., and Michael A. Gold. "Pygmalion in Work Organizations: A Meta-Analysis." *Journal of Organizational Behavior* 21, no. 8 (December 2000): 913–14.

Knight, Peter G. "'MacArthur's Eyes': Reassessing Military Intelligence Operations in the Forgotten War, June 1950–April 1951." PhD diss., Ohio State University, 2006.

Kreidberg, Marvin A., and Merton G. Henry. *History of Military Mobilization in the United States Army, 1775–1945*. Department of the Army Pamphlet 20–212. Washington, DC: Department of the Army, 1955.

Kryder, Daniel. *Divided Arsenal: Race and the American State during World War II*. Cambridge: Cambridge University Press, 2000.

Lee, Ulysses. *The Employment of Negro Troops*. U.S. Army in World War II.

Washington, DC: Office of the Chief of Military History, Department of the Army, 1966.

Lee, Young-woo. "The United States and the Formation of the Republic of Korea Army, 1945–1950." PhD diss., Duke University, 1984.

Lengel, Edward G. *To Conquer Hell: The Meuse-Argonne, 1918*. New York: Henry Holt, 2008.

Lewis, Michael M. "Lt. Gen. Ned Almond, USA: A Ground Commander's Conflicting View with Airmen over CAS Doctrine and Employment." MA thesis, School of Advanced Airpower Studies, Air University, Maxwell Air Force Base, Alabama, 1997.

Linn, Brian McAllister. *Guardians of Empire: The U.S. Army and the Pacific, 1902–1940*. Chapel Hill: University of North Carolina Press, 1997.

Litwack, Leon F. *Trouble in Mind: Black Southerners in the Age of Jim Crow*. New York: Alfred A. Knopf, 1998.

Los Angeles Tribune. "Paratroop Volunteers Named." January 17, 1944.

MacArthur, Douglas. *Reminiscences*. New York: McGraw-Hill, 1964.

MacGregor, Morris J., Jr. *Integration of the Armed Forces, 1940–1965*. Washington, DC: Center of Military History, 1981.

Manchester, William. *American Caesar: Douglas MacArthur, 1880–1964*. Boston: Little, Brown, 1978.

Marion Military Institute. "Marion Military Institute History." https://marion-military.edu/about-mmi/history.

Marshall, George C. "Profiting by War Experience." *Infantry Journal* 18, no. 1 (January 1921): 34–37.

Matheny, Michael R. *Carrying the War to the Enemy: American Operational Art to 1945*. Norman: University of Oklahoma Press, 2011.

Matloff, Maurice. "The 90-Division Gamble." In Greenfield, *Command Decisions*, 365–81.

McCaffrey, James M. *Going for Broke: Japanese American Soldiers in the War against Nazi Germany*. Norman: University of Oklahoma Press, 2013.

McGrath, John J. *The Brigade: A History; Its Organization and Employment in the US Army*. Fort Leavenworth, KS: Combat Studies Institute Press, 2004.

McGuire, Phillip, ed. *Taps for a Jim Crow Army: Letters from Black Soldiers in World War II*. Santa Barbara, CA: ABC-Clio, 1983.

Millett, Allan R. *Semper Fidelis: The History of the United States Marine Corps*. Rev. ed. New York: Free Press, 1993.

———. *The War for Korea, 1945–1950: A House Burning*. Lawrence: University of Kansas Press, 2005.

———. *The War for Korea, 1950–1951: They Came from the North*. Lawrence: University of Kansas Press, 2010.

Moenk, Jean R. *A History of Large-Scale Maneuvers in the United States, 1935–1964*. Fort Monroe, VA: Continental Army Command, 1969.

Morehouse, Maggi M. *Fighting in the Jim Crow Army: Black Men and Women Remember World War II*. Lanham, MD: Rowman and Littlefield, 2000.

Morrow, George L., et al. *The Fifty-Eighth Infantry in the World War, 1917–1918–1919*. N.p.: 58th Infantry History Association, 1919.

Mossman, Billy C. *Ebb and Flow: November 1950–July 1951*. U.S. Army in the Korean War. Washington, DC: Center of Military History, United States Army, 1990.

Motley, Mary Penick, ed. *The Invisible Soldier: The Experience of the Black Soldier, World War II*. Detroit: Wayne State University Press, 1975.

Muth, Jörg. *Command Culture: Officer Education in the U.S. Army and the German Armed Forces, 1901–1940, and the Consequences for World War II*. Denton: University of North Texas Press, 2011.

Nalty, Bernard C. *Strength for the Fight: A History of Black Americans in the Military*. New York: Free Press, 1986.

National Guard Bureau. *Annual Report of the Chief of the National Guard Bureau*. Washington, DC: National Guard Bureau, 1941.

Neiberg, Michael S. *The Second Battle of the Marne*. Bloomington: Indiana University Press, 2008.

New York Times. "Redskins Passes Top Eagles, 20–14: Baugh Sends Two Touchdown Tosses to Aguirre and One to Krueger." December 8, 1941.

Nye, Roger H. "The United States Military Academy in an Era of Educational Reform, 1900–1925." PhD diss., Columbia University, 1968.

Olson, John E. *The Philippine Scouts*. N.p.: Philippine Scout Heritage Society, 1996.

Operations Research Office, Johns Hopkins University. *Evaluation of the Clothing and Personal Equipment of the Infantry Rifleman in the Korean Winter*. Chevy Chase, MD: Johns Hopkins University, 1951.

Ottley, Roi. "92nd Had No Faith in Its Leadership." *Pittsburgh Courier*, December 21, 1946.

Palmer, Robert R., Bell I. Wiley, and William R. Keast. *The Procurement and Training of Ground Combat Troops*. U.S. Army in World War II. Washington, DC: Historical Division, Department of the Army, 1948.

Pappas, George S. *Prudens Futuri: The U.S. Army War College, 1901–1967*. Carlisle Barracks, PA: Alumni Association of the US Army War College, 1967.

Patch, Alexander M. "Machine-Gun Unit Organization." *Infantry Journal* 17, no. 2 (August 1920): 142–48.

Pickens, William. "FDR and His Negroes." *Kansas City Plaindealer*, April 14, 1933.

Poague, William Thomas. *Gunner with Stonewall: Reminiscences of William Thomas Poague*. Edited by Monroe F. Cockrell. Jackson, TN: McCowat-Mercer, 1957.

Pogue, Forrest C. *George C. Marshall: Education of a General, 1880–1939*. New York: Viking, 1963.

———. *George C. Marshall: Interviews and Reminiscences for Forrest C. Pogue*. Lexington, VA: George C. Marshall Research Foundation, 1986.

Quinn, William W. *Buffalo Bill Remembers*. Easton, MD: Wilderness Adventure, 1991.

Ramsberger, Jack F., ed. *Battle History, 473rd United States Infantry, World War II*. Italy: U.S. Army, 1945.

Reddick, L. D. "Negro Policy of the United States Army." *Journal of Negro History* 34 (January 1949): 18.

Richardson, Robert C. "Army Developments in Preparedness." *Proceedings of the Academy of Political Science* 19, no. 3 (May 1941): 9–20.

Ricks, Thomas E. *The Generals: American Military Command from World War II to Today*. New York: Penguin, 2012.

Ridgway, Matthew B. *The Korean War: How We Met the Challenge; How All-Out Asian War Was Averted; Why MacArthur Was Dismissed; Why Today's War Objectives Must Be Limited*. Garden City, NY: Doubleday, 1967.

———. *Soldier: The Memoirs of Matthew B. Ridgway*. With Harold H. Martin. New York: Harper, 1956.

Robertson, James I., Jr. *Stonewall Jackson: The Man, The Soldier, The Legend*. New York: Macmillan, 1997.

Rockingham (VA) Register. "Peculiar Local Conditions." Editorial. February 28, 1905.

Rowny, Edward L. *An American Soldier's Saga of the Korean War*. Edited by Anne Kazel-Wilcox. Washington, DC: privately printed, 2013.

———. *Smokey Joe and the General: The Tale of Gen. John E. Wood and His Protégé Lt. Ed Rowny*. Edited by Anne Kazel-Wilcox. Washington, DC: privately printed, 2013.

———. "Two Related Lives: Former Ambassador and LTG USA (Ret) Edward L. Rowny and BG John E. 'Smokey Joe' Wood." Unpublished MSS manuscript, copy in author's possession.

Ruggles, Logan E. *The Part the USS* Von Steuben *Played in the Great War*. N.p., n.d.

Sawyer, Robert K. *Military Advisors in Korea: KMAG in Peace and War*. 1962. Washington, DC: Center of Military History, 2000.

Schaller, Michael. *Douglas MacArthur: The Far Eastern General*. New York: Oxford University Press, 1989.

Schnabel, James F. *Policy and Direction: The First Year*. U.S. Army in the Korean War. Washington, DC: Office of the Chief of Military History, Department of the Army, 1972.

Shirey, Orville C. *Americans: The Story of the 442nd Combat Team* Washington, DC: Infantry Journal Press, 1947.

Shisler, Gail B. *For Country and Corps: The Life of General Oliver P. Smith*. Annapolis, MD: Naval Institute Press, 2009.

Short, Walter C. *Employment of Machine Guns*. Washington, DC: US Infantry Association, 1922.

———. "Machine Guns of an Infantry Division." *Infantry Journal* 17, no. 3 (September 1920): 261–63.

Smythe, Donald. *Pershing: General of the Armies*. Bloomington: Indiana University Press, 1986.

Sorley, Lewis. *Honor Bright: History and Origins of the West Point Honor Code and System*. New York: McGraw Hill Learning Solutions, 2009.

———. *Westmoreland: The General Who Lost Vietnam*. New York: Houghton Mifflin Harcourt, 2011.

Sparrow, John C. *History of Personnel Demobilization in the United States Army*. Washington, DC: US Army Office of Military History, 1951.

Stanton, Shelby L. *America's Tenth Legion: X Corps in Korea, 1950*. Novato, CA: Presidio, 1989.

———. *World War II Order of Battle, U.S. Army*. Rev. ed. Mechanicsburg, PA: Stackpole Books, 2006.

Starr, Chester G. *Fifth Army History*. 9 vols. Washington, DC: U.S. Government Printing Office, 1945.

Stewart, Richard W. *Staff Operations: The X Corps in Korea, December 1950*. Fort Leavenworth, KS: Combat Studies Institute Press, 1991.

Stoddard, Lothrop. *Racial Realities in Europe*. New York: Scribner, 1924.

Switzer, J. S. "Concerning Machine Guns." *Infantry Journal* 16, no. 7 (January 1920): 371–429.

Taaffe, Stephen R. *MacArthur's Korean War Generals*. Lawrence: University Press of Kansas, 2016.

Time. "Army and Navy: General Shift." September 4, 1933, 18–19.

———. "COMMAND: Sic 'Em Almond." October 23, 1950, 15–18.

Trask, David F. *The AEF and Coalition Warmaking, 1917–1918*. Lawrence: University Press of Kansas, 1993.

Truscott, Lucian K, Jr. *Command Missions: A Personal Story*. New York: Dutton, 1954.

Ulbrich, David J. *Preparing for Victory: Thomas Holcomb and the Making of the Modern Marine Corps, 1936–1943*. Annapolis, MD: Naval Institute Press, 2011.

United States. American Battle Monuments Commission. *4th Division, Summary of Operations in the World War*. Washington, DC: U.S. Government Printing Office, 1944.

———. *American Armies and Battlefields in Europe*. Washington, DC: U.S. Government Printing Office, 1938.

United States Army. *Big X in Korea*. N.p.: X Corps, U.S. Army, 1954.

———. *The Far East Command, 1 January 1947–30 June 1957*. Tokyo: Office of the Military History Officer, United States Forces in the Far East, 1957.

———. *Fifth Army at the Winter Line (15 November 1943–15 January 1944)*. 1945. Washington, DC: Center of Military History, 1990.

———. *The Final Campaign Across Northwest Italy: 14 April–2 May 1945*. Milan: Headquarters, IV Corps, U. S. Army, 1945.

———. "German Version of the History of the Italian Campaign." N.p., n.d.

———. *Historical and Pictorial Review, 41st Engineers of the United States Army.* Baton Rouge, LA: Army and Navy Publishing Company, 1941.

———. *KMAG: The United States Military Advisory Group to the Republic of Korea, 1945–1955.* Seoul: KMAG Public Information Office, 1955.

———. *Korea Handbook.* Washington: Office of the Deputy Chief of Staff, G2, Department of the Army, 1950.

———. *Leadership and the Negro Soldier.* Army Service Forces Manual, M5 (Training). Washington, DC: U.S. Government Printing Office, 1944.

———. *Pictorial History, Three Hundred Sixty-Sixth Infantry, 1941.* N.p.: Army Press, 1941.

———. *The Story of the 442nd Regimental Combat Team Composed of the 442nd Infantry Regiment, 552nd Field Artillery Battalion and 232nd Combat Engineer Company.* N.p., n.d.

———. *Terrain Handbook No. 65: Seoul and Vicinity, Korea.* Tokyo: GHQ, FECOM, Military Intelligence Section, 1950.

———. *Terrain Study No. 20: Central Korea Northeast Section.* Tokyo: GHQ, FECOM, Military Intelligence Section, 1950.

United States Army War College. Historical Section. *The Ninety-Second Division, 1917–1918: An Analytical Study.* Washington Barracks, DC: Army War College, 1923.

United States. Congress. *Biographical Directory of the United States Congress, 1774–2005.* Washington, DC: U.S. Government Printing Office, 2005.

United States. Department of the Army. Historical Division. *United States Army in the World War, 1917–1919.* Vol. 1, *Organization of the American Expeditionary Forces.* Washington, DC: U.S. Government Printing Office, 1948.

United States. Department of War. *Infantry Mobilization Training Program for Infantry Regiments at Unit Training Centers.* Mobilization Training Program no. 7-1. Washington, DC: War Department, 1942.

———. *Regulations for the Government of the Gettysburg National Military Park.* Gettysburg, PA, 1911.

United States Military Academy. *Register of Graduates and Former Cadets of the United States Military Academy, West Point, New York, Class of 1900 Centennial Edition.* West Point, NY: U.S. Military Academy, 2000.

———. *Register of the Officers and Graduates of the US Military Academy, 1852, Supplement 2010.* Cambridge, MA: Riverside Press, 2010.

Unrau, Harlan D. *Administrative History: Gettysburg National Military Park and Gettysburg National Cemetery, Pennsylvania.* Washington, DC: National Park Service, U.S. Department of the Interior, 1991.

Urwin, Gregory J. W. *The United States Cavalry: An Illustrated History, 1776–1944.* Norman: University of Oklahoma Press, 2003.

Vaughan, Curry N., Robert E. Nieman Jr., Vasco Fenili, Elmer C. Reagor, John M. Mullen, Gordon E. McQuain, and Melvin M. Jensen. "Mud, Mountains, and Armor: The First Armored Division from Rome to the Alps." Research report prepared by Committee 17, Officers Advanced Course, the Armored School, 1948–1949. Fort Knox, KY, 1949.

Villahermosa, Gilberto N. *Honor and Fidelity: The 65th Infantry in Korea, 1950–1953*. Washington, DC: Center of Military History, 2009.

Virginia Military Institute. *The Bomb*. Yearbook. Lexington, VA: Virginia Military Institute, 1915.

———. *Register of Former Cadets, Memorial Edition*. Lexington, VA: Virginia Military Institute, 1957.

———. *Roster of Graduates of the Virginia Military Institute, 1842-1919*. Lexington, VA: Virginia Military Institute, 1920.

Wade, Gary. *World War II Division Commanders*. CSI Report no. 7. Fort Leavenworth, KS: U.S. Army Command and General Staff College, 1983.

Wakamatsu, Jack K. *Silent Warriors: A Memoir of America's 442nd Regimental Combat Team*. New York: Vantage, 1995.

Wallace, Lee A. *A Guide to Virginia Military Organizations, 1861–1865*. 2nd ed. Lynchburg, VA: H. E. Howard, 1986.

Weigley, Russell F. *History of the United States Army*. Enlarged ed. Bloomington: Indiana University Press, 1984.

Whitney, Courtney. *MacArthur: His Rendezvous with History*. New York: Alfred A. Knopf, 1956.

Whitney, L. Baynard. "General Jim Crow." Calvin's Digest. *Kansas City Plaindealer*, November 1, 1940.

Wiley, Bell I. "The Building and Training of Infantry Divisions." In *United States Army in World War II: The Army Ground Forces; The Procurement and Training of Ground Combat Troops*, 429–94. Washington Center of Military History, United States Army, 1991.

Williams, Chad L. *Torchbearers of Democracy: African American Soldiers in the World War I Era*. Chapel Hill: University of North Carolina Press, 2010.

Willoughby, Charles A. "Machine Gun Known Distance Practice." *Infantry Journal* 17, no. 5 (November 1920): 498–502.

Willoughby, Charles A., and John Chamberlain. *MacArthur, 1941–1951*. New York: McGraw-Hill, 1954.

Wilson, Dale E. "Recipe for Failure: Major General Edward M. Almond and Preparation of the U.S. 92d Infantry Division for Combat in World War II." *Journal of Military History* 56 (July 1992): 473–88.

Wilson, John B. *Maneuver and Firepower: The Evolution of Divisions and Separate Brigades*. Washington, DC: Center of Military History, 1998.

Winston, George T. "The Relationship of the Whites to the Negroes." 1901. In T. Clark, *The South since Reconstruction*, 309–22.

Wise, Henry A. *Drawing Out the Man: The VMI Story*. Charlottesville: University Press of Virginia, 1978.

Wise, Jennings C. *The Military History of the Virginia Military Institute from 1839 to 1865*. Lynchburg, VA: J. P. Bell, 1915.

———. "Submarine, Blockade, and Neutral Rights." *Cadet*, May 15, 1915.

Wyant, William K. *Sandy Patch: A Biography of Lt. Gen. Alexander M. Patch.* New York: Praeger, 1991.

Y'Blood, William T., ed. *The Three Wars of Lt. Gen. George E. Stratemeyer: His Korean War Diary*. Washington, DC: Air Force History and Museums Program, 1999.

Yenne, Bill. *Rising Sons: The Japanese American GIs Who Fought for the United States in World War II*. New York: St. Martin's Press, 2007.

Zabecki, David T. *Chief of Staff: The Principal Officers Behind History's Great Commanders*. Vol. 2, *World War II to Korea and Vietnam*. Annapolis, MD: Naval Institute Press, 2008.

Index